Oracle GoldenGate 11g Complete Cookbook

Over 60 simple and easy-to-follow recipes to perform various GoldenGate administration tasks such as installing, configuring, and maintaining GoldenGate replication

Ankur Gupta

[PACKT] enterprise⌗
PUBLISHING
professional expertise distilled

BIRMINGHAM - MUMBAI

Oracle GoldenGate 11g Complete Cookbook

First published: September 2013

Production Reference: 2200913

Published by Packt Publishing Ltd.
Livery Place
35 Livery Street
Birmingham B3 2PB, UK.

ISBN 978-1-84968-614-3

www.packtpub.com

Cover Image by Karl Moore (karl@karlmoore.co.uk)

Credits

Author
Ankur Gupta

Reviewers
Judy (Shuxuan) Nie
Jos van den Oord
Gavin Soorma
Michael Verzijl

Acquisition Editor
Antony Lowe

Lead Technical Editor
Ankita Shashi

Technical Editors
Ruchita Bhanshali
Vrinda A. Bhosale
Kapil Hemnani
Mrunmayee Patil

Project Coordinators
Anurag Banerjee
Abhijit Suvarna

Proofreader
Joanna McMahon

Indexer
Priya Subramani

Graphics
Ronak Dhruv

Production Coordinator
Melwyn D'sa

Cover Work
Melwyn D'sa

About the Author

Ankur Gupta is an Oracle Database Consultant based in London. He has a Master's degree in Computer Science. He started his career as an Oracle developer and later on moved into database administration. He has been working with Oracle Technologies for over 11 years in India and the UK. Over the last 6 years, he has worked as an Oracle Consultant with some of the top companies in the UK in the areas of investment banking, retail, telecom and media.

He is an Oracle Certified Exadata, GoldenGate Specialist, and OCP 11g DBA. His main areas of interest are Oracle Exadata, GoldenGate, Dataguard, RAC, and Linux.

Outside the techie world, he is an avid cook, photographer, and enjoys travelling.

I would like to thank my wife for putting up with my long writing sessions over late nights and weekends that I spent working on this book. Without her love and support, this book would not have been possible.

My deepest gratitude to my parents for allowing me to realize my own potential. I would also like to thank my mentors Dr. Prateek Bhatia and Bikramjit Singh whose excellent teaching methods built my interest in the field of databases.

About the Reviewers

Judy (Shuxuan) Nie is a Senior SOA Consultant specializing in SOA and Java technologies. He has 14 years of experience in the IT industry that includes SOA technologies such as BPEL, ESB, SOAP, XML, and Enterprise Java technologies, Eclipse plug-ins, and other areas such as C++ cross-platform development.

Since 2010, he has been working at Rubicon Red, helping customers resolve integration issues, and design and implement highly available infrastructure platforms on Oracle VM and Exalogic.

From 2007 to 2010, he had been working in the Oracle Global Customer Support Team and focused on helping customers solve their middleware/SOA integration problems.

Before joining Oracle, he had been working for the IBM China Software Development Lab for four years as a staff software engineer, participated in several complex products on IBM Lotus Workplace, WebSphere, and Eclipse platform; and then joined the Australia Bureau of Meteorology Research Center, responsible for implementation of the Automated Thunderstorm Interactive Forecast System for Aviation and Defense.

He holds an MS in Computer Science from Beijing University of Aeronautics and Astronautics.

Jos van den Oord is an Oracle Consultant/DBA for Transfer-Solutions in the Netherlands. He has specialized in Oracle Database Management Systems since 1998, with his main interest being in Oracle RDBMS Maximum Availability Manageable Architecture Environments (Real Application Cluster, DataGuard, MAA, and Automatic Storage Management). He is a proud member of the Oracle Certified Master community, having successfully passed the exam for Database 11*g*. He prefers to work in the field of advising, implementing, and problem-solving with regards to the more difficult issues and HA topics.

Gavin Soorma is an Oracle Certified Master with over 17 years of experience. He is also an Oracle Certified Professional (versions 7.3, 8*i*, 9*i*, 10*g*, and 11*g*) as well as an Oracle Certified Expert in 10*g* RAC.

He is a regular presenter at various Oracle conferences and seminars, having presented several papers at the IOUG, South African Oracle User's Group, Oracle Open World, and the Australian Oracle User Group. Recently, at the 2013 AUSOUG held in Melbourne and Perth, he presented a paper on Oracle GoldenGate titled "Real Time Access to Real Time Information".

He is currently employed as a Senior Principal Consultant for an Oracle solution provider, OnCall DBA based in Perth, Western Australia. Prior to this, he held the position of Senior Oracle DBA and Team Lead with Bank West in Perth. Before migrating to Australia, he worked for the Emirates Airline Group IT in Dubai for over 15 years where he held the position of Technical Team Manager, Databases.

He has also written a number of tutorials and notes on Oracle GoldenGate which can be accessed via his personal blog website `http://gavinsoorma.com`.

Michael Verzijl is a Business Intelligence Consultant, specializing in Oracle Business Intelligence, Oracle Data Warehousing and Oracle GoldenGate.

He has a wide range of experience in the financial, utilities, telecom, and government industries that include BI technologies such as Oracle, Informatica, IBM Cognos, and SAP Business Objects.

Currently he is employed as a BI Consultant for Accenture in the Netherlands, specializing in Business Intelligence and Data Warehousing.

www.PacktPub.com

Support files, eBooks, discount offers, and more

You might want to visit www.PacktPub.com for support files and downloads related to your book.

Did you know that Packt offers eBook versions of every book published, with PDF and ePub files available? You can upgrade to the eBook version at www.PacktPub.com and as a print book customer, you are entitled to a discount on the eBook copy. Get in touch with us at service@packtpub.com for more details.

At www.PacktPub.com, you can also read a collection of free technical articles, sign up for a range of free newsletters and receive exclusive discounts and offers on Packt books and eBooks.

PACKTLiB®

http://PacktLib.PacktPub.com

Do you need instant solutions to your IT questions? PacktLib is Packt's online digital book library. Here, you can access, read and search across Packt's entire library of books.

Why Subscribe?

- ▸ Fully searchable across every book published by Packt
- ▸ Copy and paste, print and bookmark content
- ▸ On demand and accessible via web browser

Free Access for Packt account holders

If you have an account with Packt at www.PacktPub.com, you can use this to access PacktLib today and view nine entirely free books. Simply use your login credentials for immediate access.

Instant Updates on New Packt Books

Get notified! Find out when new books are published by following @PacktEnterprise on Twitter, or the *Packt Enterprise* Facebook page.

Table of Contents

Preface

The availability, performance, and accessibility demands of the business IT systems are increasing day-by-day. The amount of data stored by the business has grown manifolds over the years. Companies want their management information systems to be up to date with the live data in order to analyze the latest trends in customer behavior. The data replication technologies that are used to replicate the data between the systems need to be robust, high-performing, resilient, and must have minimal impact on the production systems. Oracle GoldenGate is one of the key products in the data replication industry. Oracle recently declared shifting its focus on enhancing Oracle GoldenGate as its key data replication product. Ever since this announcement was made, there has been a lot of focus on Oracle GoldenGate and companies are using it for various purposes.

There is no dearth of the material explaining the architecture and concepts of Oracle GoldenGate replication. This cookbook is a practical guide, which provides you with the steps to perform various activities in a GoldenGate environment.

The book is designed to cover the GoldenGate tasks of various complexity levels. Whether you are looking to know the process of setting up a simple GoldenGate replication, implement it in a clustered environment or planning to just perform a one-time data migration from one database environment to another, you can follow the detailed steps in the recipes in this book for that.

The purpose of this book is to provide the reader with a ready, step-by-step approach to perform various GoldenGate Administration tasks. With these recipes in hand, you will easily be able to implement and manage Oracle GoldenGate in an efficient way.

What this book covers

Chapter 1, Installation and Initial Setup, introduces Oracle GoldenGate and covers the steps in installing GoldenGate binaries. It also goes through the steps in setting up a simple GoldenGate replication.

Chapter 2, Setting up GoldenGate Replication, explains the GoldenGate setup in a more complex environment and also goes through some of the options which one would use in a production environment.

Chapter 3, DDL Replication and Initial Load, goes through the various options that are available to instantiate a target environment and also goes through the steps that one needs to follow to set up DDL replication through Oracle GoldenGate.

Chapter 4, Mapping and Manipulating Data, describes various options that one can use for performing a variety of transformations in a GoldenGate replication. It also explains how to capture errors and how to perform various mappings between different table columns in the source and target environments.

Chapter 5, Oracle GoldenGate High Availability, covers various recipes to implement GoldenGate in high availability configurations. It also includes some failover scenarios that should be followed in those configurations.

Chapter 6, Monitoring, Tuning, and Troubleshooting GoldenGate, focuses on the management of GoldenGate environments. It contains the recipes to perform a health check, measure throughput, and monitor a GoldenGate environment. It also includes a few options to enhance the performance of GoldenGate replication.

Chapter 7, Advanced Administration Tasks – I, covers some advanced maintenance tasks such as patching and upgrading GoldenGate binaries that a GoldenGate administrator would need to do at some point. It also covers how to propagate table structure changes in GoldenGate environments. We also discuss some utilities that are available in GoldenGate binaries using which you can view the contents of the extracted records and also undo the applied changes.

Chapter 8, Advanced Administration Tasks – Part II, focuses on additional advanced tasks around the setup and migration of replication to GoldenGate. It explains a few options to set up replication from the production environment without impacting the performance or jeopardizing the risk of replicating erroneous transactions to the target environment. We also cover the process of migrating an Oracle Streams replication environment to Oracle GoldenGate. It also explains the process of replicating data from MS SQL Server environments to Oracle databases using GoldenGate.

Chapter 9, GoldenGate Veridata, Director, and Monitor, focuses on the installation and configuration of some additional tools that one can buy to manage the GoldenGate environments.

What you need for this book

In order to practice the recipes in this book, you would need various machines/virtual machines which should have at least the following configuration:

- ▸ 1 * 2.0 GHZ Dual Core Intel-based CPU
- ▸ 2 GB Physical Memory
- ▸ 150 GB Hard Disk Drive Space
- ▸ Ethernet Adapter

You would also need the following software to perform the setups in various recipes:

- ▸ Oracle Enterprise Linux 6.3 – 64 Bit
- ▸ Oracle Server 11.2.0.3 for Oracle Enterprise Linux 6.0 – 64 Bit
- ▸ Oracle GoldenGate 11.2.1.0.1 and Oracle GoldenGate 11.2.1.0.3 for Oracle 11g on Linux x86_64 environment
- ▸ Oracle GoldenGate 11.2.1.0.1 and Oracle GoldenGate 11.2.1.0.3 for Oracle 11g on Windows x86_64 environment
- ▸ Oracle GoldenGate Monitor Server 11.1.1.1.0
- ▸ Oracle Jrockit – Latest version
- ▸ Oracle Weblogic – 10.3.6
- ▸ Oracle GoldenGate Director Server and Client 11.2.1.0.0
- ▸ Oracle GoldenGate Management Plugin for OEM 12c
- ▸ Oracle GoldenGate Veridata Server and Java Agent 11.2.1.0.0
- ▸ SFTP Transfer Client
- ▸ Putty

Who this book is for

Whether you are handling Oracle GoldenGate environments on a day-to-day basis or using it just for migration, this book provides the necessary information for most of the administration tasks.

The book is for Database Administrators, Architects, and Middleware Administrators who are keen to learn about various setups in Oracle GoldenGate. It also targets the Solution Architects who want to explore various high availability options in Oracle GoldenGate for Oracle RAC environments. The reader is expected to have some knowledge of Oracle databases.

Conventions

In this book, you will find a number of styles of text that distinguish between different kinds of information. Here are some examples of these styles, and an explanation of their meaning.

Code words in text, database table names, folder names, filenames, file extensions, pathnames, dummy URLs, user input, and Twitter handles are shown as follows: "We can include other contexts through the use of the `include` directive."

A block of code is set as follows:

```
EDIT PARAMS PGGTEST11
EXTRACT PGGTEST11
USERID GGATE_ADMIN@RACDB, PASSWORD GGATE_ADMIN
RMTHOST tg-oggvip1.localdomain , MGRPORT 7809
RMTTRAIL /u01/app/ggate1/dirdat/rt
TABLE scott.*;
```

When we wish to draw your attention to a particular part of a code block, the relevant lines or items are set in bold:

```
EDIT PARAMS PGGTEST11
EXTRACT PGGTEST11
USERID GGATE_ADMIN@RACDB, PASSWORD GGATE_ADMIN
RMTHOST tg-oggvip1.localdomain , MGRPORT 7809
RMTTRAIL /u01/app/ggate1/dirdat/rt
TABLE scott.*;
```

Any command-line input or output is written as follows:

```
# cp /usr/src/asterisk-addons/configs/cdr_mysql.conf.sample
    /etc/asterisk/cdr_mysql.conf
```

New terms and **important words** are shown in bold. Words that you see on the screen, in menus or dialog boxes for example, appear in the text like this: "clicking the **Next** button moves you to the next screen".

> Warnings or important notes appear in a box like this.

> Tips and tricks appear like this.

Reader feedback

Feedback from our readers is always welcome. Let us know what you think about this book—what you liked or may have disliked. Reader feedback is important for us to develop titles that you really get the most out of.

To send us general feedback, simply send an e-mail to `feedback@packtpub.com`, and mention the book title via the subject of your message.

If there is a topic that you have expertise in and you are interested in either writing or contributing to a book, see our author guide on `www.packtpub.com/authors`.

Customer support

Now that you are the proud owner of a Packt book, we have a number of things to help you to get the most from your purchase.

Downloading the example code

You can download the example code files for all Packt books you have purchased from your account at `http://www.packtpub.com`. If you purchased this book elsewhere, you can visit `http://www.packtpub.com/support` and register to have the files e-mailed directly to you.

Errata

Although we have taken every care to ensure the accuracy of our content, mistakes do happen. If you find a mistake in one of our books—maybe a mistake in the text or the code—we would be grateful if you would report this to us. By doing so, you can save other readers from frustration and help us improve subsequent versions of this book. If you find any errata, please report them by visiting `http://www.packtpub.com/submit-errata`, selecting your book, clicking on the **errata submission form** link, and entering the details of your errata. Once your errata are verified, your submission will be accepted and the errata will be uploaded on our website, or added to any list of existing errata, under the Errata section of that title. Any existing errata can be viewed by selecting your title from `http://www.packtpub.com/support`.

Piracy

Piracy of copyright material on the Internet is an ongoing problem across all media. At Packt, we take the protection of our copyright and licenses very seriously. If you come across any illegal copies of our works, in any form, on the Internet, please provide us with the location address or website name immediately so that we can pursue a remedy.

Please contact us at copyright@packtpub.com with a link to the suspected pirated material.

We appreciate your help in protecting our authors, and our ability to bring you valuable content.

Questions

You can contact us at questions@packtpub.com if you are having a problem with any aspect of the book, and we will do our best to address it.

1
Installation and Initial Setup

The following recipes will be covered in this chapter:

- ▸ Installing Oracle GoldenGate in a x86_64 Linux-based environment
- ▸ Installing Oracle GoldenGate in a Windows environment
- ▸ Enabling supplemental logging in the source database
- ▸ Supported datatypes in Oracle GoldenGate
- ▸ Preparing the source database for GoldenGate setup
- ▸ Preparing the target database for GoldenGate setup
- ▸ Setting up a Manager process
- ▸ Setting up a Classic Capture Extract process
- ▸ Setting up an Integrated Capture Extract process
- ▸ Setting up a Datapump process
- ▸ Setting up a Replicat process

Introduction

Database replication is always an interesting challenge. It requires a complex setup and strong knowledge of the underlying infrastructure, databases, and the data held in them to replicate the data efficiently without much impact on the enterprise system. Oracle GoldenGate gains a lot of its popularity from the simplicity in its setup. In this chapter we will cover the basic steps to install GoldenGate and set up various processes.

Installing Oracle GoldenGate in a x86_64 Linux-based environment

This recipe will show you how to install Oracle GoldenGate in a x86_64 Linux-based environment.

Getting ready

In order to install Oracle GoldenGate, we must have downloaded the binaries from the Oracle Technology Network website for your Linux platform. We have downloaded Oracle GoldenGate Version 11.2.0.1.0.1 in this recipe. Ensure that you check the checksum of the file once you have downloaded it.

> You can find the Oracle GoldenGate binaries for x86_64 Linux at http://www.oracle.com/technetwork/middleware/GoldenGate/downloads/index.html?ssSourceSiteId=ocomen.

How to do it...

Oracle GoldenGate binaries are installed in a directory called GoldenGate Home. This directory should be owned by the OS user (ggate) which will be the owner of GoldenGate binaries. This user must be a member of the dba group. After you have downloaded the binaries, you need to uncompress the media pack file by using the unzip utility as given in the following steps:

1. Log in to the server using the ggate account.

2. Create a directory with this user as shown in the following command:

   mkdir installation_directory

3. Change the directory to the location where you have copied the media pack file and unzip it. The media pack contains the readme files and the GoldenGate binaries file. The GoldenGate binaries file for the 64-bit x86 Linux platform is called fbs_ggs_Linux_x64_ora11g_64bit.tar.

4. Extract the contents of this file into the GoldenGate Home directory as shown in the following command:

   tar -xvf fbs_ggs_Linux_x64_ora11g_64bit.tar -C installation_directory

5. Create GoldenGate directories as follows:

   cd installation_directory

   ./ggsci

```
create subdirs

exit
```

> You must have Oracle database libraries added to the shared library environment variable, `$LD_LIBRARY_PATH` before you run `ggsci`. It is also recommended to have `$ORACLE_HOME` & `$ORACLE_SID` set to the correct Oracle instance.

How it works...

Oracle provides GoldenGate binaries in a compressed format. In order to install the binaries you unzip the compressed file, and then expand the archive file into a required directory. This unpacks all the binaries. However, GoldenGate also requires some important subdirectories under GoldenGate `Home` which are not created by default. These directories are created using the `CREATE SUBDIRS` command. The following is the list of the subdirectories that get created with this command:

Subdirectory	Contents
dirprm	It contains parameter files
dirrpt	It contains report files
dirchk	It contains checkpoint files
dirpcs	It contains process status files
dirsql	It contains SQL scripts
dirdef	It contains database definitions
dirdat	It contains trail files
dirtmp	It contains temporary files
dirout	It contains output files

> Oracle GoldenGate binaries need to be installed on both the source and target systems. The procedure for installing the binaries is the same in both environments.

Installing Oracle GoldenGate in a Windows environment

In this recipe we will go through the steps that should be followed to install the GoldenGate binaries in the Windows environment.

Getting ready

In order to install Oracle GoldenGate, we must have downloaded the binaries from the Oracle Technology Network website for your Windows platform. We have downloaded GoldenGate Version 11.2.0.1.0.1 in this recipe. Ensure that you check the checksum of the file once you have downloaded it.

> You can find the Oracle GoldenGate binaries for x86_64 Windows at `http://www.oracle.com/technetwork/middleware/GoldenGate/downloads/index.html?ssSourceSiteId=ocomen`.

How to do it...

Oracle GoldenGate binaries are installed in a directory called GoldenGate `Home`. After you have downloaded the binaries, you need to uncompress the media pack file by using the unzip utility:

1. Log in to the server as the Administrator user.
2. Create a directory for GoldenGate `Home`.
3. Unzip the contents of the media pack file to the GoldenGate `Home` directory.
4. Create GoldenGate directories as shown in the following command:

```
cd installation_directory
ggsci
create subdirs
exit
```

How it works...

Oracle provides GoldenGate binaries in a compressed format. The installation involves unzipping the file into a required directory. This unpacks all the binaries. However, GoldenGate also requires some important subdirectories under GoldenGate `Home` which are not created by default. These directories are created using the CREATE SUBDIRS command. The following is the list of the subdirectories that get created with this command:

Subdirectory	Contents
dirprm	It contains parameter files
Dirrpt	It contains report files
Dirchk	It contains checkpoint files
dirpcs	It contains process status files
dirsql	It contains SQL scripts
dirdef	It contains database definitions
dirdat	It contains trail files
dirtmp	It contains temporary files
dirout	It contains output files

Enabling supplemental logging in the source database

Oracle GoldenGate replication can be used to continuously replicate the changes from the source database to the target database. GoldenGate mines the redo information generated in the source database to extract the changes. In order to update the correct rows in the target database, Oracle needs sufficient information to be able to identify them uniquely. Since it relies on the information extracted from the redo buffers, it requires extra information columns to be logged into the redo records generated in the source database. This is done by enabling supplemental logging in the source database. This recipe explains how to enable supplemental logging in the source database.

Getting ready

We must have a list of the tables that we want to replicate between two environments.

How to do it...

Oracle GoldenGate requires supplemental logging to be enabled at the database level and table level. Use the following steps to enable the required supplemental logging:

1. Enable database supplemental logging through `sqlplus` as follows:

   ```
   ALTER DATABASE ADD SUPPLEMENTAL LOG DATA;
   ```

2. Switch a database `LOGFILE` to bring the changes into effect:

   ```
   ALTER DATABASE SWITCH LOGFILE;
   ```

3. From the GoldenGate Home, log in to GGSCI:

   `./ggsci`

4. Log in to the source database from ggsci using a user which has privileges to alter the source schema tables as shown in the following command:

   `GGSCI> DBLOGIN USERID <USER> PASSWORD <PW>`

5. Enable supplemental logging at the table level as follows:

   `GGSCI> ADD TRANDATA <SCHEMA>.<TABLE_NAME>`

6. Repeat step 5 for all the tables that you want to replicate using GoldenGate.

How it works...

Supplemental logging enables the database to add extra columns in the redo data that is required by GoldenGate to correctly identify the rows in the target database. We must enable database-level minimum supplemental logging before we can enable it at the table level. When we enable it at the table level, a supplemental log group is created for the table that consists of the columns on which supplemental logging is enabled. The columns which form a part of this group are decided based on the key constraints present on the table. These columns are decided based on the following priority order:

1. Primary key

2. First unique key alphanumerically with no nullable columns

3. First unique key alphanumerically with nullable columns

4. All columns

GoldenGate only considers unique keys which don't have any virtual columns, any user-defined types, or any function-based columns. We can also manually specify which columns we want to be a part of the supplemental log group.

> You can enable supplemental logging on all tables of a schema using the following single command:
>
> `GGSCI> ADD TRANDATA <SCHEMA>.*`
>
> If possible, do create a primary key in each source and target table that is part of the replication. The pseudo key consisting of all columns, created by GoldenGate, can be quite inefficient.

There's more...

There are two ways to enable supplemental logging. The first method is to enable it using `GGSCI`, using the `ADD TRANDATA` command. The second method is to use `sqlplus` and run the `ALTER TABLE ADD SUPPLEMENTAL LOG DATA` command. The latter method is more flexible and allows a person to specify the name of the supplemental log group. However, when you use Oracle GoldenGate to add supplemental logging it creates supplemental log group names using the format, `GGS_<TABLE_NAME>_<OBJECT_NUMBER>`. If the overall supplemental log group name is longer than 30 characters, GoldenGate truncates the table name as required. Oracle support recommends that we use the first method for enabling supplemental logging for objects to be replicated using Oracle GoldenGate. The `GGS_*` supplemental log group format enables GoldenGate to quickly identify the supplemental log groups in the database.

If you are planning to use GoldenGate to capture all transactions in the source database and convert them into `INSERT` for the target database, for example, for reporting/auditing purposes, you'll need to enable supplemental logging on all columns of the source database tables.

See also

▶ For information about how to replicate changes to a target database and maintain an audit record, refer to the recipe *Mapping the changes to a target table and storing the transaction history in a history table* in *Chapter 4, Mapping and Manipulating Data*

Supported datatypes in Oracle GoldenGate

Oracle GoldenGate has some restrictions in terms of what it can replicate. With every new release, Oracle is adding new datatypes to the list of what is supported. The list of the datatypes of the objects that you are planning to replicate should be checked against the list of supported datatypes for the GoldenGate version that you are planning to install.

Getting ready

You should have identified the various datatypes of the objects that you plan to replicate.

How to do it...

The following is a high-level list of the datatypes that are supported by Oracle GoldenGate v11.2.1.0.1:

▶ NUMBER

▶ BINARY FLOAT

▶ BINARY DOUBLE

- CHAR
- VARCHAR2
- LONG
- NCHAR
- NVARCHAR2
- RAW
- LONG RAW
- DATE
- TIMESTAMP
- CLOB
- NCLOB
- BLOB
- SECUREFILE and BASICFILE
- XML datatypes
- User defined/Abstract datatypes
- SDO_GEOMETRY, SDO_TOPO_GEOMETRY, and SDO_GEORASTER are supported

How it works...

There are some additional details that one needs to consider while evaluating the supported datatypes for a GoldenGate version. For example, the user-defined datatypes are only supported if the source and target tables have the same structures. Both Classic and Integrated Capture modes support XML types which are stored as XML, CLOB, and XML binary. However, XML type tables stored as Object Relational are only supported in Integrated Capture mode.

There's more...

The support restrictions apply to a few other factors apart from the datatypes. Some of these are as Manipulating Data:

- INSERTs, UPDATEs and DELETEs are supported on regular tables, IOTs, clustered tables and materialized views
- Tables created as EXTERNAL are not supported
- Extraction from compressed tables is supported only in Integrated Capture mode
- Materialized views created with ROWID are not supported
- Oracle GoldenGate supports replication of the sequences only in uni-directional mode

Preparing the source database for GoldenGate setup

Oracle GoldenGate architecture consists of Extract process in the source database. This process mines the redo information and extracts the changes occurring in the source database objects. These changes are then written to the trail files. There are two types of Extract processes – Classic Capture and Integrated Capture. The Extract process requires some setup to be done in the source database. Some of the steps in the setup are different depending on the type of the Extract process. GoldenGate requires a database user to be created in the source database and various privileges to be granted to this user. This recipe explains how to set up a source database for GoldenGate replication.

Getting ready

You must select a database user ID for the source database setup. For example, GGATE_ADMIN.

How to do it...

Run the following steps in the source database to set up the GoldenGate user as follows:

```
sqlplus sys/**** as sysdba
CREATE USER GGATE_ADMIN identified by GGATE_ADMIN;
GRANT CREATE SESSION, ALTER SESSION to GGATE_ADMIN;
GRANT ALTER SYSTEM TO GGATE_ADMIN;
GRANT CONNECT, RESOURCE to GGATE_ADMIN;
GRANT SELECT ANY DICTIONARY to GGATE_ADMIN;
GRANT FLASHBACK ANY TABLE to GGATE_ADMIN;
GRANT SELECT ANY TABLE TO GGATE_ADMIN;
GRANT SELECT ON DBA_CLUSTERS TO GGATE_ADMIN;
GRANT EXECUTE ON DBMS_FLASHBACK TO GGATE_ADMIN;
GRANT SELECT ANY TRANSACTION To GGATE_ADMIN;
```

The following steps are only required for Integrated Capture Extract (Version 11.2.0.2 or higher):

```
EXEC DBMS_GoldenGate_AUTH.GRANT_ADMIN_PRIVILEGE('GGATE_ADMIN');
GRANT SELECT ON SYS.V_$DATABASE TO GGATE_ADMIN;
```

The following steps are only required for Integrated Capture Extract (Version 11.2.0.1 or earlier):

```
EXEC DBMS_STREAMS_AUTH.GRANT_ADMIN_PRIVILEGE('GGATE_ADMIN');

GRANT BECOME USER TO GGATE_ADMIN;

GRANT SELECT ON SYS.V_$DATABASE TO GGATE_ADMIN;
```

Set up a TNS Entry for the source database in `$ORACLE_HOME/network/admin/tnsnames.ora`.

How it works...

The preceding commands can be used to set up the GoldenGate user in the source database. The Integrated Capture required some additional privileges as it needs to interact with the database log mining server.

You will notice that in the previous commands, we have granted SELECT ANY TABLE to the GGATE_ADMIN user. In production environments, where least required privileges policies are followed, it is quite unlikely that such a setup would be approved by the compliance team. In such cases, instead of granting this privilege, you can grant the SELECT privilege on individual tables that are a part of the source replication configuration. You can use dynamic SQL to generate such commands.

In our example schema database, we can generate the commands for all tables owned by the user SCOTT as follows:

```
select 'GRANT SELECT ON '||owner||'.'||table_name||' to GGATE_ADMIN;'
COMMAND from dba_tables where owner='SCOTT'

COMMAND
----------------------------------------------------------------

GRANT SELECT ON SCOTT.DEPT to GGATE_ADMIN;

GRANT SELECT ON SCOTT.EMP to GGATE_ADMIN;

GRANT SELECT ON SCOTT.BONUS to GGATE_ADMIN;

GRANT SELECT ON SCOTT.SALGRADE to GGATE_ADMIN;
```

There's more...

In this recipe we saw the steps required to set up a the GoldenGate user in the database. The Extract process required various privileges to be able to mine the changes from the redo data. At this stage it's worth discussing the two types of Extract processes and the differences between both.

The Classic Capture mode

The Classic Capture mode is the traditional Extract process that has been there for a while. In this mode, GoldenGate accesses the database redo logs (also, archive logs for older transactions) to capture the DML changes occurring on the objects specified in the configuration files. For this, at the OS level, the GoldenGate user must be a part of the same database group which owns the database redo logs. If the redo logs of the source database are stored in an ASM diskgroup this capture method reads it from there. This capture mode is available for other RDBMS as well. However, there are some datatypes that are not supported in Classic Capture mode. One of the biggest limitations of the Classic Capture mode is its inability to read data from the compressed tables/tablespaces.

The Integrated Capture mode

In case of the Integrated Capture mode, GoldenGate works directly with the database log mining server to receive the data changes in the form of **logical change records** (**LCRs**). An LCR is a message with a specific format that describes a database change. This mode does not require any special setup for the databases using ASM, transparent data encryption, or Oracle RAC. This feature is only available for databases on Version 11.2.0.3 or higher. This Capture mode supports extracting data from source databases using compression. It also supports various object types which were previously not supported by Classic Capture.

Integrated Capture can be configured in an online or downstream mode. In the online mode, the log miner database is configured in the source database itself. In the downstream mode, the log miner database is configured in a separate database which receives archive logs from the source database. This mode offloads the log mining load from the source database and is quite suitable for very busy production databases. If you want to use the Integrated Capture mode with a source database Version 11.2.0.2 or earlier, you must configure the Integrated Capture mode in downstream capture topology, and the downstream mining database must be on Version 11.2.0.3 or higher.

> You will need to apply a Bundle Patch specified in MOS Note 1411356.1 for full support of the datatypes offered by Integrated Capture.

See also

▸ Refer to the recipe *Setting up an Integrated Capture Extract process* later in this chapter and *Creating an Integrated Capture with a downstream database for compressed tables* in *Chapter 7, Advanced Administration Tasks – I*

Preparing the target database for GoldenGate setup

On the target side of the GoldenGate architecture, the collector processes receive the trail files shipped by the Extract/Datapump processes from the source environment. The collector process receives these files and writes them locally on the target server. For each row that gets updated in the source database, the Extract process generates a record and writes it to the trail file. The Replicat process in the target environment reads these trail files and applies the changes to the target database using native SQL calls. To be able to apply these changes to the target tables, GoldenGate requires a database user to be set up in the target database with some privileges on the target objects. The Replicat process also needs to maintain its status in a table in the target database so that it can resume in case of any failures. This recipe explains the steps required to set up a GoldenGate user in the target database.

Getting ready

You must select a database user ID for a target database setup. For example, GGATE_ADMIN, because the GoldenGate user also requires a table in the target database to maintain its status. It needs some quota assigned on a tablespace to be able to create a table. You might want to create a separate tablespace, grant quota and assign it as default for the GGATE_ ADMIN user. We will assign a GGATE_ADMIN_DAT tablespace to the GGATE_ADMIN user in this recipe.

How to do it...

Run the following steps in the target database to set up a GoldenGate user:

```
sqlplus sys/**** as sysdba

CREATE USER GGATE_ADMIN identified by GGATE_ADMIN DEFAULT TABLESPACE
GGATE_ADMIN_DAT;

ALTER USER GGATE_ADMIN QUOTA UNLIMITED ON GGATE_ADMIN_DAT;

GRANT CREATE SESSION, ALTER SESSION to GGATE_ADMIN;

GRANT CONNECT, RESOURCE to GGATE_ADMIN;

GRANT SELECT ANY DICTIONARY to GGATE_ADMIN;

GRANT SELECT ANY TABLE TO GGATE_ADMIN;

GRANT INSERT ANY TABLE, UPDATE ANY TABLE, DELETE ANY TABLE TO GGATE_
ADMIN;

GRANT CREATE TABLE TO GGATE_ADMIN;
```

How it works...

You can use these commands to set up a GoldenGate user in the target database. The GoldenGate user in the target database requires access to the database plus `update/insert/delete` privileges on the target tables to apply the changes. In the preceding commands, we have granted `SELECT ANY TABLE`, `UPDATE ANY TABLE`, `DELETE ANY TABLE`, and `INSERT ANY TABLE` privileges to the `GGATE_ADMIN` user. However, if for production database reasons your organization follows the least required privileges policy, you will need to grant these privileges on the replicated target tables individually. If the number of replicated target tables is large, you can use dynamic SQL to generate such commands. In our example `demo` database, we can generate these commands for the `SCOTT` schema objects as follows:

```
select 'GRANT SELECT, INSERT, UPDATE, DELETE ON '||owner||'.'||table_
name||' to GGATE_ADMIN;' COMMAND from dba_tables where owner='SCOTT'

COMMAND
---------------------------------------------------------------------
GRANT SELECT, INSERT, UPDATE, DELETE ON SCOTT.DEPT to GGATE_ADMIN;

GRANT SELECT, INSERT, UPDATE, DELETE ON SCOTT.EMP to GGATE_ADMIN;

GRANT SELECT, INSERT, UPDATE, DELETE ON SCOTT.SALGRADE to GGATE_ADMIN;

GRANT SELECT, INSERT, UPDATE, DELETE ON SCOTT.BONUS to GGATE_ADMIN;
```

There's more...

The replicated changes are applied to the target database on a row-by-row basis.
The Replicat process needs to maintain its status so that it can be resumed in case of failure. The checkpoints can be maintained in a database table or in a file on disk. The best practice is to create a Checkpoint table and use it to maintain the replicat status. This also enhances the performance as the replicat applies the changes to the database using asynchronous `COMMIT` with the `NOWAIT` option. If you do not use a Checkpoint table, the replicat maintains the checkpoint in a file and applies the changes to the databases using a synchronous `COMMIT` with the `WAIT` option.

Setting up a Manager process

The Manager process is a key process of a GoldenGate configuration. This process is the root of the GoldenGate instance and it must exist at each GoldenGate site. It must be running on each system in the GoldenGate configuration before any other GoldenGate processes can be started. This recipe explains how to create a GoldenGate Manager process in a GoldenGate configuration.

Getting ready

Before setting up a Manager process, you must have installed GoldenGate binaries. A Manager process requires a port number to be defined in its configuration. Ensure that you have chosen the port to be used for the GoldenGate manager instance that you are going to set up.

How to do it...

In order to configure a Manager process, you need to create a configuration file. The following are the steps to create a parameter file for the Manager process:

1. From the GoldenGate Home directory, run the GoldenGate software command line interface (GGSCI):

   ```
   ./ggsci
   ```

2. Edit the Manager process configuration as follows:

   ```
   EDIT PARAMS MGR
   ```

3. This command will open an editor window. You need to add the manager configuration parameters in this window as follows:

   ```
   PORT <PORT NO>

   DYNAMICPORTLIST <specification>

   AUTOSTART ER*

   AUTORESTART ER*, RETRIES 3, WAITMINUTES 3

   PURGEOLDEXTRACTS <specification>
   ```

   For example:

   ```
   PORT 7809

   DYNAMICPORTLIST 7810-7820, 7830

   AUTOSTART ER t*

   AUTORESTART ER t*, RETRIES 4, WAITMINUTES 4

   PURGEOLDEXTRACTS /u01/app/ggate/dirdat/tt*, USECHECKPOINTS,
   MINKEEPHOURS 2
   ```

4. Save the file and exit the editor window.

5. Start the Manager process by using the following code:

   ```
   GGSCI> START MGR
   ```

How it works...

All GoldenGate processes use a parameter file for configuration. In these files various parameters are defined. These parameters control the way the process functions. The steps to create the Manager process are broadly described as follows:

1. Log in to the GoldenGate command line interface.

2. Create a parameter file.

3. Start the Manager process.

4. When you start the Manager process you will get the following output:

```
GGSCI (prim1-ol6-112.localdomain) 2> start mgr
Manager started.
```

You can check the status of the Manager process using the `status` command as follows:

```
GGSCI (prim1-ol6-112.localdomain) 3> status mgr
Manager is running (IP port prim1-ol6-112.localdomain.7809).
```

The Manager process performs the following administrative and resource management functions:

▸ Monitor and restart Oracle GoldenGate processes

▸ Issue threshold reports, for example, when throughput slows down or when synchronization latency increases

▸ Maintain trail files and logs

▸ Report errors and events

▸ Receive and route requests from the user interface

The preceding parameters specified are defined as follows:

▸ `Port no`: This is the port used by the Manager process itself.

▸ `Dynamic port list`: Range of ports to be used by other processes in the GoldenGate instance. For example, Extract, Datapump, Replicat, and Collector processes.

▸ `Autostart ER*`: To start the GoldenGate processes when the Manager process starts.

▸ `Autorestart ER*`: To restart the GoldenGate process in case it fails. The `RETRIES` option controls the maximum number of restart attempts and the `WAITMINUTES` option controls the wait interval between each restart attempt in minutes.

▸ `Purgeoldextracts`: To configure the automatic maintenance of GoldenGate trail files. The deletion criteria is specified using `MINKEEPHOURS/MINKEEPFILES`. The GoldenGate Manager process deletes the old trail files which fall out of this criteria.

There's more...

The Manager process can be configured to perform some more administrative tasks. The following are some other key parameters that can be added to the Manager process configuration:

- ► STARTUPVALIDATONDELAY(Secs): Use this parameter to set a delay in seconds after which the Manager process checks that the processes are started after it starts up itself.

- ► LAGREPORT: The Manager process writes the lag information of a process to its report file. This parameter controls the interval after which the Manager process performs this function.

Setting up a Classic Capture Extract process

A GoldenGate Classic Capture Extract process runs on the source system. This process can be configured for initially loading the source data and for continuous replication. This process reads the redo logs in the source database and looks for changes in the tables that are defined in its configuration file. These changes are then written into a buffer in the memory. When the extract reads a commit command in the redo logs, the changes for that transaction are then flushed to the trail files on disk. In case it encounters a rollback statement for a transaction in the redo log, it discards the changes from the memory. This type of Extract process is available on all platforms which GoldenGate supports. This process cannot read the changes for compressed objects. In this recipe you will learn how to set up a Classic Capture process in a GoldenGate instance.

Getting ready

Before adding the Classic Capture Extract process, ensure that you have completed the following steps in the source database environment:

1. Enabled database minimum supplemental logging.
2. Enabled supplemental logging for tables to be replicated.
3. Set up a manager instance.
4. Created a directory for the source trail files.
5. Decided a two-letter initial for naming the source trail files.

How to do it...

The following are the steps to configure a Classic Capture Extract process in the source database:

1. From the GoldenGate `Home` directory, run the GoldenGate software command line interface (GGSCI) as follows:

   ```
   ./ggsci
   ```

2. Edit the Extract process configuration as follows:

   ```
   EDIT PARAMS EGGTEST1
   ```

3. This command will open an editor window. You need to add the extract configuration parameters in this window as follows:

   ```
   EXTRACT <EXTRACT_NAME>
   USERID <SOURCE_GG_USER>@SOURCEDB, PASSWORD ******
   EXTTRAIL <specification>
   TABLE <replicated_table_specification>;
   ```

   For example:

   ```
   EXTRACT EGGTEST1
   USERID GGATE_ADMIN@DBORATEST, PASSWORD ******
   EXTTRAIL /u01/app/ggate/dirdat/st
   TABLE scott.*;
   ```

4. Save the file and exit the editor window.

5. Add the Classic Capture Extract to the GoldenGate instance as follows:

   ```
   ADD EXTRACT <EXTRACT_NAME>, TRANLOG, <BEGIN_SPEC>
   ```
   For example:
   ```
   ADD EXTRACT EGGTEST1, TRANLOG, BEGIN NOW
   ```

6. Add the local trail to the Classic Capture configuration as follows:

   ```
   ADD EXTTRAIL /u01/app/ggate/dirdat/st, EXTRACT EGGTEST1
   ```

7. Start the Classic Capture Extract process as follows:

   ```
   GGSCI> START EXTRACT EGGTEST1
   ```

How it works...

In the preceding steps we have configured a Classic Capture Extract process to replicate all tables for a SCOTT user. For this we first configure an Extract process parameter file and add the configuration parameter to it. Once the parameter file is created, we then add the Extract process to the source manager instance. This is done using the ADD EXTRACT command in step 5. In step 6, we associate a local trail file with the Extract process and then we start it. When you start the Extract process you will see the following output:

```
GGSCI (prim1-ol6-112.localdomain) 11> start extract EGGTEST1
Sending START request to MANAGER ...
EXTRACT EGGTEST1 starting
```

You can check the status of the Extract process using the following command:

```
GGSCI (prim1-ol6-112.localdomain) 10> status extract EGGTEST1
EXTRACT EGGTEST1: STARTED
```

There's more...

There are a few additional parameters that can be specified in the extract configuration as follows:

- EOFDELAY secs: This parameter controls how often GoldenGate should check the source database redo logs for new data

- MEGABYTES <N>: This parameter controls the size of the extract trail file

- DYNAMICRESOLUTION: Use this parameter to enable extract to build the metadata for each table when the extract encounters its changes for the first time.

If your source database ie this parameter to enable extract to build the metadata for each table when the exs a very busy OLTP production system and you cannot afford to add additional load of GoldenGate process on it, you can however offload GoldenGate processing to another server by adding some extra configuration. You will need to configure the source database to ship the redo logs to a standby site and set up a GoldenGate manager instance on that server. The Extract processes will be configured to read from the archived logs on the standby system. For this you specify an additional parameter as follows:

TRANLOGOPTIONS ARCHIVEDLOGONLY ALTARCHIVEDLOGDEST <path>

> If you are using Classic Capture in ALO mode for the source database using ASM, you must store the archive log files on the standby server outside ASM to allow Classic Capture Extract to read them.

See also

▶ The recipe, *Configuring an Extract process to read from an Oracle ASM instance* and the recipe, *Setting up a GoldenGate replication with multiple process groups* in *Chapter 2, Setting up GoldenGate Replication*

Setting up an Integrated Capture Extract process

Integrated Capture is a new form of GoldenGate Extract process which works directly with the database log mining server to receive the data changes in the form of LCRs. This functionality is based on the Oracle Streams technology. For this, the GoldenGate Admin user requires access to the log miner dictionary objects. This Capture mode supports extracting data from the source databases using compression. It also supports some object types that are not supported by the Classic Capture. In this recipe, you will learn how to set up an Integrated Capture process in a GoldenGate instance.

Getting ready

Before adding the Integrated Capture Extract, ensure that you have completed the following steps in the source database environment:

1. Enabled database minimum supplemental logging.
2. Enabled supplemental logging for tables to be replicated.
3. Set up a manager instance.
4. Created a directory for source trail files.
5. Decided a two-letter initial for naming source trail files.
6. Created a GoldenGate Admin database user with extra privileges required for Integrated Capture in the source database.

How to do it...

You can follow the given steps to configure an Integrated Capture Extract process:

1. From the GoldenGate `Home` directory, run the GoldenGate software command line interface (GGSCI) as follows:

   ```
   ./ggsci
   ```

2. Edit the Extract process configuration as follows:

   ```
   EDIT PARAMS EGGTEST1
   ```

3. This command will open an editor window. You need to add the extract configuration parameters in this window as follows:

```
EXTRACT <EXTRACT_NAME>
USERID <SOURCE_GG_USER>@SOURCEDB, PASSWORD ******
TRANLOGOPTIONS MININGUSER <MINING_DB_USER>@MININGDB, &
MININGPASSWORD *****
EXTTRAIL <specification>
TABLE <replicated_table_specification>;
```

For example:

```
EXTRACT EGGTEST1
USERID GGATE_ADMIN@DBORATEST, PASSWORD ******
TRANLOGOPTIONS MININGUSER OGGMIN@MININGDB, &
MININGPASSWORD *****
EXTTRAIL /u01/app/ggate/dirdat/st
TABLE scott.*;
```

4. Save the file and exit the editor window.

5. Register the Integrated Capture Extract process to the database as follows:

```
DBLOGIN USERID <SOURCE_GG_USER>@SOURCEDB, PASSWORD ******
MININGDBLOGIN USERID <MININGUSER>@MININGDB, PASSWORD ******
REGISTER EXTRACT <EXTRACT_NAME> DATABASE
```

6. Add the Integrated Capture Extract to the GoldenGate instance as follows:

```
ADD EXTRACT <EXTRACT_NAME>, INTEGRATED TRANLOG, <BEGIN_SPEC>
```

For example:

```
ADD EXTRACT EGGTEST1, INTEGRATED TRANLOG, BEGIN NOW
```

7. Add the local trail to the Integrated Capture configuration as follows:

```
ADD EXTTRAIL /u01/app/ggate/dirdat/st, EXTRACT EGGTEST1
```

8. Start the Integrated Capture Extract process as follows:

```
GGSCI> START EXTRACT EGGTEST1
```

How it works...

The steps for configuring an Integrated Capture process are broadly the same as the ones for the Classic Capture process. We first create a parameter file in steps 1 to 4. In step 5, we add the extract to the GoldenGate instance. In step 6, we add a local extract trail file and in the next step we start the Extract process.

When you start the Extract process you will see the following output:

```
GGSCI (prim1-ol6-112.localdomain) 11> start extract EGGTEST1
Sending START request to MANAGER ...
EXTRACT EGGTEST1 starting
```

You can check the status of the Extract process using the following command:

```
GGSCI (prim1-ol6-112.localdomain) 10> status extract EGGTEST1
EXTRACT EGGTEST1: RUNNING
```

As described earlier, an Integrated Capture process can be configured with the mining dictionary in the source database or in a separate database called a downstream mining database. When you configure the Integrated Capture Extract process in the downstream mining database mode, you need to specify the following parameter in the extract configuration file:

```
TRANLOGOPTIONS MININGUSER OGGMIN@MININGDB, MININGPASSWORD *****
```

You will also need to connect to `MININGDB` using `MININGUSER` before registering the Extract process:

```
MININGDBLOGIN USERID <MININGUSER>@MININGDB, PASSWORD ******
```

This mining user has to be set up in the same way as the GoldenGate Admin user is set up in the source database.

> If you want to use Integrated Capture mode with a source database which is running on Oracle database Version 11.2.0.2 or earlier, you must configure the Integrated Capture process in the downstream mining database mode and the downstream database must be on Version 11.2.0.3 or higher.

There's more...

Some additional parameters that should be added to the extract configuration are as follows:

- ▶ `TRANLOGOPTIONS INTEGRATEDPARAMS`: Use this parameter to control how much memory you want to allocate to the log miner dictionary. This memory is allocated out of the Streams pool in the SGA:

  ```
  TRANLOGOPTIONS INTEGRATEDPARAMS (MAX_SGA_SIZE 164)
  ```

- ▶ `MEGABYTES <N>`: This parameter controls the size of the extract trail file.

- ▶ `DYNAMICRESOLUTION`: Use this parameter to enable extract to build the metadata for each table when the extract encounters its changes for the first time.

See also

▶ The recipe *Creating an Integrated Capture with a downstream database for compressed tables* in *Chapter 7, Advanced Administration Tasks – I*

Setting up a Datapump process

Datapumps are secondary Extract processes which exist only in the GoldenGate source environments. These are optional processes. When the Datapump process is not configured, the Extract process does the job of extracting and transferring the data to the target environment. When the Datapump process is configured, it relieves the main Extract process from the task of transferring the data to the target environment. The Extract process can then solely focus on extracting the changes from the source database redo and write it to local trail files.

Getting ready

Before adding the Datapump extract, you must have a manager instance running. You should have added the main extract and a local trail location to the instance configuration. You will also need the target environment details, for example, hostname, manager port no., and the remote trail file location.

How to do it...

Just like other GoldenGate processes, the Datapump process requires creating a parameter file with some parameters. The following are the steps to configure a Datapump process in a GoldenGate source environment:

1. From the GoldenGate `Home`, run the GoldenGate Software Command Line Interface (GGSCI) as follows:

   ```
   ./ggsci
   ```

2. Edit the Datapump process configuration as follows:

   ```
   EDIT PARAMS PGGTEST1
   ```

3. This command will open an editor window. You need to add the Datapump configuration parameters in this window as follows:

   ```
   EXTRACT <DATAPUMP_NAME>
   USERID <SOURCE_GG_USER>@SOURCEDB, PASSWORD ******
   RMTHOST <HOSTNAME_IP_TARGET_SYSTEM>, MGRPORT <TARGET_MGRPORT>
   RMTTRAIL <specification>
   TABLE <replicated_table_specification>;
   ```

For example:

```
EXTRACT PGGTEST1
USERID GGATE_ADMIN@DBORATEST, PASSWORD ******
RMTHOST stdby1-ol6-112.localdomain, MGRPORT 7809
RMTTRAIL /u01/app/ggate/dirdat/rt
TABLE scott.*;
```

4. Save the file and exit the editor window.

5. Add the Datapump extract to the GoldenGate instance as follows:

```
ADD EXTRACT PGGTEST1, EXTTRAILSOURCE /u01/app/ggate/dirdat/tt
```

6. Add the remote trail to the Datapump configuration as follows:

```
ADD RMTTRAIL /u01/app/ggate/dirdat/rt, EXTRACT PGGTEST1
```

7. Start the Datapump process as follows:

```
GGSCI> START EXTRACT PGGTEST1
```

How it works...

Once you have added the parameters to the Datapump parameter file and saved it, you need to add the process to the GoldenGate instance. This is done using the ADD EXTRACT command in step 5. In step 6,, we associate a remote trail with the Datapump process and in step 7 we start the Datapump process. When you start the Datapump process you will see the following output:

```
GGSCI (prim1-ol6-112.localdomain) 10> start extract PGGTEST1
Sending START request to MANAGER ...
EXTRACT PGGTEST1 starting
```

You can check the status of the Datapump process using the following command:

```
GGSCI (prim1-ol6-112.localdomain) 10> status extract PGGTEST1
EXTRACT PGGTEST1: RUNNING
```

> If you are using virtual IPs in your environment for the target host, always configure the virtual IP in the datapump RMTHOST configuration. This virtual IP should also be resolved through DNS. This will ensure automatic discovery while configuring monitoring for GoldenGate configurations.

There's more...

The following are some additional parameters/options that can be specified in the datapump configuration:

- ▶ RMTHOSTOPTIONS: Using this option for the RMTHOST parameter, you can configure additional features such as encryption and compression for trail file transfers.

- ▶ EOFDELAY secs: This parameter controls how often GoldenGate should check the local trail file for new data.

- ▶ MEGABYTES <N>: This parameter controls the size of a remote trail file.

- ▶ PASSTHRU: This parameter is used to avoid lookup in database or definitions files in datapump are not doing any conversions and so on.

- ▶ DYNAMICRESOLUTION: Use this parameter to enable extract to build the metadata for each table when the extract encounters its changes for the first time.

See also

- ▶ Refer to the recipes, *Encrypting database user passwords Encrypting the trail files* in *Chapter 2, Setting up GoldenGate Replication*

Setting up a Replicat process

The Replicat processes are the delivery processes which are configured in the target environment. These processes read the changes from the trail files on the target system and apply them to the target database objects. If there are any transformations defined in the replicat configuration, the Replicat process takes care of those transformations as well. You can define the mapping information in the replicat configuration. The Replicat process will then apply the changes to the target database based on the mappings.

Getting ready

Before setting up replicat in the target system, you must have configured and started the Manager process.

How to do it...

Follow the following steps to configure a replicat in the target environment:

1. From the GoldenGate `Home` directory, run the GoldenGate software command line interface (GGSCI) as follows:

   ```
   ./ggsci
   ```

2. Log in to the target database through GGSCI as shown in the following code:

   ```
   GGSCI> DBLOGIN, USERID <USER> PASSWORD <PW>
   ```

3. Add the Checkpoint table as shown in the following code:

   ```
   GGSCI> ADD CHECKPOINTTABLE <SCHEMA.TABLE>
   ```

4. Edit the Replicat process configuration as shown in the following code:

   ```
   GGSCI> EDIT PARAMS RGGTEST1
   ```

5. This command will open an editor window. You need to add the replicat configuration parameters in this window as shown in the following code:

   ```
   REPLICAT <REPLICAT_NAME>
   USERID <TARGET_GG_USER>@TARGETDB, PASSWORD ******
   DISCARDFILE <DISCARDFILE_SPEC>
   MAP <mapping_specification>;
   ```

   For example:

   ```
   REPLICAT RGGTEST1
   USERID GGATE_ADMIN@TGORTEST, PASSWORD ******
   DISCARDFILE /u01/app/ggate/dirrpt/RGGTEST1.dsc, APPEND, MEGABYTES 500
   MAP SCOTT.*, SCOTT.*;
   ```

6. Save the file and exit the editor.

7. Add the replicat to the GoldenGate instance as shown in the following code:

   ```
   GGSCI> ADD REPLICAT <REPLICAT> EXTTRAIL <PATH>
   ```

   For example:

   ```
   ADD REPLICAT RGGTEST1, EXTTRAIL /u01/app/ggate/dirdat/rt
   ```

8. Start the Replicat process as shown in the following code:

   ```
   GGSCI> START REPLICAT <REPLICAT>
   ```

How it works...

In the preceding procedure we first create a Checkpoint table in the target database. As the name suggests, the Replicat process uses this table to maintain its checkpoints. In case the Replicat process crashes and it is restarted, it can read this Checkpoint table and start applying the changes from the point where it left.

Once you have added a Checkpoint table, you need to create a parameter file for the Replicat process. Once the process parameter file is created, it is then added to the GoldenGate instance. At this point, we are ready to start the Replicat process and apply the changes to the target database. You should see an output similar to the following:

```
GGSCI (stdby1-ol6-112.localdomain) 10> start replicat RGGTEST1
Sending START request to MANAGER ...
REPLICAT RGGTEST1 starting
```

You can check the status of the Replicat process using the following command:

```
GGSCI (stdby1-ol6-112.localdomain) 10> status replicat RGGTEST1
REPLICAT RGGTEST1: RUNNING
```

There's more...

Following are the common parameters that are specified in the replicat configuration:

- ► DISCARDFILE: This parameter is used to specify the name of the discard file. If the Replicat process is unable to apply any changes to the target database due to any errors, it writes the record to the discard file.
- ► EOFDELAY secs: This parameter controls how often GoldenGate should check the local trail file for new data.
- ► REPORTCOUNT: This parameter controls how often the Replicat process writes its progress to the report file.
- ► BATCHSQL: This parameter is used to specify the BATCHSQL mode for replicat.
- ► ASSUMETARGETDEFS: This parameter tells the Replicat process to assume that the source and target database object structures are the same.

See also

- ► Read *Setting up GoldenGate replication between tables with different structures using defgen* recipe in *Chapter 2, Setting Up GoldenGate Replication*
- ► *Steps to configure a BATCHSQL mode recipe* in *Chapter 6, Monitoring, Tuning, and Troubleshooting GoldenGate* for further information

2
Setting up GoldenGate Replication

The following recipes will be covered in this chapter:

- ▶ Setting up a simple GoldenGate replication configuration between two single node databases
- ▶ Setting up a GoldenGate replication with multiple process groups
- ▶ Configuring an Extract process to read from an Oracle ASM instance
- ▶ Setting up a GoldenGate replication between Oracle RAC databases
- ▶ Determining the size of trail file areas
- ▶ Verifying the data transfer on the target system
- ▶ Generating encryption keys
- ▶ Encrypting database user passwords
- ▶ Encrypting the trail files
- ▶ Setting up a GoldenGate replication between tables with different structures using defgen

Introduction

There are various steps in configuring a GoldenGate environment. Some of the steps of this setup can be different for different database environments and requirements. In this chapter, we will go through the steps that should be performed for a simple replication and a complex one. We will also look into how to divide the load into multiple process groups for a busy system. Further, we will cover the set up required for ASM and RAC environments, and also how to encrypt the password and trail files. We will also look into the steps required for replication between tables with different structures.

Setting up a simple GoldenGate replication configuration between two single node databases

In this recipe we will look at how to configure GoldenGate for continuous replication between two single node databases.

Getting ready

For this setup, we make the following assumptions:

1. The source and target database have already been set up.
2. Both the databases have a schema called SCOTT which is in a consistent state. No transformations will be performed in this recipe.
3. Oracle GoldenGate binaries are already installed in both sites.
4. The extract method used in this example will be classic capture.
5. Supplemental Logging is enabled at database and table level for all the objects to be replicated.

How to do it...

We will follow these steps to set up this replication configuration.

Perform the following steps in the source database:

1. Set up the GoldenGate user. Run the following command in the source database:

```
sqlplus sys/**** as sysdba
CREATE USER GGATE_ADMIN identified by GGATE_ADMIN;
GRANT CREATE SESSION, ALTER SESSION to GGATE_ADMIN;
GRANT ALTER SYSTEM TO GGATE_ADMIN;
```

```
GRANT CONNECT, RESOURCE to GGATE_ADMIN;
GRANT SELECT ANY DICTIONARY to GGATE_ADMIN;
GRANT FLASHBACK ANY TABLE to GGATE_ADMIN;
GRANT SELECT ON DBA_CLUSTERS TO GGATE_ADMIN;
GRANT EXECUTE ON DBMS_FLASHBACK TO GGATE_ADMIN;
GRANT SELECT ANY TRANSACTION To GGATE_ADMIN;
GRANT SELECT ON SCOTT.DEPT to GGATE_ADMIN;
GRANT SELECT ON SCOTT.EMP to GGATE_ADMIN;
GRANT SELECT ON SCOTT.BONUS to GGATE_ADMIN;
GRANT SELECT ON SCOTT.SALGRADE to GGATE_ADMIN;
```

2. Set up the source GoldenGate manager process:

```
./ggsci
EDIT PARAMS MGR
PORT 7809
DYNAMICPORTLIST 7810-7820, 7830
AUTOSTART ER *
AUTORESTART ER *, RETRIES 4, WAITMINUTES 4
PURGEOLDEXTRACTS /u01/app/ggate/dirdat/st*, USECHECKPOINTS,
MINKEEPHOURS
```

3. Start the source manager process:

```
START MGR
```

4. Create a GoldenGate classic Extract process in the source environment:

```
./ggsci
EDIT PARAMS EGGTEST1
EXTRACT EGGTEST1
USERID GGATE_ADMIN@DBORATEST, PASSWORD GGATE_ADMIN
EXTTRAIL /u01/app/ggate/dirdat/st
TABLE scott.*;
```

5. Create a GoldenGate Datapump process in the source environment:

```
./ggsci
EDIT PARAMS PGGTEST1
EXTRACT PGGTEST1
USERID GGATE_ADMIN@DBORATEST, PASSWORD GGATE_ADMIN
RMTHOST stdby1-ol6-112 , MGRPORT 8809
RMTTRAIL /u01/app/ggate/dirdat/rt
TABLE scott.*;
```

6. Add the Extract process to the source manager configuration:

```
ADD EXTRACT EGGTEST1, TRANLOG, BEGIN NOW
```

7. Add the local trail to the Extract process:

```
ADD EXTTRAIL /u01/app/ggate/dirdat/st, EXTRACT EGGTEST1
```

8. Add the Datapump process to the source manager configuration:

```
ADD EXTRACT PGGTEST1, EXTTRAILSOURCE /u01/app/ggate/dirdat/st
```

9. Add the remote trail location to the Datapump process:

```
ADD RMTTRAIL /u01/app/ggate/dirdat/rt, EXTRACT PGGTEST1
```

Perform the following steps in the target database:

1. Set up the GoldenGate user:

```
sqlplus sys/**** as sysdba
CREATE USER GGATE_ADMIN identified by GGATE_ADMIN DEFAULT
TABLESPACE GGATE_ADMIN_DAT;
ALTER USER GGATE_ADMIN QUOTA UNLIMITED ON GGATE_ADMIN_DAT;
GRANT CREATE SESSION, ALTER SESSION to GGATE_ADMIN;
GRANT CONNECT, RESOURCE to GGATE_ADMIN;
GRANT SELECT ANY DICTIONARY to GGATE_ADMIN;
GRANT SELECT ANY TABLE TO GGATE_ADMIN;
GRANT CREATE TABLE TO GGATE_ADMIN;
GRANT SELECT, INSERT, UPDATE, DELETE ON SCOTT.DEPT to GGATE_ADMIN;
GRANT SELECT, INSERT, UPDATE, DELETE ON SCOTT.EMP to GGATE_ADMIN;
GRANT SELECT, INSERT, UPDATE, DELETE ON SCOTT.SALGRADE to GGATE_
ADMIN;
GRANT SELECT, INSERT, UPDATE, DELETE ON SCOTT.BONUS to GGATE_
ADMIN;
```

2. Set up target GoldenGate manager process:

```
./ggsci
EDIT PARAMS MGR
PORT 8809
DYNAMICPORTLIST 8810-8820, 8830
AUTOSTART ER *
AUTORESTART ER *, RETRIES 4, WAITMINUTES 4
STARTUPVALIDATIONDELAY 5
PURGEOLDEXTRACTS /u01/app/ggate/dirdat/rt*, USECHECKPOINTS,
MINKEEPHOURS 2
```

3. Start the target manager process:

```
START MGR
```

4. Create a checkpoint table in the target database:

    ```
    ./ggsci
    DBLOGIN, USERID GGATE_ADMIN@TGORTEST PASSWORD *****
    ADD CHECKPOINTTABLE
    ```

5. Create a GoldenGate Replicat process in the target environment:

    ```
    ./ggsci
    EDIT PARAMS RGGTEST1
    REPLICAT RGGTEST1
    USERID GGATE_ADMIN@TGORTEST, PASSWORD GGATE_ADMIN
    DISCARDFILE /u01/app/ggate/dirrpt/RGGTEST1.dsc,append,MEGABYTES
    500
    ASSUMETARGETDEFS
    MAP SCOTT.*, TARGET SCOTT.*;
    ```

    ❑   Add the Replicat process to the target manager configuration:

    ```
    ADD REPLICAT RGGTEST1, EXTTRAIL /u01/app/ggate/dirdat/rt,
    BEGIN NOW, CHECKPOINTTABLE CHECKPOINT
    ```

    Perform the following steps in the source database:

6. Start the Extract and Datapump process:

    ```
    START EXTRACT EGGTEST1
    START EXTRACT PGGTEST1
    ```

    Perform the following steps in the target database:

7. Start the Replicat process:

    ```
    START REPLICAT RGGTEST1
    ```

How it works...

The replication configuration requires set up in both the source and target environments. In each database, GoldenGate requires an Admin user which it connects to the database. In the preceding steps, we first set up a GoldenGate Admin user in the source database and grant it necessary privileges. After this we create a GoldenGate manager instance in the source environment and start it. Then we create an Extract and a Datapump process in the source environment. Then we add the Extract process, extract trail, and Datapump process to the manager configuration. We also need to associate the remote trail location to the Datapump process to enable it to transfer the files to the target server.

After this we set up the GoldenGate Admin user in the target database with necessary privileges. We then create the manager instance in the target environment and start it. After this we create a Replicat process in the target environment. The Replicat processes require a checkpoint table in the target database to maintain checkpoints. We then create a checkpoint table in the GGATE_ADMIN schema. Then we create a Replicat process and add it to the target manager configuration.

Once all the setup is done, we need to start the Extract, Datapump, and Replicat processes to enable the continuous replication.

There's more...

The Datapump process, as we know, is always an optional process in the GoldenGate configuration. This process is mainly used to offload the task of TCP/IP network transfer and data transformation from the main Extract process. Using Datapump also provides recoverability benefits in case of network failures.

Although a Datapump process is always used in the production environments, one of the practical scenarios where it offers further advantages is when replicating between systems which are on two different networks. In such an environment, you can configure an Extract and Datapump on the source server. The source server Datapump then ships the trail files to an intermediary server, which can see both networks and where there is an additional Datapump that reads the trail files, and transfers them on to the target server. The Datapump process can also do the transformations on the intermediary server as long as both the source and target databases use the same character set.

See also

> ▸ See *Setting up a GoldenGate replication between tables with different structures using defgen* recipe later in this chapter

Setting up a GoldenGate replication with multiple process groups

If your source system is a very busy OLTP system, with a high rate of data changes, then you will find that a single set of GoldenGate processes is not sufficient to replicate the load to the target environment in real time. In such a situation Oracle recommends splitting the load into multiple process groups.

Getting ready

For this recipe we will use the `Order Entry` demo schema. This schema has been created in both source and target databases, and is in the same state. The GoldenGate binaries, the GoldenGate Admin user, and manager instance have also been set up in the source and target environment.

How to do it...

In this recipe we will set up the following configuration for replicating the `Order Entry` schema:

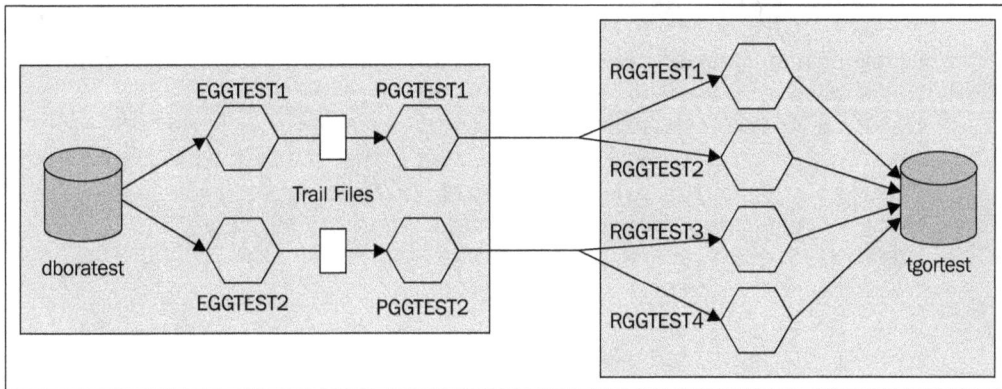

As you can see from the preceding diagram, the replication setup performed here will consist of two Extract processes, two Datapumps, and four Replicat processes.

Perform the following steps in the source database:

1. Create the first Extract process `EGGTEST1` in the source environment:

    ```
    ./ggsci
    EDIT PARAMS EGGTEST1
    EXTRACT EGGTEST1
    USERID GGATE_ADMIN@DBORATEST, PASSWORD GGATE_ADMIN
    EXTTRAIL /u01/app/ggate/dirdat/EGGTEST1/st
    TABLE oe.warehouses,FILTER (@RANGE (1,2));
    TABLE oe.subcategory_ref_list_nestedtab,FILTER (@RANGE (1,2));
    TABLE oe.purchaseorder,FILTER (@RANGE (1,2));
    TABLE oe.promotions,FILTER (@RANGE (1,2));
    TABLE oe.product_ref_list_nestedtab,FILTER (@RANGE (1,2));
    TABLE oe.product_information,FILTER (@RANGE (1,2));
    TABLE oe.product_descriptions,FILTER (@RANGE (1,2));
    TABLE oe.order_items,FILTER (@RANGE (1,2));
    ```

```
      TABLE oe.orders,FILTER (@RANGE (1,2));
      TABLE oe.lineitem_table,FILTER (@RANGE (1,2));
      TABLE oe.inventories,FILTER (@RANGE (1,2));
      TABLE oe.customers,FILTER (@RANGE (1,2));
      TABLE oe.categories_tab,FILTER (@RANGE (1,2));
      TABLE oe.action_table,FILTER (@RANGE (1,2));
```

2. Create the second Extract process EGGTEST2 in the source environment:

```
   ./ggsci
   EDIT PARAMS EGGTEST2
   EXTRACT EGGTEST2
   USERID GGATE_ADMIN@DBORATEST, PASSWORD GGATE_ADMIN
   EXTTRAIL /u01/app/ggate/dirdat/EGGTEST2/st
   TABLE oe.warehouses,FILTER (@RANGE (2,2));
   TABLE oe.subcategory_ref_list_nestedtab,FILTER (@RANGE (2,2));
   TABLE oe.purchaseorder,FILTER (@RANGE (2,2));
   TABLE oe.promotions,FILTER (@RANGE (2,2));
   TABLE oe.product_ref_list_nestedtab,FILTER (@RANGE (2,2));
   TABLE oe.product_information,FILTER (@RANGE (2,2));
   TABLE oe.product_descriptions,FILTER (@RANGE (2,2));
   TABLE oe.order_items,FILTER (@RANGE (2,2));
   TABLE oe.orders,FILTER (@RANGE (2,2));
   TABLE oe.lineitem_table,FILTER (@RANGE (2,2));
   TABLE oe.inventories,FILTER (@RANGE (2,2));
   TABLE oe.customers,FILTER (@RANGE (2,2));
   TABLE oe.categories_tab,FILTER (@RANGE (2,2));
   TABLE oe.action_table,FILTER (@RANGE (2,2));
```

3. Create the first Datapump process PGGTEST1 in the source environment:

```
   EDIT PARAMS PGGTEST1
   EXTRACT PGGTEST1
   USERID GGATE_ADMIN@DBORATEST, PASSWORD GGATE_ADMIN
   RMTHOST stdby1-ol6-112 , MGRPORT 8809
   RMTTRAIL /u01/app/ggate/dirdat/PGGTEST1/rt
   TABLE oe.*
```

4. Create the second Datapump process PGGTEST2 in the source environment:

```
   EDIT PARAMS PGGTEST2
   EXTRACT PGGTEST2
   USERID GGATE_ADMIN@DBORATEST, PASSWORD GGATE_ADMIN
   RMTHOST stdby1-ol6-112 , MGRPORT 8809
   RMTTRAIL /u01/app/ggate/dirdat/PGGTEST2/rt
   TABLE oe.*
```

5. Add both the Extract processes to the source manager configuration:

```
ADD EXTRACT EGGTEST1, TRANLOG, BEGIN NOW
ADD EXTRACT EGGTEST2, TRANLOG, BEGIN NOW
```

6. Add both the local trail locations to the Extract processes:

```
ADD EXTTRAIL /u01/app/ggate/dirdat/EGGTEST1/st, EXTRACT EGGTEST1
ADD EXTTRAIL /u01/app/ggate/dirdat/EGGTEST2/st, EXTRACT EGGTEST2
```

7. Add the Datapump processes to the source manager configuration:

```
ADD EXTRACT PGGTEST1, EXTTRAILSOURCE /u01/app/ggate/dirdat/
EGGTEST1/st
ADD EXTRACT PGGTEST2, EXTTRAILSOURCE /u01/app/ggate/dirdat/
EGGTEST2/st
```

8. Add the remote trail locations to the Datapump process:

```
ADD RMTTRAIL /u01/app/ggate/dirdat/PGGTEST1/rt, EXTRACT PGGTEST1
ADD RMTTRAIL /u01/app/ggate/dirdat/PGGTEST2/rt, EXTRACT PGGTEST2
```

Perform the following steps in the target database:

1. Create a checkpoint table in the target database:

```
./ggsci
DBLOGIN, USERID GGATE_ADMIN@TGORTEST PASSWORD *****
ADD CHECKPOINTTABLE
```

2. Create the first GoldenGate Replicat process in the target environment:

```
./ggsci
EDIT PARAMS RGGTEST1
REPLICAT RGGTEST1
USERID GGATE_ADMIN@TGORTEST, PASSWORD GGATE_ADMIN
DISCARDFILE /u01/app/ggate/dirrpt/RGGTEST1.dsc,append,MEGABYTES
500
ASSUMETARGETDEFS
MAP oe.warehouses, TARGET oe.warehouses, FILTER (@RANGE (1,2));
MAP oe.subcategory_ref_list_nestedtab, TARGET oe.subcategory_ref_
list_nestedtab, FILTER (@RANGE (1,2));
MAP oe.purchaseorder, TARGET oe.purchaseorder, FILTER (@RANGE
(1,2));
MAP oe.promotions, TARGET oe.promotions, FILTER (@RANGE (1,2));
MAP oe.product_ref_list_nestedtab, TARGET oe.product_ref_list_
nestedtab, FILTER (@RANGE (1,2));
MAP oe.product_information, TARGET oe.product_information, FILTER
(@RANGE (1,2));
MAP oe.product_descriptions, TARGET oe.product_descriptions,
FILTER (@RANGE (1,2));
```

```
MAP oe.order_items, TARGET oe.order_items, FILTER (@RANGE (1,2));
MAP oe.orders, TARGET oe.orders, FILTER (@RANGE (1,2));
MAP oe.lineitem_table, TARGET oe.lineitem_table, FILTER (@RANGE
(1,2));
MAP oe.inventories, TARGET oe.inventories, FILTER (@RANGE (1,2));
MAP oe.customers, TARGET oe.customers, FILTER (@RANGE (1,2));
MAP oe.categories_tab, TARGET oe.categories_tab, FILTER (@RANGE
(1,2));
MAP oe.action_table, TARGET oe.action_table, FILTER (@RANGE
(1,2));
```

3. Create the second GoldenGate Replicat process in the target environment:

```
./ggsci
EDIT PARAMS RGGTEST2
REPLICAT RGGTEST2
USERID GGATE_ADMIN@TGORTEST, PASSWORD GGATE_ADMIN
DISCARDFILE /u01/app/ggate/dirrpt/RGGTEST2.dsc,append,MEGABYTES
500
ASSUMETARGETDEFS
MAP oe.warehouses, TARGET oe.warehouses, FILTER (@RANGE (2,2));
MAP oe.subcategory_ref_list_nestedtab, TARGET oe.subcategory_ref_
list_nestedtab, FILTER (@RANGE (2,2));
MAP oe.purchaseorder, TARGET oe.purchaseorder, FILTER (@RANGE
(2,2));
MAP oe.promotions, TARGET oe.promotions, FILTER (@RANGE (2,2));
MAP oe.product_ref_list_nestedtab, TARGET oe.product_ref_list_
nestedtab, FILTER (@RANGE (2,2));
MAP oe.product_information, TARGET oe.product_information, FILTER
(@RANGE (2,2));
MAP oe.product_descriptions, TARGET oe.product_descriptions,
FILTER (@RANGE (2,2));
MAP oe.order_items, TARGET oe.order_items, FILTER (@RANGE (2,2));
MAP oe.orders, TARGET oe.orders, FILTER (@RANGE (2,2));
MAP oe.lineitem_table, TARGET oe.lineitem_table, FILTER (@RANGE
(2,2));
MAP oe.inventories, TARGET oe.inventories, FILTER (@RANGE (2,2));
MAP oe.customers, TARGET oe.customers, FILTER (@RANGE (2,2));
MAP oe.categories_tab, TARGET oe.categories_tab, FILTER (@RANGE
(2,2));
MAP oe.action_table, TARGET oe.action_table, FILTER (@RANGE
(2,2));
```

4. Create the third GoldenGate Replicat process in the target environment:

```
./ggsci
EDIT PARAMS RGGTEST3
REPLICAT RGGTEST3
USERID GGATE_ADMIN@TGORTEST, PASSWORD GGATE_ADMIN
DISCARDFILE /u01/app/ggate/dirrpt/RGGTEST3.dsc,append,MEGABYTES
500
ASSUMETARGETDEFS
MAP oe.warehouses, TARGET oe.warehouses, FILTER (@RANGE (1,2));
MAP oe.subcategory_ref_list_nestedtab, TARGET oe.subcategory_ref_
list_nestedtab, FILTER (@RANGE (1,2));
MAP oe.purchaseorder, TARGET oe.purchaseorder, FILTER (@RANGE
(1,2));
MAP oe.promotions, TARGET oe.promotions, FILTER (@RANGE (1,2));
MAP oe.product_ref_list_nestedtab, TARGET oe.product_ref_list_
nestedtab, FILTER (@RANGE (1,2));
MAP oe.product_information, TARGET oe.product_information, FILTER
(@RANGE (1,2));
MAP oe.product_descriptions, TARGET oe.product_descriptions,
FILTER (@RANGE (1,2));
MAP oe.order_items, TARGET oe.order_items, FILTER (@RANGE (1,2));
MAP oe.orders, TARGET oe.orders, FILTER (@RANGE (1,2));
MAP oe.lineitem_table, TARGET oe.lineitem_table, FILTER (@RANGE
(1,2));
MAP oe.inventories, TARGET oe.inventories, FILTER (@RANGE (1,2));
MAP oe.customers, TARGET oe.customers, FILTER (@RANGE (1,2));
MAP oe.categories_tab, TARGET oe.categories_tab, FILTER (@RANGE
(1,2));
MAP oe.action_table, TARGET oe.action_table, FILTER (@RANGE
(1,2));
```

5. Create the fourth GoldenGate Replicat process in the target environment:

```
./ggsci
EDIT PARAMS RGGTEST4
REPLICAT RGGTEST4
USERID GGATE_ADMIN@TGORTEST, PASSWORD GGATE_ADMIN
DISCARDFILE /u01/app/ggate/dirrpt/RGGTEST4.dsc,append,MEGABYTES
500
ASSUMETARGETDEFS
MAP oe.warehouses, TARGET oe.warehouses, FILTER (@RANGE (2,2));
MAP oe.subcategory_ref_list_nestedtab, TARGET oe.subcategory_ref_
list_nestedtab, FILTER (@RANGE (2,2));
MAP oe.purchaseorder, TARGET oe.purchaseorder, FILTER (@RANGE
(2,2));
MAP oe.promotions, TARGET oe.promotions, FILTER (@RANGE (2,2));
```

```
MAP oe.product_ref_list_nestedtab, TARGET oe.product_ref_list_
nestedtab, FILTER (@RANGE (2,2));
MAP oe.product_information, TARGET oe.product_information, FILTER
(@RANGE (2,2));
MAP oe.product_descriptions, TARGET oe.product_descriptions,
FILTER (@RANGE (2,2));
MAP oe.order_items, TARGET oe.order_items, FILTER (@RANGE (2,2));
MAP oe.orders, TARGET oe.orders, FILTER (@RANGE (2,2));
MAP oe.lineitem_table, TARGET oe.lineitem_table, FILTER (@RANGE
(2,2));
MAP oe.inventories, TARGET oe.inventories, FILTER (@RANGE (2,2));
MAP oe.customers, TARGET oe.customers, FILTER (@RANGE (2,2));
MAP oe.categories_tab, TARGET oe.categories_tab, FILTER (@RANGE
(2,2));
MAP oe.action_table, TARGET oe.action_table, FILTER (@RANGE
(2,2));
```

6. Add the Replicat processes to the target manager configuration:

```
ADD REPLICAT RGGTEST1, EXTTRAIL /u01/app/ggate/dirdat/PGGTEST1/rt,
BEGIN NOW
ADD REPLICAT RGGTEST2, EXTTRAIL /u01/app/ggate/dirdat/PGGTEST1/rt,
BEGIN NOW
ADD REPLICAT RGGTEST3, EXTTRAIL /u01/app/ggate/dirdat/PGGTEST2/rt,
BEGIN NOW
ADD REPLICAT RGGTEST4, EXTTRAIL /u01/app/ggate/dirdat/PGGTEST2/rt,
BEGIN NOW
```

Perform the following steps in the source database:

1. Start the Extract and Datapump processes:

```
START EXTRACT EGGTEST1
START EXTRACT EGGTEST2
START EXTRACT EGGTEST1
START EXTRACT PGGTEST2
```

Perform the following steps in the target database:

1. Start the Replicat processes:

```
START REPLICAT RGGTEST1
START REPLICAT RGGTEST2
START REPLICAT RGGTEST3
START REPLICAT RGGTEST4
```

How it works...

In this example, we have split the extract load into two streams using the FILTER clause with a RANGE option. The FILTER clause is used to refine the changes that a GoldenGate process looks for. The RANGE function distributes the load evenly into multiple streams by calculating the hash value of the key columns in the table. By using both of these options each Extract process only processes half the load. Each Extract process writes its trail files to a separate directory under $GG_HOME/dirdat/ and is configured with a dedicated Datapump process on the source server. These Datapump processes then transfer the trail files to the remote server and write them to separate directories there. The replicat load on the target server is split into four parallel streams. The first two Replicat processes (RGGTEST1 and RGGTEST2) apply the changes captured by the first Extract process (EGGTEST1) on the source server. The next two Replicat processes (RGGTEST3 and RGGTEST4) apply the changes captured by the second Extract process (EGGTEST2) on the source server.

There's more...

You would configure multiple processes to enhance the GoldenGate performance. In most cases you would find that it is the Replicat process that is causing the bottleneck and needs intervention. There are many performance enhancements in the latest release of Oracle GoldenGate. However, at times you would find that adding additional process groups is the only way of achieving the desired replication lag targets. There are various ways to determine how to split tables between various processes which are as follows:

- You can specify different tables in different processes
- General rule of thumb is to keep related tables together
- Tables with referential integrity constraints should always be kept in the same process group
- You can use the RANGE function to logically split the load of related tables into multiple streams
- If a single process is not able to handle the load of high rate of change on a single table, then you should split its load using the RANGE clause

See also

- See the *Splitting the replication load into multiple process groups for optimal performance* recipe in *Chapter 6, Monitoring, Tuning, and Troubleshooting GoldenGate*

Configuring an Extract process to read from an Oracle ASM instance

If your `source` database is on ASM and the archive logs reside in an ASM diskgroup, the GoldenGate extract requires some additional configuration to be able to read them. In this recipe we will look at the additional parameters that you need to specify in the extract parameter file for this.

How to do it...

The setup required for reading archive logs from ASM depends on the version of the source database.

For Oracle 10gR2 (10.2.0.5 or later) / Oracle 11gR2 (11.2.0.2 or later):

1. Modify the extract parameter files to use the `TRANSLOGOPTIONS` parameter:

```
./ggsci
EDIT PARAMS EGGTEST1
EXTRACT EGGTEST1
USERID GGATE_ADMIN@DBORATEST, PASSWORD AADAAAAAAAAAAAFAQCFIIDLCUEL
FNFECLITBSCAHYBBHHEUGKDNICDCCDCFELJDJFFEAUHUBFGWIUJGCAJJDNDPDZEOHG
ILBIIWCUIBHHGPBKBHB, AES256, ENCRYPTKEY dbkey1
EXTTRAIL /u01/app/ggate/dirdat/st
TRANSLOGOPTIONS DBLOGREADER
TABLE scott.*;
```

2. Save the file and exit the editor window.

3. Start the Extract process:

```
GGSCI> START EGGTEST1
```

For Oracle 10gR2 (10.2.0.4 or earlier) / Oracle 11gR2(11.2.0.1 or earlier):

1. Add the following entry to `tnsnames.ora` to enable a bequeath connection for ASM:

```
ASM =
(DESCRIPTION =
(ADDRESS = (PROTOCOL = BEQ)
(PROGRAM = <ORACLE_HOME>/bin/oracle)
(ARGV0 = oracle+ASM1)
(ARGS = '(DESCRIPTION=(LOCAL=YES)(ADDRESS=(PROTOCOL=BEQ)))')
(ENVS = 'ORACLE_HOME=<ORACLE_HOME>/asm,ORACLE_SID=+ASM1')
)
(CONNECT_DATA =
(SERVICE_NAME = +ASM) (INSTANCE_NAME = +ASM1)))
```

2. Encrypt the ASM sys user password:

```
./ggsci
encrypt password helloworld AES256, encryptkey dbkey1
Encrypted password:  AADAAAAAAAAAAAKAHBABQBPFFEVGRHGIFFBAQHSHGD
CHKCTFFCQHKCPCFCKJSGPIPJWDQAGHRCQBZEQFOGUELCTDPDEJMBDJBJWAOGE
JJEQHBCEF
Algorithm used:  AES256
```

3. Modify the process parameter files to use the TRANSLOGOPTIONS parameter with an encrypted password:

```
./ggsci
EDIT PARAMS EGGTEST1
EXTRACT EGGTEST1
USERID GGATE_ADMIN@DBORATEST, PASSWORD
AADAAAAAAAAAAAFAQCFIIDLCUELFNFECLITBSCA
HYBBHHEUGKDNICDCCDCFELJDJFFEAUHUBFGWIUJGCAJJDNDPDZEOHGILBIIWC
UIBHHGPBKBHB, AES256, ENCRYPTKEY dbkey1
EXTTRAIL /u01/app/ggate/dirdat/st
TRANLOGOPTIONS ASMUSER SYS@ASM, ASMPASSWORD
AADAAAAAAAAAAAFAQCFIIDLCUELFNFECLITBSC
AHYBBHHEUGKDNICDCCDCFELJDJFFEAUHUBFGWIUJGCAJJDNDPDZEOHGIL
BIIWCUIBHHGPBKBHB, AES256, ENCRYPTKEY dbkey1
TABLE scott.*;
```

4. Save the file and exit the editor window.

5. Start the Extract process:

```
GGSCI> START EGGTEST1
```

How it works...

For the newer Oracle 10gR2 and 11gR2 versions, GoldenGate connects through the database instance to read the archived log files in the ASM diskgroup. This enables the Extract process to read the archived logs in a much more efficient way than the old way of accessing it directly through an ASM instance.

If your database is on Oracle 10gR2 (10.2.0.5 or earlier) or 11g (11.2.0.1 or earlier), then you must configure an ASM user with sysdba privileges in the extract configuration to enable it to login to an ASM instance and read the redo/archived logs. You can specify the ASM user password in the extract configuration file, however, the best practice is to encrypt the password using the encrypt tool, as done in step 2 in the previous section, and specify the generated key in the parameter files.

> Although in the newer Oracle releases you don't need to configure the ASM user in the extract configuration, it is recommended to configure both the ways to enable the extract to continue processing archived logs in the event of a database instance not being available.
>
> TRANSLOGOPTIONS DBLOGREADER
>
> -- TRANSLOGOPTIONS ASMUSER SYS@ASM, PASSWORD *****
>
> If the `source` database instance is not available and you still have archived logs which have not yet been mined, you can swap the `TRANSLOGOPTIONS` parameters to allow extract to access the ASM instance directly.

Setting up a GoldenGate replication between Oracle RAC databases

High Availability is the buzz word in today's world. The systems need to be available all the time. The applications store their data in the databases, so it becomes quite critical for the databases to be fault tolerant and always available. **Oracle RAC** is a popular choice when companies want to build resilience in their systems. More and more applications are becoming RAC aware and it is quite common to see companies migrating most of their applications to Oracle RAC-based database environments.

Replicating the data between Oracle RAC databases requires some additional setup. In this recipe we will look into what configuration steps are required to setup replication between Oracle RAC environments. We will not cover the set up required to make the GoldenGate replication highly available itself as there are many ways to do it and will be covered in separate recipes in *Chapter 5, Oracle GoldenGate High Availability*.

Getting ready

This recipe assumes that GoldenGate has already been installed in the source and target environment. Both the source and target databases are **2 Node Oracle RAC 11.2.0.3** databases. In both environments, GoldenGate has been installed in a shared filesystem /u01.

How to do it...

Perform the following steps in the source database:

1. Create an Extract process EGGTEST1 in the source environment:

   ```
   ./ggsci
   EXTRACT EGGTEST1
   USERID GGATE_ADMIN@RACDB, PASSWORD GGATE_ADMIN
   ```

```
TRANSLOGOPTIONS DBLOGREADER
EXTTRAIL /u01/app/ggate/dirdat/st
TABLE scott.*;
```

2. Create a GoldenGate Datapump process in the source environment:

```
./ggsci
EDIT PARAMS PGGTEST1
EXTRACT PGGTEST1
USERID GGATE_ADMIN@RACDB, PASSWORD GGATE_ADMIN
RMTHOST tg-oggvip.localdomain , MGRPORT 8809
RMTTRAIL /u01/app/ggate/dirdat/rt
TABLE scott.*;
```

3. Add the Extract process to the source manager configuration:

```
ADD EXTRACT EGGTEST1, THREADS 2, TRANLOG, BEGIN NOW
```

4. Add the local trail to the Extract process:

```
ADD EXTTRAIL /u01/app/ggate/dirdat/st, EXTRACT EGGTEST1, MEGABYTES
100
```

5. Add the Datapump process to the source manager configuration:

```
ADD EXTRACT PGGTEST1, EXTTRAILSOURCE /u01/app/ggate/dirdat/st
```

6. Add the remote trail location to the Datapump process:

```
ADD RMTTRAIL /u01/app/ggate/dirdat/rt, EXTRACT PGGTEST1, MEGABYTES
100
```

7. Start the Extract and Datapump process:

```
START EXTRACT EGGTEST1
START EXTRACT PGGTEST1
```

Perform the following steps in the target database:

1. Create a GoldenGate Replicat process in the target environment:

```
./ggsci
EDIT PARAMS RGGTEST1
REPLICAT RGGTEST1
USERID GGATE_ADMIN@TGRACDB, PASSWORD GGATE_ADMIN
DISCARDFILE /u01/app/ggate/dirrpt/RGGTEST1.dsc,append,MEGABYTES
500
ASSUMETARGETDEFS
MAP SCOTT.*, TARGET SCOTT.*;
```

2. Add the Replicat process to the target manager configuration:

```
ADD REPLICAT RGGTEST1, EXTTRAIL /u01/app/ggate/dirdat/
rt,CHECKPOINTTABLE CHECKPOINT, BEGIN NOW
```

3. Start the Replicat process:

```
START REPLICAT RGGTEST1
```

How it works...

The setup assumes that Oracle GoldenGate is already installed in the source and target environment, and a GoldenGate manager instance has been set up as well. We create an extract parameter file. Since this database is running on Oracle ASM, we need to specify the `TRANSLOGOPTIONS DBLOGREADER` parameter to enable the Extract process to read the archive log from ASM. We then create a Datapump process parameter file. The key thing to note in the Datapump configuration in the case of the Oracle RAC-based target system is the name of the remote host. The GoldenGate manager resource should be configured on a Virtual IP in the target environment and this Virtual IP should be specified as the remote host in the source Datapump configuration.

In an RAC environment, you need to specify the threads parameter while adding the Extract process to the GoldenGate manager configuration.

The TNS entry used in the replicat configuration should be configured using the TAF policies in your environment.

You can also use GoldenGate to set up replication between two environments when only one of them is clustered.

See also

For information on how to configure GoldenGate in an RAC environment see the following receipes in *Chapter 5, Oracle GoldenGate High Availability*:

- ▸ *Creating a highly available GoldenGate configuration using Oracle Clusterware and ACFS*

- ▸ *Creating a highly available GoldenGate configuration using Oracle Clusterware and OCFS2*

- ▸ *Creating a highly available GoldenGate configuration using Oracle Clusterware and DBFS*

Determining the size of trail file areas

You would most likely create an Extract process with a dedicated Datapump process in the source environment. The Datapump process can suffer an outage in case of any network issue. However, it, resumes the trail file transfer to the remote site when it is up again. In such a situation you would want the Extract process to continue extracting the data into the trail files on the source system.

The trail files are stored in the filesystem which would be finite in space. The size of the trail file area will determine how many trail files can be stored, which in effect will determine how long the Extract process can continue generating the trail files while the Datapump process is down. This will determine the overall network outage capacity of your replication infrastructure. Clearly, it is quite important to size the trail file areas appropriately to avoid the situations where the Extract process has to be stopped because of lack of available space on the filesystem.

In this recipe we will go through the method which you can use to calculate the required trail file area sizes for your environment.

How to do it...

1. Calculate the trail file area size using the following formula:

   ```
   Trail file area size = Redo Log Volume in an hour X Maximum number
   of hours downtime X .4
   ```

How it works...

For this formula, you need to determine the amount of redo logs generated in the busiest period for your system and the maximum amount of replication downtime that you can bear for your target system. Oracle recommends multiplying the product of these with .4 as usually GoldenGate requires only 40 percent of the data from the archive logs.

You should however, test the size of trail files generated for a period and measure it with the size of the archive files generated to determine the correct ratio for your system.

Since GoldenGate stores Object Names with each update in trail files, if the names of the objects in your system are quite long, you may find that the ratio of trail file size to archive log size is much higher than 4:10.

General rule of thumb for sizing the trail files is keeping them same as the Archive Log size. Keeping it too small will cause very frequent switches which will cause performance overhead.

Verifying the data transfer on the target system

This recipe will show you how to verify data transfer on a target system.

Getting ready

For this recipe we will use the continuous replication setup for the SCOTT schema done in *Setting up a simple GoldenGate replication configuration between two single node databases* earlier in this chapter.

How to do it...

Perform the following steps in the source database:

1. Check the number of employees whose salary is greater than 3000:

    ```
    SQL> select * from EMP where sal>3000;

    EMPNO  ENAME   JOB       MGR   HIREDATE   SAL  COMM  DEPTNO
    -----  -----   ---       ---   --------   ---  ----  ------
    7839   KING    PRESIDENT       17-NOV-81  5000          10
    ```

2. Perform some updates in the source database. Here we increase the salary for all employees by 1000:

    ```
    SQL> update SCOTT.EMP set sal=sal+1000;
    14 rows updated.

    SQL> commit;
    Commit complete.
    ```

3. Check the Extract process statistics:

    ```
    GGSCI (prim1-ol6-112.localdomain) 3> stats EGGTEST1 hourly

    Sending STATS request to EXTRACT EGGTEST1 ...

    Start of Statistics at 2012-10-18 10:58:58.

    Output to /u01/app/ggate/dirdat/st:

    Extracting from SCOTT.EMP to SCOTT.EMP:

    *** Hourly statistics since 2012-10-18 10:56:09 ***
    ```

```
               Total inserts                        0.00
               Total updates                       14.00
               Total deletes                        0.00
               Total discards                       0.00
               Total operations                    14.00
```

        End of Statistics.

4. Check the Datapump Process Statistics:

```
        GGSCI (prim1-ol6-112.localdomain) 2> stats pggtest1 hourly

        Sending STATS request to EXTRACT PGGTEST1 ...

        Start of Statistics at 2012-10-18 11:03:15.

        Output to /u01/app/ggate/dirdat/rt:

        Extracting from SCOTT.EMP to SCOTT.EMP:

        *** Hourly statistics since 2012-10-18 10:57:13 ***
               Total inserts                        0.00
               Total updates                       14.00
               Total deletes                        0.00
               Total discards                       0.00
               Total operations                    14.00
```

        End of Statistics.

Perform the following steps in the target database:

1. Check the Replicat Process Statistics:

```
        GGSCI (stdby1-ol6-112.localdomain) 2> stats rggtest1 hourly

        Sending STATS request to REPLICAT RGGTEST1 ...

        Start of Statistics at 2012-10-18 11:05:05.

        Replicating from SCOTT.EMP to SCOTT.EMP:

        *** Hourly statistics since 2012-10-18 10:58:07 ***
               Total inserts                        0.00
               Total updates                       14.00
               Total deletes                        0.00
               Total discards                       0.00
               Total operations                    14.00
```

        End of Statistics.

2. Again, check the number of employees whose salary is greater than 3000:

```
SQL> select * from emp where sal>3000;

EMPNO  ENAME  JOB       MGR  HIREDATE   SAL   COMM  DEPTNO
-----  -----  ---       ---  --------   ---   ----  ------
 7566  JONES  MANAGER  7839  02-APR-81  3975           20
 7698  BLAKE  MANAGER  7839  01-MAY-81  3850           30
 7782  CLARK  MANAGER  7839  09-JUN-81  3450           10
 7788  SCOTT  ANALYST  7566  09-DEC-82  4000           20
 7839  KING   PRESIDENT      17-NOV-81  6000           10
 7902  FORD   ANALYST  7566  03-DEC-81  4000           20

6 rows selected.
```

How it works...

In this recipe, we perform an update in the source environment and verify the changes in the target environment. We use the stats command to see the volume statistics of a Replicat process.

The stats command only lists the volume statistics for the tables for which the process found any changes. The stats command has the following syntax:

```
STATS {EXTRACT | REPLICAT | ER} {<group | wildcard>}[TABLE {<name |
wildcard>}] [TOTAL | DAILY | HOURLY | LATEST]
```

for example:

```
STATS REPLICAT RGGTEST1 TABLE SCOTT.EMP HOURLY
```

There's more...

You can use the stats command to list the summary of the volume statistics with the following syntax:

```
STATS {EXTRACT | REPLICAT | ER} {<group | wildcard>},TOTALSONLY
<table>
```

for example:

```
STATS REPLICAT RGGTEST1 TOTALSONLY SCOTT.*
```

Another popular use of the stats command is to check the progress rate of a GoldenGate process:

```
STATS REPLICAT RGGTEST1 REPORTRATE HR
```

This command will show the hourly, daily, and total (since startup) processing summary for that replicat as follows:

```
*** Total statistics since 2012-10-18 11:56:35 ***
    Total inserts/hour:                    0.00
    Total updates/hour:                   37.66
    Total deletes/hour:                    0.00
    Total discards/hour:                   0.00
    Total operations/hour:                37.66
```

Generating encryption keys

GoldenGate uses encryption keys for encrypting the passwords and trail files. You can use default keys or define custom encryption keys. Oracle recommends using custom encryption keys for encrypting passwords and trail files. In this recipe you will learn how to generate encryption keys using the `keygen` tool.

How to do it...

1. As the GoldenGate software owner, change the current directory to GoldenGate Home directory:

    `cd $GG_HOME`

2. Generate the encryption key using the `keygen` utility:

    `./keygen <length> <number>`
    for example

    `./keygen 128 1`

3. Copy the generated encryption key to the ENCKEYS file under `$GG_HOME` and give this key a logical name:

    `dbkey1 0xC2052964C5C2C1309FEF5042E306716A`

4. If you are going to use encryption for encrypting the trail files or for Datapump transfers, then you must copy the ENCKEYS file to the target server:

    `scp $GG_HOME/ENCKEYS stdby1-ol6-112:/u01/app/ggate/`

How it works...

The encryption keys are generated using the `keygen` utility which is enclosed in the GoldenGate binaries. You can generate encryption keys of various lengths using this utility. All keys must be stored with a logical name in the `ENCKEYS` file under GoldenGate Home. It is from this file that the GoldenGate resolves the logical key name to the actual key value.

Encrypting database user passwords

GoldenGate requires an Oracle user password to connect to the source and target databases. In this recipe you will learn how to encrypt the database passwords using the `ENCRYPT` utility.

Getting ready

You need to generate the encryption keys and store them in the `ENCKEYS` file before generating encrypted passwords. Follow the steps in the *Generating encryption keys* recipe to generate and store a 256-bit key called `dbkey1` in the `ENCKEYS` file.

> Although you can generate encrypted passwords using the `DEFAULT` encryption keys, Oracle recommends using custom encryption keys for all production systems.

How to do it...

Encrypting the database user password involves the following steps:

1. From GoldenGate Home, run the **GoldenGate Software Command Line Interface (GGSCI)**:

   ```
   ./ggsci
   ```

2. Run the `ENCRYPT PASSWORD` command as follows:

   ```
   ENCRYPT PASSWORD *** <ALGORITHM> ENCRYPTKEY <key|DEFAULT>
   ```

   for example:

   ```
   ENCRYPT PASSWORD TIGER AES256 dbkey1
   Encrypted password:  AADAAAAAAAAAAAFAQCFIIDLCUELFNFECLITBSCAHYBBHHE
   UGKDNICDCCDCFELJDJFFEAUHUBFGWIUJGCAJJDNDPDZEOHGILBIIWCUIBHHGPBKBHB
   Algorithm used:  AES256
   ```

3. Stop the Extract process:

```
GGSCI> STOP EGGTEST1
```

4. Modify the process parameter files to use the encrypted password:

```
./ggsci
EDIT PARAMS EGGTEST1
EXTRACT EGGTEST1
USERID GGATE_ADMIN@DBORATEST, PASSWORD
ADAAAAAAAAAAAAFAQCFIIDLCUELFNFECLITBSCAHYBBHHEU
GKDNICDCCDCFELJDJFFEAUHUBFGWIUJGCAJJDNDPDZEOHGILBIIWCUIBHHGPBKBHB,
AES256, ENCRYPTKEY dbkey1
EXTTRAIL /u01/app/ggate/dirdat/st
TABLE scott.*;
```

5. Save the file and exit the editor window.

6. Start the Extract process:

```
GGSCI> START EGGTEST1
```

How it works...

GoldenGate requires a connection to the source and target databases using the Admin user. As always recommended, one should never hard code the database user passwords in the configuration files. Here we use the ENCRYPT PASSWORD command to encrypt a database user password. You can use one of the four algorithms (AES128, AES192, AES256, BLOWFISH) to encrypt the password. If you plan to use a DEFAULT encryption key, then you can only use the BLOWFISH algorithm. If you want to use the AES algorithm then you must generate a custom encryption key of appropriate length and store it in the ENCKEYS file under the GoldenGate Home directory. You can use one of the following algorithms for encrypting the password:

- AES128 uses the AES-128 cipher, which has a key size of 128 bits
- AES192 uses the AES-192 cipher, which has a key size of 192 bits
- AES256 uses the AES-256 cipher, which has a key size of 256 bits
- BLOWFISH uses Blowfish encryption with a 64-bit block size and a variable length key size from 32 bits to 128 bits

Encrypting the trail files

The trail files are the key component in the GoldenGate configuration. Since these files hold the data that is extracted by the Extract process, keeping them in the default format poses a security risk. We can overcome this security risk by encrypting the trail files using various algorithms. In this recipe we will learn how to configure the automatic encryption of the trail files.

Getting ready

You need to generate the encryption keys and store them in the ENCKEYS file before encrypting the trail files. Follow the steps in the Generating encryption keys recipe to generate and store a 256-bit key called dbkey1 in the ENCKEYS file.

How to do it...

Here are the steps to configure the encryption and decryption of trail files.

Perform the following steps in the source environment:

1. From GoldenGate Home, run the GoldenGate Software Command Line Interface (GGSCI):

   ```
   ./ggsci
   ```

2. Edit the Extract process configuration:

   ```
   EDIT PARAMS EGGTEST1
   ```

3. Add the ENCRYPTTRAIL command before the EXTTRAIL command to the parameter file as follows:

   ```
   EXTRACT EGGTEST1
   USERID GGATE_ADMIN@DBORATEST, PASSWORD ******
   ENCRYPTTRAIL AES256 KEYNAME dbkey1
   EXTTRAIL /u01/app/ggate/dirdat/st
   TABLE scott.*;
   ```

4. Save the file and exit the editor window.

5. Stop and start the Extract process:

   ```
   GGSCI> STOP EXTRACT EGGTEST1
   GGSCI> START EXTRACT EGGTEST1
   ```

6. Edit the Datapump parameter file as follows:

```
./ggsci
EDIT PARAMS EGGTEST1
EXTRACT PGGTEST1
USERID GGATE_ADMIN@DBORATEST, PASSWORD GGATE_ADMIN
DECRYPTTRAIL AES256 KEYNAME dbkey1
RMTHOST stdby1-ol6-112 , MGRPORT 8809
ENCRYPTTRAIL AES256 KEYNAME dbkey1
RMTTRAIL /u01/app/ggate/dirdat/rt
TABLE scott.*;
```

7. Restart the Datapump process:

```
GGSCI> STOP EXTRACT PGGTEST1
GGSCI> START EXTRACT PGGTEST1
```

Perform the following steps in the target environment:

1. Add the DECRYPTTRAIL command before the MAP command to the parameter file as follows:

```
./ggsci
EDIT PARAMS RGGTEST1
REPLICAT RGGTEST1
USERID GGATE_ADMIN@TGORTEST, PASSWORD GGATE_ADMIN
DISCARDFILE /u01/app/ggate/dirrpt/RGGTEST1.dsc,append,MEGABYTES
500
ASSUMETARGETDEFS
DECRYPTTRAIL AES256 KEYNAME dbkey1
MAP SCOTT.*, TARGET SCOTT.*;
```

2. Save the file and exit the editor window.

3. Stop and start the Replicat process:

```
GGSCI> STOP REPLICAT RGGTEST1
GGSCI> START REPLICAT RGGTEST1
```

How it works...

In the preceding steps we have configured the trail file encryption in the source environment. The extract file encrypts the data as it writes it to the trail files. The Datapump process then decrypts it using the encryption key provided in the ENCKEYS file and then re-encrypts it after applying the filter parameter, if defined. The encrypted file is then transferred to the target server. The Replicat process then uses the custom key to decrypt the data in the trail files and applies it to the target database.

Setting up a GoldenGate replication between tables with different structures using defgen

By default, GoldenGate expects the table definitions in your source and target environments to be similar. However, this may not always be the case. If you have defined the mapping between different tables in the source and target environments or the mapped tables have dissimilar structures, you would need to do some extra configuration to make GoldenGate replication work. In this recipe we will look into the additional steps that are required for this.

Getting ready

For this recipe we will use the continuous replication setup for the SCOTT schema done in the *Setting up a simple GoldenGate replication configuration between two single node databases* recipe earlier in this chapter. We will create two additional tables in the target database with the following structures:

▶ EMP_DIFFCOL_ORDER: EMP table with different column order

▶ EMP_EXTRACOL: EMP table with an additional column LAST_UPDATE_TIME

We will replicate the EMP table in the source database to three tables in the target database (EMP, EMP_DIFFCOL_ORDER, EMP_EXTRACOL).

How to do it...

Once you have created two new tables in the target schema, you can follow the following steps to set up a replication between tables with different structures.

Perform the following steps in the source environment:

1. Create a parameter file for defgen:

```
./ggsci
EDIT PARAMS defs
DEFSFILE ./dirdef/defs.def
USERID ggs_admin@dboratest, PASSWORD ******
TABLE SCOTT.EMP;
TABLE SCOTT.DEPT;
TABLE SCOTT.BONUS;
TABLE SCOTT.DUMMY;
TABLE SCOTT.SALGRADE;
```

2. Generate the definitions file:

```
./defgen paramfile ./dirprm/defs.prm
```

3. Push the definitions file to the target server using `scp`:

```
scp ./dirdef/defs.def stdby1-ol6-112:/u01/app/ggate/dirdef/
```

4. The Extract process parameter file should look like this:

```
EXTRACT EGGTEST1
USERID GGATE_ADMIN@DBORATEST, PASSWORD GGATE_ADMIN
EXTTRAIL /u01/app/ggate/dirdat/st
TABLE SCOTT.*;
```

5. The Datapump process parameter file should look like this:

```
EXTRACT PGGTEST1
USERID GGATE_ADMIN@DBORATEST, PASSWORD GGATE_ADMIN
RMTHOST stdby1-ol6-112 , MGRPORT 8809
RMTTRAIL /u01/app/ggate/dirdat/rt
TABLE SCOTT.*;
```

Perform the following steps in the target environment:

1. Edit the Replicat process configuration as follows:

```
./ggsci
EDIT PARAMS RGGTEST1
REPLICAT RGGTEST1
USERID GGATE_ADMIN@TGORTEST, PASSWORD GGATE_ADMIN
DISCARDFILE /u01/app/ggate/dirrpt/RGGTEST1.dsc,append,MEGABYTES
500
SOURCEDEFS ./dirdef/defs.def
MAP SCOTT.BONUS, TARGET SCOTT.BONUS;
MAP SCOTT.SALGRADE, TARGET SCOTT.SALGRADE;
MAP SCOTT.DEPT, TARGET SCOTT.DEPT;
MAP SCOTT.DUMMY, TARGET SCOTT.DUMMY;
MAP SCOTT.EMP, TARGET SCOTT.EMP;
MAP SCOTT.EMP,TARGET SCOTT.EMP_DIFFCOL_ORDER;
MAP SCOTT.EMP, TARGET SCOTT.EMP_EXTRACOL, COLMAP(USEDEFAULTS,
LAST_UPDATE_TIME = @DATENOW ());
```

2. Start the Replicat process.

How it works...

The default parameter ASSUMETARGETDEFS only works when the tables in the replication configuration have exactly the same structures in the source and target databases. However, when this is not the case, you need to use the SOURCEDEFS/TARGETDEFS parameter with the reference to the definitions file. This file is generated using the defgen utility which is shipped as a part of GoldenGate binaries by Oracle.

Defgen utility: This utility extracts the table structure information and writes it to a file called definitions file. The utility requires a parameter file with the following information:

- ▸ Database login information
- ▸ Definition file name and path
- ▸ Table list

Definitions file: This file is generated using the defgen utility and contains the table structure information. It can be generated for the source database or the target database.

For an Oracle database system, you would mostly generate the source database definitions file and transfer it to the target system. This is because most of the transformations occur in the target system and are done by the Replicat process. The only exception where you would need to generate a target database definitions file is if you are performing the transformation on an intermediary system where you would need to provide both the source and the target database definitions files.

See also

- ▸ The *Setting up a GoldenGate replication with mapping between different columns* recipe in *Chapter 4, Mapping and Manipulating Data*
- ▸ The *Table structure changes in GoldenGate environments with different table definitions* recipe in *Chapter 7, Advanced Administration Tasks – I*

3
DDL Replication and Initial Load

We will cover the following recipes in this chapter:

▸ Performing an initial setup required for GoldenGate DDL replication

▸ Setting up a GoldenGate DDL replication and verifying the changes

▸ Performing an initial load using GoldenGate

▸ Performing an initial load using an extract file to the GoldenGate's replicat method

▸ Loading data using trail files to the Replicat process method

▸ Loading data with files to the database utility method

▸ Loading data with the GoldenGate direct load method

▸ Loading data with bulk load to the SQL loader method

Introduction

Replication technologies are mostly used to synchronize the data changes between two or more environments. However, there are a few environments where applications modify the structures of the objects along with the data. In such cases, the job of replication technologies extends from just copying DMLs to replicating these structural changes as well. Oracle GoldenGate supports replication of DDL and DML changes between environments.

Before starting the replication between two environments, it is quite important to have a consistent point. The process of creating a synchronous state in a target environment is called an initial load or instantiation. GoldenGate offers many methods to perform an initial load.

In this chapter, we will look into the setup required, and the methods for performing a DDL replication and initial load using GoldenGate.

Performing an initial setup required for GoldenGate DDL replication

When GoldenGate is used for DDL replication, the Extract process on the source system requires some metadata tables. Hence, to enable the DDL replication in a source environment, you need to run some scripts to do an initial setup which, in turn, creates these metadata objects.

In this recipe, we will look at how to perform the initial setup required for enabling the DDL replication in a GoldenGate environment.

Getting ready

We will use the GGATE_ADMIN schema for this setup.

How to do it...

Run the following scripts in the source environment:

1. Change the directory to GoldenGate Home as follows:

   ```
   cd /u01/app/ggate
   ```

2. Log in to sqlplus as sysdba as shown in the following command:

   ```
   sqlplus sys/**** as sysdba
   ```

3. Run the marker_setup.sql script:

   ```
   SQL> @marker_setup.sql
   ```

4. This script will prompt for GoldenGate Admin schema name, enter it when prompted:

   ```
   Enter Oracle GoldenGate schema name:GGATE_ADMIN
   ```

5. Run the ddl_setup.sql script as shown in the following command:

   ```
   SQL> @ddl_setup.sql
   ```

6. This script will prompt for the GoldenGate Admin schema name, enter it when prompted:

   ```
   Enter Oracle GoldenGate schema name:GGATE_ADMIN
   ```

7. Run the role_setup.sql script:

   ```
   SQL> @role_setup.sql
   ```

8. Enter the GoldenGate Admin schema name, when prompted:

   ```
   Enter Oracle GoldenGate schema name:GGATE_ADMIN
   ```

9. Grant the GoldenGate DDL role to the GoldenGate Admin user as follows:

   ```
   SQL> GRANT GGS_GGSUSER_ROLE TO GGATE_ADMIN;
   ```

10. Run the `ddl_enable.sql` script as shown in the following command:

    ```
    SQL> @ddl_enable.sql
    ```

11. Create a `Globals` file as shown in the following command:

    ```
    GGSCI (prim1-ol6-112.localdomain) 1> edit params ./GLOBALS
    GGSCHEMA GGATE_ADMIN
    ```

12. Save and close the file.

How it works...

The initial setup required for replicating DDL changes in a GoldenGate configuration is done in the source environment. GoldenGate binaries include the scripts that are installed in the GoldenGate `Home` directory. The scripts are run as shown in the following command:

```
SQL> @marker_setup.sql

Marker setup script

You will be prompted for the name of a schema for the Oracle GoldenGate
database objects.

NOTE: The schema must be created prior to running this script.

NOTE: Stop all DDL replication before starting this installation.

Enter Oracle GoldenGate schema name:GGATE_ADMIN

Marker setup table script complete, running verification script...

Please enter the name of a schema for the GoldenGate database objects:

Setting schema name to GGATE_ADMIN

MARKER TABLE

-------------------------------

OK

MARKER SEQUENCE

-------------------------------

OK

Script complete.


SQL> @ddl_setup.sql

GoldenGate DDL Replication setup script

Verifying that current user has privileges to install DDL Replication...

You will be prompted for the name of a schema for the Oracle GoldenGate
```

database objects.

NOTE: For an Oracle 10g source, the system recycle bin must be disabled. For Oracle 11g and later, it can be enabled.

NOTE: The schema must be created prior to running this script.

NOTE: Stop all DDL replication before starting this installation.

Enter Oracle GoldenGate schema name:GGATE_ADMIN

Working, please wait ...

Spooling to file ddl_setup_spool.txt

Checking for sessions that are holding locks on Oracle Golden Gate metadata tables ...

Check complete.

Using GGATE_ADMIN as an Oracle GoldenGate schema name.

Working, please wait ...

....

....

DDL replication setup script complete, running verification script...

Please enter the name of a schema for the GoldenGate database objects:

Setting schema name to GGATE_ADMIN

LOCATION OF DDL TRACE FILE

---/

u01/app/oracle/diag/rdbms/dboratest/dboratest/trace/ggs_ddl_trace.log

Analyzing installation status...

STATUS OF DDL REPLICATION

--SUCCESSFUL installation of DDL Replication software components

Script complete.

SQL> @role_setup.sql

GGS Role setup script

This script will drop and recreate the role GGS_GGSUSER_ROLE

To use a different role name, quit this script and then edit the params. sql script to change the gg_role parameter to the preferred name. (Do not run the script.)

You will be prompted for the name of a schema for the GoldenGate database objects.

NOTE: The schema must be created prior to running this script.

NOTE: Stop all DDL replication before starting this installation.

```
Enter GoldenGate schema name:GGATE_ADMIN

Wrote file role_setup_set.txt

PL/SQL procedure successfully completed.

Role setup script complete
```

Grant this role to each user assigned to the Extract, GGSCI, and Manager processes, by using the following SQL command:

```
GRANT GGS_GGSUSER_ROLE TO <loggedUser>
```

Where <loggedUser> is the user assigned to the GoldenGate processes.

```
SQL> @ddl_enable.sql

Trigger altered.
```

There's more...

The DDL setup scripts by default follow a fixed naming convention in which all objects names start with GGS_. If you want to change the names of the tables created as a part of this setup due to some organization standards or security reasons, you can do so by modifying the params.sql script which is supplied as a part of GoldenGate binaries. All the DDL initial setup scripts read this script for setting the values of the object names.

See also

 ▸ The next recipe, *Setting up a GoldenGate DDL replication and verifying the changes*

Setting up a GoldenGate DDL replication and verifying the changes

In a default GoldenGate setup, all DMLs are captured in the source environment and all DMLs and DDLs are applied in the target environment. However, unless you start extracting the DDL statements in source, there would not be any DDL statements to apply at the target environment by replicat. Extracting the DDLs in source requires some extra configuration. In this recipe we will look into the additional parameters/setup required for performing the DDL replication.

Getting ready

For this recipe the following setup must be in place:

1. Source and target databases with the SCOTT sample schema.

2. DDL replication initial setup as explained in the previous recipe, *Performing an initial setup required for GoldenGate DDL replication*.

How to do it...

Following are the steps to configure DDL synchronization between the source and target environments.

Perform the following steps in the source environment:

1. Start the GoldenGate command line interface by using the following code:

   ```
   ./ggsci
   ```

2. Stop the Extract and Datapump processes if they are running as shown in the following command:

   ```
   GGSCI> STOP EXTRACT EGGTEST1
   GGSCI> STOP EXTRACT PGGTEST1
   ```

3. Edit the extract parameter file as follows:

   ```
   ./ggsci
   EDIT PARAMS EGGTEST1
   EXTRACT EGGTEST1
   USERID GGATE_ADMIN@DBORATEST, PASSWORD ******
   EXTTRAIL /u01/app/ggate/dirdat/st
   DDL INCLUDE MAPPED OBJNAME SCOTT.*
   TABLE SCOTT.*;
   ```

4. Start the Extract process as shown in the following command:

   ```
   GGSCI> START EGGTEST1
   ```

5. Start the Datapump process as shown in the following command:

   ```
   GGSCI> START PGGTEST1
   ```

Perform the following steps in the target environment:

1. Start the GoldenGate command line interface by using the following command:

   ```
   ./ggsci
   ```

2. Stop the Replicat process as shown in the following command:

   ```
   GGSCI> STOP REPLICAT RGGTEST1
   ```

3. Grant the necessary privileges to the GoldenGate Admin user to enable it to replicate DDL changes to the target environment as shown in the following command:

   ```
   SQL> GRANT ALTER on SCOTT.EMP to GGATE_ADMIN;
   ```

4. Start the Replicat process as shown in the following command:

```
GGSCI> START REPLICAT RGGTEST1
```

5. Check the structure of the EMP table in the target environment as shown in the following command:

```
SQL> DESC SCOTT.EMP
```

Name	Null?	Type
EMPNO	NOT NULL	NUMBER(4)
ENAME		VARCHAR2(10)
JOB		VARCHAR2(9)
MGR		NUMBER(4)
HIREDATE		DATE
SAL		NUMBER(7,2)
COMM		NUMBER(7,2)
DEPTNO		NUMBER(2)

After you complete the preceding steps, perform the following steps in the source environment:

1. Check the structure of the EMP table in the source environment as shown in the following command:

```
SQL> DESC SCOTT.EMP
```

Name	Null?	Type
EMPNO	NOT NULL	NUMBER(4)
ENAME		VARCHAR2(10)
JOB		VARCHAR2(9)
MGR		NUMBER(4)
HIREDATE		DATE
SAL		NUMBER(7,2)
COMM		NUMBER(7,2)
DEPTNO		NUMBER(2)

2. Perform a DDL operation on the EMP table as shown in the following command:

```
SQL> ALTER TABLE EMP ADD CITY VARCHAR(25);
```

3. Verify the modified structure in the source environment as shown in the following command:

```
SQL> DESC SCOTT.EMP
Name                        Null?              Type

 ----------------------------------------------- --------- -----

EMPNO                       NOT NULL           NUMBER(4)
ENAME                                          VARCHAR2(10)
JOB                                            VARCHAR2(9)
MGR                                            NUMBER(4)
HIREDATE                                       DATE
SAL                                            NUMBER(7,2)
COMM                                           NUMBER(7,2)
DEPTNO                                         NUMBER(2)
CITY                                           VARCHAR2(25)
```

Perform the following steps in the target environment:

1. Verify the modified structure in the target environment as shown in the following command:

```
SQL> DESC SCOTT.EMP
Name                        Null?              Type

 ----------------------------------------------- --------- -----

EMPNO                       NOT NULL           NUMBER(4)
ENAME                                          VARCHAR2(10)
JOB                                            VARCHAR2(9)
MGR                                            NUMBER(4)
IREDATE                                        DATE
SAL                                            NUMBER(7,2)
COMM                                           NUMBER(7,2)
DEPTNO                                         NUMBER(2)
CITY                                           VARCHAR2(25)
```

How it works...

The DDL INCLUDE parameter enables the Extract process to extract any structural changes for all SCOTT objects. When the ALTER TABLE statement is run to add a column to the EMP table, this DDL change is extracted by the EGGTEST1 Extract process and then transferred to the target site by the PGGTEST1 Datapump process. The GoldenGate Admin user needs to be granted some extra privileges to allow it to apply the DDL changes to the target database objects. In this example, we have only granted it the ALTER privileges on the EMP table. Then the Replicat process picks up the DDL change from the trail file and applies it to the target database.

> In this example we haven't modified the replicat parameter file to include any DDL parameter. This is because DDL replication is enabled by default at the replicat level. However, you might need to include some of the additional DDLOPTIONS parameters based on your requirements for which you might need to add it to the replicat parameter file.

There's more...

When you set up a GoldenGate DDL replication, there are some additional aspects that you should consider. Some of these are as follows:

Extra privileges that are required for the GoldenGate Admin user

When you replicate DDL using GoldenGate, you can synchronize the changes to existing objects as well as to the new objects that get created in the source environment. For the changes to the existing objects, the GoldenGate Admin user will need the appropriate privilege on the object whose structure is modified in the source environment, for example, ALTER on the EMP table as in this example.

For creating new objects in various schemas, you need to grant the CREATE ANY TABLE privilege to the GoldenGate Admin user.

Filtering and mapping

There are many options in GoldenGate for mapping and filtering various DDL changes to different objects/schemas. The filtering is mainly done at the extract level by specifying various options to the DDL INCLUDE and DDL EXCLUDE parameter. You can filter on the basis of object name, type, DDL type, or you can even search for a particular string in the DDL statement. Once the filtered changes are captured by the Extract process and sent to the target environment, the replicat then applies them on the basis of the mapping rules defined in its parameter file. You only define the mapping for the source and target objects in the replicat parameter file once. GoldenGate applies both DML and DDL changes based on these mapping rules to the target objects. Following is an example of how these parameters can be used:

```
DDL INCLUDE OBJNAME "SCOTT.*"
DDL EXCLUDE OBJNAME "SCOTT.*"
```

You can specify the INCLUDE clause on its own, but if you want to use an EXCLUDE parameter you must specify at least one INCLUDE parameter.

Additional DDLOPTIONS

The following are some of the additional important `DDLOPTIONS`:

▶ `DDLOPTIONS ADDTRANDATA`: If you have configured DDL replication, GoldenGate will create the new objects in the target environment. However, these objects will not have Supplemental Logging groups created by default due to which it will not be able to extract any DML changes that occur on these objects. Using the `DDLOPTIONS ADDTRANDATA` option ensures Supplemental Logging is enabled on the newly created objects that GoldenGate is replicating. It also updates the supplemental log groups when `ALTER TABLE` is run.

▶ `DDLOPTIONS REPORT`: This option can be used to write extra information about DDL changes processed by a GoldenGate process to its report file.

Performing an initial load using GoldenGate

So far we have seen how to replicate the changes that occur in a source environment continuously to the target environment. GoldenGate applies these changes using the standard SQL calls to the target database. The success of these statements depends on the state of the data within the database. For this it is imperative that your source and target databases are in a synchronous state before you start the continuous replication between them. If your target database tables are not in the same state as the source database tables, it is quite possible that certain statements will fail. A simple example of this case is when you try to apply an `UPDATE` statement to the target database that was run in the source database. If the row that you are trying to update does not exist in the target environment, the statement will fail.

There are many methods available to instantiate target database/schemas. You can use the non-GoldenGate methods to do this. However, in this recipe and the following recipes we will focus on the methods/options in GoldenGate to do an initial load. We will also discuss the advantages of using the GoldenGate methods over other methods.

In this recipe, we will look into the overall procedure of instantiation or initial load for the GoldenGate replication.

Getting ready

You can use GoldenGate to perform an initial load while it is capturing the on-going changes in the source production database. This enables you to perform the instantiation without any downtime in the source database. In order to perform such an instantiation of the target database using Oracle GoldenGate, there are the following prerequisites:

1. The continuous replication setup must be done and the Extract/Datapump processes must be started prior to starting the initial load using GoldenGate. This is done to ensure that any changes that are happening in the source database are captured by the Extract process while the initial load Extract process is busy replicating the consistent state of the database, as it was when the initial load was started.

2. You should disable the DDL replication before starting an initial load process.

3. The data in the target tables to be instantiated should be deleted prior to the start of the initial load.

4. You should remove any indexes and disable any constraints in the target environment.

5. If you are configuring a continuous replication with an initial load process, you should add the `HANDLECOLLISIONS` parameter to the replicat configuration. Due to the overlap of time between the initial load and the online synchronization, there can be few collisions in the target database. This parameter will handle such collisions and will convert the DMLs appropriately. For example, if the Replicat process encounters an `INSERT` statement for a record that already exists in the target database, this parameter will convert that `INSERT` statement to an `UPDATE` statement. Any missing rows for which the Replicat process finds an `UPDATE` or `DELETE` record in the trail file are ignored by this parameter.

6. You should split the instantiation load between multiple processes for optimal performance.

How to do it...

The high-level steps for setting up an initial load are as follows:

1. If the source database from which you are doing an instantiation is going to remain active while the initial load will run, you need to set up a continuous data replication configuration as explained in the recipes, *Setting up a simple GoldenGate replication configuration between two single node databases* and *Setting up a GoldenGate replication with multiple process groups* in *Chapter 2, Setting up GoldenGate Replication*, using a Classic or Integrated Capture. Make sure that you add the `HANDLECOLLISIONS` parameter to the replicat configuration.

2. Based on the size of the database, select a GoldenGate initial load method.

3. Set up the configuration for an initial load method.

4. Copy the table structures if not present in the target environment.

5. Start the initial load processes.

6. If you are replicating any sequences, you should flush them in the source database.

7. Verify that the initial load is complete and all data has been replicated to the target environment.

8. Enable the constraints and create the indexes.

9. Enable the DDL replication, if there was any configured in this environment.

10. Verify that all data that was generated up to the time when initial load completed has been applied by the replicat, and then stop the continuous replication replicat and turn off the `HANDLECOLLISIONS` parameter and start it again.

How it works...

In this recipe, we will see the overall procedure of performing an initial load using GoldenGate. For this we first set up a continuous replication configuration. This is to ensure that all the changes originating from the source database are being captured while the initial load is run. Then we configure and start the initial load process. Once the data load has completed, we start applying the captured changes using the continuous Replicat process. We can also enable the DDL replication at this stage. Once all the changes are applied in the target environment, we can turn off the `HANDLECOLLISSIONS` parameter and restart the Replicat process.

There's more...

Broadly, the methods for initial load can be divided into two categories: GoldenGate-based and External methods.

You can use non-GoldenGate or External methods to perform an initial load. Some of the examples of these methods for Oracle databases are: Oracle Datapump, export/import, Rman backup/restore, and ETL tools. But all of these methods do not offer the facility of keeping the source database active while the initial load is being done. These methods require you to stop the application load on the source database to get a consistent image. This is because if you keep them active they do not offer a way of identifying and applying the new changes that occurred ever since the initial load process started.

GoldenGate methods offer a substantial benefit over the External methods. While the initial load is performed, you can continue running the application and perform changes in the source database. In the source environment there are two sets of Extract processes. First extract process extracts the data for the initial load and transfers it to the target environment. The second set of extract processes are configured to extract all the changes that are performed after the initial load has started and transfer these changes to the target environment. At the destination side, the changes are applied once the initial load is complete. You can perform various transformations in the initial load process which is not possible with External methods. GoldenGate offers some parameters such as `HANDLECOLLISSIONS` that can be used to manage the data inconsistencies in the target database while the initial load process runs, and after that the current changes are applied to the target database.

If your source and target databases are on different platforms, you can use some External methods to perform instantiation. These methods, however, do not allow any transformations to be done at the individual table/column level. These features are available in some of the GoldenGate methods even when they are used for heterogeneous databases.

Within GoldenGate the following are the various methods for initial load:

- Extract file to the Replicat method
- Trail to the Replicat method
- File to the database utility method
- GoldenGate direct load method
- Direct bulk load to the SQL loader method

Extract file to the Replicat method

This method is mainly suited for simple instantiation jobs or where the database is small. In this method, the Extract process on the source database extracts the data from the database and writes it to the trail files on the target server. The Replicat process on the target server applies transformations, if any, and then applies the records to the target database. There is a limit of 2 GB on the extract file size due to which this method is only suitable for small initial load jobs.

Trail to the Replicat method

In this method an initial load extract is configured on the source system. This initial load extract is configured to write trail files to the target environment. The size and the maximum number of trail files are configured in the initial load Extract process configuration file. The key advantage of this method is that you can use it to instantiate the datasets which are larger than 2 GB.

File to the database utility method

In this method an initial load extract is configured on the source system. This is where all the transformations need to be done because there is no replicat in this method. This extract writes the extracted data in one of the formats, that is, ASCII, Comma Separated Values, XML, or SQL. On the target side, a database utility then reads this file and loads the data into the database. The key advantage of this method is that it can be used to load data into other databases, as on the target side it's a simple load from the data files which are in an industry standard format that is supported by many available RDBMS, for example, the file can be read by Oracle's SQL * Loader, Microsoft's BCP, DTS, SQL **Server Integration Services** (**SSIS**) utility, or IBM's Load Utility (LOADUTIL).

GoldenGate direct load method

This is the most flexible method. In this method, you configure an Extract process in the source environment which communicates directly to the Replicat process in the target environment. The Extract process transfers the extracted data to the Replicat. The Replicat process then applies the received data using the native SQL calls to the target database. Because there are no external components involved in this method, this method can be used to load data between various types of databases. You can perform various transformations as well that are supported by GoldenGate. The disadvantage of this method is that it does not support extraction of LOB or LONG data, user-defined types, or any other datatypes which are longer than 4 KB in size. This method is much slower than the other GoldenGate initial load methods.

Direct bulk load to SQL loader method

In this method you configure an initial load Extract process on the source system. This Extract process communicates with an initial load Replicat process on the target system. The Replicat process communicates with the SQL * Loader on the target system and SQL * Loader loads the data into the target database using the direct path loading which bypasses the SQL parsing. The advantage of this method is that you can use the direct path loading which provides very fast results. The disadvantage of this method is that it only supports Oracle as the target database because SQL * Loader is only available with Oracle. Moreover, this method does not support any data encryption, LOB or LONG datatypes, and materialized views with LOBs.

See also

Depending on the type of GoldenGate initial load method that you want to use for your environment, you can see the following recipes in this chapter:

- *Performing an initial load using an extract file to the GoldenGate's replicat method*
- *Loading data using trail files to the Replicat process method*
- *Loading data with files to the database utility method*
- *Loading data with the GoldenGate direct load method*
- *Loading data with bulk load to the SQL loader method*

Performing an initial load using an extract file to the GoldenGate's replicat method

In this recipe we will look into the detailed steps of instantiating a target database from a source database using the GoldenGate extract file to the replicat method. For this, we will instantiate the EMP table with 1 million rows to the target database while it gets updated with various transactions. We will also verify at the end of the initial load that all of these changes have been applied to the target as well.

Getting ready

For this recipe we will use the following setup:

1. Create a modified version of the EMP table that is delivered in the SCOTT demo schema with Oracle binaries in the source and target databases. You can use the following DDL statement to create the EMP table:

   ```
   CREATE TABLE EMP (

   EMPNO NUMBER(10) PRIMARY KEY,

   ENAME VARCHAR2(25),

   JOB VARCHAR2(25),

   MGR NUMBER(10),

   HIREDATE DATE,

   SAL NUMBER(20,2),

   COMM NUMBER(20,2),

   DEPTNO NUMBER(10),

   CITY VARCHAR2(25));
   ```

2. Use the following script to load 1 million rows into this table:

   ```
   BEGIN

   FOR I IN 1..250000 LOOP

   INSERT INTO EMP VALUES (0+I,'TOM'||I,'WORKER',7369,TO_DATE('07-11-
   2012','DD-MM-YYYY'),10000+I,I,10,'LONDON');

   INSERT INTO EMP VALUES (250000+I,'BOB'||I,'DBA',7499,TO_DATE('07-
   11-2012','DD-MM-YYYY'),260000+I,I,10,'PARIS');

   INSERT INTO EMP VALUES (500000+I,'ALEX'||I,'DEVELOPER',7521,TO_
   DATE('07-11-2012','DD-MM-YYYY'),500000+I,I,10,'TOKYO');

   INSERT INTO EMP VALUES (750000+I,'SAM'||I,'SALESMAN',7934,TO_
   DATE('07-11-2012','DD-MM-YYYY'),750000+I,I,10,'BOSTON');

   END LOOP;

   COMMIT;

   END;
   ```

3. Enable Supplemental Logging for the EMP table in the source database.

4. Grant SELECT on the EMP table to the GGATE_ADMIN user in the source database.

5. Grant INSERT, UPDATE, and DELETE on the EMP table to the GGATE_ADMIN user in the target database.

How to do it...

The following are the steps for a continuous replication setup:

1. Follow the steps in the *Setting up a simple GoldenGate replication configuration between two single node databases* recipe in *Chapter 2, Setting up GoldenGate Replication* to set up continuous replication for the EMP table.

2. Modify the replicat RGGTEST1 configuration to add the HANDLECOLLISIONS parameter as shown in the following command:

    ```
    ./ggsci
    STOP REPLICAT RGGTEST1
    EDIT REPLICAT RGGTEST1
    REPLICAT RGGTEST1
    USERID GGATE_ADMIN@TGORTEST, PASSWORD GGATE_ADMIN
    DISCARDFILE /u01/app/ggate/dirrpt/RGGTEST1.dsc,append,MEGABYTES
    500
    ASSUMETARGETDEFS
    HANDLECOLLISIONS
    MAP SCOTT.emp, TARGET SCOTT.emp;
    ```

3. Ensure that you do not start the RGGTEST1 replicat at this stage.

The following are the steps to set up an initial load:

1. Create a GoldenGate initial load Extract process in the source environment as shown in the following command:

    ```
    ./ggsci
    EDIT PARAMS EXTINIT
    EXTRACT EXTINIT
    SOURCEISTABLE
    USERID GGATE_ADMIN@DBORATEST, PASSWORD GGATE_ADMIN
    RMTHOST stdby1-ol6-112, MGRPORT 8809
    RMTFILE ./dirdat/extinit.dat, PURGE
    TABLE SCOTT.EMP;
    ```

2. Add the initial load Extract process to the source manager configuration as follows:

    ```
    GGSCI> ADD EXTRACT EXTINIT, SOURCEISTABLE
    ```

3. Create a GoldenGate initial load Replicat process in the target environment as shown in the following command:

```
./ggsci

EDIT PARAMS RPTINIT

REPLICAT RPTINIT

SPECIALRUN

USERID GGATE_ADMIN@TGORTEST, PASSWORD GGATE_ADMIN

EXTFILE ./dirdat/extinit.dat

DISCARDFILE ./dirrpt/rptinit.dsc, PURGE

ASSUMETARGETDEFS

MAP SCOTT.EMP, TARGET SCOTT.EMP;

END RUNTIME
```

4. Add the initial load Replicate process to the target manager configuration as shown in the following command:

```
GGSCI> ADD REPLICAT RPTINIT, EXTFILE ./dirdat/extinit.dat
```

5. Before starting the initial load, check the data in the source database as shown in the following command:

```
SQL> SELECT CITY,COUNT(*) FROM EMP GROUP BY CITY;

CITY                COUNT(*)

-----------------------------------

LONDON              250000

PARIS               250000

TOKYO               250000

BOSTON              250000
```

6. On the source system, start the EXTINIT Extract process as shown in the following command:

```
GGSCI> START EXTRACT EXTINIT
```

7. On the target system, start the RPTINIT Replicat process as shown in the following command:

```
GGSCI> START REPLICAT RPTINIT
```

8. Run the following UPDATE/DELETE statement in the source system:

```
SQL> DELETE EMP WHERE EMPNO>650000 and CITY='TOKYO';

SQL> UPDATE EMP SET CITY='SHANGHAI' where CITY='TOKYO';

SQL> COMMIT;
```

9. Once the initial load Replicat process is done, check the data in the target database as shown in the following command:

```
SQL> SELECT CITY, COUNT(*) FROM EMP GROUP BY CITY;
CITY                   COUNT(*)
-------------------------------
LONDON                 250000
PARIS                  250000
TOKYO                  250000
BOSTON                 250000
```

10. Check the updated state of data in the source environment:

```
SQL> SELECT CITY, COUNT(*) FROM EMP GROUP BY CITY;
CITY                   COUNT(*)
-------------------------------
LONDON                 250000
PARIS                  250000
SHANGHAI               150000
BOSTON                 250000
```

11. Start the change delivery Replicat process in the target environment as shown in the following command:

```
GGSCI> START REPLICAT RGGTEST1
```

12. Check the state of the Replicat process once it has processed all the trail files. Check the data in the target database to ensure that all the changes are copied across as shown in the following command:

```
SQL> SELECT CITY, COUNT(*) FROM EMP GROUP BY CITY;
CITY                   COUNT(*)
-------------------------------
LONDON                 250000
PARIS                  250000
SHANGHAI               150000
BOSTON                 250000
```

13. Now that the initial load is complete, we will update the `RGGTEST1` Replicat process to turn off `HANDLECOLLISIONS` as shown in the following command:

```
GGSCI> SEND REPLICAT RGGTEST1, NOHANDLECOLLISIONS
GGSCI> EDIT PARAMS RGGTEST1
REPLICAT RGGTEST1
USERID GGATE_ADMIN@TGORTEST, PASSWORD GGATE_ADMIN
DISCARDFILE /u01/app/ggate/dirrpt/RGGTEST1.dsc,append,MEGABYTES
```

```
500
ASSUMETARGETDEFS
MAP SCOTT.EMP, TARGET SCOTT.EMP;
```

How it works...

In this recipe we first configure the processes for continuous replication following the steps from a recipe in *Chapter 2, Setting up GoldenGate Replication*. Once that is done, we modify the Replicat process to add the HANDLECOLLISIONS parameter. The key thing to note in this procedure is that we do not start the Replicat process at this stage. After this we configure an initial load extract. The use of the SOURCEISTABLE parameter tells the GoldenGate extract to read the data from the database itself and not from the redo logs/archived logs. In this method, the Extract process writes directly to a file in the target environment called the extract file. This file is then read by the initial load replicat which is configured in the target environment. The use of the SPECIALRUN and EXTFILE parameters tells GoldenGate that this replicat is for initial load purposes and not for continuous replication. The extract data is applied to the target EMP table by this process, after which it stops. Then we start the RGGTEST1 replicat which will apply the changes generated by the UPDATE and DELETE statement that we run in step 10. After these changes are applied, the data in the target EMP table is in the same state as the data in the source EMP table.

There's more...

You can check the status of the initial load Extract process using the following command:

```
GGSCI> INFO EXTRACT *, TASKS
EXTRACT   EXTINIT  Last Started 2012-11-08 12:08  Status STOPPED
Checkpoint Lag       Not Available
Log Read Checkpoint Table SCOTT.EMP
                2012-11-08 12:09:11  Record 1000000
Task             SOURCEISTABLE
```

Loading data using trail files to the Replicat process method

In this recipe we will look into the detailed steps of instantiating a target database from a source database using the GoldenGate trail files to the replicat method. For this, we will instantiate the EMP table with 1 million rows to the target database while it gets updated with various transactions. We will also verify at the end of the initial load that all of these changes have been applied to the target as well.

Getting ready

For this recipe we will use the following setup:

1. Create a modified version of the EMP table that is delivered in the SCOTT demo schema with Oracle binaries in the source and target databases. You can use the following DDL statement to create the EMP table:

```
CREATE TABLE EMP (
EMPNO NUMBER(10) PRIMARY KEY,
ENAME VARCHAR2(25),
JOB VARCHAR2(25),
MGR NUMBER(10),
HIREDATE DATE,
SAL NUMBER(20,2),
COMM NUMBER(20,2),
DEPTNO NUMBER(10),
CITY VARCHAR2(25));
```

2. Use the following script to load 1 million rows into this table:

```
BEGIN
FOR I IN 1..250000 LOOP
INSERT INTO EMP VALUES (0+I,'TOM'||I,'WORKER',7369,TO_DATE('07-11-
2012','DD-MM-YYYY'),10000+I,I,10,'LONDON');
INSERT INTO EMP VALUES (250000+I,'BOB'||I,'DBA',7499,TO_DATE('07-
11-2012','DD-MM-YYYY'),260000+I,I,10,'PARIS');
INSERT INTO EMP VALUES (500000+I,'ALEX'||I,'DEVELOPER',7521,TO_
DATE('07-11-2012','DD-MM-YYYY'),500000+I,I,10,'TOKYO');
INSERT INTO EMP VALUES (750000+I,'SAM'||I,'SALESMAN',7934,TO_
DATE('07-11-2012','DD-MM-YYYY'),750000+I,I,10,'BOSTON');
END LOOP;
COMMIT;
END;
```

3. Enable Supplemental Logging for the EMP table in the source database.

4. Grant SELECT on the EMP table to the GGATE_ADMIN user in the source database.

5. Grant INSERT, UPDATE, and DELETE on the EMP table to the GGATE_ADMIN user in the target database.

How to do it...

The following are the steps for a continuous replication setup:

1. Follow the steps in the *Setting up a simple GoldenGate replication configuration between two single node databases* recipe in *Chapter 2, Setting up GoldenGate Replication* to set up the continuous replication for the EMP table.

2. Modify the replicat RGGTEST1 configuration to add the HANDLECOLLISIONS parameter as shown in the following command:

```
./ggsci
STOP REPLICAT RGGTEST1
EDIT REPLICAT RGGTEST1
REPLICAT RGGTEST1
USERID GGATE_ADMIN@TGORTEST, PASSWORD GGATE_ADMIN
DISCARDFILE /u01/app/ggate/dirrpt/RGGTEST1.dsc,append,MEGABYTES
500
ASSUMETARGETDEFS
HANDLECOLLISIONS
MAP SCOTT.emp, TARGET SCOTT.emp;
```

3. Ensure that you do not start the RGGTEST1 replicat at this stage.

The following are the steps to set up an initial load:

1. Create a GoldenGate initial load Extract process in the source environment as shown in the following command:

```
./ggsci
EDIT PARAMS EXTINIT
EXTRACT EXTINIT
SOURCEISTABLE
USERID GGATE_ADMIN@DBORATEST, PASSWORD GGATE_ADMIN
RMTHOST stdby1-ol6-112, MGRPORT 8809
RMTFILE :/dirdat/ri, maxfiles 1000, megabytes 10
TABLE SCOTT.EMP;
```

2. Add the initial load Extract process to the source manager configuration as shown in the following command:

```
GGSCI> ADD EXTRACT EXTINIT, SOURCEISTABLE
```

3. Create the GoldenGate initial load Replicat process in the target environment as shown in the following command:

```
./ggsci
EDIT PARAMS RPTINIT
REPLICAT RPTINIT
USERID GGATE_ADMIN@TGORTEST, PASSWORD GGATE_ADMIN
DISCARDFILE ./dirrpt/rptinit.dsc, PURGE
ASSUMETARGETDEFS
MAP SCOTT.EMP, TARGET SCOTT.EMP;
```

4. Add the initial load Replicate process to the target manager configuration as shown in the following command:

```
GGSCI> ADD REPLICAT RPTINIT, EXTTRAIL ./dirdat/ri, nodbcheckpoint
```

5. Before starting the initial load, check the data in the source database:

```
SQL> SELECT CITY,COUNT(*) FROM EMP GROUP BY CITY;
CITY                   COUNT(*)
----------------------------------
LONDON                 250000
PARIS                  250000
TOKYO                  250000
BOSTON                 250000
```

6. On the source system, start the EXTINIT Extract process as shown in the following command:

```
GGSCI> START EXTRACT EXTINIT
```

7. On the target system, start the RPTINIT Replicat process as shown in the following command:

```
GGSCI> START REPLICAT RPTINIT
```

8. Run the following UPDATE/DELETE statement in the source system as shown in the following command:

```
SQL> DELETE EMP WHERE EMPNO>650000 and CITY='TOKYO';
SQL> UPDATE EMP SET CITY='SHANGHAI' where CITY='TOKYO';
SQL> COMMIT;
```

9. Once the initial load Replicat process is done, check the data in the target database as shown in the following command:

```
SQL> SELECT CITY, COUNT(*) FROM EMP GROUP BY CITY;

CITY                    COUNT(*)

-------------------------------

LONDON                  250000

PARIS                   250000

TOKYO                   250000

BOSTON                  250000
```

10. Check the updated state of data in the source environment as shown in the following command:

```
SQL> SELECT CITY, COUNT(*) FROM EMP GROUP BY CITY;

CITY                    COUNT(*)

-------------------------------

LONDON                  250000

PARIS                   250000

SHANGHAI                150000

BOSTON                  250000
```

11. Start the change delivery Replicat process in the target environment as shown in the following command:

```
GGSCI> START REPLICAT RGGTEST1
```

12. Check the state of the Replicat process once it has processed all the trail files. Check the data in the target database to ensure that all the changes are copied across as shown in the following command:

```
SQL> SELECT CITY, COUNT(*) FROM EMP GROUP BY CITY;

CITY                    COUNT(*)

-------------------------------

LONDON                  250000

PARIS                   250000

SHANGHAI                150000

BOSTON                  250000
```

13. Now that the initial load is complete, we will update the `RGGTEST1` Replicat process to turn off `HANDLECOLLISIONS` as shown in the following command:

```
GGSCI> SEND REPLICAT RGGTEST1, NOHANDLECOLLISIONS

GGSCI> EDIT PARAMS RGGTEST1

REPLICAT RGGTEST1

USERID GGATE_ADMIN@TGORTEST, PASSWORD GGATE_ADMIN

DISCARDFILE /u01/app/ggate/dirrpt/RGGTEST1.dsc,append,MEGABYTES
500

ASSUMETARGETDEFS

MAP SCOTT.EMP, TARGET SCOTT.EMP;
```

How it works...

In this recipe we first configure the processes for continuous replication following the steps from a Setting up a simple GoldenGate replication configuration between two single node databases recipe in *Chapter 2, Setting up GoldenGate Replication*. Once that is done, we modify the Replicat process to add the `HANDLECOLLISIONS` parameter. The key thing to note in this procedure is that we do not start the Replicat process at this stage. After this we configure an initial load extract. The use of the `SOURCEISTABLE` parameter tells the GoldenGate extract to read the data from the database itself and not from the redo logs/archived logs. In this method, the Extract process writes directly to the trail files in the target environment. In this example, these trail files are limited in size by 10 MB. The number of trail files is limited to 1,000. These trail files are then read by the initial load replicat that is configured in the target environment. The Replicat process in this method is a regular Replicat process as it is configured for a continuous replication. The extract data is applied to the target `EMP` table by this process. Then we start the `RGGTEST1` replicat that will apply the changes generated by the `UPDATE` and `DELETE` statement that we ran in step 10. After these changes are applied, the data in the target `EMP` table is in the same state as the data in the source `EMP` table.

Loading data with files to the database utility method

In this recipe we will look into the detailed steps of instantiating a target database from a source database using the GoldenGate extract file to the database utility method. Although this method can be used to load the data into a variety of databases, for example, Microsoft SQL Server and Oracle DB2, we will focus on loading the data into the target Oracle database using the SQL * Loader. For this, we will instantiate the `EMP` table with 1 million rows to the target database while it gets updated with various transactions. We will also verify at the end of the initial load that all of these changes have been applied to the target as well.

Getting ready

For this recipe we will use the following setup:

1. Create a modified version of the EMP table that is delivered in the SCOTT demo schema with Oracle binaries in the source and target databases. You can use the following DDL statement to create the EMP table:

    ```
    CREATE TABLE EMP (
    EMPNO NUMBER(10) PRIMARY KEY,
    ENAME VARCHAR2(25),
    JOB VARCHAR2(25),
    MGR NUMBER(10),
    HIREDATE DATE,
    SAL NUMBER(20,2),
    COMM NUMBER(20,2),
    DEPTNO NUMBER(10),
    CITY VARCHAR2(25));
    ```

2. Use the following script to load 1 million rows into this table:

    ```
    BEGIN
    FOR I IN 1..250000 LOOP
    INSERT INTO EMP VALUES (0+I,'TOM'||I,'WORKER',7369,TO_DATE('07-11-
    2012','DD-MM-YYYY'),10000+I,I,10,'LONDON');
    INSERT INTO EMP VALUES (250000+I,'BOB'||I,'DBA',7499,TO_DATE('07-
    11-2012','DD-MM-YYYY'),260000+I,I,10,'PARIS');
    INSERT INTO EMP VALUES (500000+I,'ALEX'||I,'DEVELOPER',7521,TO_
    DATE('07-11-2012','DD-MM-YYYY'),500000+I,I,10,'TOKYO');
    INSERT INTO EMP VALUES (750000+I,'SAM'||I,'SALESMAN',7934,TO_
    DATE('07-11-2012','DD-MM-YYYY'),750000+I,I,10,'BOSTON');
    END LOOP;
    COMMIT;
    END;
    ```

3. Enable supplemental logging for the EMP table in the source database.

4. Grant SELECT on the EMP table to the GGATE_ADMIN user in the source database.

5. Grant INSERT, UPDATE, and DELETE on the EMP table to the GGATE_ADMIN user in the target database.

How to do it...

The following are the steps for a continuous replication setup:

1. Follow the steps in the *Setting up a simple GoldenGate replication configuration between two single node databases* recipe in *Chapter 2, Setting up GoldenGate Replication* to set up the continuous replication for the EMP table.

2. Modify the replicat RGGTEST1 configuration to add the HANDLECOLLISIONS parameter as shown in the following command:

   ```
   ./ggsci
   STOP REPLICAT RGGTEST1
   EDIT REPLICAT RGGTEST1
   REPLICAT RGGTEST1
   USERID GGATE_ADMIN@TGORTEST, PASSWORD GGATE_ADMIN
   DISCARDFILE /u01/app/ggate/dirrpt/RGGTEST1.dsc,append,MEGABYTES
   500
   ASSUMETARGETDEFS
   HANDLECOLLISIONS
   MAP SCOTT.EMP, TARGET SCOTT.EMP;
   ```

3. Ensure that you don't start the RGGTEST1 replicat at this stage.

The following are the steps for setting up an initial load:

1. Create a GoldenGate initial load Extract process in the source environment as shown in the following command:

   ```
   ./ggsci
   EDIT PARAMS EXTINIT
   EXTRACT EXTINIT
   SOURCEISTABLE
   USERID GGATE_ADMIN@DBORATEST, PASSWORD GGATE_ADMIN
   FORMATASCII, SQLLOADER
   RMTHOST stdby1-ol6-112, MGRPORT 8809
   RMTFILE ./dirdat/extinit.dat, PURGE
   TABLE SCOTT.EMP;
   ```

2. Add the initial load Extract process to the source manager configuration as shown in the following command:

   ```
   GGSCI> ADD EXTRACT EXTINIT, SOURCEISTABLE
   ```

3. Create a GoldenGate initial load Replicat process in the target environment as shown in the following command:

```
./ggsci
EDIT PARAMS RPTINIT
GENLOADFILES sqlldr.tpl
USERID GGATE_ADMIN@TGORTEST, PASSWORD GGATE_ADMIN
EXTFILE ./dirdat/extinit.dat
ASSUMETARGETDEFS
MAP SCOTT.EMP, TARGET SCOTT.EMP;
```

4. Run the following command to generate the files for the SQL loader:

```
cd $GG_HOME
./replicat paramfile ./dirprm/rptinit.prm reportfile ./dirrpt/
RPTINIT.rpt
```

5. The preceding command will generate two files called EMP.run and EMP.ctl in $GG_HOME.

6. Modify the contents of EMP.ctl and change the name of the EMP table to fully qualified SCOTT.EMP.

7. Before starting the initial load, check the data in the source database as shown in the following command:

```
SQL> SELECT CITY,COUNT(*) FROM EMP GROUP BY CITY;

CITY                 COUNT(*)
----------------------------------
LONDON               250000
PARIS                250000
TOKYO                250000
BOSTON               250000
```

8. On the source system, start the EXTINIT Extract process as shown in the following command:

```
GGSCI> START EXTRACT EXTINIT
```

9. Run the following UPDATE/DELETE statement in the source system:

```
SQL> DELETE EMP WHERE EMPNO>650000 and CITY='TOKYO';
SQL> UPDATE EMP SET CITY='SHANGHAI' where CITY='TOKYO';
SQL> COMMIT;
```

10. Once the `EXTINIT` Extract process finishes in step 8, start the SQL * Loader job to load the data in the `EMP` table as shown in the following command:

```
cd $GG_HOME
./EMP.run
```

11. Wait for the SQL loader job to finish, then check the data in the target database as shown in the following command:

```
SQL> SELECT CITY,COUNT(*) FROM EMP GROUP BY CITY;

CITY                  COUNT(*)

---------------------------------

LONDON                250000

PARIS                 250000

TOKYO                 250000

BOSTON                250000
```

12. Check the updated state of data in the source environment as shown in the following command:

```
SQL> SELECT CITY,COUNT(*) FROM EMP GROUP BY CITY;

CITY                  COUNT(*)

---------------------------------

LONDON                250000

PARIS                 250000

SHANGHAI              150000

BOSTON                250000
```

13. Start the change delivery Replicat process in the target environment as shown in the following command:

```
GGSCI> START REPLICAT RGGTEST1
```

14. Check the state of the Replicat process once it has processed all the trail files. Check the data in the target database to ensure that all the changes are copied across as shown in the following command:

```
SQL> SELECT CITY,COUNT(*) FROM EMP GROUP BY CITY;

CITY                  COUNT(*)

---------------------------------

LONDON                250000

PARIS                 250000

SHANGHAI              150000

BOSTON                250000
```

15. Now that the initial load is complete, we will update the `RGGTEST1` Replicat process to turn off `HANDLECOLLISIONS` as shown in the following command:

```
GGSCI> SEND REPLICAT RGGTEST1, NOHANDLECOLLISIONS

GGSCI> EDIT PARAMS RGGTEST1

REPLICAT RGGTEST1

USERID GGATE_ADMIN@TGORTEST, PASSWORD GGATE_ADMIN

DISCARDFILE /u01/app/ggate/dirrpt/RGGTEST1.dsc,APPEND,MEGABYTES
500

ASSUMETARGETDEFS

MAP SCOTT.EMP, TARGET SCOTT.EMP;
```

How it works...

In this recipe we first configure the processes for continuous replication following the steps from a Setting up a simple GoldenGate replication configuration between two single node databases recipe in *Chapter 2, Setting up GoldenGate Replication*. Once that is done, we will modify the Replicat process to add the `HANDLECOLLISIONS` parameter. The key thing to note in this procedure is that we do not start the Replicat process at this stage. After this we configure an initial load extract. The use of the `SOURCEISTABLE` parameter tells the GoldenGate extract to read the data from the database itself and not from the redo logs/archived logs. The `FORMATASCII` and `SQLLOADER` parameters are used to write the destination file in the ASCII format on the target server. This parameter must be specified before the `RMTFILE` parameter in the extract configuration.

We then create an initial load replicat on the target system. The `GENLOADFILES` parameter is used to denote that we want to generate SQL loader files using the Replicat process. GoldenGate does this by referring to a template file called `sqlldr.tpl` which is shipped with the GoldenGate binaries by Oracle.

Then we start the initial load extract, which creates the `ASCII` file on the target server. Afterwards, we update the data in the source system to generate some changes while the initial load extracts the data from the database.

Then we start the SQL loader process to load the data and verify that all the data from source has been copied to the target environment.

This is followed by starting the `RGGTEST1` replicat that applies the DML changes to the target `EMP` table. Finally we verify that the data in the target `EMP` table matches the one in the source `EMP` table.

There's more...

You can use this method to load the data into a non-Oracle target database. For this you will need to change the FORMATASCII parameter as follows:

```
FORMATASCII, BCP
```

While generating the loader files on the target system, you will need to specify the appropriate template for the database that you are loading into, for example, db2cntl.tpl for DB2 and bcpfmt.tpl for SQL Server.

See also

▸ See the recipe *Cross RDBMS replication using GoldenGate* in *Chapter 8, Advanced Administration Tasks – Part II*

Loading data with the GoldenGate direct load method

In this recipe we will look at how to perform an initial load using the GoldenGate direct load method.

Getting ready

For this recipe we will use the following setup:

1. Create a modified version of the EMP table that is delivered in the SCOTT demo schema with Oracle binaries in the source and target databases. You can use the following DDL statement to create the EMP table:

```
CREATE TABLE EMP (
EMPNO NUMBER(10) PRIMARY KEY,
ENAME VARCHAR2(25),
JOB VARCHAR2(25),
MGR NUMBER(10),
HIREDATE DATE,
SAL NUMBER(20,2),
COMM NUMBER(20,2),
DEPTNO NUMBER(10),
CITY VARCHAR2(25));
```

2. Use the following script to load 1 million rows into this table:

```
BEGIN

FOR I IN 1..250000 LOOP

INSERT INTO EMP VALUES (0+I,'TOM'||I,'WORKER',7369,TO_DATE('07-11-
2012','DD-MM-YYYY'),10000+I,I,10,'LONDON');

INSERT INTO EMP VALUES (250000+I,'BOB'||I,'DBA',7499,TO_DATE('07-
11-2012','DD-MM-YYYY'),260000+I,I,10,'PARIS');

INSERT INTO EMP VALUES (500000+I,'ALEX'||I,'DEVELOPER',7521,TO_
DATE('07-11-2012','DD-MM-YYYY'),500000+I,I,10,'TOKYO');

INSERT INTO EMP VALUES (750000+I,'SAM'||I,'SALESMAN',7934,TO_
DATE('07-11-2012','DD-MM-YYYY'),750000+I,I,10,'BOSTON');

END LOOP;

COMMIT;

END;
```

3. Enable Supplemental Logging for the EMP table in the source database.

4. Grant SELECT on the EMP table to the GGATE_ADMIN user in the source database.

5. Grant INSERT, UPDATE, and DELETE on the EMP table to the GGATE_ADMIN user in the target database.

How to do it...

The following are the steps to set up a continuous replication:

1. Follow the steps in the *Setting up a simple GoldenGate replication configuration between two single node databases* recipe in *Chapter 2, Setting up GoldenGate Replication* to set up the continuous replication for the EMP table.

2. Modify the replicat RGGTEST1 configuration to add the HANDLECOLLISIONS parameter as shown in the following command:

```
./ggsci

STOP REPLICAT RGGTEST1

EDIT REPLICAT RGGTEST1

REPLICAT RGGTEST1

USERID GGATE_ADMIN@TGORTEST, PASSWORD GGATE_ADMIN

DISCARDFILE /u01/app/ggate/dirrpt/RGGTEST1.dsc,append,MEGABYTES
500

ASSUMETARGETDEFS

HANDLECOLLISIONS

MAP SCOTT.emp, TARGET SCOTT.emp;
```

3. The `RGGTEST1` replicat must be stopped at this stage.

The following are the steps to set up an initial load replication:

1. Add the initial load Extract process to the source manager configuration:

   ```
   GGSCI> ADD EXTRACT EXTINIT, SOURCEISTABLE
   ```

2. Create a GoldenGate initial load Extract process in the source environment as shown in the following command:

   ```
   ./ggsci
   EDIT PARAMS EXTINIT
   EXTRACT EXTINIT
   SOURCEISTABLE
   USERID GGATE_ADMIN@DBORATEST, PASSWORD GGATE_ADMIN
   RMTHOST stdby1-ol6-112, MGRPORT 8809
   RMTTASK REPLICAT, GROUP RPTINIT
   TABLE SCOTT.EMP;
   ```

3. Add the initial load replicat to the target manager configuration as shown in the following command:

   ```
   GGSCI> ADD REPLICAT RPTINIT, SPECIALRUN
   ```

4. Create a GoldenGate initial load Replicat process in the target environment as shown in the following command:

   ```
   ./ggsci
   EDIT PARAMS RPTINIT
   REPLICAT RPTINIT
   USERID GGATE_ADMIN@TGORTEST, PASSWORD GGATE_ADMIN
   ASSUMETARGETDEFS
   MAP SCOTT.EMP, TARGET SCOTT.EMP;
   ```

5. Before starting the initial load, check the data in the source database as shown in the following command:

   ```
   SQL> SELECT CITY,COUNT(*) FROM EMP GROUP BY CITY;

   CITY               COUNT(*)
   ----------------------------------
   LONDON               250000
   PARIS                250000
   TOKYO                250000
   BOSTON               250000
   ```

6. On the source system, start the EXTINIT Extract process. The Manager process on the target system will automatically start the initial load replicat as shown in the following command:

    ```
    GGSCI> START EXTRACT EXTINIT
    ```

7. Run the following UPDATE/DELETE statement in the source system:

    ```
    SQL> DELETE EMP WHERE EMPNO>650000 and CITY='TOKYO';

    SQL> UPDATE EMP SET CITY='SHANGHAI' where CITY='TOKYO';

    SQL> COMMIT;
    ```

8. Check the status of the EXTINIT Extract process as shown in the following command:

    ```
    GGSCI> VIEW REPORT EXTINIT
    ```

9. Once the initial load Extract process finishes, check the data in the target database as shown in the following command:

    ```
    SQL> SELECT CITY,COUNT(*) FROM EMP GROUP BY CITY;

    CITY                    COUNT(*)
    ---------------------------------

    LONDON                    250000

    PARIS                     250000

    TOKYO                     250000

    BOSTON                    250000
    ```

10. Check the updated state of data in the source environment:

    ```
    SQL> SELECT CITY,COUNT(*) FROM EMP GROUP BY CITY;

    CITY                    COUNT(*)
    ------------------------------------

    LONDON                    250000

    PARIS                     250000

    SHANGHAI                  150000

    BOSTON                    250000
    ```

11. Start the change delivery Replicat process in the target environment as shown in the following command:

    ```
    GGSCI> START REPLICAT RGGTEST1
    ```

12. Check the state of the Replicat process once it has processed all the trail files. Check the data in the target database to ensure that all changes are copied across as shown in the following command:

```
SQL> SELECT CITY,COUNT(*) FROM EMP GROUP BY CITY;

CITY                    COUNT(*)

---------------------------------

LONDON                  250000

PARIS                   250000

SHANGHAI                150000

BOSTON                  250000
```

13. Now that the initial load is complete, we will update the RGGTEST1 Replicat process to turn off HANDLECOLLISIONS as shown in the following command:

```
GGSCI> SEND REPLICAT RGGTEST1, NOHANDLECOLLISIONS

GGSCI> EDIT PARAMS RGGTEST1

REPLICAT RGGTEST1

USERID GGATE_ADMIN@TGORTEST, PASSWORD GGATE_ADMIN

DISCARDFILE /u01/app/ggate/dirrpt/RGGTEST1.dsc,append,MEGABYTES
500

ASSUMETARGETDEFS

MAP SCOTT.EMP, TARGET SCOTT.EMP;
```

How it works...

In this method, an initial load extract in the source environment communicates directly to an initial load replicat in the target environment. The Extract process extracts the data from the source database and passes it on to the initial load replicat. The Replicat process processes this data in large chunks and converts them into the INSERT statements and applies them to the target database. The key thing to note in this method is that we do not manually start the initial load Replicat process. The initial load Extract process communicates with the Manager process in the target environment, and the Manager process starts the initial load Replicat process for the duration of the data load after which it is stopped.

In this demo, we first configure the processes for continuous change delivery by following the steps from the Setting up a simple GoldenGate replication configuration between two single node databases recipe in *Chapter 2, Setting up GoldenGate Replication*. We then modify the Replicat process to add the HANDLECOLLISIONS parameter, and then stop the Replicat process. Then we configure the processes for initial load. In the initial load extract parameter file, we specify the SOURCEISTABLE parameter. This parameter specifies that the data will be extracted from the source database and not from the redo logs/archived logs. The RMTTASK REPLICAT and GROUP RPTINIT parameters tell the extract to transfer the data to the

Replicat process in the target environment that will be started dynamically by the Manager process. The data is then broken into large chunks and converted into the INSERT statements and loaded into the target database by the Replicat process. While this data is loaded, we run few DMLs in the source database to generate some changes. These changes are processed by the EGGTEST1 extract and trail files transferred by the PGGTEST1 datapump to the target server. Once all the data is loaded by the initial load processes, EXTINIT/RPTINIT, we start the RGGTEST1 replicat that applies the DML changes to the target EMP table.

At the end we verify that the data in the target EMP table matches the one in the source EMP table.

There's more...

The key benefit of this method is that you can perform transformations in the extract configuration or in the replicat configuration. This method is, however, much slower as compared to other GoldenGate initial load methods.

Loading data with bulk load to the SQL loader method

The GoldenGate bulk load to the SQL loader method consists of an initial load Extract process which communicates with an initial load Replicat process. This process is started automatically by the destination Manager process. The Replicat process then coordinates with the SQL loader API and uses it to load the data into the target database. In this recipe, we will look into the detailed steps of how to use this method to perform an instantiation of the source database.

Getting ready

For this recipe we will use the following setup:

1. Create a modified version of the EMP table that is delivered in the SCOTT demo schema with Oracle binaries in the source and target databases. You can use the following DDL statement to create the EMP table:

```
CREATE TABLE EMP (
EMPNO NUMBER(10) PRIMARY KEY,
ENAME VARCHAR2(25),
JOB VARCHAR2(25),
MGR NUMBER(10),
HIREDATE DATE,
SAL NUMBER(20,2),
COMM NUMBER(20,2),
DEPTNO NUMBER(10),
CITY VARCHAR2(25));
```

2. Use the following script to load 1 million rows into this table:

```
BEGIN
FOR I IN 1..250000 LOOP
INSERT INTO EMP VALUES (0+I,'TOM'||I,'WORKER',7369,TO_DATE('07-11-
2012','DD-MM-YYYY'),10000+I,I,10,'LONDON');
INSERT INTO EMP VALUES (250000+I,'BOB'||I,'DBA',7499,TO_DATE('07-
11-2012','DD-MM-YYYY'),260000+I,I,10,'PARIS');
INSERT INTO EMP VALUES (500000+I,'ALEX'||I,'DEVELOPER',7521,TO_
DATE('07-11-2012','DD-MM-YYYY'),500000+I,I,10,'TOKYO');
INSERT INTO EMP VALUES (750000+I,'SAM'||I,'SALESMAN',7934,TO_
DATE('07-11-2012','DD-MM-YYYY'),750000+I,I,10,'BOSTON');
END LOOP;
COMMIT;
END;
```

3. Enable Supplemental Logging for the `EMP` table in the source database.

4. Grant `SELECT` on the `EMP` table to the `GGATE_ADMIN` user in the source database.

5. Grant `INSERT`, `UPDATE`, and `DELETE` on the `EMP` table to the `GGATE_ADMIN` user in the target database.

6. Grant `LOCK ANY TABLE` to the `GGATE_ADMIN` user in the target database.

How to do it...

Follow the given steps to perform a source to target database initial load using the GoldenGate bulk load to the SQL loader method.

The following are the steps to set up a continuous replication:

1. Follow the steps in the *Setting up a simple GoldenGate replication configuration between two single node databases* recipe in *Chapter 2, Setting up GoldenGate Replication* to set up the continuous replication for the `EMP` table.

2. Modify the replicat `RGGTEST1` configuration to add the `HANDLECOLLISIONS` parameter as shown in the following command:

```
./ggsci
STOP REPLICAT RGGTEST1
EDIT REPLICAT RGGTEST1
REPLICAT RGGTEST1
USERID GGATE_ADMIN@TGORTEST, PASSWORD GGATE_ADMIN
DISCARDFILE /u01/app/ggate/dirrpt/RGGTEST1.dsc,append,MEGABYTES
```

```
500

ASSUMETARGETDEFS

HANDLECOLLISIONS

MAP SCOTT.emp, TARGET SCOTT.emp;
```

3. The `RGGTEST1` replicat must be stopped at this stage.

The following are the steps to set up an initial load replication:

1. Add the initial load Extract process to the source manager configuration as shown in the following command:

```
GGSCI> ADD EXTRACT EXTINIT, SOURCEISTABLE
```

2. Create a GoldenGate initial load Extract process in the source environment as shown in the following command:

```
./ggsci

EDIT PARAMS EXTINIT

EXTRACT EXTINIT

USERID GGATE_ADMIN@DBORATEST, PASSWORD GGATE_ADMIN

RMTHOST stdby1-ol6-112, MGRPORT 8809

RMTTASK REPLICAT, GROUP RPTINIT

TABLE SCOTT.EMP;
```

3. Add the initial load replicat to the target manager configuration as shown in the following command:

```
GGSCI> ADD REPLICAT RPTINIT, SPECIALRUN
```

4. Create a GoldenGate initial load Replicat process in the target environment as shown in the following command:

```
./ggsci

EDIT PARAMS RPTINIT

REPLICAT RPTINIT

USERID GGATE_ADMIN@TGORTEST, PASSWORD GGATE_ADMIN

BULKLOAD

ASSUMETARGETDEFS

MAP SCOTT.EMP, TARGET SCOTT.EMP;
```

5. Before starting the initial load, check the data in the source database as shown in the following command:

```
SQL> SELECT CITY,COUNT(*) FROM EMP GROUP BY CITY;

CITY                    COUNT(*)
-------------------------------------

LONDON                  250000

PARIS                   250000

TOKYO                   250000

BOSTON                  250000
```

6. On the source system, start the `EXTINIT` Extract process. The Manager process on the target system will automatically start the initial load replicat as shown in the following command:

```
GGSCI> START EXTRACT EXTINIT
```

7. Run the following `UPDATE/DELETE` statement in the source system as shown in the following command:

```
SQL> DELETE EMP WHERE EMPNO>650000 and CITY='TOKYO';

SQL> UPDATE EMP SET CITY='SHANGHAI' WHERE CITY='TOKYO';

SQL> COMMIT;
```

8. Check the status of the `EXTINIT` Extract process as shown in the following command:

```
GGSCI> VIEW REPORT EXTINIT
```

9. Once the initial load Extract process finishes, check the data in the target database as shown in the following command:

```
SQL> SELECT CITY,COUNT(*) FROM EMP GROUP BY CITY;

CITY                    COUNT(*)
-------------------------------------

LONDON                  250000

PARIS                   250000

TOKYO                   250000

BOSTON                  250000
```

10. Check the updated state of data in the source environment as shown in the following command:

```
SQL> SELECT CITY,COUNT(*) FROM EMP GROUP BY CITY;

CITY                    COUNT(*)

--------------------------------

LONDON                  250000

PARIS                   250000

SHANGHAI                150000

BOSTON                  250000
```

11. Start the change delivery Replicat process in the target environment as shown in the following command:

```
GGSCI> START REPLICAT RGGTEST1
```

12. Check the state of the Replicat process once it has processed all the trail files. Check the data in the target database to ensure that all changes are copied across as shown in the following command:

```
SQL> SELECT CITY,COUNT(*) FROM EMP GROUP BY CITY;

CITY                    COUNT(*)

--------------------------------

LONDON                  250000

PARIS                   250000

SHANGHAI                150000

BOSTON                  250000
```

13. Now that the initial load is complete, we will update the RGGTEST1 Replicat process to turn off HANDLECOLLISIONS as shown in the following command:

```
GGSCI> SEND REPLICAT RGGTEST1, NOHANDLECOLLISIONS

GGSCI> EDIT PARAMS RGGTEST1

REPLICAT RGGTEST1

USERID GGATE_ADMIN@TGORTEST, PASSWORD GGATE_ADMIN

DISCARDFILE /u01/app/ggate/dirrpt/RGGTEST1.dsc,append,MEGABYTES
500

ASSUMETARGETDEFS

MAP SCOTT.EMP, TARGET SCOTT.EMP;
```

How it works...

This method is quite similar to the direct load method. Here, an initial load extract in the source environment communicates directly to an initial load replicat in the target environment. The Extract process extracts the data from the source database and passes it on to the initial load replicat. The initial load Replicat process uses the SQL * Loader binaries to load the data into the database using the bulk load method. Just as with the direct load method, we don't manually start the Replicat process. It is started automatically by the target Manager process. The use of the SQL loader by the replicat is implicit and happens with a single parameter in the replicat configuration called BULKLOAD. Once the data is loaded into the target database by the Replicat process, it is stopped by the Manager process.

In this demo, we first configure the processes for continuous change delivery by following the steps from the recipe in *Chapter 2, Setting up GoldenGate Replication*. We then modify the Replicat process to add the HANDLECOLLISIONS parameter, and then stop the Replicat process. Then we configure the processes for initial load. In the initial load extract parameter file, we specify the SOURCEISTABLE parameter. This parameter specifies that the data will be extracted from the source database and not from the redo logs/archived logs. The RMTTASK REPLICAT and GROUP RPTINIT parameter tells the extract to transfer the data to the Replicat process in the target environment that will be started dynamically by the Manager process. The data is loaded into the target database by the RPTINIT replicat using SQL * Loader. While this data is loaded, we run a few DMLs in the source database to generate some changes. These changes are processed by the EGGTEST1 extract and trail files transferred by the PGGTEST1 datapump to the target server. Once all the data is loaded by the initial load processes, EXTINIT/RPTINIT, we start the RGGTEST1 replicat that applies the DML changes to the target EMP table. Finally, we verify that the data in the target EMP table matches the one in the source EMP table.

4

Mapping and Manipulating Data

The following recipes will be covered in this chapter:

- ▸ Setting up a GoldenGate replication with mapping between different columns
- ▸ Adding custom fields for a replicated record using tokens
- ▸ Adding custom fields to a replicated record using `SQLEXEC`
- ▸ Filtering the records using the `FILTER` and `WHERE` clause
- ▸ Mapping the changes to a target table and storing the transaction history in a history table
- ▸ Creating a GoldenGate configuration to run a Shell script when an end-of-day processing record is replicated
- ▸ Creating an exception handler to record the erroneous transactions in a GoldenGate configuration

Introduction

When GoldenGate is used in some of the topologies where the source and target systems are not identical, you would most likely be required to perform some additional configuration. GoldenGate has got many additional parameters and options using which you can set up complex mappings and filtering. Data Lifecycle management is becoming an important part of the overall IT strategy of various companies. The regulatory requirements in some industries require the businesses to maintain a record of upto seven years or even longer. In such cases if you keep all the data in main database tables it can cause performance problems. Using GoldenGate you can track the changes applied on a table to maintain a transaction history without much impact on the production system. It also allows you to track the replication errors using exception handling.

Using GoldenGate macros, you can write the process configuration parameters once and reuse them in multiple parameter files in a single environment. This is quite helpful if you have written some complex transformations which need to be used in multiple objects.

In this chapter we will look into the various mapping, filtering, and exception handling options available in GoldenGate. We will also see an example of how to maintain the transaction history of a table.

Setting up a GoldenGate replication with mapping between different columns

In some of the GoldenGate topologies, you would probably have different table structures in the source and target environment. Different structures can include different table names, different column order, or different column names. When you want to map the data from a source table to a target table in which the column names are not the same, you need to specify some extra parameters in the Replicat process groups. In this recipe we will look into how this can be done.

Getting ready

For this recipe we will use the continuous replication setup for the SCOTT schema done in the *Setting up a simple GoldenGate replication configuration between two single node databases* recipe earlier in *Chapter 2, Setting up GoldenGate Replication*. We will rename two columns in the target EMP table as follows:

```
SQL> ALTER TABLE EMP RENAME COLUMN SAL TO SALARY;
SQL> ALTER TABLE EMP RENAME COLUMN COMM TO COMMISSION;
```

After this, the source and the target EMP tables should be as follows:

Source EMP Table	Target EMP Table
EMPNO	EMPNO
ENAME	ENAME
JOB	JOB
MGR	MGR
HIREDATE	HIREDATE
SAL	SALARY
COMM	COMMISSION
DEPTNO	DEPTNO

How to do it...

Once you have modified the EMP table in the target environment, you can follow the following steps to set up a replication between these tables.

Steps to be performed in the source environment are as follows:

1. Create a parameter file for defgen:

    ```
    ./ggsci
    EDIT PARAMS defs
    DEFSFILE ./dirdef/defs.def
    USERID ggs_admin@dboratest, PASSWORD ******
    TABLE SCOTT.EMP;
    TABLE SCOTT.DEPT;
    TABLE SCOTT.BONUS;
    TABLE SCOTT.DUMMY;
    TABLE SCOTT.SALGRADE;
    ```

2. Generate the definitions file:

    ```
    ./defgen paramfile ./dirprm/defs.prm
    ```

3. Push the definitions file to the target server using scp:

    ```
    scp ./dirdef/defs.def stdby1-ol6-112:/u01/app/ggate/dirdef/
    ```

4. The Extract process parameter file should look as follows:

    ```
    EXTRACT EGGTEST1
    USERID GGATE_ADMIN@DBORATEST, PASSWORD GGATE_ADMIN
    EXTTRAIL /u01/app/ggate/dirdat/st
    TABLE scott.*;
    ```

5. The Datapump process parameter file should look as follows:

    ```
    EXTRACT PGGTEST1
    USERID GGATE_ADMIN@DBORATEST, PASSWORD GGATE_ADMIN
    RMTHOST stdby1-ol6-112 , MGRPORT 8809
    RMTTRAIL /u01/app/ggate/dirdat/rt
    TABLE scott.*;
    ```

6. Start the Extract and Datapump processes.

Steps to be performed in the target environment are as follows:

1. Edit the Replicat process configuration as follows:

```
./ggsci
EDIT PARAMS RGGTEST1
REPLICAT RGGTEST1
USERID GGATE_ADMIN@TGORTEST, PASSWORD GGATE_ADMIN
DISCARDFILE /u01/app/ggate/dirrpt/RGGTEST1.dsc,append,MEGABYTES
500
SOURCEDEFS ./dirdef/defs.def
MAP SCOTT.BONUS, TARGET SCOTT.BONUS;
MAP SCOTT.SALGRADE, TARGET SCOTT.SALGRADE;
MAP SCOTT.DEPT, TARGET SCOTT.DEPT;
MAP SCOTT.DUMMY, TARGET SCOTT.DUMMY;
MAP SCOTT.EMP, TARGET SCOTT.EMP, COLMAP(USEDEFAULTS, SAL=SALARY,
COMM=COMMISSION);
```

2. Start the Replicat process.

How it works...

The default GoldenGate configuration that includes the `Table` and `Map` commands with just the source and target table names assumes that the table structures in both the source and target databases are similar. In some circumstances, you would need to replicate between two tables where the column names are different. For this, you would need to define additional options with the `MAP` command in the replicat parameter file to define an explicit match between the source and target database tables. In the earlier set of steps, we have got a modified version of the `EMP` table in the target database. This table has two columns which are named differently from the one in the source database. The `COLMAP` option with the `MAP` command is used to define the relationship between the `SAL` and `SALARY` columns and the `COMM` and `COMMISSION` columns. As we have already seen in a previous recipe *Setting up GoldenGate replication between the tables with different structures using defgen* in *Chapter 2, Setting up GoldenGate Replication*, when you replicate using GoldenGate between two tables which have different structures, you need to generate the definitions file for one environment and refer it in the configuration of the other environment. This definitions file is generated using the defgen utility. This utility exports the table structure information and writes it to a file. This file is then transferred to the other environment and referred to in the GoldenGate configuration. In this example, we also generate a `defs.def` file, transfer it to the target machine and then refer it in the replicat configuration using the `SOURCEDEFS` parameter.

There's more...

There are some additional ways of specifying the column mapping. Depending on the requirements and the number of mappings to be defined, you can use one of the following methods:

Source environment mapping

So far, we have seen how to define the mapping of the source objects in the target environment parameter files. In some situations, it might be better to define the mappings in the source environment. For example, if you are using GoldenGate in a consolidation topology, where changes from multiple source systems are merged into a target system, it would be easier to generate a single target definitions file and refer it in all the source systems than having to generate and manage a separate one for each source system. However, do keep in mind that mapping does add overheads to an environment. So if your source environment is a very busy production environment where you cannot afford to add any more overheads, then it would be a better decision to define mappings on the target side.

The mappings are defined in the source environment extract parameter file as:

```
EXTRACT EGGTEST1
USERID GGATE_ADMIN@DBORATEST, PASSWORD GGATE_ADMIN
EXTTRAIL /u01/app/ggate/dirdat/st
TARGETDEFS ./dirdef/defs.def
TABLE SCOTT.BONUS, TARGET SCOTT.BONUS;
TABLE SCOTT.SALGRADE, TARGET SCOTT.SALGRADE;
TABLE SOTT.DEPT, TARGET SCOTT.DEPT;
TABLE SCOTT.DUMMY, TARGET SCOTT.DUMMY;
TABLE SCOTT.EMP, TARGET SCOTT.EMP, COLMAP(USEDEFAULTS, SAL=SALARY,
COMM=COMMISSION);
```

Defining global mappings

If you have multiple tables in the target environment which have different column names from the ones in the source environment for the same data set, then rather than defining the column mapping for each table individually, you can use global mapping. In case of global mapping, you define the column mappings using COLMATCH in the parameter files. This is followed by all the TABLE or MAP statements depending on whether you are defining the mappings in the source or target environment:

```
COLMATCH NAMES SALARY = SAL
COLMATCH NAMES COMMISSION = COMM
MAP SCOTT.EMP, TARGET SCOTT.EMP COLMAP(USEDEFAULTS);
ADDITIONAL TABLE MAP STATEMENTS GO HERE
```

Defining mappings using prefix/suffix

If the only difference between the column names of the source and target environment tables is a suffix or a prefix, then you can use COLMATCH with the PREFIX or SUFFIX option to instruct GoldenGate to ignore them. You can do that as follows:

```
COLMATCH PREFIX DWH_
COLMATCH SUFFIX _TGT
MAP SCOTT.EMP, TARGET SCOTT.EMP COLMAP(USEDEFAULTS);
ADDITIONAL TABLE MAP STATEMENTS GO HERE
```

In this example, GoldenGate will ignore the defined suffix DWH_ and prefix _TGT in the source and target columns.

> [🔆 Use COLMATCH RESET to turn off any active global
> column mappings in a parameter file.]

See also

▸ The *Setting up a GoldenGate replication with mapping between different columns* recipe in *Chapter 4, Mapping and Manipulating Data*

Adding custom fields for a replicated record using tokens

In this recipe we will look at how we use GoldenGate tokens to add additional information to an extracted record and map it to the table in the target environment.

Getting ready

For this recipe, we will use the following CUST table. This table is created in the source and target databases under the SCOTT schema. In the target database, the table has an additional column to denote the name of the source database from which this change originated.

Source CUST Table	Target CUST Table
CUST_ID	CUST_ID
ACCOUNT_ID	ACCOUNT_ID
CUST_NAME	CUST_NAME
BALANCE	BALANCE
	CHANGE_ORIGIN

How to do it...

Steps to be performed in the source environment are as follows:

1. Create an Extract process parameter file as follows:

```
EXTRACT EGGTEST1
USERID GGATE_ADMIN@DBORATEST, PASSWORD GGATE_ADMIN
EXTTRAIL /u01/app/ggate/dirdat/st
TABLE scott.CUST, TOKENS (TK_ORIGIN = @GETENV("DBENVIRONMENT" ,
"DBNAME" ));
```

2. The Datapump process parameter file should be as follows:

```
EXTRACT PGGTEST1
USERID GGATE_ADMIN@DBORATEST, PASSWORD GGATE_ADMIN
RMTHOST stdby1-ol6-112 , MGRPORT 8809
RMTTRAIL /u01/app/ggate/dirdat/rt
TABLE scott.CUST;
```

3. Start the Extract and Datapump process.

Steps to be performed in the target environment are as follows:

1. Edit the Replicat process configuration as follows:

```
./ggsci
EDIT PARAMS RGGTEST1
REPLICAT RGGTEST1
USERID GGATE_ADMIN@TGORTEST, PASSWORD GGATE_ADMIN
DISCARDFILE /u01/app/ggate/dirrpt/RGGTEST1.dsc,append,MEGABYTES
500
ASSUMETARGETDEFS
MAP SCOTT.CUST, TARGET SCOTT.CUST, COLMAP(USEDEFAULTS, CHANGE_
ORIGIN = @TOKEN ("TK_ORIGIN"));
```

2. Start the Replicat process.

How it works...

In this example, the Extract process in the source environment will extract the changes for the CUST table. The TOKENS clause in the TABLE parameter in the extract configuration will extract the database name from the source GoldenGate environment and add it to a token called TK_ORIGIN. This token is added to the extract record and to the trail file on the source system. The Datapump process will read this trail file and write the changes to the remote trail file on the target environment.

The replicated records are read by the Replicat process RGGTEST1 on the target server. In the replicat configuration, we have specified the COLMAP option as COLMAP (USEDEFAULTS, CHANGE_ORIGIN = @TOKEN ("TK_ORIGIN")). The USEDEFAULTS parameter will map the default source columns to the ones in the target CUST table. We have an additional column called CHANGE_ORIGIN in the CUST table. This column is mapped to a token called TK_ORIGIN which was added by the Extract process in the source environment. The Replicat process reads this configuration and replicates the records to the target CUST table.

The replicated records in the target table will look as follows:

```
oracle@stdby1-ol6-112:~/Desktop                    _ □ ×

File  Edit  View  Search  Terminal  Help

SQL> select * from cust;

  CUST_ID ACCOUNT_ID CUST_NAME         BALANCE CHANGE_ORIGIN
---------- ---------- ---------------- ---------- --------------------
        1        100 MICHAEL              5000 DBORATES
        2        103 SANDY               10000 DBORATES
        3        101 RAJ                100000 DBORATES
        5       2132 ROGER               20000 DBORATES
        6       2133 RICHARD             35000 DBORATES

SQL>
```

There's more...

There are various tokens that you can generate and add to the replicated records in the target database. Using these tokens you can add some critical information which can be used for various purposes, for example auditing, reporting, and so on.

Some of the most widely used user tokens are:

Name of OS User	@GETENV("GGENVIRONMENT","OSUSERNAME")
Process Group Name	@GETENV("GGENVIRONMENT", "GROUPNAME"))
Process Group Type	@GETENV("GGENVIRONMENT", "GROUPTYPE"))
Hostname	@GETENV ("GGENVIRONMENT","HOSTNAME")
Database name	@GETENV ("DBENVIRONMENT","DBNAME")
Database Username	@GETENV ("DBENVIRONMENT","DBUSER")
Record Commit Time	@GETENV("GGHEADER","COMMITTIMESTAMP")
Update Before/After Indicator	@GETENV(("GGHEADER","BEFOREAFTERINDICATOR"))
Table Name	@GETENV ("GGHEADER", "TABLENAME")
Archive Log Sequence	@GETENV ("GGHEADER", "LOGRBA")
Archive Log Position In file	@GETENV ("GGHEADER", "LOGPOSITION")
Database Error Number	@GETENV ("LASTERR", "DBERRNUM")
Database Error Message	@GETENV ("LASTERR", "DBERRMSG")
GoldenGate Operation Type	@GETENV ("LASTERR", "OPTYPE")
GoldenGate Error Type	@GETENV ("LASTERR", "ERRTYPE")

One of the most popular uses of the tokens is to track the commit timestamp of a GoldenGate record as it passes through various GoldenGate processes. This is quite useful to check the overall state of GoldenGate replication and this process can be used to check the lag between various processes.

See also

▶ See the *Script to perform a regular scheduled healthcheck of a live GoldenGate configuration* recipe in *Chapter 6, Monitoring, Tuning, and Troubleshooting GoldenGate*

Adding custom fields to a replicated record using SQLEXEC

In this recipe we will look into how we can use SQLEXEC to populate a column using an SQL statement in the GoldenGate replication.

Getting ready

For this recipe we will use the EMP table that is delivered in the SCOTT schema with Oracle binaries. In the target environment, the EMP table has an extra column called AVG_SAL which will be the average salary of an employee's department calculated using SQL ran by SQLEXEC.

Source EMP Table	Target EMP Table
EMPNO	EMPNO
ENAME	ENAME
JOB	JOB
MGR	MGR
HIREDATE	HIREDATE
SAL	SAL
COMM	COMM
DEPTNO	DEPTNO
	AVG_SAL

How to do it...

We will follow the following steps to demonstrate the use of the `SQLEXEC` command.

Run the following in the source environment:

1. Create an Extract process parameter file as follows:

```
EXTRACT EGGTEST1
USERID GGATE_ADMIN@DBORATEST, PASSWORD GGATE_ADMIN
EXTTRAIL /u01/app/ggate/dirdat/st
TABLE scott.EMP;
```

2. The Datapump process parameter file should look as follows:

```
EXTRACT PGGTEST1
USERID GGATE_ADMIN@DBORATEST, PASSWORD GGATE_ADMIN
RMTHOST stdby1-ol6-112 , MGRPORT 8809
RMTTRAIL /u01/app/ggate/dirdat/rt
TABLE scott.EMP;
```

3. Start the Extract and Datapump process.

Steps for the target environment are as follows:

1. Edit the Replicat process configuration as follows:

```
./ggsci
EDIT PARAMS RGGTEST1
REPLICAT RGGTEST1
USERID GGATE_ADMIN@TGORTEST, PASSWORD GGATE_ADMIN
DISCARDFILE /u01/app/ggate/dirrpt/RGGTEST1.dsc,append,MEGABYTES
500
ASSUMETARGETDEFS
MAP SCOTT.EMP, TARGET SCOTT.EMP, &
SQLEXEC (ID lookavg, QUERY &
"SELECT AVG(SAL) avgsal FROM SCOTT.EMP WHERE DEPTNO =(SELECT
DEPTNO FROM EMP WHERE EMPNO = :EMP_ID)" &
PARAMS (EMP_ID = EMPNO)), &
COLMAP (USEDEFAULTS, AVG_SAL = @GETVAL(lookavg.avgsal);
```

2. Start the Replicat process.

How it works...

The source environment setup in this recipe consists of a simple Extract and a Datapump process configuration. In the target environment, we have modified the demo EMP table and added an extra column called AVG_SAL to it. The replicated configuration consists of a MAP statement with SQLEXEC and COLMAP clauses. The SQLEXEC command is used in the query mode in this example. It runs an SQL statement which retrieves the average salary of an employee's department. Each SQLEXEC clause is identified by an ID. In this case, we have assigned lookavg as ID to the SQLEXEC clause. The employee's department information is passed as a parameter to the SQLEXEC query. The database then runs the SQL query and returns the value of the average salary in avgsal. This value is then populated into the AVG_SAL by the COLMAP clause.

There's more...

The power of the SQLEXEC command lies in its ability to interact with the database directly. It can do this in three ways:

- Run an SQL statement as a part of a TABLE/MAP command
- Run a stored procedure as a part of a TABLE/MAP command
- Run a global SQL statement/procedure

We have already seen how we can use the SQLEXEC command to run an SQL statement as a part of a MAP command to retrieve and populate a value in the target table. Let's now look at how we can use SQLEXEC to run a stored procedure with table mapping and to directly execute the SQL/stored procedure.

Running a stored procedure with SQLEXEC

In order to use the SQLEXEC to run a stored procedure, you would first need to create the stored procedure and grant execute privileges on this store procedure to the GGATE_ADMIN user. We create a demo stored procedure to perform the same task as we did using the SQL Query in the earlier section:

```
CREATE PROCEDURE AVG_SAL( EMP_ID IN NUMBER, AVGSAL OUT NUMBER) IS
BEGIN
SELECT AVG(SAL) INTO AVGSAL FROM SCOTT.EMP WHERE DEPTNO= (SELECT
DEPTNO FROM SCOTT.EMP WHERE EMPNO=EMP_ID);
END;

MAP SCOTT.EMP, TARGET SCOTT.EMP, &
SQLEXEC (SPNAME AVG_SAL, &
PARAMS (EMP_ID = EMPNO)), &
COLMAP (USEDEFAULTS, AVG_SAL = @GETVAL(AVG_SAL.AVGSAL);
```

When SQLEXEC is used to run a stored procedure, you use the SPNAME option and pass the required parameters using the PARAMS clause.

Running a global SQL statement/procedure

You can also use SQLEXEC to run an SQL statement or a stored procedure. This is when you want to run them without the aim of returning a value, that is, you want to run them to perform an action and not to ascertain a value. An example of this would be to run a batch reports generation procedure once the data load is done:

```
MAP SCOTT.EMP, TARGET SCOTT.EMP;
SQLEXEC "call generate_end_of_day_reports ()";
```

Filtering the records using the FILTER and WHERE clause

One of the most powerful features of GoldenGate is the ability to replicate the data which can be chosen on the basis of built-in logic in its parameter files. There is a FILTER command using which this can be done. FILTER is a very versatile command, as you can define complex logic to select the data based on conditions.

In this recipe we will look at how you can use the FILTER command to select the records to be replicated by a Replicat process. We will also look at some examples of various filter conditions.

Getting ready

For this recipe, we will use the following CUST table. This table is created in the source and target databases under the SCOTT schema. There is an additional table in the target database called CUST_PREMIER which has a similar structure to the CUST table.

Source CUSTTable	Target CUSTTable	Target CUST_PREMIER
CUST_ID	CUST_ID	CUST_ID
ACCOUNT_ID	ACCOUNT_ID	ACCOUNT_ID
CUST_NAME	CUST_NAME	CUST_NAME
BALANCE	BALANCE	BALANCE

How to do it...

Following is an example to demonstrate the use of the FILTER command in GoldenGate replication.

Perform the following steps in the source environment:

1. Create an Extract process parameter file as follows:

```
EXTRACT EGGTEST1
USERID GGATE_ADMIN@DBORATEST, PASSWORD GGATE_ADMIN
EXTTRAIL /u01/app/ggate/dirdat/st
TABLE SCOTT.CUST;
```

2. The Datapump process parameter file should look like this:

```
EXTRACT PGGTEST1
USERID GGATE_ADMIN@DBORATEST, PASSWORD GGATE_ADMIN
RMTHOST stdby1-ol6-112 , MGRPORT 8809
RMTTRAIL /u01/app/ggate/dirdat/rt
TABLE scott.CUST;
```

3. Start the Extract and Datapump process.

Steps to be performed in the target environment are as follows:

1. Edit the Replicat process configuration as follows:

```
./ggsci
EDIT PARAMS RGGTEST1
REPLICAT RGGTEST1
USERID GGATE_ADMIN@TGORTEST, PASSWORD GGATE_ADMIN
DISCARDFILE /u01/app/ggate/dirrpt/RGGTEST1.dsc,append,MEGABYTES
500
ASSUMETARGETDEFS
MAP SCOTT.CUST, TARGET SCOTT.CUST ;
MAP SCOTT.CUST, TARGET SCOTT.CUST_PREMIER, FILTER (BALANCE
>100000);
```

2. Start the Replicat process.

How it works...

The aim of this GoldenGate configuration is to do the following:

- Replicate all data from the source CUST table to the target CUST table
- Replicate all records from the source CUST table to the target CUST_PREMIER table only for customers having a balance of more than 1,00,000

To perform this replication, we configure a simple Extract and Datapump process in the source environment. These processes extract and ship all the records for the CUST table to the target server. On the target side, in the replicat parameter file, there are two map statements. One of these maps the records to the target CUST table and the second one maps the records to the CUST_PREMIER table. The FILTER clause in the second map statement will filter and apply only the records where the value of the balance column is greater than 1,00,000.

There's more...

You can define different conditions using arithmetic, relational, and conjunction operators in the FILTER command. Some of the examples of using the FILTER command are as follows:

▶ Filter all records where Sum of Salary and Commission is greater than 1000

```
FILTER (@COMPUTE (SAL + COMM) > 1000);
```

▶ Filter all rows where Employee name is SMITH

```
FILTER (@STREQ ("ENAME", 'SMITH') > 0);
```

▶ Filter all rows where Commission is not null

```
FILTER (COMM <> @NULL);
```

▶ Filter all rows where Commission is not null and salary is greater than 10000

```
FILTER ((COMM <> @NULL) AND (SAL > 10000));
```

You can also filter specific DML statements using the FILTER command as follows:

▶ Filter all Insert Statements where SAL is greater than 10000

```
FILTER (ON INSERT, SAL > 10000);
```

▶ Ignore all Insert Statements where SAL is greater than 10000

```
FILTER (IGNORE INSERT, SAL > 10000);
```

> You can use GoldenGate global parameters IGNOREUPDATES, IGNOREDELETES, IGNOREINSERTS to ignore specific DML statements from a number of tables.

Using the Where clause

You can also use the WHERE clause to filter the replicated records. The WHERE clause works in the same way as the FILTER clause except you cannot filter on statement types using WHERE. Some examples of using the WHERE clause are as follows:

▶ Filter all Insert statements where SAL is greater than 10000

```
WHERE (SAL > 10000);
```

- Filter all records where SAL is present and greater than 10,000

```
WHERE (SAL = @PRESENT, SAL > 10000);
```

Filtering in the source environment

So far we have seen how to filter the records in the Replicat process configuration. You can also filter the data in the source environment, that is in the Extract or Datapump process. The only difference in the filtering in source environment is that instead of specifying the FILTER clause with the MAP command, you would need to specify it with the TABLE command as:

```
TABLE scott.emp, FILTER (SAL > 1000);
```

If you are only replicating some of the data based on filtering conditions then it would be better to filter on the source system, as lesser data will need to be transferred over the network.

Filtering the records into parallel groups

You can use the FILTER clause to divide the replication load into multiple process groups. The data load is divided equally into the number of streams defined in the FILTER clause.

See also

- See the *Setting up a GoldenGate replication with multiple process groups* recipe in *Chapter 2, Setting up GoldenGate Replication* using the FILTER clause

Mapping the changes to a target table and storing the transaction history in a history table

Many businesses, these days, have a requirement to keep a transaction history of the data. This could be due to regulatory requirements or even for management reporting. Oracle GoldenGate's flexible architecture allows you to track the old value of a record before a change is applied to it. You can then map these changes to a different table to maintain a transaction history.

In this recipe we will look into how we can track the changes occurring on a source database table and replicate them to a target database table and also maintain the transaction history in a separate table.

Getting ready

For this recipe we will set up a replication between the EMP table in the SCOTT demo schema that is delivered in the $ORACLE_HOME/sqlplus/demo/demobld.sql script by Oracle.

We will also create an additional table in the target environment called EMP_TXN_HISTORY with the following structure:

EMP_TXN_HISTORY
EMPNO
ENAME
JOB
MGR
HIREDATE
SAL
COMM
DEPTNO
TIMESTAMP
OPERATION
BEFORE_AFTER

How to do it...

Perform the following steps in the source environment:

1. Add supplemental logging for all columns for the EMP table:

   ```
   SQL> ALTER TABLE EMP ADD SUPPLEMENTAL LOG DATA (ALL) COLUMNS;
   ```

2. Create an Extract process parameter file as follows:

   ```
   EXTRACT EGGTEST1
   USERID GGATE_ADMIN@DBORATEST, PASSWORD GGATE_ADMIN
   EXTTRAIL /u01/app/ggate/dirdat/st
   GETUPDATEBEFORES
   NOCOMPRESSDELETES
   TABLE SCOTT.EMP;
   ```

3. The Datapump process parameter file should look like this:

   ```
   EXTRACT PGGTEST1
   USERID GGATE_ADMIN@DBORATEST, PASSWORD GGATE_ADMIN
   RMTHOST stdby1-ol6-112 , MGRPORT 8809
   RMTTRAIL /u01/app/ggate/dirdat/rt
   GETUPDATEBEFORES
   TABLE SCOTT.EMP;
   ```

4. Start the Extract and Datapump process.

Steps for the target environment are as follows:

1. Create a Replicat process configuration as follows:

```
./ggsci
EDIT PARAMS RGGTEST1
REPLICAT RGGTEST1
USERID GGATE_ADMIN@TGORTEST, PASSWORD GGATE_ADMIN
DISCARDFILE /u01/app/ggate/dirrpt/RGGTEST1.dsc,append,MEGABYTES
500
ASSUMETARGETDEFS
MAP SCOTT.EMP, TARGET SCOTT.EMP ;
```

2. Create another Replicat process as follows:

```
./ggsci
EDIT PARAMS RGGTEST1
REPLICAT RGGTEST2
USERID GGATE_ADMIN@TGORTEST, PASSWORD GGATE_ADMIN
DISCARDFILE /u01/app/ggate/dirrpt/RGGTEST2.dsc,append,MEGABYTES
500
ASSUMETARGETDEFS
INSERTALLRECORDS
MAP SCOTT.EMP, TARGET SCOTT.EMP_TXN_HISTORY, COLMAP &
(USEDEFAULTS,TXN_DATE = @GETENV ("GGHEADER", & "COMMITTIMESTAMP"),
&
OPERATION = @GETENV ("GGHEADER", "OPTYPE"), &
BEFORE_AFTER = @GETENV ("GGHEADER", & "BEFOREAFTERINDICATOR"));
```

3. Start the Replicat processes:

```
GGSCI> START RGGTEST*
```

4. Run some DML statements in the source environment as follows:

```
INSERT INTO EMP VALUES (7999,'MICHAEL','CLERK',7782,sysda
te,2900,300,10);
UPDATE EMP SET SAL=SAL+1000 where EMPNO=7999;
UPDATE EMP SET COMM=COMM+500 where EMPNO=7999;
DELETE EMP WHERE EMPNO=7999;
COMMIT;
```

5. Verify the transaction history in the EMP_TXN_HISTORY table:

```
SELECT * FROM EMP_TXN_HISTORY;
```

How it works...

The first step in this recipe is to add supplemental logging on all columns on the EMP table in the source database. This is to enable the database to write the redo information of all columns and not just the key columns in case of updates and deletes. This is required for the Extract process to retrieve all the values which will be used to generate the old image of the records that will get updated.

After this we create an Extract process with the following two additional parameters:

> ► GETUPDATEBEFORES: This parameter is used to include the before image of the updated columns in the trail files. Without this parameter, GoldenGate by default only writes the new values of the update columns with the key columns required to identify the row in the target environment.

> ► NOCOMPRESSDELETES: For all delete statements, by default, GoldenGate only writes the primary key columns to the trail file. This allows GoldenGate to correctly identify the records in the target environment and, at the same time, minimize the size of the information to be written to the trail file. However, when you want to generate the transaction history for a table, you would want to store the old values for all the columns. Using this parameter, Oracle GoldenGate writes all the columns of the deleted record to the trail file.

The Datapump configuration also contains the GETUPDATEBEFORES parameter as otherwise it will only transfer the after images of the affected records.

On the target environment side, we create two Replicat processes. The first process RGGTEST1 replicates the changes to the target EMP table.

The second process RGGTEST2 writes the transaction history records to the target EMP_TXN_HISTORY table. This process converts all the operations that it reads from the trail files into INSERT due to the INSERTALLRECORDS parameter and inserts them in to the transaction history table. The transaction history table has got three extra column: TXN_DATE, OPERATION, BEFORE_AFTER. The values for these columns are extracted from the default system tokens and added to the replicated record.

Before the data updates, here are the records in the EMP table:

```
┌─────────────────────────────────────────────────────────────────────────────┐
│ ▣    ggate@prim1-ol6-112:/u01/app/oracle/product/11.2.0/dbhome_1/sqlplus/demo  _ □ × │
├─────────────────────────────────────────────────────────────────────────────┤
│ File  Edit  View  Search  Terminal  Help                                       │
│ SQL> select * from emp;                                                        │
│                                                                                │
│     EMPNO ENAME      JOB         MGR HIREDATE       SAL      COMM     DEPTNO    │
│ ---------- ---------- --------- ---------- --------- ---------- ---------- ---- │
│      7934 MILLER     CLERK      7782 23-JAN-82      1300               10       │
│      7369 SMITH      CLERK      7902 17-DEC-80       800               20       │
│      7499 ALLEN      SALESMAN   7698 20-FEB-81      1600       300     30       │
│      7521 WARD       SALESMAN   7698 22-FEB-81      1250       500     30       │
│      7566 JONES      MANAGER    7839 02-APR-81      2975               20       │
│      7654 MARTIN     SALESMAN   7698 28-SEP-81      1250      1400     30       │
│      7698 BLAKE      MANAGER    7839 01-MAY-81      2850               30       │
│      7782 CLARK      MANAGER    7839 09-JUN-81      2450               10       │
│      7788 SCOTT      ANALYST    7566 09-DEC-82      3000               20       │
│      7839 KING       PRESIDENT       17-NOV-81      5000               10       │
│      7844 TURNER     SALESMAN   7698 08-SEP-81      1500         0     30       │
│      7876 ADAMS      CLERK      7788 12-JAN-83      1100               20       │
│      7900 JAMES      CLERK      7698 03-DEC-81       950               30       │
│      7902 FORD       ANALYST    7566 03-DEC-81      3000               20       │
│                                                                                │
│ 14 rows selected.                                                              │
│                                                                                │
│ SQL> ▮                                                                         │
└─────────────────────────────────────────────────────────────────────────────┘
```

Since we only updated and dropped a new record in the EMP table; the data in the source EMP table after running the DML statements remains the same. However, if we query the EMP_TXN_HISTORY table in step 5, it looks as follows:

```
┌─────────────────────────────────────────────────────────────────────────────┐
│ ▣              oracle@stdby1-ol6-112:~/Desktop                        _ □ × │
├─────────────────────────────────────────────────────────────────────────────┤
│ File  Edit  View  Search  Terminal  Help                                       │
│ SQL> SELECT * FROM EMP_TXN_HISTORY;                                            │
│                                                                                │
│   EMPNO ENAME    JOB      MGR HIREDATE     SAL    COMM  DEPTNO TXN_DATE  OPERATION        BEFORE_AFT │
│ -------- -------- ------- ---- --------- ------- ------ ------- --------- --------------- ---------- │
│    7999 MICHAEL  CLERK   7782 22-NOV-12   2900    300     10 22-NOV-12 INSERT          AFTER  │
│    7999 MICHAEL  CLERK   7782 22-NOV-12   2900    300     10 22-NOV-12 SQL COMPUPDATE  BEFORE │
│    7999 MICHAEL  CLERK   7782 22-NOV-12   3900    300     10 22-NOV-12 SQL COMPUPDATE  AFTER  │
│    7999 MICHAEL  CLERK   7782 22-NOV-12   3900    300     10 22-NOV-12 SQL COMPUPDATE  BEFORE │
│    7999 MICHAEL  CLERK   7782 22-NOV-12   3900    800     10 22-NOV-12 SQL COMPUPDATE  AFTER  │
│    7999 MICHAEL  CLERK   7782 22-NOV-12   3900    800     10 22-NOV-12 DELETE          BEFORE │
│                                                                                │
│ 6 rows selected.                                                               │
│                                                                                │
│ SQL> ▮                                                                         │
└─────────────────────────────────────────────────────────────────────────────┘
```

As you can see from this output, for each update statement there were two rows inserted into this table. One of them is with the old values and the second one is for the new values of the updated columns. The final delete statement resulted in only a BEFORE record with all the columns of the record that were deleted.

Without this transaction history, there is no trace of this inserted, updated, deleted record in the main EMP table. However, by maintaining a transaction history like this, you can trace all the activity that occurred on the original table records.

See also

▶ See the *Steps to re-instantiate a failed GoldenGate configuration* recipe in *Chapter 6, Monitoring, Tuning, and Troubleshooting GoldenGate*

Creating a GoldenGate configuration to run a Shell script when an end-of-day processing record is replicated

GoldenGate offers a feature called EVENTMARKER using which you can build some events into the process group configuration based on which certain actions will be performed. In this recipe, we will demonstrate how we can run a job in the target environment based on what is replicated to the target tables. This is quite useful in cases where you would run a replication load and would want to perform an activity which is dependent on the successful completion of the data load.

Getting ready

For this recipe, we will create the following table in both the source and target databases:

SOURCE DATABASE	TARGET DATABASE
PROCESS_STATUS	PROCESS_STATUS
TIMESTAMP	TIMESTAMP
STATE	STATE

We will also assume that we have a script called Update_Balances.sh in the target environment which runs a batch process to update balances once the load for the day has completed.

How to do it...

Let's look at an example of how we can run a script in the target environment based on the values of a replicated record.

Perform the following steps in the source environment:

1. Create an Extract process parameter file as follows:

```
EXTRACT EGGTEST1
USERID GGATE_ADMIN@DBORATEST, PASSWORD GGATE_ADMIN
EXTTRAIL /u01/app/ggate/dirdat/st
TABLE SCOTT.*;
```

2. The Datapump process parameter file should look as follows:

```
EXTRACT PGGTEST1
USERID GGATE_ADMIN@DBORATEST, PASSWORD GGATE_ADMIN
RMTHOST stdby1-ol6-112 , MGRPORT 8809
RMTTRAIL /u01/app/ggate/dirdat/rt
TABLE SCOTT.*;
```

3. Start the Extract and Datapump process.

Steps to be performed in the target environment are as follows:

1. Edit the Replicat process configuration as follows:

```
./ggsci
EDIT PARAMS RGGTEST1
REPLICAT RGGTEST1
USERID GGATE_ADMIN@TGORTEST, PASSWORD GGATE_ADMIN
DISCARDFILE /u01/app/ggate/dirrpt/RGGTEST1.dsc,append,MEGABYTES
500
ASSUMETARGETDEFS
MAP SCOTT.BONUS, TARGET SCOTT.BONUS;
MAP SCOTT.SALGRADE, TARGET SCOTT.SALGRADE;
MAP SCOTT.DEPT, TARGET SCOTT.DEPT;
MAP SCOTT.DUMMY, TARGET SCOTT.DUMMY;
MAP SCOTT.EMP, TARGET SCOTT.EMP;
MAP SCOTT.EMP,TARGET SCOTT.EMP_DIFFCOL_ORDER;
MAP SCOTT.PROCESS_STATUS, TARGET SCOTT.PROCESS_STATUS, FILTER (@
STREQ(STATE, "EOD COMPLETE")=1, &
EVENTACTIONS (SHELL "Update_Balances.sh")
```

2. Start the Replicat process.

How it works...

In this example, we use a PROCESS_STATUS table which is created solely to record the state of Load. The extract parameter file contains a simple configuration which extracts the data, and writes it to local trail files. These trail files are read and transferred to the target environment by the Datapump process PGGTEST1. The data load is loaded into the source system. Once the data load is complete, a record is inserted into the PROCESS_STATUS table as:

```
INSERT INTO PROCESS_STATUS VALUES (SYSDATE, 'EOD COMPLETE');
COMMIT;
```

This record is extracted by the EGGTEST1 process and transferred to the target environment by the PGGTEST1 process. On the target side, the RGGTEST1 Replicat process reads this record from the trail file and matches it with the condition specified in the FILTER clause. When the value for the STATE column equals "EOD COMPLETE", it runs the Shell script "Update_Balances.sh". The key thing to note here is that the GGATE_ADMIN user must have an execute privilege on this Shell script. And the Shell script must return a return status 0 on successful completion.

Another example of running a Shell script after completing end of processing would be to kick off a database backup. You can also use this feature to notify the team about a successful completed load by running a script which sends a status email.

There's more...

There are many other instances where using event marking is quite beneficial. Some of the other practical applications of this feature are:

- You can use EVENTACTIONS to trace the data for some particular values of a replicated record using the TRACE option.
- To switch from the initial load to change synchronization without causing downtime to the source database.
- Write warnings to the GoldenGate Logs when a condition is true, for example when the process lag is over a certain limit, or when the data replicated is incorrect. Such records can even be written to a discard file using the DISCARD option.
- Use EVENTACTIONS to stop a GoldenGate process, for example when the last record for the day is replicated using the STOP option.
- Use EVENTACTIONS to track, log, and ignore certain operations on crucial data, for example the DELETE statements on some data that you wouldn't expect to be run in a production system. This can be done using the IGNORE and LOG options.

See also

- The *Creating an exception handler to record the erroneous transactions in a GoldenGate configuration* recipe in *Chapter 4, Mapping and Manipulating Data*
- The *Script to perform a regular scheduled healthcheck of a live GoldenGate Configuration* recipe in *Chapter 6, Monitoring, Tuning, and Troubleshooting GoldenGate*

Creating an exception handler to record the erroneous transactions in a GoldenGate configuration

The success of one-way replication between two environments is dependent on the state of the data in the target environment. If the record that the Replicat process is trying to update does not exist in the target database, the replication will certainly fail. If the data set is small, it is easy to verify that the data in the target environment is in the expected state. However, when the volume of the data increases, it gets tougher and the chances of getting issues in the replication increase manifold. When such errors happen, the Replicat process stops and there can be a pile up of pending changes that still need to be applied to the target environment. In order to avoid the pile up of pending transactions, it might be better to track the error, keep a record of erroneous records, and carry on with the replication.

GoldenGate offers a powerful way of managing such errors. In this recipe we will look at how to map such exceptions and continue the replication.

Getting ready

For this recipe, we will use the SCOTT.EMP table that is delivered in demo scripts with Oracle binaries. We will also delete a row from the EMP table in the target environment to simulate the data inconsistency by generating an UPDATE operation on the missing record. We will also create an additional table to record the exception records as follows:

EMP_EXCEPTIONS
EMPNO
ENAME
JOB
MGR
HIREDATE
SAL
COMM
DEPTNO
ERRDATE
OPTYPE
DBERRNO
DBERRMSG

How to do it...

Let's see how we can use the exception handler to trap the errors.

Perform the following steps in the source environment:

1. Create an Extract process parameter file as follows:

    ```
    EXTRACT EGGTEST1
    USERID GGATE_ADMIN@DBORATEST, PASSWORD GGATE_ADMIN
    EXTTRAIL /u01/app/ggate/dirdat/st
    NOCOMPRESSDELETES
    GETUPDATEBEFORES
    TABLE SCOTT.EMP;
    ```

2. The Datapump process parameter file should look like this:

    ```
    EXTRACT PGGTEST1
    USERID GGATE_ADMIN@DBORATEST, PASSWORD GGATE_ADMIN
    RMTHOST stdby1-ol6-112 , MGRPORT 8809
    RMTTRAIL /u01/app/ggate/dirdat/rt
    GETUPDATEBEFORES
    TABLE SCOTT.EMP;
    ```

3. Start the Extract and Datapump process.

Steps to be performed in the target environment are as follows:

1. Create an EXCEPTIONS TABLE in the target environment as follows:

    ```
    CREATE TABLE EMP_EXCEPTIONS
    ( EMPNO NUMBER(4),
    ENAME VARCHAR(10),
    JOB VARCHAR(9),
    MGR VARCHAR(4),
    HIREDATE DATE,
    SAL NUMBER(7,2),
    COMM NUMBER(7,2),
    DEPTNO NUMBER(2),
    ERRDATE DATE,
    OPTYPE VARCHAR(20),
    DBERRNO NUMBER(6),
    DBERRMSG VARCHAR(4000));
    ```

2. Grant Insert on the Exceptions table to the GGATE_ADMIN user:

    ```
    GRANT INSERT ON SCOTT.EMP_EXCEPTIONS to GGATE_ADMIN;
    ```

3. Edit the Replicat process configuration as follows:

```
./ggsci
EDIT PARAMS RGGTEST1
REPLICAT RGGTEST1
USERID GGATE_ADMIN@TGORTEST, PASSWORD GGATE_ADMIN
ASSUMETARGETDEFS
REPERROR (DEFAULT, EXCEPTION)
MAP SCOTT.EMP, TARGET SCOTT.EMP;
INSERTALLRECORDS
MAP SCOTT.EMP, SCOTT.EMP_EXCEPTIONS, EXCEPTIONSONLY,
COLMAP (USEDEFAULTS,
ERRDATE = @DATENOW(),
OPTYPE = @GETENV("LASTERR", "OPTYPE"),
DBERRNUM = @GETENV("LASTERR", "DBERRNUM"),
DBERRMSG = @GETENV("LASTERR", "DBERRMSG"));
```

4. Delete a row from the target EMP table:

```
DELETE EMP WHERE EMPNO=7902;
COMMIT;
```

5. Start the Replicat process:

```
GGSCI> START RGGTEST1
```

In the source environment, run the following steps:

1. Run an UPDATE in the source environment:

```
UPDATE EMP SET SAL=SAL+100 where EMPNO=7902;
COMMIT;
```

Run the following steps in the target environment:

1. Verify the state of the RGGTEST1 Replicat process:

```
GGSCI > STATUS RGGTEST1
REPLICAT RGGTEST1: RUNNING
```

2. Verify the data in EMP_EXCEPTIONS:

```
SELECT * FROM EMP_EXCEPTIONS;
```

How it works...

In this example, we have created an EXCEPTION table for the main EMP table. In addition to all the columns of the EMP table, this table has the following four additional columns:

- ▸ ERRDATE: Date when exception occurred
- ▸ OPTYPE: Type of statement that failed
- ▸ DBERRNUM: Error code of the exception
- ▸ DBERRMSG: Actual error message

Then we delete a row from the target table using the DELETE statement in step 1 from the target environment. The Extract process configuration contains two parameters: GETUPDATEBEFORES and NOCOMPRESSDELETES. GETUPDATEBEFORES instructs GoldenGate to add the old values of the updated records to the trail file. With NOCOMPRESSDELETES, GoldenGate adds all the columns of the deleted rows to the trail file records. The replicat configuration also contains some additional new parameters:

- ▸ REPERROR (DEFAULT, EXCEPTION): This parameter drives the Replicat process' behavior when it encounters an error. The DEFAULT keyword means for all errors, and the EXCEPTION keyword denotes that the exception procedure should be followed for the error.
- ▸ INSERTALLRECORDS: With this parameter, GoldenGate will convert all the statements into inserts.

The second MAP statement is only applicable in the case of exceptions. Here we map the default columns of the EMP table to the EMP_EXCEPTIONS table and also extract some additional metadata and map it to the columns of the EMP_EXCEPTIONS table.

When we run the update statement and the Replicat process reads it from the trail file, it tries to apply it to the target environment, but since the record does not exist in the target environment, it results in ORA-01403: no data found. However, because we have defined an exception handler, GoldenGate adds this row to the EMP_EXCEPTIONS table using the second MAP statement and the Replicat process continues.

Here are the contents of the EMP_EXCEPTIONS table:

```
oracle@stdby1-ol6-112:~/Desktop                                    _ □ ×
File  Edit  View  Search  Terminal  Help

SQL> SELECT * FROM EMP_EXCEPTIONS;

EMPNO ENAME   JOB       MGR  HIREDATE   SAL  COMM DEPTNO ERRDATE   OPTYPE       DBERRNO DBERRMSG
----- ------- --------- ---- --------- ----- ---- ------ --------- -----------  ------- --------------------------------
 7902 FORD    ANALYST   7566 03-DEC-81  3100          20 23-NOV-12 SQL COMPUPDATE   1403 OCI Error ORA-01403: no data f
                                                                                        ound, SQL <UPDATE "SCOTT"."EMP
                                                                                        " SET "ENAME" = :a1,"JOB" = :a
                                                                                        2,"MGR" = :a3,"HIREDATE" = :a4
                                                                                        ,"SAL" = :a5,"COMM" = :a6,"DEP
                                                                                        TNO" = :a7 WHERE "EMPNO" = :b0
                                                                                        >

SQL> █
```

There's more...

So far we have seen how to handle an exception for a single table. The main drawback of this method is that you would need to create an exception table for each replicated table and hence would need to define exception handling for each one as well. This process can become quite cumbersome if the number of replicated tables is quite large. GoldenGate has two other methods using which you can define exception handling for a large number of tables in a much simpler way:

MAPEXCEPTION method

This method uses a single `Exception` table for mapping the exceptions of all the replicated tables. The `Exception` table must be a superset of all the tables, that is, it should have all the columns of all the tables. You can also add additional metadata columns to this table. The `MAP` statements in the replicat configuration for this method would like:

```
MAP SCOTT.*, TARGET SCOTT.*,
MAPEXCEPTION (TARGET SCOTT.ALLEXCEPTIONS,
COLMAP(USEDEFAULTS,
TABLE_NAME = @GETENV("GGENV", "TABLENAME"),
ERRDATE = @DATENOW(),
OPTYPE = @GETENV("LASTERR", "OPTYPE"),
DBERRNUM = @GETENV("LASTERR", "DBERRNUM"),
DBERRMSG = @GETENV("LASTERR", "DBERRMSG"));
```

This method might not be suitable in cases where you have many columns in the tables as the `Exception` table will become very wide.

Handle exceptions with a MACRO

You can also create a generic `Exception` table only to track the metadata information with the failing SQL statement. You would need to define the mapping for each table in that case as we did in the example in this recipe. Another option is to define a `MACRO` and reuse it for all the tables. That way you only need to define the mapping information once. Here is an example of how to write a macro to map the exception metadata to an `Exception` table called ALLEXCEPTIONS:

```
EDIT PARAMS EXCEPTION_HANDLER.mac

MACRO #EXCEPTION_HANDLER
BEGIN
, TARGET GGATE_ADMIN.ALLEXCEPTIONS
, COLMAP ( REPLICAT_NAME = @GETENV("GGENVIRONMENT", "GROUPNAME"))
, TABLE_NAME = @GETENV ("GGHEADER", "TABLENAME")
, ERRNO = @GETENV ("LASTERR", "DBERRNUM")
, DBERRMSG = @GETENV ("LASTERR", "DBERRMSG")
```

```
, OPTYPE = @GETENV ("LASTERR", "OPTYPE")
, ERRTYPE = @GETENV ("LASTERR", "ERRTYPE")
, LOGRBA = @GETENV ("GGHEADER", "LOGRBA")
, LOGPOSITION = @GETENV ("GGHEADER", "LOGPOSITION")
, COMMITTIMESTAMP = @GETENV ("GGHEADER", "COMMITTIMESTAMP"))
, INSERTALLRECORDS
, EXCEPTIONSONLY;
END;
```

This will create a file called `EXCEPTION_HANDLER.mac` under `$GG_HOME/dirprm`. You would then include this file in the replicat `RGGTEST1` config as:

```
include ./dirprm/EXCEPTION_HANDLER.mac
```

You can use the following statement to `MAP` the exceptions of a table to this generic `EXCEPTION` table defined in the macro:

```
REPERROR (DEFAULT, EXCEPTION)
MAP SCOTT.EMP, TARGET SCOTT.EMP;
MAP SCOTT.EMP #EXCEPTION_HANDLER()
```

The macro contents will be substituted in place of the `#EXCEPTION_HANDLER()` call in the replicat configuration, thereby completing the `MAP` statement which is applicable for `EXCEPTIONSONLY`. Because we are using `INSERTALLRECORDS` in the macro, it will convert all statements to inserts and insert them into the exception table.

The drawback of this method is that you would only capture the metadata information about the error and would not record the actual column values of the affected rows. Moreover, the `DBERRMSG` column can only hold statements up to 4000 bytes long.

See also

▶ The *Steps to re-instantiate a failed GoldenGate configuration recipe* in *Chapter 6, Monitoring, Tuning, and Troubleshooting GoldenGate*

5
Oracle GoldenGate High Availability

In this chapter we will cover the following recipes:

- ► Choosing a GoldenGate high availability option
- ► Creating a highly available GoldenGate configuration using Oracle Clusterware and ACFS
- ► Creating a highly available GoldenGate configuration using Oracle Clusterware and OCFS2
- ► Creating a highly available GoldenGate configuration using Oracle Clusterware and DBFS
- ► Manually switching over Oracle Clusterware-based configuration to the other node
- ► Automatic failover of a DBFS-based configuration
- ► Creating a set of parallel load balanced, highly available GoldenGate configurations using Oracle Clusterware and DBFS

Introduction

Over the years, the availability requirements of business applications has considerably grown. Any company with or even without an online presence requires its systems, websites, and applications to be available round the clock. This can be due to their e-commerce business, their branches across the globe or merely due to the scale of operations. Ensuring such availability times requires the underlying hardware and software systems to be fault tolerant. When Oracle GoldenGate is implemented in an enterprise infrastructure it requires some extra configuration to work in a highly available fashion. In this chapter we will look into the additional steps involved in setting up Oracle GoldenGate in Oracle RAC environments. We will also cover the steps required to configure the failover of the GoldenGate processes.

Choosing a GoldenGate high availability option

One of the most important tasks in increasing the availability of any technology is choosing the correct method. There are often a number of ways to make the system immune to different types of failures. Choosing the correct type of system resilience ensures realistic availability times. One of the most common causes of failure is the breakdown of the actual hardware system on which the system is running. In order to overcome such a failure, the most common approach is to move the failed resources to another surviving available piece of kit. This is achieved, for example, using watchdog software, which monitors the state of the processes and triggers the failover in case the process dies. Also, when you are configuring Oracle GoldenGate in an Oracle RAC environment, you need to perform some additional steps to make it work with a cluster database. In this recipe, we will look into the overall process of how GoldenGate high availability works and the resources required for configuring GoldenGate in an Oracle RAC environment. We will also look into various options that we have available to share the required resources between redundant systems.

Getting ready

When you are configuring Oracle GoldenGate in a high availability mode, there are some key things that you should be aware of:

- Oracle GoldenGate replication can only run in active-passive mode
- In order to ensure data consistency, the processes should start from the point where they stop
- The Manager process is the parent process of all worker processes: Extract, Datapump, Collector, and Replicat
- Any dependent processes, for example monitoring, should automatically fail over with the GoldenGate processes

How to do it...

There are three fundamental resources that are required for a GoldenGate high availability solution:

- Virtual IP
- Shared storage
- Action script

These resources are managed by a cluster software; for example, Oracle Clusterware, HP Service Guard, Veritas Cluster Software, IBM cluster software. By associating the replication to a Virtual IP rather than a physical IP, you enable the cluster software to fail over the replication processes to the other nodes in the cluster. When the processes fail over to the other nodes in the cluster, they should resume from the point of the failure. This requires some of the files in the GoldenGate configuration to be available on the shared storage. There are many options available for a shared storage. For example, OCFS2, ACFS, DBFS, NFS. Some of them are available on all nodes of the cluster all the time, and others require the filesystems to be mounted on the node where the processes are started.

Regardless of the cluster software and the shared storage option used, you would configure the GoldenGate resources in the following dependency hierarchy:

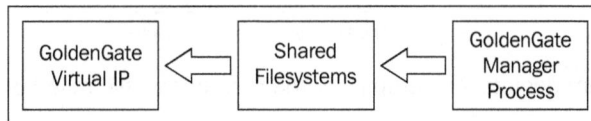

How it works...

As you can see from the preceding dependency diagram, all GoldenGate resources are dependent on the Virtual IP. In case of any hardware problems with the node where GoldenGate is currently running, the cluster software starts the Virtual IP on any other node of the cluster. All the dependent resources of the GoldenGate Virtual IP are also started on the new node. This failover operation is demonstrated in the following diagrams:

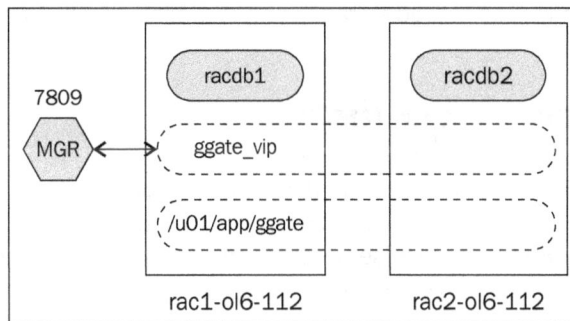

Oracle GoldenGate resources before failover

The preceding diagram depicts the initial setup where all GoldenGate resources are running on the first node of the cluster.

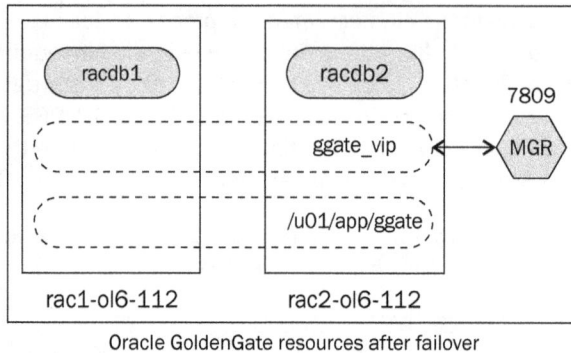

Oracle GoldenGate resources after failover

The preceding diagram depicts the setup after the resources have failed over to the second node of the cluster.

Whatever cluster software you use, it would require an action script to query and maintain the status of the resource, managed by the cluster for the GoldenGate Manager process. Once the cluster software gets the status of the Manager process, it can then decide whether or not it needs to initiate a failover. All GoldenGate processes are configured to autostart with the Manager process using the AUTOSTART parameter.

There's more...

Let's briefly look at the various shared storage options available from Oracle when using Oracle Clusterware.

Oracle Cluster File System (OCFS2)

OCFS2 is POSIX-compliant and Oracle's general purpose filesystem. This filesystem is only available on Linux platforms. When configured, the mount points created using this filesystem remain available on all the nodes of the cluster, so there is no need to fail over the filesystems to the surviving nodes. However, because GoldenGate processes only run on one of the nodes of the cluster, this cluster-wide availability is a bit risky as files can be modified from any of the nodes of the cluster. If you are using OCFS2 as a shared storage filesystem for your GoldenGate setup, you should ensure that the changes to the GoldenGate files from other nodes (where GoldenGate is not running) are restricted/controlled. For example, if someone modifies the checkpoint file of a GoldenGate process from another node, the process may undergo abend as GoldenGate will not be able to determine its last known state.

Database File System (DBFS)

The Database File System as the name suggests refers to a filesystem that is created on top of objects that are stored within the database (Oracle). The files that you place in a DBFS filesystem are stored as SecureFile LOBs in the database. This filesystem repository can only be created in a Linux environment and is the only supported method of high availability in an Oracle Exadata environment. This method requires a database in the cluster to be created. The DBFS filesystem is then mounted only on one of the nodes of the cluster. The GoldenGate Manager resource is configured as a dependent of this database, which in turn would be a dependent of the GoldenGate Virtual IP. This filesystem can only be configured in an Oracle 11gR2 database. The use of this filesystem does add to the complexity of the overall GoldenGate replication architecture and requires additional tuning.

ASM Cluster File System (ACFS)

The Oracle ASM Cluster File System is built on top of the ASM functionality of the Oracle database. It is available on multiple platforms and fits very well with the rest of the components of the Oracle database technology stack. The filesystem is created by creating a volume in an ASM diskgroup and mounting it at OS level. ACFS takes advantages of better reliability and distribution of data as it sits on top of Oracle ASM. This filesystem is only available for Oracle databases 11gR2 and above. This filesystem is mounted on all nodes of the cluster and does not require a combined failover with the GoldenGate Manager/ GoldenGate VIP resources.

See also

- ▸ The *Creating a highly available GoldenGate configuration using Oracle Clusterware and OCFS2* recipe
- ▸ The *Creating a highly available GoldenGate configuration using Oracle Clusterware and DBFS* recipe
- ▸ The *Creating a highly available GoldenGate configuration using Oracle Clusterware and ACFS* recipe

Creating a highly available GoldenGate configuration using Oracle Clusterware and ACFS

In this recipe we will see how to create a GoldenGate configuration using ACFS as a shared storage filesystem and Oracle Clusterware to manage the high availability.

Getting ready

For this recipe, we have a two-node Oracle RAC 11.2.0.3 database in the source environment. The new ACFS filesystem for GoldenGate will be created on the DATA diskgroup. We would also need an additional IP on the public network in the cluster as that will be used for GoldenGate's high availability and communication. This IP (192.168.0.220) has been added to /etc/hosts on both nodes with a ggate_vip alias.

How to do it...

The following steps show how we can create an ACFS filesystem, install GoldenGate on it and configure it for high availability using Oracle Clusterware. The high availability setup required in the target environment would be similar to that of the source environment.

Follow these steps to set up an ACFS filesystem:

1. Log in as the Grid Infrastructure Software Owner on the first node of the cluster. (Oracle user in our case.)

2. Set the environment to +ASM1 using oraenv:

   ```
   [oracle@rac1-ol6-112 ~]$ . oraenv
   ORACLE_SID = [oracle] ? +ASM1
   The Oracle base has been set to /u01/app/oracle
   ```

3. As a root user, load the ACFS drivers:

   ```
   cd $ORACLE_HOME/bin
   acfsload start
   ```

4. Perform steps 1 to 3 on the second node of the cluster.

5. Run the ASM Configuration Assistant, using the following command:

   ```
   asmca
   ```

This should take you to the following screen:

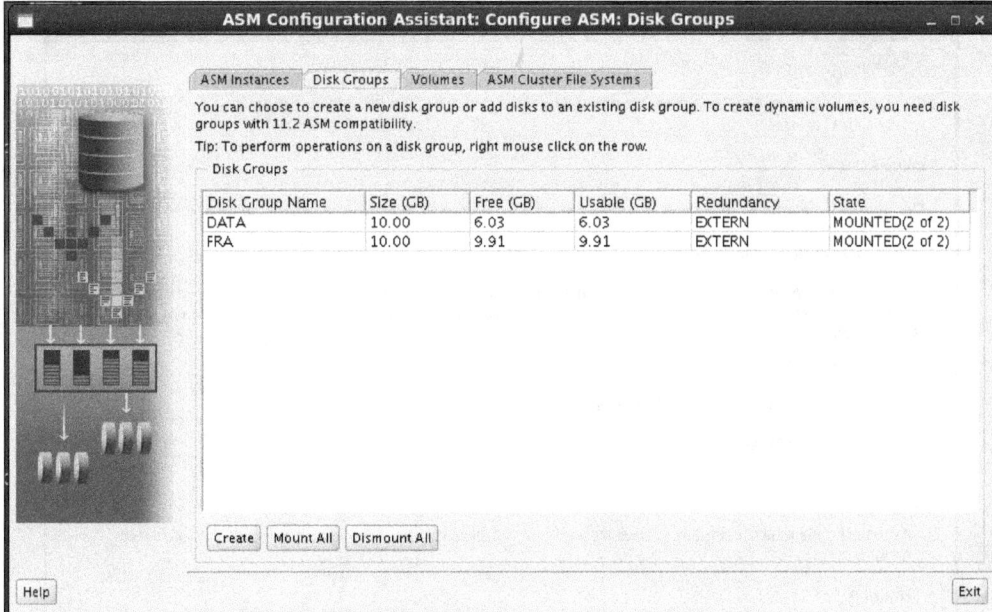

6. Click on **ASM Cluster File Systems**:

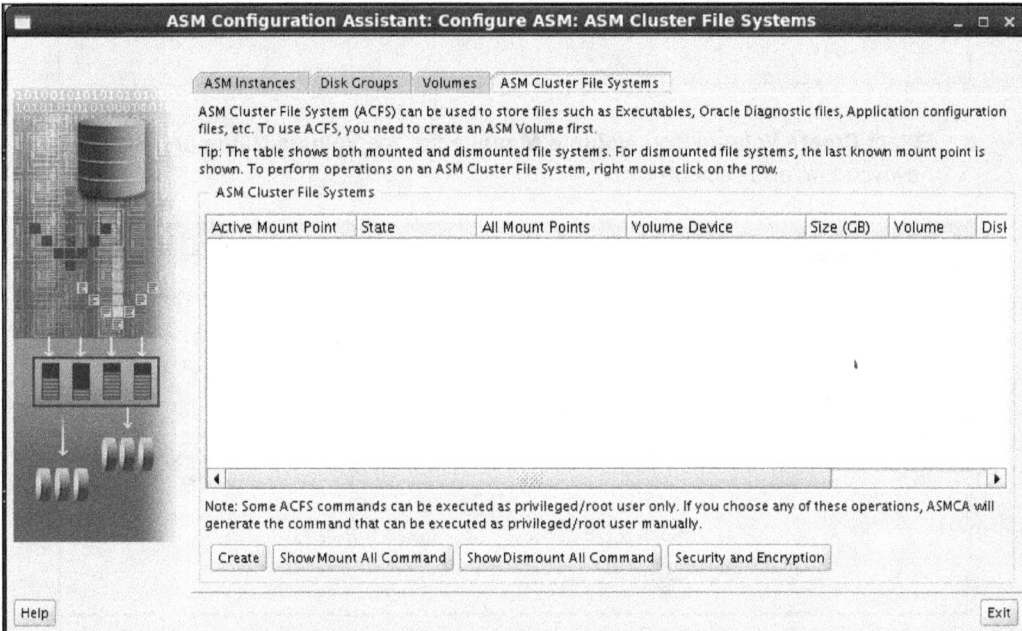

7. Click on **Create**:

8. Select **Create Volume** from **Volume Menu**, enter the **Volume Name** and **Size** in the new window, and click on OK:

9. Choose the **General Purpose File System** option on the next screen. Make sure that **Register Mount Point** is selected and click on **OK**.

10. The ACFS filesystem name is `ggate-3`.

11. Click on **OK** and exit from ASMCA.

12. As a root user, run the following command on both the nodes to mount the ACFS filesystem:

```
/bin/mount -t acfs /dev/asm/ggate-3 /u01/app/ggate
```

The steps to install GoldenGate on the ACFS filesystem are as follows:

1. Now that we have created an ACFS filesystem, we need to install GoldenGate on this filesystem by extracting the binaries media file:

```
tar -xvf fbs_ggs_Linux_x64_ora11g_64bit.tar -C /u01/app/ggate
```

2. Create GoldenGate subdirectories:

```
cd /u01/app/ggate
./ggsci
GGSCI> CREATE SUBDIRS
```

3. Follow the steps from the *Setting up a GoldenGate replication between Oracle RAC databases* recipe in *Chapter 2, Setting up GoldenGate Replication*, to set up Manager, Extract, and Datapump processes.

The steps to configure GoldenGate high availability are as follows:

1. Run the following commands to create an Application VIP for GoldenGate and set the correct permissions:

```
/u01/app/grid/bin/appvipcfg create -network=1 -ip=192.168.0.220
-vipname=ggate_vip -user=root
```

```
root@rac1-ol6-112:~                                          _ □ ×
File  Edit  View  Search  Terminal  Help
[root@rac1-ol6-112 ~]# /u01/app/grid/bin/appvipcfg create -network=1 -ip=192.168.0.220 -vipnam
e=ggate_vip -user=root
Production Copyright 2007, 2008, Oracle.All rights reserved
2012-12-05 20:17:36: Creating Resource Type
2012-12-05 20:17:36: Executing /u01/app/grid/bin/crsctl add type app.appvip_net1.type -basetyp
e ora.cluster_vip_net1.type -file /u01/app/grid/crs/template/appvip.type
2012-12-05 20:17:36: Executing cmd: /u01/app/grid/bin/crsctl add type app.appvip_net1.type -ba
setype ora.cluster_vip_net1.type -file /u01/app/grid/crs/template/appvip.type
2012-12-05 20:17:40: Create the Resource
2012-12-05 20:17:40: Executing /u01/app/grid/bin/crsctl add resource ggate_vip -type app.appvi
p_net1.type -attr "USR_ORA_VIP=192.168.0.220,START_DEPENDENCIES=hard(ora.net1.network) pullup(
ora.net1.network),STOP_DEPENDENCIES=hard(ora.net1.network),ACL='owner:root:rwx,pgrp:root:r-x,o
ther::r--,user:root:r-x',HOSTING_MEMBERS=rac1-ol6-112.localdomain,APPSVIP_FAILBACK="
2012-12-05 20:17:40: Executing cmd: /u01/app/grid/bin/crsctl add resource ggate_vip -type app.
appvip_net1.type -attr "USR_ORA_VIP=192.168.0.220,START_DEPENDENCIES=hard(ora.net1.network) pu
llup(ora.net1.network),STOP_DEPENDENCIES=hard(ora.net1.network),ACL='owner:root:rwx,pgrp:root:
r-x,other::r--,user:root:r-x',HOSTING_MEMBERS=rac1-ol6-112.localdomain,APPSVIP_FAILBACK="
[root@rac1-ol6-112 ~]# ▓
```

2. Change the permissions so that the Oracle user can manage the VIP:

```
/u01/app/grid/bin/crsctl setperm resource ggate_vip -u
user:oracle:r-x
```

3. Start the GoldenGate VIP:

```
/u01/app/grid/bin/crsctl start resource ggate_vip
```

4. Create an action script called `GoldenGate_action.scr` to allow Clusterware to manage the GoldenGate Manager resource. Copy this script to the `scripts` directory located at `/u01/app/ggate`.

5. Create a GoldenGate Manager resource:

```
/u01/app/grid/bin/crsctl add resource ggate_mgr -type cluster_
resource -attr "ACTION_SCRIPT=/u01/app/grid/crs/script/GoldenGate_
action.scr, CHECK_INTERVAL=30, START_DEPENDENCIES='hard(ggate_
vip,ora.racdb.db) pullup(ggate_vip)'STOP_DEPENDENCIES='hard(ggate_
vip)' SCRIPT_TIMEOUT=300, RESTART_ATTEMPTS=6"
```

6. Set the correct permissions on the Manager resource:

```
/u01/app/grid/bin/crsctl setperm resource ggate_mgr -o ggate
```

7. Stop the Manager process:

```
GGSCI> STOP MGR
```

8. Start the Manager resource to start the Manager process:

```
/u01/app/grid/bin/crsctl start resource ggate_mgr
```

How it works...

In this recipe, we first create an ACFS filesystem called `ggate-3` on the data diskgroup. This filesystem is then mounted on `/u01/app/ggate` for installing GoldenGate on both nodes. We then install GoldenGate on this filesystem and create the subdirectories. The next step is to create Manager, Extract, and Datapump processes with autostart mode enabled. So far we have configured the GoldenGate processes in a non-cluster mode. In order to configure the high availability in the next step, we first create a GoldenGate Application VIP using the `appvipcfg` command. You must have an IP allocated for this purpose by your network administrator. Using a Virtual IP allows the processes to fail over to the other node as they are not configured to connect to a physical host. In the next step we create a GoldenGate Manager resource using the action script. This script allows Oracle Clusterware to perform the necessary functions in order to manage the GoldenGate Manager resource. Once the GoldenGate Manager resource is created we need to restart the GoldenGate processes using the `crsctl` commands.

Creating a highly available GoldenGate configuration using Oracle Clusterware and OCFS2

In this recipe we will see how to create a GoldenGate configuration using OCFS2 as a shared storage filesystem and Oracle Clusterware to manage the high availability.

Getting ready

For this recipe, we have a two-node Oracle RAC 11.2.0.3 database in the source environment. We also have an additional unused shared disk /dev/sdf1, which will be used for hosting the GoldenGate binaries and other files. The OCFS2 filesystem will be created on this shared disk. We would also need an additional IP on the public network in the cluster as that will be used for GoldenGate high availability and communication. This IP (192.168.0.220) has been added to the /etc/hosts on both nodes with a ggate_vip alias.

How to do it...

In the following steps, we will configure GoldenGate in an OCFS2 filesystem and configure it for high availability using Oracle Clusterware. The high availability setup required in the target environment would be similar to that of the source environment.

The steps to set up an OCFS2 filesystem are as follows:

1. Download and install the appropriate Oracle OCFS packages for your kernel environment in all nodes of the cluster. For OEL 6 and above you can only download them from Oracle's Unbreakable Linux Network. For previous Oracle versions you can download them from http://oss.oracle.com/projects/ocfs2/:

```
root@rac2-ol6-112:/u01/downloads
File  Edit  View  Search  Terminal  Help

[root@rac2-ol6-112 downloads]# rpm -Uvh ocfs2console-1.6.4-1.el6.x86_64.rpm \
> ocfs2-tools-1.6.4-1.el6.x86_64.rpm
Preparing...                ########################################### [100%]
   1:ocfs2-tools            ########################################### [ 50%]
   2:ocfs2console           ########################################### [100%]
[root@rac2-ol6-112 downloads]#
[root@rac2-ol6-112 downloads]#
[root@rac2-ol6-112 downloads]#
[root@rac2-ol6-112 downloads]#
```

2. Configure OCFS2 using the `ocfs2console` utility. Start the `ocfs2console` utility as follows.

```
[root@rac1-ol6-112 ~]# ocfs2console
```

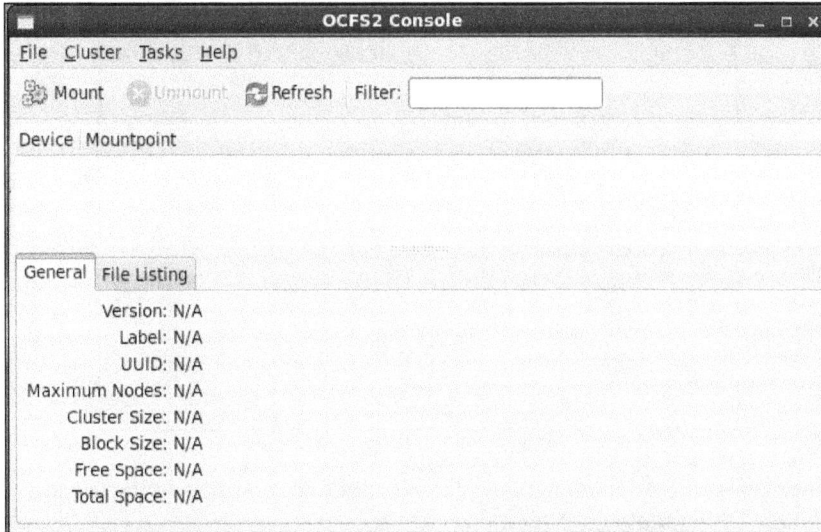

3. Navigate to **Cluster** | **Configure Nodes** from the menu and you will be presented with a Node Configuration window as follows:

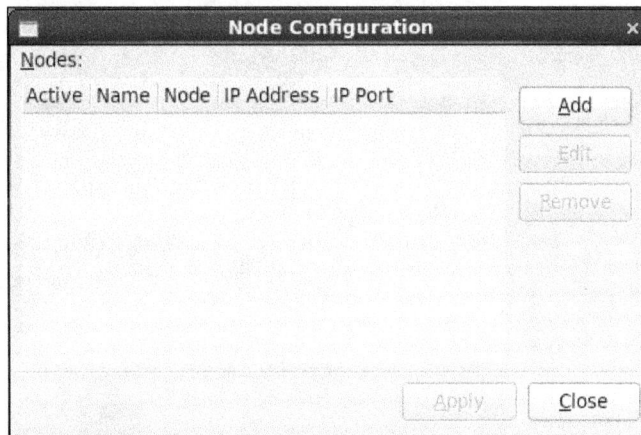

4. Click on the **Add** button and enter the information of both nodes, one by one as follows, and click on **Apply**. The node name must match the output of the hostname command on the host. Oracle recommends that you specify the private interconnected IPs for this configuration.

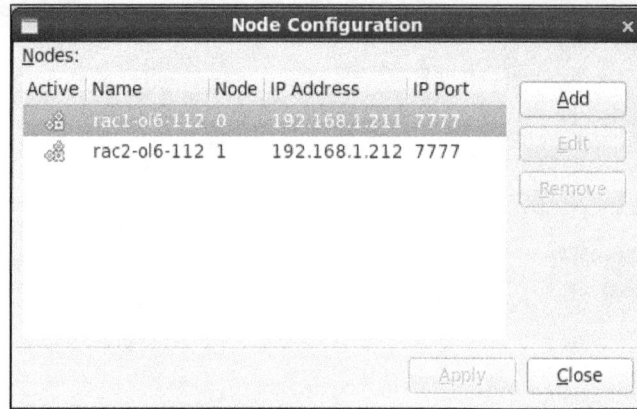

5. Propagate the cluster configuration to the other node by navigating to the **Cluster | Propagate** configuration:

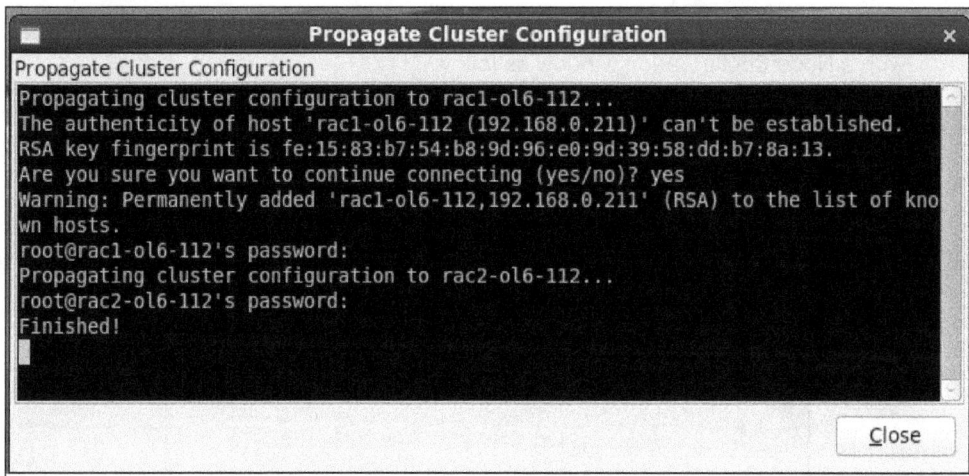

6. Configure the O2CB stack to start automatically at boot time on both the nodes. This step will start the cluster services as well.

```
[root@rac1-ol6-112 ocfs2]# /etc/init.d/o2cb configure
Configuring the O2CB driver.

This will configure the on-boot properties of the O2CB driver.
```

The following questions will determine whether the driver is loaded on
boot. The current values will be shown in brackets ('[]').
Hitting
<ENTER> without typing an answer will keep that current value.
Ctrl-C will abort.

Load O2CB driver on boot (y/n) [y]: y
Cluster stack backing O2CB [o2cb]:
Cluster to start on boot (Enter "none" to clear) [ocfs2]:
Specify heartbeat dead threshold (>=7) [31]:
Specify network idle timeout in ms (>=5000) [30000]:
Specify network keepalive delay in ms (>=1000) [2000]:
Specify network reconnect delay in ms (>=2000) [2000]:
Writing O2CB configuration: OK
Loading filesystem "configfs": OK
Mounting configfs filesystem at /sys/kernel/config: OK
Loading stack plugin "o2cb": OK
Loading filesystem "ocfs2_dlmfs": OK
Mounting ocfs2_dlmfs filesystem at /dlm: OK
Setting cluster stack "o2cb": OK
Starting O2CB cluster ocfs2: OK
[root@rac1-ol6-112 ocfs2]#

7. Create an OCFS2 filesystem on the /dev/sdf1 shared disk:

```
[root@rac1-ol6-112 app]# mkdir -p /u01/app/ggate
[root@rac1-ol6-112 app]# mkfs.ocfs2 -b 4K -C 4K -N 2 -L /u01/app/
ggate /dev/sdf1
mkfs.ocfs2 1.6.4
Cluster stack: classic o2cb
Label: /u01/app/ggate
Features: sparse backup-super unwritten inline-data strict-
journal-super xattr
Block size: 4096 (12 bits)
Cluster size: 4096 (12 bits)
Volume size: 5362847744 (1309289 clusters) (1309289 blocks)
Cluster groups: 41 (tail covers 19049 clusters, rest cover 32256
clusters)
Extent allocator size: 4194304 (1 groups)
Journal size: 67108864
Node slots: 2
Creating bitmaps: done
Initializing superblock: done
Writing system files: done
Writing superblock: done
```

```
Writing backup superblock: 2 block(s)
Formatting Journals: done
Growing extent allocator: done
Formatting slot map: done
Formatting quota files: done
Writing lost+found: done
mkfs.ocfs2 successful
```

8. Mount the filesystem using the **mount** command:

    ```
    mount /dev/sdf1 /u01/app/ggate
    ```

9. Add the following line `/etc/fstab` to automatically mount this filesystem at boot time:

    ```
    /dev/sdf1   /u01/app/ggate   ocfs2  _netdev,datavolume   0 0
    ```

10. Repeat steps 8 and 9 on node 2.

The steps to install GoldenGate on the OCFS2 filesystem are as follows:.

1. Now that we have created an OCFS2, we need to install GoldenGate on this filesystem by extracting the binaries media file:

    ```
    tar -xvf fbs_ggs_Linux_x64_ora11g_64bit.tar -C /u01/app/ggate
    ```

2. Create GoldenGate subdirectories:

    ```
    cd /u01/app/ggate
    ./ggsci
    GGSCI> CREATE SUBDIRS
    ```

3. Follow the steps from the *Setting up a GoldenGate replication between Oracle RAC databases* recipe in *Chapter 2, Setting up GoldenGate Replication*, to set up Manager, Extract, and Datapump processes.

The steps to configure GoldenGate high availability are as follows:

1. Run the following commands to create an Application VIP for GoldenGate and set the correct permissions:

    ```
    /u01/app/grid/bin/appvipcfg create -network=1 -ip=192.168.0.220
    -vipname=ggate_vip -user=root
    ```

```
root@rac1-ol6-112:~                                    _ □ ×

File  Edit  View  Search  Terminal  Help
[root@rac1-ol6-112 ~]# /u01/app/grid/bin/appvipcfg create -network=1 -ip=192.168.0.220 -vipnam
e=ggate_vip -user=root
Production Copyright 2007, 2008, Oracle.All rights reserved
2012-12-05 20:17:36: Creating Resource Type
2012-12-05 20:17:36: Executing /u01/app/grid/bin/crsctl add type app.appvip_net1.type -basetyp
e ora.cluster_vip_net1.type -file /u01/app/grid/crs/template/appvip.type
2012-12-05 20:17:36: Executing cmd: /u01/app/grid/bin/crsctl add type app.appvip_net1.type -ba
setype ora.cluster_vip_net1.type -file /u01/app/grid/crs/template/appvip.type
2012-12-05 20:17:40: Create the Resource
2012-12-05 20:17:40: Executing /u01/app/grid/bin/crsctl add resource ggate_vip -type app.appvi
p_net1.type -attr "USR_ORA_VIP=192.168.0.220,START_DEPENDENCIES=hard(ora.net1.network) pullup(
ora.net1.network),STOP_DEPENDENCIES=hard(ora.net1.network),ACL='owner:root:rwx,pgrp:root:r-x,o
ther::r--,user:root:r-x',HOSTING_MEMBERS=rac1-ol6-112.localdomain,APPSVIP_FAILBACK="
2012-12-05 20:17:40: Executing cmd: /u01/app/grid/bin/crsctl add resource ggate_vip -type app.
appvip_net1.type -attr "USR_ORA_VIP=192.168.0.220,START_DEPENDENCIES=hard(ora.net1.network) pu
llup(ora.net1.network),STOP_DEPENDENCIES=hard(ora.net1.network),ACL='owner:root:rwx,pgrp:root:
r-x,other::r--,user:root:r-x',HOSTING_MEMBERS=rac1-ol6-112.localdomain,APPSVIP_FAILBACK="
[root@rac1-ol6-112 ~]# ▮
```

2. Change the permissions so that the Oracle user can manage the VIP:

    ```
    /u01/app/grid/bin/crsctl setperm resource ggate_vip -u
    user:oracle:r-x
    ```

3. Start the GoldenGate VIP:

    ```
    /u01/app/grid/bin/crsctl start resource ggate_vip
    ```

4. Create an action script called `GoldenGate_action.scr` to allow Clusterware
    to manage the GoldenGate Manager resource. Copy this script to the `scripts`
    directory located at `/u01/app/ggate`.

5. Create a GoldenGate Manager resource:

    ```
    /u01/app/grid/bin/crsctl add resource ggate_mgr -type cluster_
    resource -attr "ACTION_SCRIPT=/u01/app/grid/crs/script/GoldenGate_
    action.scr, CHECK_INTERVAL=30, START_DEPENDENCIES='hard(ggate_
    vip,ora.racdb.db) pullup(ggate_vip)'STOP_DEPENDENCIES='hard(ggate_
    vip)' SCRIPT_TIMEOUT=300, RESTART_ATTEMPTS=6"
    ```

6. Set the correct permissions on the Manager resource:

    ```
    /u01/app/grid/bin/crsctl setperm resource ggate_mgr -o ggate
    ```

7. Stop the Manager process:

    ```
    GGSCI> STOP MGR
    ```

8. Start the Manager resource to start the Manager process:

    ```
    /u01/app/grid/bin/crsctl start resource ggate_mgr
    ```

How it works...

In this recipe, we configure an OCFS2 filesystem `/u01/app/ggate` for installing GoldenGate. For this we first download the required packages for the kernel version of the OS that we are using. Once the packages are installed, we then configure the OCFS2 cluster using the `ocfs2console` utility. Once the filesystem is created it is mounted on both the nodes. We then install GoldenGate on this filesystem and create the subdirectories. The next step is to create Manager, Extract, and Datapump processes with autostart mode enabled. So far we have configured the GoldenGate processes in a non-cluster mode. In order to configure the high availability in the next step, we first create a GoldenGate Application VIP using the `appvipcfg` command. You must have an IP allocated for this purpose by your network administrator. Using a Virtual IP allows the processes to fail over to the other node as these are not configured to connect to a physical host. In the next step we create a GoldenGate Manager resource using the action script. This script allows Oracle Clusterware to perform the necessary functions in order to manage the GoldenGate Manager resource. Once the GoldenGate Manager resource is created we need to restart the GoldenGate processes using the `crsctl` commands.

Creating a highly available GoldenGate configuration using Oracle Clusterware and DBFS

In this recipe we will go through the steps needed to create a GoldenGate configuration in an Oracle RAC environment using Oracle Clusterware and DBFS.

Getting ready

For this recipe, we have a two-node Oracle RAC 11.2.0.3 database in the source environment. We have also created a database called `dbfsdb`, which will be used to create the DBFS repository according to the following specifications:

▸ **Flashback** should be disabled for the DBFS database

▸ **Compatible Parameter** must be set to **11.2.0.2** or higher

▸ **Database Character Set** should be set to **AL32UTF8**

▸ **Parallel_Max_Servers** should be set to **2**

For this illustration, we have created the database on the same diskgroup as `racdb`. We would also need an additional IP on the public network in the cluster as that will be used for GoldenGate high availability and communication. This IP (`192.168.0.220`) has been added to the `/etc/hosts` on both nodes with a `ggate_vip` alias.

How to do it...

In the following steps, we will create a DBFS repository in the dbfsdb database and then create the filesystems required for setting up GoldenGate. We will then configure the GoldenGate Manager resource in conjunction with the DBFS database resource in the Oracle Clusterware. This recipe only contains the steps required to perform this setup in the source environment. You would need to perform a similar setup in the target environment if your target database is an Oracle RAC database and you want to configure GoldenGate in high availability configuration using DBFS.

The steps to create a DBFS repository in the dbfsdb database are as follows:

1. Create a repository tablespace as follows:

    ```
    CREATE TABLESPACE DBFS_TB DATAFILE '+DATA' SIZE 2G;
    ```

2. Create a user for the DBFS repository schema:

    ```
    CREATE USER DBFS IDENTIFIED BY DBFS123 DEFAULT TABLESPACE DBFS_TB
    QUOTA UNLIMITED ON DBFS_TB;
    ```

3. Grant the necessary privileges to the DBFS user:

    ```
    GRANT CREATE SESSION, CREATE TABLE, CREATE PROCEDURE, DBFS_ROLE TO
    DBFS;
    ```

4. As a DBFS user, run the script to create the DBFS repository:

    ```
    cd $ORACLE_HOME/rdbms/admin
    sqlplus DBFS/DBFS123
    @dbfs_create_filesystem_advanced dbfs_tb ggate nocompress
    nodeduplicate noencrypt non-partition
    ```

The steps to mount the DBFS filesystem using dbfs_client are as follows:

1. Run the following commands as a root user to fix the library links issue on both nodes:

    ```
    mkdir /usr/local/lib
    cd /usr/local/lib
    ln -s $ORACLE_HOME/lib/libnnz11.so /usr/local/lib/libnnz11.so
    ln -s $ORACLE_HOME/lib/libclntsh.so.11.1 /usr/local/lib/libclntsh.
    so.11.1
    ln -s /lib64/libfuse.so.2 /usr/local/lib/libfuse.so
    ln -s /lib64/libfuse.so.2 /usr/local/lib64/libfuse.so
    echo /usr/local/lib >> /etc/ld.so.conf.d/usr_local_lib.conf
    echo /usr/local/lib64 >> /etc/ld.so.conf.d/usr_local_lib.conf
    ldconfig
    ```

2. Run the following commands to create the DBFS mount point on both nodes:

```
usermod -a -G fuse oracle
mkdir /oggdbfs
chown oracle:oinstall /oggdbfs
echo user_allow_other > /etc/fuse.conf
```

3. Restart the Oracle Clusterware on all nodes for the updated fuse permissions to take effect:

```
crsctl stop cluster -all
crsctl start cluster -all
```

4. Download the `mount_dbfs.sh` scripts from MOS Note 1054431.1 and copy them to `$GRID_HOME/crs/script`. This script will be used for mounting the DBFS filesystem.

5. Modify the `mount_dbfs.sh` script with the following information for your environment;

```
DBNAME=dbfsdb
MOUNT_POINT=/oggdbfs
DBFS_USER=dbfs
ORACLE_HOME=/u01/app/oracle/product/11.2.0/dbhome_1
DBFS_PASSWD=DBFS123
```

6. Change the permissions and ownership on the script as follows:

```
chown oracle:oinstall $GRID_HOME/crs/script/mount_dbfs.sh
chmod 740 $GRID_HOME/crs/script/mount_dbfs.sh
```

7. Copy the script on the other node of the cluster as:

```
scp $GRID_HOME/crs/script/mount_dbfs.sh rac2-ol6-112:$GRID_HOME/
crs/script/
```

8. Create a shortcut for `dbfs_client` on `/sbin`:

```
ln -s /u01/app/oracle/product/11.2.0/dbhome_1/bin/dbfs_client /
sbin/mount.dbfs
```

9. Add an entry to `/etc/fstab` on both nodes:

```
echo '/sbin/mount.dbfs  #/@DBFSDB /oggdbfs fuse rw,user,direct_
io,allow_other,wallet,noauto 0 0' >> /etc/fstab
```

The steps for the Clusterware resource setup to mount the DBFS and GoldenGate resources are as follows:

1. Create the GoldenGate VIP resource:

```
/u01/app/grid/bin/appvipcfg create -network=1 -ip=192.168.0.220
-vipname=ggate_vip -user=root
```

2. Change the permissions so that the Oracle user can manage the VIP:

```
/u01/app/grid/bin/crsctl setperm resource ggate_vip -o ggate
```

3. Start the GoldenGate VIP:

```
/u01/app/grid/bin/crsctl start resource ggate_vip
```

4. As Grid Software Owner, create the DBFS Cluster resource as follows:

```
export DBNAME=dbfsdb
export ORACLE_HOME=/u01/app/grid
export ACTION_SCRIPT=/u01/app/grid/crs/script/mount-dbfs.sh
/u01/app/grid/bin/crsctl add resource ggate_dbfs -type
cluster_resource  -attr "ACTION_SCRIPT=$ACTION_SCRIPT,
CHECK_INTERVAL=30,START_DEPENDENCIES='hard(ora.$DBNAME.db)
pullup(ggate_vip,ora.$DBNAME.db)attraction(ggate_vip)',  STOP_
DEPENDENCIES='hard(ora.$DBNAME.db)', SCRIPT_TIMEOUT=300, RESTART_
ATTEMPTS=0"
```

5. Start the DBFS resource as follows:

```
/u01/app/grid/bin/crsctl start res ggate_dbfs
```

6. After this /oggdbfs should be mounted on the first node.

7. Create an action script to allow Clusterware to manage the GoldenGate Manager resource. Copy this script to the /u01/app/ggate/scripts directory. You can download this script from MOS Note ID 1313703.1.

8. Create a GoldenGate Manager resource:

```
/u01/app/grid/bin/crsctl add resource ggate_mgr -type cluster_
resource -attr "ACTION_SCRIPT=/u01/app/grid/crs/script/GoldenGate_
action.scr, CHECK_INTERVAL=30, START_DEPENDENCIES='hard(ggate_
vip,ora.dbfsdb.db,ggate_dbfs)pullup(ggate_vip)attraction(ggate_
dbfs)' STOP_DEPENDENCIES='hard(ggate_vip,ggate_dbfs)' SCRIPT_
TIMEOUT=300,RESTART_ATTEMPTS=6"
```

9. Set the correct permissions on the Manager resource:

```
/u01/app/grid/bin/crsctl setperm resource ggate_mgr -o oracle
```

The steps to install GoldenGate and create processes in a DBFS environment are as follows:

1. Create a directory on the local filesystem to install Oracle GoldenGate binaries:

```
mkdir /u01/app/ggate
chown ggate:ggate /u01/app/ggate
```

2. Extract the binaries in this directory:

```
cd /u01/app/ggate/
tar -xvf fbo_ggs_Linux_x64_ora11g_64bit.tar
```

3. Create the subdirectories:

```
./ggsci
 create subdirs
```

4. Move the GoldenGate subdirectories to the DBFS filesystem:

```
mkdir -p /oggdbfs/ggate
cd /u01/app/ggate
mv dirprm /oggdbfs/ggate/
mv dirpcs /oggdbfs/ggate/
mv dirrpt /oggdbfs/ggate/
mv dirdat /oggdbfs/ggate/
mv dirout /oggdbfs/ggate/
mv dirtmp /oggdbfs/ggate/
mv dirdef /oggdbfs/ggate/
mv dirsql /oggdbfs/ggate/
mv dirchk /oggdbfs/ggate/
cd ggate
ln -s /oggdbfs/ggate/dirprm ./
ln -s /oggdbfs/ggate/dirpcs ./
ln -s /oggdbfs/ggate/dirrpt ./
ln -s /oggdbfs/ggate/dirdat ./
ln -s /oggdbfs/ggate/dirout ./
ln -s /oggdbfs/ggate/dirtmp ./
ln -s /oggdbfs/ggate/dirdef ./
ln -s /oggdbfs/ggate/dirsql ./
ln -s /oggdbfs/ggate/dirchk ./
```

5. Perform steps 1 to 4 on the other node of the cluster.

6. Follow the steps from the *Setting up a GoldenGate replication between Oracle RAC databases* recipe in *Chapter 2, Setting up GoldenGate Replication*, to set up Manager, Extract, and Datapump processes.

7. Stop the Manager process.

8. Start the GoldenGate Manager resource:

```
crsctl start resource ggate_mgr
```

How it works...

In this first part of this recipe, we create a DBFS repository in the DBFS database. This is created in a DBFS schema which resides in its own tablespace. The script `dbfs_create_filesystem_advanced` creates all the relevant objects required for creating/maintaining a DBFS filesystem in the `dbfsdb` database.

```
oracle@rac1-ol6-112:/u01/app/oracle/product/11.2.0/dbhome_1/rdbms/adr _ □ ×

File  Edit  View  Search  Terminal  Help
SQL> connect DBFS/DBFS123
Connected.
SQL> @dbfs_create_filesystem_advanced dbfs_tb ggate nocompress nodeduplicate noe
ncrypt non-partition
No errors.
--------
CREATE STORE:
begin dbms_dbfs_sfs.createFilesystem(store_name => 'FS_GGATE', tbl_name =>
'T_GGATE', tbl_tbs => 'dbfs_tb', lob_tbs => 'dbfs_tb', do_partition => false,
partition_key => 1, do_compress => false, compression => '', do_dedup => false,
do_encrypt => false); end;
--------
REGISTER STORE:
begin dbms_dbfs_content.registerStore(store_name=> 'FS_GGATE', provider_name =>
'sample1', provider_package => 'dbms_dbfs_sfs'); end;
--------
MOUNT STORE:
begin dbms_dbfs_content.mountStore(store_name=>'FS_GGATE',
store_mount=>'ggate'); end;
--------
CHMOD STORE:
declare m integer; begin m := dbms_fuse.fs_chmod('/ggate', 16895); end;
No errors.
SQL>
```

After this, we perform the required OS level setup to mount the DBFS filesystem. This requires some links for the binaries to be created and setup of the `mount_dbfs.sh` script. We perform these steps on both nodes of the cluster.

In the next section we will set up the required Clusterware resources for Application VIP, DBFS, and the GoldenGate Manager process. The resources are set up in the following order:

GoldenGate VIP >> DBFS Database >>DBFS Resource >> GoldenGate Manager

In the resource configuration, we specify the dependencies which must be present for the resource to start. This is required to ensure that Clusterware would only try to start the Manager resource on the node where the DBFS filesystem is mounted. This setup also ensures, that in the event of a node failure, when the Application VIP relocates to the other node, the resources dependent on the VIP would also move with the VIP to the other node.

Once the required Clusterware configuration is done and the DBFS filesystem is mounted, the GoldenGate binaries are installed on a local filesystem on both nodes. After this, we create the links for GoldenGate subdirectories to the directories in the DBFS filesystem. Following this, we will create the processes parameter files and start the Manager resource using `crsctl`. The Manager process would automatically start all the Extract/Replicat processes. At the end of the setup, the resources in the Cluster configuration would look as follows:

```
                    oracle@rac1-ol6-112:/oggdbfs/ggate/dirpcs        _  □  ×
 File  Edit  View  Search  Terminal  Help

[oracle@rac1-ol6-112 dirpcs]$ crsctl status resource ggate_vip
NAME=ggate_vip
TYPE=app.appvip_net1.type
TARGET=ONLINE
STATE=ONLINE on rac1-ol6-112

[oracle@rac1-ol6-112 dirpcs]$ crsctl status resource ggate_dbfs
NAME=ggate_dbfs
TYPE=cluster_resource
TARGET=ONLINE
STATE=ONLINE on rac1-ol6-112

[oracle@rac1-ol6-112 dirpcs]$ crsctl status resource ggate_mgr
NAME=ggate_mgr
TYPE=cluster_resource
TARGET=ONLINE
STATE=ONLINE on rac1-ol6-112

[oracle@rac1-ol6-112 dirpcs]$ ▌
```

See also

▶   The *Automatic failover of a DBFS-based configuration* recipe later in this chapter

Manually switching over Oracle Clusterware-based configuration to the other node

In this recipe we will look at the steps/methods of relocating the GoldenGate resources to the other nodes of the cluster.

Getting ready

For this recipe we will refer to the setup performed in the *Creating a highly available GoldenGate configuration using Oracle Clusterware and OCFS2* recipe.

How to do it...

In order to move the GoldenGate resources to the other node of the cluster, we need to move the underlying parent resource—GoldenGate Application VIP. This is done as follows:

1. Check the status of the GoldenGate resources:

   ```
   crsctl status resource ggate_vip
   crsctl status resource ggate_mgr
   ```

2. As Oracle user, run the following command to relocate the VIP resource:

   ```
   crsctl relocate resource ggate_mgr -n rac2-ol6-112 -f
   ```

3. Check the status of the GoldenGate resources:

   ```
   crsctl status resource ggate_vip
   crsctl status resource ggate_mgr
   ```

How it works...

Before running the relocate command, the status of the GoldenGate resources is as follows:

```
[oracle@rac1-ol6-112 ~]$ crsctl status resource ggate_vip
NAME=ggate_vip
TYPE=app.appvip_net1.type
TARGET=ONLINE
STATE=ONLINE on rac1-ol6-112

[oracle@rac1-ol6-112 ~]$ crsctl status resource ggate_mgr
NAME=ggate_mgr
TYPE=cluster_resource
TARGET=ONLINE
STATE=ONLINE on rac1-ol6-112
```

The status of the Manager process can be checked as follows:

```
GGSCI (rac1-ol6-112.localdomain) 1> status mgr
Manager is running (IP port rac1-ol6-112.localdomain.7809).
```

Because we have created a Clusterware resource for the GoldenGate Manager process, it is controlled by the Clusterware.

In step 2, we issue a relocate command as follows:

```
[oracle@rac1-ol6-112 ~]# crsctl relocate resource ggate_mgr -n rac2-ol6-112 -f
CRS-2673: Attempting to stop 'ggate_mgr' on 'rac1-ol6-112'
CRS-2677: Stop of 'ggate_mgr' on 'rac1-ol6-112' succeeded
```

```
CRS-2673: Attempting to stop 'ggate_vip' on 'rac1-ol6-112'
CRS-2677: Stop of 'ggate_vip' on 'rac1-ol6-112' succeeded
CRS-2672: Attempting to start 'ggate_vip' on 'rac2-ol6-112'
CRS-2676: Start of 'ggate_vip' on 'rac2-ol6-112' succeeded
CRS-2672: Attempting to start 'ggate_mgr' on 'rac2-ol6-112'
CRS-2676: Start of 'ggate_mgr' on 'rac2-ol6-112' succeeded
```

Once the relocation is complete, the Manager process and the VIP is started on the second node of the cluster.

```
[oracle@rac1-ol6-112 ~]$ crsctl status resource ggate_vip
NAME=ggate_vip
TYPE=app.appvip_net1.type
TARGET=ONLINE
STATE=ONLINE on rac2-ol6-112

[oracle@rac1-ol6-112 ~]$ crsctl status resource ggate_mgr
NAME=ggate_mgr
TYPE=cluster_resource
TARGET=ONLINE
STATE=ONLINE on rac2-ol6-112
```

Automatic failover of a DBFS-based configuration

In this recipe we will look into the underlying working of how the Clusterware performs an automatic failover of the GoldenGate resources when the active node where the GoldenGate Manager process is running fails.

Getting ready

In this recipe we will refer to the setup performed in the *Creating a highly available GoldenGate configuration using Oracle Clusterware and DBFS* recipe.

How to do it...

For the purpose of this recipe, we will demonstrate the failure of the active node of the cluster by powering it off. The scenario demonstrated in this recipe refers to a natural occurrence of the failure event in the real world.

1. We will shut down the first node of the cluster where the ggate_vip, ggate_mgr, ggate_dbfs resources are currently online.

2. In order to shut down the machine, in the Virtual Machine Window, navigate to **Machine | ACPI Shutdown**:

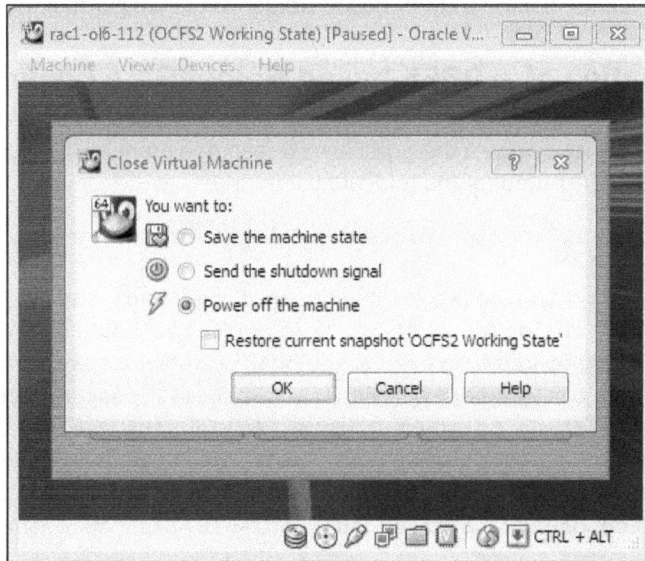

3. Select **Power off the Machine** and click on **OK**.

How it works...

We have seen from the configuration steps of the DBFS setup that the DBFS/GoldenGate Manager process is a singleton resource. This means that at any point in time, these resources can only be active on only one node of the cluster. In this recipe we have seen that before stopping the `rac1-ol6-112` machine, all resources are active on this node. In the previous steps we stop this machine, which will trigger the failover of these resources to the other node of the cluster. These resources are configured in the Oracle Clusterware configuration in the following hierarchal relationship.

ggate_vip << ggate_dbfs << ggate_mgr

So when the first node of the cluster is unavailable, Clusterware notices that the `ggate_vip` is not reachable anymore. It then initiates the startup of the `ggate_vip` resource on the second node of the cluster. Because the other two resources are dependent on the `ggate_vip` resource, it initiates their clean up on the first node and startup on the second node. Once the failover is complete, `ggate_dbfs` is online on the second node of the cluster and `/oggdbfs` filesystem is available as well. When the GoldenGate Manager resource comes online, it starts the other processes—Extract/Replicat—on the second node of the cluster, by reading their checkpoint locations from the `dirchk` directory. So, after the failover, replication continues from the second node of the cluster.

Let's look at the steps to relocate a DBFS-based GoldenGate configuration manually:

Manual relocation of a DBFS-based GoldenGate configuration

In order to understand how Clusterware actually performs the switchover of the resources behind the scenes, we will relocate the ggate_vip resource manually to the second node of the cluster. Here is the output of the relocate command:

```
[root@rac1-ol6-112 script]# crsctl relocate resource ggate_vip -n
rac2-ol6-112 -f
CRS-2673: Attempting to stop 'ggate_mgr' on 'rac1-ol6-112'
CRS-2677: Stop of 'ggate_mgr' on 'rac1-ol6-112' succeeded
CRS-2673: Attempting to stop 'ggate_vip' on 'rac1-ol6-112'
CRS-2677: Stop of 'ggate_vip' on 'rac1-ol6-112' succeeded
CRS-2672: Attempting to start 'ggate_vip' on 'rac2-ol6-112'
CRS-2676: Start of 'ggate_vip' on 'rac2-ol6-112' succeeded
CRS-2673: Attempting to stop 'ggate_dbfs' on 'rac1-ol6-112'
CRS-2677: Stop of 'ggate_dbfs' on 'rac1-ol6-112' succeeded
CRS-2672: Attempting to start 'ggate_dbfs' on 'rac2-ol6-112'
CRS-2676: Start of 'ggate_dbfs' on 'rac2-ol6-112' succeeded
CRS-2672: Attempting to start 'ggate_mgr' on 'rac2-ol6-112'
CRS-2676: Start of 'ggate_mgr' on 'rac2-ol6-112' succeeded
```

Creating a set of parallel load balanced, highly available GoldenGate configurations using Oracle Clusterware and DBFS

In the previous recipes in this chapter we have seen how we can configure Oracle GoldenGate in a clustered database environment. If there are multiple databases in the cluster that you want to replicate the data to/from, you can configure multiple Replicat processes for various databases running under a single Manager process. A single instance of Oracle GoldenGate can only be active on one of the nodes of the cluster. This means that the replication load of all the databases will be on the single node of the cluster. In such circumstances it is better to configure multiple instances of Oracle GoldenGate in the cluster as, in such a configuration, we can split the replication load between different nodes of the cluster.

In this recipe we will see how we can configure multiple instances of GoldenGate with DBFS repositories to balance the replication load between multiple nodes of the cluster.

Getting ready

For this recipe, we have created two-node Oracle RAC 11.2.0.3 databases (`racdb` and `testdb`) in the source environment. We have also created two databases called `dbfsdb1` and `dbfsdb2` which will be used to create the DBFS repositories according to the following specifications:

- ▸ **Flashback** should be disabled for DBFS databases
- ▸ **Compatible Parameter** must be set to **11.2.0.2** or higher
- ▸ **Database Character Set** should be set to **AL32UTF8**
- ▸ **Parallel_Max_Servers** should be set to **2**

For this illustration, we have created all the databases on the same diskgroup (+DATA). We would also need two additional IPs on the public network in the cluster as that will be used for GoldenGate high availability and communication. These IPs (192.168.0.220 and 192.168.0.320) have been added to /etc/hosts on both nodes with ggate1_vip and ggate2_vip aliases respectively.

The setup would look like this:

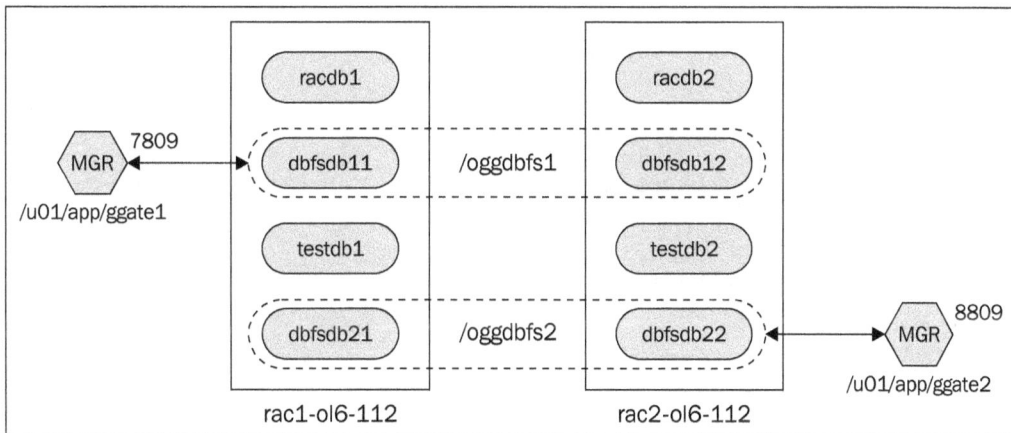

How to do it...

Follow these steps to build the setup illustrated in the preceding section:

1. Follow the steps in the *Creating a highly available GoldenGate configuration using Oracle Clusterware and DBFS* recipe earlier in this chapter to create the first DBFS repository and first instance of Oracle GoldenGate. The information in the following table should be used while performing the setup:

Setting	Value
DBFS Mount Point	`/oggdbfs1`
Mount Script	`mount_dbfs1.sh`
DB Name	`dbfsdb1`
DBFS_USER	`dbfs`
Oracle Home	`/u01/app/oracle/product/11.2.0/dbhome_1`
GoldenGate Home	`/u01/app/ggate1`
DBFS_PASSWD	`DBFS123`
DBFS Resource Name	`ggate1_dbfs`
ggate_vip	`192.168.0.220`
Ggate VIP Name	`ggate1_vip`
Ggate Manager Resource	`ggate1_mgr`

2. Stop the Manager resource for the first GoldenGate instance as GoldenGate owner:

    ```
    crsctl stop resource ggate_mgr
    ```

3. Update the GoldenGate Home in all the process configuration files as follows:

    ```
    EDIT PARAMS MGR
    PORT 8809
    DYNAMICPORTLIST 8810-8820, 8830
    AUTOSTART ER *
    AUTORESTART ER *, RETRIES 4, WAITMINUTES 4
    PURGEOLDEXTRACTS /u01/app/ggate1/dirdat/st*, USECHECKPOINTS,
    MINKEEPHOURS

    EDIT PARAMS EGGTEST11
    EXTRACT EGGTEST1
    USERID GGATE_ADMIN@RACDB, PASSWORD GGATE_ADMIN
    TRANSLOGOPTIONS DBLOGREADER
    EXTTRAIL /u01/app/ggate1/dirdat/st
    TABLE scott.*;
    ```

```
EDIT PARAMS PGGTEST11
EXTRACT PGGTEST11
USERID GGATE_ADMIN@RACDB, PASSWORD GGATE_ADMIN
RMTHOST tg-oggvip1.localdomain , MGRPORT 7809
RMTTRAIL /u01/app/ggate1/dirdat/rt
TABLE scott.*;
```

4. Follow the steps in the *Creating a highly available GoldenGate configuration using Oracle Clusterware and DBFS* recipe to create the second DBFS repository and second instance of Oracle GoldenGate. The information in the following table should be used while performing this setup:

Setting	Value
DBFS Mount Point	/oggdbfs2
Mount Script	mount_dbfs2.sh
DB Name	dbfsdb2
DBFS_USER	dbfs
Oracle Home	/u01/app/oracle/product/11.2.0/dbhome_1
GoldenGate Home	/u01/app/ggate2
DBFS_PASSWD	DBFS123
DBFS Resource Name	ggate2_dbfs
Ggate_vip	192.168.0.320
Ggate VIP Name	ggate2_vip
Ggate Manager Resource	ggate2_mgr

5. Stop the Manager process for the second GoldenGate instance.

6. Edit the process parameter files as follows:

```
EDIT PARAMS MGR
PORT 8809
DYNAMICPORTLIST 8810-8820, 8830
AUTOSTART ER *
AUTORESTART ER *, RETRIES 4, WAITMINUTES 4
PURGEOLDEXTRACTS /u01/app/ggate2/dirdat/st*, USECHECKPOINTS,
MINKEEPHOURS

EDIT PARAMS EGGTEST21
EXTRACT EGGTEST21
USERID GGATE_ADMIN@TESTDB, PASSWORD GGATE_ADMIN
TRANSLOGOPTIONS DBLOGREADER
EXTTRAIL /u01/app/ggate2/dirdat/st
TABLE scott.*;
```

```
EDIT PARAMS PGGTEST21
EXTRACT PGGTEST21
USERID GGATE_ADMIN@TESTDB, PASSWORD GGATE_ADMIN
RMTHOST tg-oggvip2.localdomain , MGRPORT 7809
RMTTRAIL /u01/app/ggate2/dirdat/rt
TABLE scott.*;
```

7. Start the GoldenGate VIP, DBFS resource, and GoldenGate Manager resources for the first instance on the first node as follows:

```
rac1-ol6-112$ crsctl start resource ggate1_vip -n rac1-ol6-112
rac1-ol6-112$ crsctl start resource ggate1_dbfs -n rac1-ol6-112
rac1-ol6-112$ crsctl start resource ggate1_mgr -n rac1-ol6-112
```

8. Start the GoldenGate VIP, DBFS resource, and GoldenGate Manager resources for the second instance on the second node as follows:

```
rac2-ol6-112$ crsctl start resource ggate2_vip -n rac2-ol6-112
rac2-ol6-112$ crsctl start resource ggate2_dbfs -n rac2-ol6-112
rac2-ol6-112$ crsctl start resource ggate2_mgr -n rac2-ol6-112
```

How it works...

In this recipe, we create two GoldenGate instances with their dedicated Clusterware resources. As explained earlier in this recipe, the main motive of this type of setup is to spread the replication load between multiple nodes of the cluster. In the real world when there are numerous databases in a cluster and if the data has to be replicated from most or all of them, there is a considerable replication load on the server. In such cases, it is quite helpful to segregate the load of these processes onto the other nodes of the cluster. At the same time, all of these GoldenGate instances need to be able to fail over to the other nodes of the cluster in case of loss of a node. In this recipe we are mainly following the steps from the *Creating a highly available GoldenGate configuration using Oracle Clusterware and DBFS* recipe to create two GoldenGate instances. The key thing to note here is that we need to design the configuration by taking into consideration the possibility of both GoldenGate instances running on a single node of the cluster. For this, we need to ensure that the ports, among others, are defined separately for both of these instances. In our setup, both GoldenGate instances run on different ports so there would not be any conflicts between them.

See also

▸ The *Splitting the replication load into multiple process groups for optimal performance* recipe in *Chapter 6, Monitoring, Tuning, and Troubleshooting GoldenGate*

6
Monitoring, Tuning, and Troubleshooting GoldenGate

In this chapter we will cover the following recipes:

- ▶ Steps to configure a BATCHSQL mode
- ▶ Splitting the replication load into multiple process groups for optimal performance
- ▶ Optimizing the network settings for a GoldenGate configuration
- ▶ Performing a healthcheck of a live GoldenGate configuration
- ▶ Script to perform a regular scheduled healthcheck of a GoldenGate configuration
- ▶ Steps to measure throughput of a GoldenGate configuration
- ▶ Steps to re-instantiate a failed GoldenGate configuration
- ▶ Steps to implement a Heartbeat mechanism for a GoldenGate replication

Introduction

Performance tuning is a key part of any IT implementation. When you install an application with its default options, they sometimes might not deliver the best performance. This is where having detailed knowledge allows the administrator to configure it in a way to achieve best performance. Tuning involves evaluating the current setup and making changes for improving the performance. Like any technology, the design of GoldenGate replication can affect the end result performance quite a bit.

Once you have implemented GoldenGate in your environment, you will need to monitor it to ensure that the replication is working as expected. If any of the processes are not running, you will need to troubleshoot them to find the real cause.

In this chapter, we will learn various aspects of replication design that one should consider for optimal performance while implementing GoldenGate. We will also learn some additional parameters using which the performance of GoldenGate replication can be improved. We will also cover the techniques using which the replication configurations can be monitored and the ways to troubleshoot the issues that might occur in the replication.

Steps to configure a BATCHSQL mode

In this recipe we will discuss a batch processing mode for the Replicat process using which the performance of the target replication environment can be improved. We will also discuss the additional options that can be specified in this mode.

How to do it...

The **BATCHSQL** mode can be configured by adding the following parameters in the replicat configuration file:

```
REPLICAT RGGTEST1
USERID GGATE_ADMIN@TGORTEST, PASSWORD GGATE_ADMIN
DISCARDFILE /u01/app/ggate/dirrpt/RGGTEST1.dsc,append,MEGABYTES 500
ASSUMETARGETDEFS
MAP SCOTT.*, TARGET SCOTT.*;
BATCHSQL BATCHPERQUEUE 100, OPSPERBATCH 200
```

How it works...

By default, the Replicat process processes one SQL statement at a time. Compared to the Extract process, the Replicat process has to re-construct the SQL statements by reading them from the trail files. Once this is done, these statements are applied to the target database. Overall, this process is slower than the rate at which the GoldenGate extract is able to read the log files, extract the changes and write them to the trail files. Due to this, sometimes there can be a considerable lag in the Replicat process operation.

GoldenGate offers an additional mode in which the Replicat process can be configured called the BATCHSQL mode. In this mode the Replicat process groups similar statements for the same objects in groups called batches. These batches are prepared in memory and applied to the target database in one go. The criteria for grouping the statements are that they should perform the same operation on the same target table with the same column list.

This method is most suitable for statements that generate very small data change, that is, 100 bytes. Oracle documentation suggests that as the size of the change generated by the SQL statement grows, the benefits achieved by the BATCHSQL mode starts decreasing. When the size of change for each SQL grows upto 5000 bytes, the benefits of the BATCHSQL mode start to diminish.

The Replicat process in this mode cache more SQL statements in memory, therefore, the memory requirements of the Replicat process in this mode increases. GoldenGate provides some additional parameters with the BATCHSQL mode using which you can control how many SQL statements are cached and how much memory is used by this mode, before the batches in the queue are applied to the target database. The following are the additional parameters:

- ► BATCHESPERQUEUE: This parameter controls the maximum number of batches that are stored in a memory queue. The default value of this parameter is 50 bytes. The range for this parameter's value is between 1 byte and 1,000 bytes.

- ► BATCHTRANSOPS: This parameter controls the maximum number of batch operations that can be grouped into transactions before a commit is issued. The default value of this parameter is 1,000 bytes and the range is between 1 byte and 100,000 bytes.

- ► BYTESPERQUEUE: This parameter controls the maximum number of bytes that can be allocated to a queue. The default value of this parameter is 20 MB and one can set a value between 1 MB and 1 GB..

- ► OPSPERBATCH: This parameter controls the maximum number of row operations that can be grouped into a batch. The default value of this parameter is 1,200 bytes and the range is between 1 byte and 100,000 bytes.

- ► OPSPERQUEUE: This parameter controls the maximum number of row operations in all batches of a queue. The default value of this parameter is 1,200 bytes and the range is between 1 byte and 100,000 bytes.

There's more...

The BATCHSQL mode increases performance by grouping similar transactions, and applying them in one go to the target database. Oracle has a built-in exception handling in this mode. In case one of the statements in the batch fails, the whole batch is rolled back and the Replicat process reverts to the standard mode. It then reads those statements again and applies them one-by-one. This whole procedure happens automatically.

In addition to the previous parameters, one can configure additional exception handling in this mode using the BATCHERRORMODE parameter. The BATCHERRORMODE parameter works in a similar way in the BATCHSQL mode as HANDLECOLLISSIONS works. If an Insert statement fails, GoldenGate converts it into an Update statement and tries to update the target record. If a Delete statement fails, GoldenGate just ignores it.

When using BATCHSQL mode, it is best to create a separate Replicat process for tables with a row size greater than 25 Kilobytes, tables containing any LONG or LOB datatypes, and tables with more than one unique key, besides the primary key, as the BATCHSQL mode treats them as exceptions. If you include them in a Replicat process that is configured in the BATCHSQL mode, the Replicat process will not gain any performance benefits as it would switch to the default mode.

See also

▶ See the next recipe, *Splitting the replication load into multiple process groups for optimal performance*

Splitting the replication load into multiple process groups for optimal performance

You will often notice that when replication is implemented in very busy systems, a single Extract/Replicat process is not sufficient to keep up with the rate of change. In most cases, you will find that it is the Replicat process that is causing the bottleneck. This is due to the fact that the Replicat or Apply process works in a serial fashion. All the changes read from the trail files are re-constructed into the SQL statements. These statements are then run in the target database one-by-one. Unless you have deliberately created a configuration with a set delay between the systems, it is usually desired to have the least lag between the source and target environments. The performance of a replication technology is often judged by the rate at which it is capable of keeping the changes replicated from the source environment to the target environment, even when the systems are under peak loads. One of the easiest ways to measure this is by measuring the lag between the systems at peak times. Once you have identified that the lag between the systems is unacceptable and the replication load needs to be split into multiple processes, the next task is to identify how to split the load. In this recipe, we will look into various things that should be considered while splitting the load into multiple processes. This recipe is not focused on the actual syntaxes of creating additional process groups.

How to do it...

In order to split the replication load into multiple processes, the key thing to decide is how to split the tables into multiple groups. There are various ways to determine this; however, you can choose the one which is most suitable to your environment:

1. Identify the most updated tables in the database by querying `v$segment_statistics`. The following is a sample query to find the top 20 tables with the highest write activity since the database was last restarted:

```
SELECT OWNER, OBJECT_NAME, VALUE AS TOTAL_WRITES
FROM V$SEGMENT_STATISTICS
```

```
WHERE STATISTIC_NAME IN ('PHYSICAL WRITES')
ORDER BY TOTAL_WRITES DESC)
WHERE ROWNUM <=20;
```

2. If the tables identified in the preceding step belong to separate schemas, create additional processes and configure different schemas in them.

3. Try to keep the related schemas together in the same process.

4. Keep the DDL and DML for tables in the same process group.

5. Ensure that all the tables with referential integrity constraints are in the same process group.

6. If there is a single table that is very heavily updated, you can create a separate dedicated process for it.

7. If a single process is not able to handle the load of such a busy table, you should split its load into multiple processes using the @RANGE function.

8. If you are using the BATCHSQL mode, create a separate process group for tables with a row size greater than 25 Kilobytes, tables containing any LONG or LOB datatypes, and tables with more than one unique key, besides the primary key, as the BATCHSQL mode treats them as exceptions.

9. If more than three Replicat processes are reading the same set of trail files, split the Extract/Datapump process into multiple processes with dedicated trail files.

How it works...

GoldenGate processes work in serial mode to maintain database integrity. If the amount of changes replicated is high, there can sometimes be a bottleneck, especially in the Replicat process where it has to apply the changes to the target database. One of the most basic tasks that can be done in tuning GoldenGate is to add additional processes. In most cases, you will need to add additional processes in a target environment. Due to this, in most cases you will find that the target environment has more processes than the source environment.

Different tables can be split into separate processes. It is quite important that you split the tables into multiple processes in a correct way. Adding additional processes can significantly improve the replication performance. However, one should remember that each additional process consumes OS resources, that is, memory and CPU. Each GoldenGate process consumes around 55 MB of memory. Hence, creating unnecessary additional processes will be a wastage of these resources and can have a negative performance impact on the system.

You can split any of the Extract, Datapump, and Replicat processes into multiple groups. The following is an example of a GoldenGate configuration with multiple process groups:

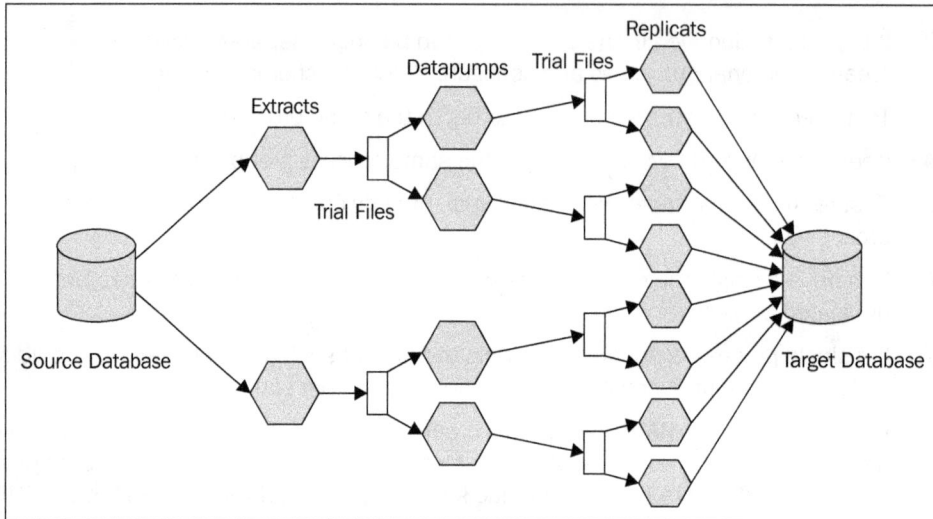

In the preceding diagram, we can see that there are two **Extracts** processes in the source environment, each one writes to its own set of **Trail Files**. Each of these trail file sets is read by two parallel **Datapumps** processes which write the trail files to the **Target Database**. On the target server we have four sets of **Trail Files**. There are eight **Replicats** processes in total in the target environment. Out of these eight Replicat processes, two dedicated Replicat processes read each set of trail files and apply the changes to the **Target Database**.

There's more...

Let us look at some additional parameters using which the replication load can be split into multiple processes.

The RANGE function

Imagine if you are running a very busy application whose data model is highly normalized and you cannot split the tables between different process groups as it will jeopardize the integrity of the target database. In such a situation, you want to split the replicat load into multiple processes, but at the same time you don't want to split the tables. You can achieve this by using the @RANGE function.

The RANGE function works in a similar way as Hash Partitioning in Oracle. You have to specify the total number of ranges (partitions) that you want to create in the process parameter configuration and also which range of the data that process belongs to. The @RANGE function will calculate a hash value of the columns specified in the configuration. If you don't specify any columns, it calculates the hash value of the primary key column of the table. The rows of the tables included in the replication are equally distributed between all the processes which form a part of the ranges.

The following is the syntax of the @RANGE function:

```
FILTER (@RANGE (X,Y))
```

Where X is the range number for the process and Y is the total number of ranges.

The following is an example of two Replicat processes in which the data is split using the @Range function:

```
REPLICAT RGGTEST1
USERID GGATE_ADMIN@TGORTEST, PASSWORD GGATE_ADMIN
DISCARDFILE /u01/app/ggate/dirrpt/RGGTEST1.dsc,append,MEGABYTES 500
ASSUMETARGETDEFS
MAP SCOTT.EMP, TARGET SCOTT.EMP, FILTER (@RANGE (1,2));
MAP SCOTT.BONUS, TARGET SCOTT.BONUS, FILTER (@RANGE (1,2));
MAP SCOTT.DEPT, TARGET SCOTT.DEPT, FILTER (@RANGE (1,2));
MAP SCOTT.SALGRADE, TARGET SCOTT.SALGRADE, FILTER (@RANGE (1,2));
REPLICAT RGGTEST2
USERID GGATE_ADMIN@TGORTEST, PASSWORD GGATE_ADMIN
DISCARDFILE /u01/app/ggate/dirrpt/RGGTEST1.dsc,append,MEGABYTES 500
ASSUMETARGETDEFS
MAP SCOTT.EMP, TARGET SCOTT.EMP, FILTER (@RANGE (2,2));
MAP SCOTT.BONUS, TARGET SCOTT.BONUS, FILTER (@RANGE (2,2));
MAP SCOTT.DEPT, TARGET SCOTT.DEPT, FILTER (@RANGE (2,2));
MAP SCOTT.SALGRADE, TARGET SCOTT.SALGRADE, FILTER (@RANGE (2,2));
```

> When you use FILTER (@RANGE) function to split the load between multiple processes, you cannot use a schema name.* qualifier to include all the tables in the schema. You have to specify each table name individually. For example, In order to include all the tables for SCOTT schema, you cannot specify SCOTT.* qualifier with the FILTER function, instead you have to specify each SCOTT table individually as it is done in this recipe.

See also

- The *Setting up a GoldenGate replication with multiple process groups recipe* in *Chapter 2, Setting up GoldenGate Replication*

Optimizing the network settings for a GoldenGate configuration

You can use GoldenGate to replicate data between two schemas within the same database; however, in most cases you will use GoldenGate to replicate the data between two databases that are running on different systems. These systems can be quite far from each other in different locations. One of the key functions performed by the GoldenGate processes is transferring the files to the remote destination. Even though you have the best tuned database with a well-tuned GoldenGate Replicat process, it will not apply any changes if they are not transferred to the target system by the Extract/Datapump process. In order to transfer the data efficiently and make the best use of the network, there are certain things that you need to consider and tune at the GoldenGate and operating system level. In this recipe, we will look at the configuration required to ensure an efficient transfer of GoldenGate trail files between two systems.

Getting ready

Tuning or changing some of these parameters may require administrator-level privileges at the operating system level. Depending upon your environment, you might need to involve the System Administrator team to do this.

How to do it...

The following are the key parameters that can be tuned for a GoldenGate configuration:

1. You should always configure at least one Datapump process for each extract to alleviate the job of data transfer from the Extract process.

2. Configure the TCPBUFSIZE and TCPFLUSHBYTES option for the RMTHOST parameter. The default value of TCPBUFSIZE is 30,000 bytes and it is not adequate for high-speed networks. In order to determine the optimal value of TCPBUFSIZE for your environment, determine the average **Round-Trip Time (RTT)** as follows:

```
[ggate@prim1-ol6-112 ~]$ ping -c 3 stdby1-ol6-112
PING stdby1-ol6-112.localdomain (192.168.0.11) 56(84) bytes of
data.
64 bytes from stdby1-ol6-112.localdomain (192.168.0.11): icmp_
seq=1 ttl=64 time=1.22 ms
64 bytes from stdby1-ol6-112.localdomain (192.168.0.11): icmp_
seq=2 ttl=64 time=0.765 ms
64 bytes from stdby1-ol6-112.localdomain (192.168.0.11): icmp_
seq=3 ttl=64 time=0.520 ms
--- stdby1-ol6-112.localdomain ping statistics ---
3 packets transmitted, 3 received, 0% packet loss, time 2003ms
rtt min/avg/max/mdev = 0.520/0.836/1.223/0.291 ms
```

3. Multiply the average RTT with the bandwidth of your network.

    In our example, the network bandwidth is 100 Mbps and the average RTT is 0.836 milliseconds as follows:

    ```
    TCPBUFSIZE =.0836 seconds * 100000000 Bits per seconds =
       8360000 Bits =8360000/8 = 1045000 Bytes
    ```

4. Configure the parameters in the Datapump parameter file. The `TCPFLUSHBYTES` parameter should be at least equal to `TCPBUFSIZE` as shown in the following code:

    ```
    RMTHOST stdby1-ol6-112 , MGRPORT 8809, TCPBUFSIZE 1045000,
       TCPFLUSHBYTES 1045000
    ```

5. Configure the appropriate values for OS maximum socket buffer sizes. These should be at least equal to the values of `TCPBUFSIZE`. For a Linux environment, the following parameters in `/etc/sysctl.conf` will need tuning/adjusting:

    net.core.rmem_max

    net.core.wmem_max

    net.ipv4.tcp_rmem

    net.ipv4.tcp_wmem

6. If even after modifying the previous settings, there is a big lag in the transfer of files to the remote system, you can configure the Datapump process to compress the trail files for network transfer. This can be done using the `COMPRESS` option with the `RMTHOST` parameter as follows:

    ```
    RMTHOST stdby1-ol6-112 , MGRPORT 8809, COMPRESS
    ```

    GoldenGate compression compresses the trail files by a factor 1:4. Enabling the compression option adds extra processing load to the server, so you would see an increase in the CPU usage.

How it works...

Network speeds like any other part of IT infrastructure are improving with time. One of the features of GoldenGate is to replicate the data between systems that are physically located in different geographical locations on two different sides of the world. If the underlying system is a very busy OLTP system and the distance between the systems is massive, sometimes there can be a delay in the data transfer between the systems.

Tuning the network for an efficient transfer for the trail files is an important task. GoldenGate uses the TCP/IP protocol for transfer of the trail files. You should always create at least one Datapump process in the extract configuration. Without that, the extract will be doing both the data extraction and data transfer tasks. This can sometimes cause a bottleneck if there are too many changes occurring in the database.

The next step is to determine the appropriate value for the TCPBUFSIZE parameter. This parameter should be configured in all the Datapumps and the processes should be restarted.

Similarly, you will also need to ensure that the underlying operating system has been configured to handle the TCP data efficiently. For this, you will need to modify some parameters that can be different from one platform to another.

If the network speed in your infrastructure is not enough to handle the transfer load of the trail files and you are observing considerable lag, you should enable the compression of the trail files. This might not be desirable in some cases as it will add some overheads that will lead to higher CPU usage on the server.

Performing a healthcheck of a live GoldenGate configuration

Like any technology, once implemented, GoldenGate forms a key part of enterprise infrastructure. It is responsible for synchronizing the state of some data between two or more systems. For a GoldenGate administrator, it is quite important to know the status of replication configuration. This can have an impact on the state of data in the destination system to some extent. In case the administrator finds any issue with the replication, he can then follow corrective measures to fix it and bring the systems back into synchronization. In this recipe, we will look into various steps that you can follow to ensure that a GoldenGate configuration is running fine. This recipe does not cover the steps required to check the performance of a GoldenGate configuration.

How to do it...

The state of a GoldenGate replication can be checked by performing the following steps on both source and target systems:

1. Check the GoldenGate event logger file ggserr.log for any error or warning messages. You can find these messages using the egrep command as shown in the following code:

    ```
    cd /u01/app/ggate
    egrep -i 'WARNING|ERROR' ggserr.log | more
    ```

2. Using the GoldenGate command line interface, check the status of the processes as follows:

    ```
    GGSCI (prim1-ol6-112.localdomain) 1> status *
    EXTRACT EGGTEST1: RUNNING
    EXTRACT PGGTEST1: ABENDED
    ```

    The status of all processes should be RUNNING.

3. If the status of any of the processes is not RUNNING, check the Process Report files under $GG_HOME/dirrpt/. For example, for the PGGTEST1 process that has an ABENDED status you should look for the error in the /u01/app/ggate/dirrpt/ PGGTEST1.rpt report file.

4. If the process is abended due to any data issue, you will see an ORA-error in the Process Report file. GoldenGate writes failed record information to the discard file.

5. If all the processes are running, check the lag between the systems as shown in the following code:

```
GGSCI (prim1-ol6-112.localdomain) 1> lag *
Sending GETLAG request to EXTRACT EGGTEST1 ...
Last record lag: 5 seconds.
At EOF, no more records to process.
Sending GETLAG request to EXTRACT PGGTEST1 ...
Last record lag: 6 seconds.
At EOF, no more records to process.
```

6. Sometimes there can be an issue with the underlying database due to which the GoldenGate processes can abend. The state of the database can be checked from the database alert log.

How it works...

As we saw in the previous recipe, there are mainly six steps to conduct a healthcheck of a GoldenGate configuration.

Every GoldenGate instance has an event logger file called ggserr.log. In the first step we see how we can query the error/warning messages from this file. GoldenGate writes all informational, warning and error messages to this file in a sequence. This file is a good starting point to check the overall status of the replication. GoldenGate writes the information about the following events to this file:

- All the GGSCI commands that have been issued in this instance
- GoldenGate processes startup/shutdown
- All errors are recorded
- Any warnings
- Any informational messages

The following is an example of the messages from `ggserr.log`:

```
2012-09-24 18:47:30  ERROR   OGG-00664  Oracle GoldenGate Capture for
Oracle, eggtest1.prm:  OCI Error during OCIServerAttach (status = 12162-
ORA-12162: TNS:net service name is incorrectly specified).

2012-09-24 18:47:30  ERROR   OGG-01668  Oracle GoldenGate Capture for
Oracle, eggtest1.prm:  PROCESS ABENDING.

2012-09-24 18:47:30  INFO    OGG-00975  Oracle GoldenGate Manager for
Oracle, mgr.prm:  client_start_er_prog failed.

2012-09-24 18:47:30  WARNING OGG-01742  Oracle GoldenGate Command
Interpreter for Oracle:  Command sent to MGR MGR returned with an ERROR
response.

2012-09-24 18:49:51  INFO    OGG-00987  Oracle GoldenGate Command
Interpreter for Oracle:  GGSCI command (ggate): start egg*.

2012-09-24 18:49:51  INFO    OGG-00963  Oracle GoldenGate Manager for
Oracle, mgr.prm:  Command received from GGSCI on host localhost (START
EXTRACT EGGTEST1 ).

2012-09-24 18:49:51  INFO    OGG-00992  Oracle GoldenGate Capture for
Oracle, eggtest1.prm:  EXTRACT EGGTEST1 starting.

2012-09-24 18:49:51  INFO    OGG-03035  Oracle GoldenGate Capture for
Oracle, eggtest1.prm:  Operating system character set identified as UTF-
8. Locale: en_US, LC_ALL
```

In the next step, we run the `ggsci` command to check the status of all processes in this GoldenGate instance. A status other than `RUNNING` implies that there is an issue. If the status of any of the processes is not `RUNNING`, you can look into the report files for each process. All processes have a dedicated report file under the `dirrpt` folder. GoldenGate writes all statistical information of a process in the report file. Also, whenever the status of a process changes, the report file is updated with appropriate information. So this is a good place to find the detailed information about the reason of process failure. Every time you restart a process the report files are rolled over and a new one is created. The following is an example of an error from the `PGGTEST1.rpt` file:

```
2013-02-20 20:00:43  ERROR   OGG-01232  Receive TCP params error: TCP/IP
error 104 (Connection reset by peer).

***************************************************************
*                    ** Run Time Statistics **
***************************************************************
Report at 2013-02-20 20:00:43 (activity since 2013-02-20 19:55:33)

Output to /u01/app/ggate/dirdat/rt:

From Table SCOTT.EMP:
    #           inserts:          0
    #           updates:        168
```

```
#            befores:      168
#            deletes:      0
#            discards:     0
Last log location read:
     FILE:       /u01/app/ggate/dirdat/st000032
     SEQNO:      32
     RBA:        72281
     TIMESTAMP:  Not Available
     EOF:        YES
     READERR:    400
```

When a process abends due to any Oracle error or any data validation issue, the records are discarded and the details of the failed records are written in the discard file. If the data loss is not acceptable to the business, the information in the discard file is very critical. This is where you can see the details of the error occurred while processing the failed records. The following is an example of the discard file from the RGGTEST1 replicat. The error shown in this case is an instance when replicat couldn't find the records it was trying to update in the target database:

```
Oracle GoldenGate Delivery for Oracle process started, group RGGTEST1
discard file opened: 2013-02-21 18:58:35
Current time: 2013-02-21 18:58:41
Discarded record from action ABEND on error 1403
OCI Error ORA-01403: no data found, SQL <UPDATE "SCOTT"."EMP" SET
"ENAME" = :a1,"JOB" = :a2,"MGR" = :a3,"HIREDATE" = :a4,"SAL" =
:a5,"COMM" = :a6,"DEPTNO" = :a7 WHERE "EMPNO" = :b0>
Aborting transaction on ./dirdat/rt beginning at seqno 30 rba 14033
error at seqno 30 rba 19750
Problem replicating SCOTT.EMP to SCOTT.EMP
Record not found
Mapping problem with compressed update record (target format)...
EMPNO = 7902
ENAME = FORD
JOB = ANALYST
MGR = 7566
HIREDATE = 1981-12-03 00:00:00
SAL = 3100.00
COMM = NULL
DEPTNO = 20
```

A `RUNNING` status of the GoldenGate replication does not necessarily mean that the replication is working efficiently. Sometimes, the process status is `RUNNING`, but due to some issues, the speed of data replication drops down. In order to check whether the records generated in the database are being processed efficiently by the replication, we use the `LAG` command. The `LAG` command reports the difference in seconds from the time the records were generated to the time when it was processed by the GoldenGate process.

If there is an issue with the underlying database, you can check its alert log. The core database issues and alert log scanning are out of the scope of this book.

See also

> ▶ See the next recipe, *Script to perform a regular scheduled healthcheck of a live GoldenGate configuration*

Script to perform a regular scheduled healthcheck of a live GoldenGate configuration

Automation is a key part of every IT administrator's job role. When you perform the same task again and again, after a while it becomes monotonous. From a company's perspective this is not the most efficient use of their human capital especially when things can be automated and computers can be used to perform such tasks. Once the systems are live in production, the teams work round the clock to ensure they are up all the time. A lot of proactive work is done to identify any faults that might jeopardize the availability of the systems. Ensuring the availability of a GoldenGate replication requires regular monitoring and healthchecks. We saw in the previous recipe how to perform a manual healthcheck of a GoldenGate configuration. In this recipe, we will see how to automate some of the checks so that the report are sent in e-mail regularly.

Getting ready

The script provided in this recipe requires the following:

> ▶ `Mailx` configuration
> ▶ GoldenGate user to have the privileges to schedule jobs through the `cron` files

How to do it...

The steps to schedule a regular healthcheck are as follows:

1. Edit the following script `status_report.sh` and set the appropriate values for the environment variables, that is, `ORACLE_HOME`, `GG_HOME`, `MAIL_LIST`, and `REPORT_FILE`.

2. Schedule a `crontab` entry to enable regular running of this script, for example, to run it daily at midnight:

   ```
   00 00 * * * /u01/app/ggate/scripts/status_report.sh
   ```

3. The contents of the script are as follows:

   ```
   #!/bin/bash
   # Written by Ankur Gupta
   # status_report.sh
   export ORACLE_HOME=/u01/app/oracle/product/11.2.0/dbhome_1
   export GG_HOME=/u01/app/ggate
   export LD_LIBRARY_PATH=$ORACLE_HOME/lib:$GG_HOME
   export MAIL_LIST=dbas@company.com
   export REPORT_FILE=/u01/app/ggate/status_report.txt
   export HOSTNAME=`hostname`
   list_all ()
   {
     cd $GG_HOME
     ./ggsci > /tmp/all_processes.txt <<EOF
     info *
     exit
     EOF
   }
   status ()
   {
     cd $GG_HOME
     ./ggsci > /tmp/proc_stat.txt <<EOF
     status $1
     exit
     EOF
   }
   ```

```
lag ()
{
  cd $GG_HOME
  ./ggsci > /tmp/lag.txt <<EOF
  lag $1
  exit
  EOF
}
printf "%-19s \t %-8s \t %-10s %-19s \n" Time Process Status Lag
> $REPORT_FILE
echo "=============================================================
================" >> $REPORT_FILE
list_all
for process in `egrep 'EXTRACT|REPLICAT' /tmp/all_processes.txt |
awk {' print $2 '}`
do
status $process
export STATUS=`grep $process /tmp/proc_stat.txt | awk -F:
  {'print $2'} | tr -d ' '`
if [ $STATUS == 'RUNNING' ]; then
lag $process
export EOF=`grep EOF /tmp/lag.txt| wc -l`
  if [ $EOF -eq 1 ]; then
    LAG_STATUS="Reached End of File"
  else
    export LAG_STATUS=`grep "Last record lag" /tmp/lag.txt | awk
-F: {'print $2'} | tr -d '.' `
  fi
else
  export LAG_STATUS="CHECK PROCESS STATUS"
fi
Timestamp=`date "+%d-%m-%y %H:%M:%S"`
printf "%-19s \t %-8s \t %-10s %-19s \n" "$Timestamp" "$process"
"$STATUS" "$LAG_STATUS" >> $REPORT_FILE
done
# Email the Report to the Mailing List
mail -s "Daily GoldenGate Replication Status Report for $HOSTNAME"
$MAIL_LIST < $REPORT_FILE
```

How it works...

The preceding script works by first listing all the processes in the GoldenGate instance in a temporary file under /tmp. Then we query the status and lag of each of these processes, and add the output to a report file. The report file is then e-mailed at each run of the script. The script sends an e-mail with the following output:

```
Time                    Process     Status     Lag
=====================================================================
24-02-13 00:00:00       RGGTEST1    RUNNING    2 seconds
24-02-13 00:00:00       RGGTEST2    RUNNING    Reached End of File
24-02-13 00:00:01       RGGTEST3    STOPPED    CHECK PROCESS STATUS
24-02-13 00:00:01       RGGTEST4    STOPPED    CHECK PROCESS STATUS
```

See also

▸ See the recipe, *Steps to implement a Heartbeat mechanism for the GoldenGate replication* later in this chapter

Steps to measure throughput of a GoldenGate configuration

One of the important tasks in operational maintenance of an infrastructure component is to measure its performance. Once you have the statistics, you can compare them to the expected results, and then take the necessary steps to fix the deviation. GoldenGate replication is often used to replicate a large amount of data between systems. Even if you don't have any noticeable performance degradation, you will sometimes need to know how well the replication is performing. When it comes to measuring the performance of GoldenGate replication, one of the aspects is the throughput. There are two types of throughput that you can measure in a GoldenGate configuration, namely, **data throughput** and **operational throughput**. In this recipe, we will look into various steps using which you can measure both of them. We will also discuss how this information can be used for tuning the performance of replication and also how to resolve issues.

Getting ready

For this recipe we will refer to the setup done in the *Setting up a simple GoldenGate replication configuration between two single node databases* recipe in *Chapter 2, Setting up GoldenGate Replication*

How to do it...

The steps to measure the data throughput of replication processes are as follows:

1. Login to GGSCI.

2. Execute the `info` command as shown in the following code:

   ```
   GGSCI (stdby1-ol6-112.localdomain) 8> info rggtest1

   REPLICAT  RGGTEST1  Last Started 2013-02-23 18:44   Status RUNNING

   Checkpoint Lag     00:00:00 (updated 00:00:02 ago)

   Log Read Checkpoint  File ./dirdat/rt000031

   2013-02-23 18:55:15.992584  RBA 280707
   ```

3. Note down the RBA from the preceding output, that is, RBA 280707 in this case.

4. Wait for one minute and re-run the `info` command:

   ```
   GGSCI (stdby1-ol6-112.localdomain) 9> info rggtest1

   REPLICAT  RGGTEST1  Last Started 2013-02-23 18:44   Status RUNNING

   Checkpoint Lag        00:00:00 (updated 00:00:03 ago)

   Log Read Checkpoint  File ./dirdat/rt000031

   2013-02-23 18:56:06.994400  RBA 33999984
   ```

5. Note down the RBA from the previous output, that is, RBA 33999984.

6. Subtract the RBA from the 4th step and the one from the 2nd step as follows:

   ```
   33999984-280707 = 33879327 bytes per Minute
                   = 32.3 MB per Minute
   ```

The steps to measure the operational throughput are as follows:

1. Login to GGSCI.

2. Execute the STATS command for the process:

   ```
   GGSCI (stdby1-ol6-112.localdomain) 10> stats rggtest1, totalsonly
   SCOTT.*

   Sending STATS request to REPLICAT RGGTEST1 ...

   Start of Statistics at 2013-02-23 19:19:10.

   Cumulative totals for specified table(s):

   *** Total statistics since 2013-02-23 19:12:48 ***

     Total inserts                          0.00
     Total updates                       8494.00
     Total deletes                          0.00
     Total discards                         0.00
   ```

```
    Total operations                    8494.00
    Total update collisions             2358.00
 *** Daily statistics since 2013-02-23 19:12:48 ***
    Total inserts                          0.00
    Total updates                       8494.00
    Total deletes                          0.00
    Total discards                         0.00
    Total operations                    8494.00
    Total update collisions             2358.00
 *** Hourly statistics since 2013-02-23 19:12:48 ***
    Total inserts                          0.00
    Total updates                       8494.00
    Total deletes                          0.00
    Total discards                         0.00
    Total operations                    8494.00
    Total update collisions             2358.00
 *** Latest statistics since 2013-02-23 19:12:48 ***
    Total inserts                          0.00
    Total updates                       8494.00
    Total deletes                          0.00
    Total discards                         0.00
    Total operations                    8494.00
    Total update collisions             2358.00
 End of Statistics.
```

How it works...

In the preceding steps we saw how we can measure the throughput for a GoldenGate Replicat process. In the steps for data throughput, we measure the data throughput of a GoldenGate replication process. Measuring data throughput tells you how much data was processed by each process. This is quite useful information to measure the trends of the replication performance.

The operational throughput means the number of DDL, delete, insert, update, discard, and collision operations per second that have happened in a given period. This is very useful to match the exact number and type of operations that occurred in source to the ones that have been replicated to target. In the preceding example, we run the stats with a totalsonly parameter for SCOTT. * tables. This provides us with a combined summary of the operations of all the tables for a SCOTT user.

There's more...

In order to measure the data throughput trend of a GoldenGate process, you can use the following solution. Here we have a script called `log_data_throughput.sh` that measures the throughput of all processes running in a GoldenGate instance and logs the output to a file called `data_througput_history.txt`:

```bash
#!/bin/bash -x
# Written by Ankur Gupta
# log_data_throughput.sh
export ORACLE_HOME=/u01/app/oracle/product/11.2.0/dbhome_1
export LD_LIBRARY_PATH=$LD_LIBRARY_PATH:$ORACLE_HOME/lib
export GG_HOME=/u01/app/ggate
export LOG_FILE=/u01/app/ggate/data_throughput_history.txt
info ()
{
cd $GG_HOME
./ggsci > /tmp/info.txt <<EOF
info $1
exit
EOF
}
list_all ()
{
cd $GG_HOME
./ggsci > /tmp/all_processes.txt <<EOF
info *
exit
EOF
}
list_all
for process in `egrep 'EXTRACT|REPLICAT' /tmp/all_processes.txt |
awk {' print $2 '}`
do
info $process
export START=`grep RBA /tmp/info.txt | awk {'print $4'}`
sleep 30
info $process
```

```
export STOP=`grep RBA /tmp/info.txt | awk {'print $4'}`
SPEED=$(($STOP-$START))
SPEED=$(($SPEED*60/1024/1024))
TIMESTAMP=`date "+%d-%m-%y %H:%M"`
echo "${process} ${TIMESTAMP} ${SPEED}MB/HR" >> $LOG_FILE
done
```

Schedule this script in `crontab` to run every hour. The output file (`data_throughput_history.txt`) will then have the output as shown in the following command:

```
RGGTEST1 24-02-13 08:00 43MB/HR
RGGTEST2 24-02-13 08:01 43MB/HR
RGGTEST3 24-02-13 08:02 44MB/HR
RGGTEST4 24-02-13 08:03 43MB/HR
RGGTEST1 24-02-13 09:00 45MB/HR
RGGTEST2 24-02-13 09:01 43MB/HR
RGGTEST3 24-02-13 09:02 44MB/HR
RGGTEST4 24-02-13 09:03 44MB/HR
RGGTEST1 24-02-13 10:00 42MB/HR
RGGTEST2 24-02-13 10:01 42MB/HR
RGGTEST3 24-02-13 10:02 43MB/HR
RGGTEST4 24-02-13 10:03 43MB/HR
RGGTEST1 24-02-13 11:00 46MB/HR
RGGTEST2 24-02-13 11:01 41MB/HR
RGGTEST3 24-02-13 11:02 45MB/HR
RGGTEST4 24-02-13 11:03 44MB/HR
RGGTEST1 24-02-13 12:00 43MB/HR
RGGTEST2 24-02-13 12:01 41MB/HR
RGGTEST3 24-02-13 12:02 44MB/HR
RGGTEST4 24-02-13 12:03 43MB/HR
```

You can then use this information for reporting or monitoring purposes. You can also import this information into Microsoft Excel to draw any graphs to see the performance trends over a long period of time.

Stats command options

There are various options that you can specify with the STATS command. The overall syntax for the STATS command is as follows:

```
STATS <PROCESS_TYPE> <group name>
[, <statistic>]
[, TABLE <table>]
[, TOTALSONLY <table spec>]
[, REPORTCDR]
[, REPORTDETAIL | NOREPORTDETAIL]
[, REPORTRATE <time units>]
[, ... ]
```

In the preceding command:

<PROCESS_TYPE> is Extract or Replicat, <group name> is either the name of a process or a wildcard to specify multiple processes.

TABLE <table> is the name of the table(s) for which you want to see the statistics.

TOTALSONLY <table spec> is used if you want to see the combined summary of all the tables specified using the table clause.

REPORTCDR is used if you want to see the conflict detection and resolution statistics in case of multimaster replication.

REPORTDETAIL|NOREPORTDETAIL is used to control whether to show the statistics of operations that got any collision errors.

REPORTRATE is used if you want to see the statistics in the form of processing rate and not as absolute figures.

The following are the examples of the STATS command with these options:

```
GGSCI (stdby1-ol6-112.localdomain) 7> stats *
Sending STATS request to REPLICAT RGGTEST1 ...
Start of Statistics at 2013-02-24 16:19:06.
Replicating from SCOTT.EMP to SCOTT.EMP:
*** Total statistics since 2013-02-23 19:12:48 ***
    Total inserts                         0.00
    Total updates                   1309164.00
    Total deletes                         0.00
    Total discards                        0.00
```

```
    Total operations                    1309164.00
    Total update collisions               93511.00
*** Daily statistics since 2013-02-24 00:00:00 ***
    Total inserts                             0.00
    Total updates                       1233244.00
    Total deletes                             0.00
    Total discards                            0.00
    Total operations                    1233244.00
    Total update collisions               88089.00
*** Hourly statistics since 2013-02-24 16:00:00 ***
    Total inserts                             0.00
    Total updates                         73636.00
    Total deletes                             0.00
    Total discards                            0.00
    Total operations                      73636.00
    Total update collisions                5259.00
*** Latest statistics since 2013-02-23 19:12:48 ***
    Total inserts                             0.00
    Total updates                       1309164.00
    Total deletes                             0.00
    Total discards                            0.00
    Total operations                    1309164.00
    Total update collisions               93511.00
Replicating from SCOTT.DEPT to SCOTT.DEPT:
*** Total statistics since 2013-02-23 19:12:48 ***
    Total inserts                             0.00
    Total updates                        374044.00
    Total deletes                             0.00
    Total discards                            0.00
    Total operations                     374044.00
    Total update collisions              374044.00
*** Daily statistics since 2013-02-24 00:00:00 ***
    Total inserts                             0.00
    Total updates                        352356.00
    Total deletes                             0.00
    Total discards                            0.00
```

```
   Total operations                          352356.00
   Total update collisions                   352356.00
*** Hourly statistics since 2013-02-24 16:00:00 ***
   Total inserts                                  0.00
   Total updates                              21039.00
   Total deletes                                  0.00
   Total discards                                 0.00
   Total operations                           21039.00
   Total update collisions                    21039.00
*** Latest statistics since 2013-02-23 19:12:48 ***
   Total inserts                                  0.00
   Total updates                             374044.00
   Total deletes                                  0.00
   Total discards                                 0.00
   Total operations                          374044.00
   Total update collisions                   374044.00
End of Statistics.
GGSCI (stdby1-ol6-112.localdomain) 8> STATS RGGTEST1,
TOTAL, HOURLY, TABLE SCOTT.EMP, REPORTRATE HR, REPORTDETAIL
Sending STATS request to REPLICAT RGGTEST1 ...
Start of Statistics at 2013-02-24 16:23:20.
Replicating from SCOTT.EMP to SCOTT.EMP:
*** Total statistics since 2013-02-23 19:12:48 ***
   Total inserts/hour:                            0.00
   Total updates/hour:                        62606.02
   Total deletes/hour:                            0.00
   Total discards/hour:                           0.00
   Total operations/hour:                     62606.02
   Total update collisions /hour:              4471.82
*** Hourly statistics since 2013-02-24 16:00:00 ***
   Total inserts/hour:                            0.00
   Total updates/hour:                       231864.66
   Total deletes/hour:                            0.00
   Total discards/hour:                           0.00
   Total operations/hour:                    231864.66
   Total update collisions /hour:             16559.74
End of Statistics
```

See also

▶ See the recipe *Performing a healthcheck of a live GoldenGate configuration* earlier in this chapter

Steps to re-instantiate a failed GoldenGate configuration

A network outage between the systems can sometimes break the synchronization between the databases. GoldenGate replication is quite good in recovering from short outages. However, if the outage is long and the amount of change caused in the source database is high, there can be instances where the GoldenGate replication cannot recover itself, and the administrator will need to re-instantiate the target environment. In this recipe, we will look into the steps that you can follow to re-sync a GoldenGate configuration when there is a network outage or some issue with the target database/system.

Getting ready

For this recipe we will refer to the setup done in the *Setting up a simple GoldenGate replication configuration between two single node databases* recipe in *Chapter 2, Setting up GoldenGate Replication*. The scenario demonstrated in this recipe is a broken replication due to a long network outage. The trail file area on the source system filled up causing the extract to abend. Due to the long outage in replication, some of the archive logs are no longer present on the disk on the source server. Due to this the replication cannot be resumed with just a simple restart of the Extract/Datapump processes.

How to do it...

The steps to re-instantiate a broken GoldenGate replication configuration are as follows:

1. Stop the Replicat process in the target environment if it is running by using the following command:

   ```
   GGSCI> STOP REPLICAT RGGTEST1
   ```

2. Truncate the tables in the target database that you are replicating using the following commands:

   ```
   SQL> TRUNCATE TABLE SCOTT.EMP;
   SQL> TRUNCATE TABLE SCOTT.DEPT;
   SQL> TRUNCATE TABLE SCOTT.SALGRADE;
   SQL> TRUNCATE TABLE SCOTT.BONUS;
   ```

3. Note down the current timestamp from the source database:

   ```
   SQL> SELECT TO_CHAR(SYSDATE,'YYYY-MM-DD HH24:MI:SS') from dual;
   TO_CHAR(SYSDATE,'YY
   -------------------
   2013-02-26 15:50:02
   ```

4. Note down the `current_scn` from the source database as follows:

   ```
   SQL> SELECT CURRENT_SCN FROM V$DATABASE;
   CURRENT_SCN
   -----------
      11547294
   ```

5. Create a `/u01/app/ggate/expdp` directory for taking a Datapump Export on both the servers, as follows:

   mkdir /u01/app/ggate/expdp

6. Create a directory object in the source database as follows:

   ```
   SQL> CREATE DIRECTORY EXPIMP as '/u01/app/ggate/expdp';
   Directory created.
   SQL> GRANT READ, WRITE, EXECUTE on Directory EXPIMP to system;
   Grant succeeded.
   ```

7. Run Datapump Export to backup the tables that we are replicating:

   ```
   [oracle@prim1-ol6-112 ggate]$ expdp userid=system schemas=SCOTT
   FLASHBACK_SCN=11547294 DIRECTORY=EXPIMP DUMPFILE=EXPDP.dmp
   LOGFILE=EXPDP.log

   Export: Release 11.2.0.3.0 - Production on Tue Feb 26 16:03:39
   2013

   Copyright (c) 1982, 2011, Oracle and/or its affiliates. All rights
   reserved.

   Password:

   Connected to: Oracle Database 11g Enterprise Edition Release
   11.2.0.3.0 - 64bit Production

   With the Partitioning, OLAP, Data Mining and Real Application
   Testing options

   FLASHBACK automatically enabled to preserve database integrity.

   Starting "SYSTEM"."SYS_EXPORT_SCHEMA_01":  userid=system/********
   schemas=SCOTT FLASHBACK_SCN=11547294 DIRECTORY=EXPIMP
   DUMPFILE=EXPDP.dmp LOGFILE=EXPDP.log

   Estimate in progress using BLOCKS method...

   Processing object type SCHEMA_EXPORT/TABLE/TABLE_DATA
   ```

```
Total estimation using BLOCKS method: 192 KB

Processing object type SCHEMA_EXPORT/USER

Processing object type SCHEMA_EXPORT/SYSTEM_GRANT

Processing object type SCHEMA_EXPORT/ROLE_GRANT

Processing object type SCHEMA_EXPORT/DEFAULT_ROLE

Processing object type SCHEMA_EXPORT/PRE_SCHEMA/PROCACT_SCHEMA

Processing object type SCHEMA_EXPORT/TABLE/TABLE

Processing object type SCHEMA_EXPORT/TABLE/CONSTRAINT/CONSTRAINT

Processing object type SCHEMA_EXPORT/TABLE/INDEX/STATISTICS/INDEX_
STATISTICS

Processing object type SCHEMA_EXPORT/TABLE/STATISTICS/TABLE_
STATISTICS

   exported "SCOTT"."DEPT"     5.929 KB        4 rows
   exported "SCOTT"."EMP"       8.648 KB       16 rows
   exported "SCOTT"."SALGRADE"  5.859 KB        5 rows
   exported "SCOTT"."BONUS"     0 KB            0 rows

Master table "SYSTEM"."SYS_EXPORT_SCHEMA_01" successfully loaded/
unloaded

******************************************************Dump file
set for SYSTEM.SYS_EXPORT_SCHEMA_01 is:

   /u01/app/ggate/expdp/EXPDP.dmp

Job "SYSTEM"."SYS_EXPORT_SCHEMA_01" successfully completed at
16:05:08
```

8. Create a directory object in the database in the target database:

   ```
   SQL> CREATE DIRECTORY EXPIMP AS '/u01/app/ggate/expdp';

   Directory created.

   SQL> GRANT READ,WRITE,EXECUTE ON DIRECTORY EXPIMP TO SYSTEM;

   Grant succeeded.
   ```

9. Copy the dump file from the source to the target server as follows:

   ```
   scp /u01/app/ggate/expdp/expdp.dmp stdby1-ol6-112:/u01/app/ggate/
   expdp/
   ```

10. Import the dump file into the target database as follows:

    ```
    [oracle@stdby1-ol6-112 expdp]$ impdp userid=system
    directory=expimp dumpfile=EXPDP.dmp logfile=IMPDP.dmp full=y
    table_exists_action=REPLACE

    Import: Release 11.2.0.3.0 - Production on Tue Feb 26 16:20:51
    2013
    ```

```
Copyright (c) 1982, 2011, Oracle and/or its affiliates. All rights
reserved.
```

```
Password:
```

```
Connected to: Oracle Database 11g Enterprise Edition Release
11.2.0.3.0 - 64bit Production
```

```
With the Partitioning, OLAP, Data Mining and Real Application
Testing options
```

```
Master table "SYSTEM"."SYS_IMPORT_FULL_01" successfully loaded/
unloaded
```

```
Starting "SYSTEM"."SYS_IMPORT_FULL_01":  userid=system/********
directory=expimp dumpfile=EXPDP.dmp logfile=IMPDP.dmp full=y
table_exists_action=REPLACE
```

```
Processing object type SCHEMA_EXPORT/USER
```

```
ORA-31684: Object type USER:"SCOTT" already exists
```

```
Processing object type SCHEMA_EXPORT/SYSTEM_GRANT
```

```
Processing object type SCHEMA_EXPORT/ROLE_GRANT
```

```
Processing object type SCHEMA_EXPORT/DEFAULT_ROLE
```

```
Processing object type SCHEMA_EXPORT/PRE_SCHEMA/PROCACT_SCHEMA
```

```
Processing object type SCHEMA_EXPORT/TABLE/TABLE
```

```
Processing object type SCHEMA_EXPORT/TABLE/TABLE_DATA
```

```
   imported "SCOTT"."DEPT" 5.929 KB       4 rows
```

```
   imported "SCOTT"."EMP"  8.648 KB      16 rows
```

```
   imported "SCOTT"."SALGRADE" 5.859 KB  5 rows
```

```
   imported "SCOTT"."BONUS"     0 KB       0 rows
```

```
Processing object type SCHEMA_EXPORT/TABLE/CONSTRAINT/CONSTRAINT
```

```
Processing object type SCHEMA_EXPORT/TABLE/INDEX/STATISTICS/INDEX_
STATISTICS
```

```
Processing object type SCHEMA_EXPORT/TABLE/STATISTICS/TABLE_
STATISTICS
```

```
Job "SYSTEM"."SYS_IMPORT_FULL_01" completed with 1 error(s) at
16:21:05
```

11. Alter the Extract and Datapump on the source server as follows:

```
GGSCI> ALTER EXTRACT EGGTEST1, BEGIN 2013-02-26 15:50:02
```

```
GGSCI> ALTER EXTRACT PGGTEST1, BEGIN 2013-02-26 15:50:02
```

12. Remove all the trail files from the `dirdat` directory on the source server except the last generated trail file.

13. Start Extract and Datapump on server A as follows:

```
GGSCI> START EXTRACT EGGTEST1
GGSCI> START EXTRACT PGGTEST1
```

14. Start the Replicat process on server B from the SCN noted in step 4 as follows:

```
GGSCI> START REPLICAT RGGTEST1, AFTERCSN 11547294
```

15. Check whether the data is getting replicated on both sides by running stats or not as follows:

```
GGSCI (prim1-ol6-112.localdomain) 3> STATS EGGTEST1, TOTAL, TABLE
SCOTT.*

Sending STATS request to EXTRACT EGGTEST1 ...

Start of Statistics at 2013-02-26 22:34:00.

Output to /u01/app/ggate/dirdat/st:

Extracting from SCOTT.EMP to SCOTT.EMP:

*** Total statistics since 2013-02-26 22:01:04 ***

   Total inserts                        0.00
   Total updates                       16.00
   Total deletes                        0.00
   Total discards                       0.00
   Total operations                    16.00

End of Statistics.

GGSCI (prim1-ol6-112.localdomain) 4> STATS PGGTEST1, TOTAL, TABLE
SCOTT.*

Sending STATS request to EXTRACT PGGTEST1 ...

Start of Statistics at 2013-02-26 22:34:18.

Output to /u01/app/ggate/dirdat/rt:

Extracting from SCOTT.EMP to SCOTT.EMP:

*** Total statistics since 2013-02-26 22:01:05 ***

   Total inserts                        0.00
   Total updates                       16.00
   Total deletes                        0.00
   Total discards                       0.00
   Total operations                    16.00

End of Statistics.

GGSCI (stdby1-ol6-112.localdomain) 8> STATS RGGTEST1, TOTAL, TABLE
SCOTT.*

Sending STATS request to REPLICAT RGGTEST1 ...
```

```
Start of Statistics at 2013-02-26 22:36:54.
Replicating from SCOTT.EMP to SCOTT.EMP:
*** Total statistics since 2013-02-26 22:09:22 ***
  Total inserts                          0.00
  Total updates                         16.00
  Total deletes                          0.00
  Total discards                         0.00
  Total operations                      16.00
End of Statistics.
```

How it works...

All GoldenGate processes maintain their checkpoints at filesystem level (or a table in the case of Replicat). Using this checkpoint information, a GoldenGate process can resume its job from the point it left at the time of failure. Sometimes due to a network issue or any other issue, the outage can be long, due to which it might not be possible to resume the replication, for example, in the case of Extract, as long as you have all the archive logs available on the disk that have still not been mined, GoldenGate should be able to resume the Extract process. If the source system is a very busy OLTP system, keeping the archive logs on the disk for the duration of the outage might not be an option and due to this, it may not be feasible to resume the replication.
In such scenarios, you will need to re-instantiate the tables that you are replicating in the target database. In this recipe, we have covered the steps that you can follow to re-instantiate the target database objects without causing an outage to the source database.

In this procedure, we first stop the Replicat process in the target system. After this we clear all the data in the replicated objects by truncating the tables. At this time, we note the SCN and timestamp of the source database. In step 6, we run an export of the replicated tables. In this example, we are replicating the objects owner by a SCOTT user. The dump file is then transferred on to the target system. Then we import the dump file into the target database. At this time, we have re-instantiated the objects in the target database to the state at which SCN was noted as we saw in step 3. We now re-point the Extract processes to start from the timestamp which was noted in step 4. In this scenario, our trail file area has filled up so we delete the trail files except the latest one as that will be required by the Extract process to resume its functioning. After this we start the Extract and Datapump processes. Then we start the Replicat process on the target system and instruct it to start applying the changes from the SCN that was noted in step 3. Now the replication should be back in sync. We verify that it is working by checking the stats of all three processes.

See also

▸ See the next recipe, *Steps to implement a Heartbeat mechanism for the GoldenGate replication*

Steps to implement a Heartbeat mechanism for the GoldenGate replication

A GoldenGate configuration consists of multiple processes each of which perform specific functions. Even though these processes are loosely coupled and maintain their respective checkpoints, an issue with one of them can cause the overall replication for that particular stream to fail. This behavior is not confined to just an issue that will cause a failure, it also persists to an issue which causes delay to one of the processes. So, if the Extract process is overloaded and there is a delay in reading data from the redo stream, the downstream Datapump and Replicat processes will receive the data only at that speed. Although monitoring the lag of an individual process can certainly highlight the sudden spikes in lag times, it will not provide a breakdown of what stage of the replication is causing the majority of the lag. This is where you need to implement a technique called **Heartbeat**. In this recipe, we will look into the detailed steps that you can follow to implement Heartbeat in your GoldenGate configuration. We will also cover how to query the Heartbeat information and check how much was the lag caused by each GoldenGate process.

Getting ready

For this recipe we will refer to the setup done in the *Setting up a simple GoldenGate replication configuration between two single node databases* recipe in *Chapter 2, Setting up GoldenGate Replication*. This recipe assumes that there is a tablespace called `GGATE_DATA` in both the source and target environments. This tablespace is assigned as a default tablespace for the `GGATE_ADMIN` user.

If you don't have a `GGATE_DATA` tablespace in your source or target database, you can create one as shown in the following command:

```
SQL> CREATE TABLESPACE GGATE_DATA DATAFILE '/u01/app/oracle/oradata/
dboratest/ggate_data01.dbf' SIZE 200M AUTOEXTEND ON;

Tablespace created.

SQL> ALTER USER GGATE_ADMIN DEFAULT TABLESPACE GGATE_DATA;

User altered.

SQL> ALTER USER GGATE_ADMIN QUOTA UNLIMITED ON GGATE_DATA;

User altered.
```

How to do it...

The following are the steps to set up a Heartbeat mechanism in the replication environment:

1. Connect to SQLPLUS as sysdba in the source database.

2. Run the following commands to grant required privileges to the GGATE_ADMIN user in the source database:

```
SQL> GRANT SELECT ON V_$INSTANCE TO GGATE_ADMIN;

Grant succeeded.

SQL> GRANT SELECT ON V_$DATABASE TO GGATE_ADMIN;

Grant succeeded.
```

3. Create a Heartbeat table in the source database as follows:

```
SQL> CREATE TABLE GGATE_ADMIN.GGS_HEARTBEAT

( ID NUMBER ,
  SRC_DB VARCHAR2(30),
  EXTRACT_NAME varchar2(8),
  SOURCE_COMMIT TIMESTAMP,
  TARGET_COMMIT TIMESTAMP,
  CAPTIME TIMESTAMP,
  CAPLAG NUMBER,
  PMPTIME TIMESTAMP,
  PMPGROUP VARCHAR2(8 BYTE),
  PMPLAG NUMBER,
  DELTIME TIMESTAMP,
  DELGROUP VARCHAR2(8 BYTE),
  DELLAG NUMBER,
  TOTALLAG NUMBER,
thread number,
update_timestamp timestamp,
EDDLDELTASTATS number,
EDMLDELTASTATS number,
RDDLDELTASTATS number,
RDMLDELTASTATS number,
CONSTRAINT HEARTBEAT_PK PRIMARY KEY (THREAD) ENABLE

) TABLESPACE GGATE_DATA

/Table created.
```

4. Insert the Heartbeat record in this table using the following command:

```
SQL> INSERT INTO GGATE_ADMIN.GGS_HEARTBEAT(THREAD) SELECT THREAD#
FROM V$INSTANCE;

1 row created.

SQL> COMMIT;

Commit complete.
```

5. Login to `GGSCI` and add Supplemental Logging for this new table in the source environment as follows:

```
GGSCI (prim1-ol6-112.localdomain) 1> DBLOGIN USERID GGATE_ADMIN@
DBORATEST

Password:

Successfully logged into database.

GGSCI (prim1-ol6-112.localdomain) 2> ADD TRANDATA GGATE_ADMIN.GGS_
HEARTBEAT

Logging of supplemental redo data enabled for table GGATE_ADMIN.
GGS_HEARTBEAT.
```

6. Create a procedure in the source database to update the Heartbeat record as follows:

```
SQL> CREATE OR REPLACE PROCEDURE GGATE_ADMIN.GG_UPDATE_HB_TAB IS

V_THREAD_NUM NUMBER;

V_DB_UNIQUE_NAME VARCHAR2 (128);

BEGIN

SELECT THREAD#, DB_UNIQUE_NAME INTO V_THREAD_NUM, V_DB_UNIQUE_NAME
FROM V$INSTANCE, V$DATABASE;

UPDATE GGATE_ADMIN.GGS_HEARTBEAT SET UPDATE_TIMESTAMP =
SYSTIMESTAMP ,SRC_DB = V_DB_UNIQUE_NAME WHERE THREAD = V_THREAD_
NUM;

COMMIT;

END;

/

Procedure created.
```

7. Create a scheduler job in the source database to update the Heartbeat record every minute as follows:

```
SQL> BEGIN

SYS.DBMS_SCHEDULER.CREATE_JOB (

JOB_NAME => '"GGATE_ADMIN"."GGS_HB"',

JOB_TYPE => 'STORED_PROCEDURE',

JOB_ACTION => '"GGATE_ADMIN"."GG_UPDATE_HB_TAB"',

NUMBER_OF_ARGUMENTS => 0,

START_DATE => NULL,

REPEAT_INTERVAL => 'FREQ=MINUTELY',

END_DATE => NULL,

JOB_CLASS => '"SYS"."DEFAULT_JOB_CLASS"',

ENABLED => FALSE,
```

```
AUTO_DROP => FALSE,

COMMENTS => 'GoldenGate Heartbeat Update Job',

CREDENTIAL_NAME => NULL,

DESTINATION_NAME => NULL);

SYS.DBMS_SCHEDULER.SET_ATTRIBUTE(NAME => '"GGATE_ADMIN"."GGS_
HB"',ATTRIBUTE => 'RESTARTABLE', VALUE => TRUE);

SYS.DBMS_SCHEDULER.SET_ATTRIBUTE(NAME => '"GGATE_ADMIN"."GGS_HB"',
ATTRIBUTE => 'LOGGING_LEVEL', VALUE => DBMS_SCHEDULER.LOGGING_
OFF);

SYS.DBMS_SCHEDULER.ENABLE(NAME => '"GGATE_ADMIN"."GGS_HB"');

END;

/

PL/SQL procedure successfully completed.
```

8. Log in to the target database and create a sequence for the `History` table as follows:

```
SQL> CREATE SEQUENCE GGATE_ADMIN.SEQ_GGS_HEARTBEAT_ID INCREMENT BY
1 START WITH 1 ORDER;

Sequence created.
```

9. Create the `Heartbeat` table in the target database as follows:

```
SQL> CREATE TABLE GGATE_ADMIN.GGS_HEARTBEAT

(ID NUMBER ,SRC_DB VARCHAR2(30),
EXTRACT_NAME varchar2(8),SOURCE_COMMIT TIMESTAMP,
TARGET_COMMIT TIMESTAMP,
CAPTIME TIMESTAMP,
CAPLAG NUMBER,
PMPTIME TIMESTAMP,
PMPGROUP VARCHAR2(8 BYTE),
PMPLAG NUMBER,
DELTIME TIMESTAMP,
DELGROUP VARCHAR2(8 BYTE),
DELLAG NUMBER,
TOTALLAG NUMBER,
thread number,
update_timestamp timestamp,
EDDLDELTASTATS number,
EDMLDELTASTATS number,
RDDLDELTASTATS number,
RDMLDELTASTATS number,
CONSTRAINT GGS_HEARTBEAT_PK PRIMARY KEY (DELGROUP) ENABLE

) Tablespace GGATE_DATA;

Table created.
```

10. Create a sequence for the `Heartbeat_History` table in the target database as follows:

```
SQL> CREATE SEQUENCE GGATE_ADMIN.SEQ_GGS_HEARTBEAT_HIST INCREMENT
BY 1 START WITH 1 ORDER ;

Sequence created.
```

11. Create a `Heartbeart_History` table in the target database as follows:

```
SQL> CREATE TABLE GGATE_ADMIN.GGS_HEARTBEAT_HISTORY

(ID NUMBER ,
SRC_DB VARCHAR2(30),
EXTRACT_NAME varchar2(8),
SOURCE_COMMIT TIMESTAMP,
TARGET_COMMIT TIMESTAMP,
CAPTIME TIMESTAMP,
CAPLAG NUMBER,
PMPTIME TIMESTAMP,
PMPGROUP VARCHAR2(8 BYTE),
PMPLAG NUMBER,
DELTIME TIMESTAMP,
DELGROUP VARCHAR2(8 BYTE),
DELLAG NUMBER,
TOTALLAG      NUMBER,
thread number,
update_timestamp timestamp,
EDDLDELTASTATS        number,
EDMLDELTASTATS        number,
RDDLDELTASTATS        number,
RDMLDELTASTATS        number,
CONSTRAINT GGS_HEARTBEAT_HIST_PK PRIMARY KEY (ID) ENABLE

);

Table created.
```

12. Create a trigger to update the `Lag` columns for the `Heartbeat` table as follows:

```
SQL> CREATE OR REPLACE TRIGGER GGATE_ADMIN.GGS_HEARTBEAT_TRIG

BEFORE INSERT OR UPDATE ON GGATE_ADMIN.GGS_HEARTBEAT

FOR EACH ROW

BEGIN

SELECT SEQ_GGS_HEARTBEAT_ID.NEXTVAL

INTO :NEW.ID

FROM DUAL;

SELECT SYSTIMESTAMP

INTO :NEW.TARGET_COMMIT
```

```
FROM DUAL;

SELECT TRUNC(TO_NUMBER(SUBSTR((:NEW.CAPTIME - :NEW.SOURCE_COMMIT
),1, INSTR(:NEW.CAPTIME - :NEW.SOURCE_COMMIT,' ')))) * 86400

+ TO_NUMBER(SUBSTR((:NEW.CAPTIME - :NEW.SOURCE_COMMIT),
INSTR((:NEW.CAPTIME - :NEW.SOURCE_COMMIT),' ')+1,2) * 3600

+ TO_NUMBER(SUBSTR((:NEW.CAPTIME - :NEW.SOURCE_COMMIT),
INSTR((:NEW.CAPTIME - :NEW.SOURCE_COMMIT),' ')+4,2) ) * 60

+ TO_NUMBER(SUBSTR((:NEW.CAPTIME - :NEW.SOURCE_COMMIT),
INSTR((:NEW.CAPTIME - :NEW.SOURCE_COMMIT),' ')+7,2))

+ TO_NUMBER(SUBSTR((:NEW.CAPTIME - :NEW.SOURCE_COMMIT),
INSTR((:NEW.CAPTIME - :NEW.SOURCE_COMMIT),' ')+10,6)) / 1000000

INTO :NEW.CAPLAG

FROM DUAL;

SELECT TRUNC(TO_NUMBER(SUBSTR((:NEW.PMPTIME - :NEW.CAPTIME),1,
INSTR(:NEW.PMPTIME - :NEW.CAPTIME,' ')))) * 86400

+ TO_NUMBER(SUBSTR((:NEW.PMPTIME - :NEW.CAPTIME), INSTR((:NEW.
PMPTIME - :NEW.CAPTIME),' ')+1,2)) * 3600

+ TO_NUMBER(SUBSTR((:NEW.PMPTIME - :NEW.CAPTIME), INSTR((:NEW.
PMPTIME - :NEW.CAPTIME),' ')+4,2) ) * 60

+ TO_NUMBER(SUBSTR((:NEW.PMPTIME - :NEW.CAPTIME), INSTR((:NEW.
PMPTIME - :NEW.CAPTIME),' ')+7,2))

+ TO_NUMBER(SUBSTR((:NEW.PMPTIME - :NEW.CAPTIME), INSTR((:NEW.
PMPTIME - :NEW.CAPTIME),' ')+10,6)) / 1000000

INTO :NEW.PMPLAG

FROM DUAL;

SELECT TRUNC(TO_NUMBER(SUBSTR((:NEW.DELTIME - :NEW.PMPTIME),1,
INSTR(:NEW.DELTIME - :NEW.PMPTIME,' ')))) * 86400

+ TO_NUMBER(SUBSTR((:NEW.DELTIME - :NEW.PMPTIME), INSTR((:NEW.
DELTIME - :NEW.PMPTIME),' ')+1,2)) * 3600

+ TO_NUMBER(SUBSTR((:NEW.DELTIME - :NEW.PMPTIME), INSTR((:NEW.
DELTIME - :NEW.PMPTIME),' ')+4,2) ) * 60

+ TO_NUMBER(SUBSTR((:NEW.DELTIME - :NEW.PMPTIME), INSTR((:NEW.
DELTIME - :NEW.PMPTIME),' ')+7,2))

+ TO_NUMBER(SUBSTR((:NEW.DELTIME - :NEW.PMPTIME), INSTR((:NEW.
DELTIME - :NEW.PMPTIME),' ')+10,6)) / 1000000

INTO :NEW.DELLAG

FROM DUAL;

SELECT TRUNC(TO_NUMBER(SUBSTR((:NEW.TARGET_COMMIT - :NEW.SOURCE_
COMMIT),1, INSTR(:NEW.TARGET_COMMIT - :NEW.SOURCE_COMMIT,' ')))) *
86400

+ TO_NUMBER(SUBSTR((:NEW.TARGET_COMMIT - :NEW.SOURCE_COMMIT),
```

```
INSTR((:NEW.TARGET_COMMIT - :NEW.SOURCE_COMMIT),' ')+1,2)) * 3600

+ TO_NUMBER(SUBSTR((:NEW.TARGET_COMMIT - :NEW.SOURCE_COMMIT),
INSTR((:NEW.TARGET_COMMIT - :NEW.SOURCE_COMMIT),' ')+4,2) ) * 60

+ TO_NUMBER(SUBSTR((:NEW.TARGET_COMMIT - :NEW.SOURCE_COMMIT),
INSTR((:NEW.TARGET_COMMIT - :NEW.SOURCE_COMMIT),' ')+7,2))

+ TO_NUMBER(SUBSTR((:NEW.TARGET_COMMIT - :NEW.SOURCE_COMMIT),
INSTR((:NEW.TARGET_COMMIT - :NEW.SOURCE_COMMIT),' ')+10,6)) /
1000000

INTO :NEW.TOTALLAG

FROM DUAL;

END ;

/

Trigger created.
```

13. Create a trigger to update the Lag columns for the Heartbeat_History table in the target database as follows:

```
SQL> CREATE OR REPLACE TRIGGER GGATE_ADMIN.GGS_HEARTBEAT_TRIG_HIST

BEFORE INSERT OR UPDATE ON GGATE_ADMIN.GGS_HEARTBEAT_HISTORY

FOR EACH ROW

BEGIN

SELECT SEQ_GGS_HEARTBEAT_HIST.NEXTVAL

INTO :NEW.ID

FROM DUAL;

SELECT SYSTIMESTAMP

INTO :NEW.TARGET_COMMIT

FROM DUAL;

SELECT TRUNC(TO_NUMBER(SUBSTR((:NEW.CAPTIME - :NEW.SOURCE_COMMIT
),1, INSTR(:NEW.CAPTIME - :NEW.SOURCE_COMMIT,' ')))) * 86400

+ TO_NUMBER(SUBSTR((:NEW.CAPTIME - :NEW.SOURCE_COMMIT),
INSTR((:NEW.CAPTIME - :NEW.SOURCE_COMMIT),' ')+1,2)) * 3600

+ TO_NUMBER(SUBSTR((:NEW.CAPTIME - :NEW.SOURCE_COMMIT),
INSTR((:NEW.CAPTIME - :NEW.SOURCE_COMMIT),' ')+4,2) ) * 60

+ TO_NUMBER(SUBSTR((:NEW.CAPTIME - :NEW.SOURCE_COMMIT),
INSTR((:NEW.CAPTIME - :NEW.SOURCE_COMMIT),' ')+7,2))

+ TO_NUMBER(SUBSTR((:NEW.CAPTIME - :NEW.SOURCE_COMMIT),
INSTR((:NEW.CAPTIME - :NEW.SOURCE_COMMIT),' ')+10,6)) / 1000000

INTO :NEW.CAPLAG

FROM DUAL;

SELECT TRUNC(TO_NUMBER(SUBSTR((:NEW.PMPTIME - :NEW.CAPTIME),1,
```

```
           INSTR(:NEW.PMPTIME - :NEW.CAPTIME,' ')))) * 86400

+ TO_NUMBER(SUBSTR((:NEW.PMPTIME - :NEW.CAPTIME), INSTR((:NEW.
PMPTIME - :NEW.CAPTIME),' ')+1,2)) * 3600

+ TO_NUMBER(SUBSTR((:NEW.PMPTIME - :NEW.CAPTIME), INSTR((:NEW.
PMPTIME - :NEW.CAPTIME),' ')+4,2) ) * 60

+ TO_NUMBER(SUBSTR((:NEW.PMPTIME - :NEW.CAPTIME), INSTR((:NEW.
PMPTIME - :NEW.CAPTIME),' ')+7,2))

+ TO_NUMBER(SUBSTR((:NEW.PMPTIME - :NEW.CAPTIME), INSTR((:NEW.
PMPTIME - :NEW.CAPTIME),' ')+10,6)) / 1000000

INTO :NEW.PMPLAG

FROM DUAL;

SELECT TRUNC(TO_NUMBER(SUBSTR((:NEW.DELTIME - :NEW.PMPTIME),1,
INSTR(:NEW.DELTIME - :NEW.PMPTIME,' ')))) * 86400

+ TO_NUMBER(SUBSTR((:NEW.DELTIME - :NEW.PMPTIME), INSTR((:NEW.
DELTIME - :NEW.PMPTIME),' ')+1,2)) * 3600

+ TO_NUMBER(SUBSTR((:NEW.DELTIME - :NEW.PMPTIME), INSTR((:NEW.
DELTIME - :NEW.PMPTIME),' ')+4,2) ) * 60

+ TO_NUMBER(SUBSTR((:NEW.DELTIME - :NEW.PMPTIME), INSTR((:NEW.
DELTIME - :NEW.PMPTIME),' ')+7,2))

+ TO_NUMBER(SUBSTR((:NEW.DELTIME - :NEW.PMPTIME), INSTR((:NEW.
DELTIME - :NEW.PMPTIME),' ')+10,6)) / 1000000

INTO :NEW.DELLAG

FROM DUAL;

SELECT TRUNC(TO_NUMBER(SUBSTR((:NEW.TARGET_COMMIT - :NEW.SOURCE_
COMMIT),1, INSTR(:NEW.TARGET_COMMIT - :NEW.SOURCE_COMMIT,' ')))) *
86400

+ TO_NUMBER(SUBSTR((:NEW.TARGET_COMMIT - :NEW.SOURCE_COMMIT),
INSTR((:NEW.TARGET_COMMIT - :NEW.SOURCE_COMMIT),' ')+1,2)) * 3600

+ TO_NUMBER(SUBSTR((:NEW.TARGET_COMMIT - :NEW.SOURCE_COMMIT),
INSTR((:NEW.TARGET_COMMIT - :NEW.SOURCE_COMMIT),' ')+4,2) ) * 60

+ TO_NUMBER(SUBSTR((:NEW.TARGET_COMMIT - :NEW.SOURCE_COMMIT),
INSTR((:NEW.TARGET_COMMIT - :NEW.SOURCE_COMMIT),' ')+7,2))

+ TO_NUMBER(SUBSTR((:NEW.TARGET_COMMIT - :NEW.SOURCE_COMMIT),
INSTR((:NEW.TARGET_COMMIT - :NEW.SOURCE_COMMIT),' ')+10,6)) /
1000000

INTO :NEW.TOTALLAG

FROM DUAL;

END ;

/

Trigger created.
```

14. Stop the replication process in the source and target environment by the following command:

```
GGSCI> STOP ER *
```

15. Edit the Extract Parameter file in the source environment and add the Heartbeat table in the list as follows:

```
EXTRACT EGGTEST1

USERID GGATE_ADMIN@DBORATEST, PASSWORD GGATE_ADMIN

EXTTRAIL /u01/app/ggate/dirdat/st

TABLE SCOTT.*;

TABLE GGATE_ADMIN.GGS_HEARTBEAT,

TOKENS (

CAPGROUP = @GETENV ("GGENVIRONMENT", "GROUPNAME"),

CAPTIME =  @DATE ("YYYY-MM-DD HH:MI:SS.FFFFFF","JTS",@GETENV
("JULIANTIMESTAMP")),

EDDLDELTASTATS = @GETENV ("DELTASTATS", "DDL"),

EDMLDELTASTATS = @GETENV ("DELTASTATS", "DML")

);
```

16. Edit the Datapump Parameter file and add the Heartbeat table to the list as follows:

```
EXTRACT PGGTEST1

USERID GGATE_ADMIN@DBORATEST, PASSWORD GGATE_ADMIN

RMTHOST 192.168.0.11 , MGRPORT 8809

RMTTRAIL /u01/app/ggate/dirdat/rt

NOPASSTHRU

TABLE GGATE_ADMIN.GGS_HEARTBEAT,

TOKENS (

PMPGROUP = @GETENV ("GGENVIRONMENT","GROUPNAME"),

PMPTIME = @DATE ("YYYY-MM-DD HH:MI:SS.FFFFFF","JTS",@GETENV
("JULIANTIMESTAMP"))

);

PASSTHRU

TABLE SCOTT.*;
```

17. Edit the Replicat Parameter file in the target environment and add the mapping information for the `Heartbeat` and `Heartbeat_History` tables as follows:

```
REPLICAT RGGTEST1

USERID GGATE_ADMIN@TGORTEST, PASSWORD GGATE_ADMIN

DISCARDFILE /U01/APP/GGATE/DIRRPT/RGGTEST1.DSC,APPEND,MEGABYTES
500

ASSUMETARGETDEFS

MAP SCOTT.*, TARGET SCOTT.*;

MAP GGATE_ADMIN.GGS_HEARTBEAT, TARGET GGATE_ADMIN.GGS_HEARTBEAT,

KEYCOLS (DELGROUP),

INSERTMISSINGUPDATES,

COLMAP (USEDEFAULTS,

ID = 0,

SOURCE_COMMIT = @GETENV ("GGHEADER", "COMMITTIMESTAMP"),

EXTRACT_NAME = @TOKEN ("CAPGROUP"),

CAPTIME = @TOKEN ("CAPTIME"),

PMPGROUP = @TOKEN ("PMPGROUP"),

PMPTIME = @TOKEN ("PMPTIME"),

DELGROUP = @GETENV ("GGENVIRONMENT", "GROUPNAME"),

DELTIME =  @DATE ("YYYY-MM-DD HH:MI:SS.FFFFFF","JTS",@GETENV
("JULIANTIMESTAMP")),

EDDLDELTASTATS = @TOKEN ("EDDLDELTASTATS"),

EDMLDELTASTATS = @TOKEN ("EDMLDELTASTATS"),

RDDLDELTASTATS = @GETENV ("DELTASTATS", "DDL"),

RDMLDELTASTATS = @GETENV ("DELTASTATS", "DML")

);

MAP GGATE_ADMIN.GGS_HEARTBEAT, TARGET GGATE_ADMIN.GGS_HEARTBEAT_
HISTORY,

KEYCOLS (ID),

INSERTALLRECORDS,

COLMAP (USEDEFAULTS,

ID = 0,

SOURCE_COMMIT = @GETENV ("GGHEADER", "COMMITTIMESTAMP"),

EXTRACT_NAME = @TOKEN ("CAPGROUP"),

CAPTIME = @TOKEN ("CAPTIME"),

PMPGROUP = @TOKEN ("PMPGROUP"),

PMPTIME = @TOKEN ("PMPTIME"),
```

```
DELGROUP = @GETENV ("GGENVIRONMENT", "GROUPNAME"),
DELTIME =  @DATE ("YYYY-MM-DD HH:MI:SS.FFFFFF","JTS",@GETENV
("JULIANTIMESTAMP")),
EDDLDELTASTATS = @TOKEN ("EDDLDELTASTATS"),
EDMLDELTASTATS = @TOKEN ("EDMLDELTASTATS"),
RDDLDELTASTATS = @GETENV ("DELTASTATS", "DDL"),
RDMLDELTASTATS = @GETENV ("DELTASTATS", "DML")
);
```

18. Start the Extract and Datapump in the source environment as follows:

    ```
    GGSCI (prim1-ol6-112.localdomain) 11> START EXTRACT EGGTEST1
    Sending START request to MANAGER ...
    EXTRACT EGGTEST1 starting
    GGSCI (prim1-ol6-112.localdomain) 12> START EXTRACT PGGTEST1
    Sending START request to MANAGER ...
    EXTRACT PGGTEST1 starting
    ```

19. Start the Replicat process in the target environment as follows:

    ```
    GGSCI (stdby1-ol6-112.localdomain) 2> START REPLICAT RGGTEST1
    Sending START request to MANAGER ...
    REPLICAT RGGTEST1 starting
    ```

20. Verify whether the Heartbeat is working by querying the GGS_HEARTBEAT
    and GGS_HEARTBEAT_HISTORY tables in the target environment as follows:

    ```
    SQL> SELECT CAPLAG,PMPLAG, DELLAG FROM GGATE_ADMIN.GGS_HEARTBEAT;
        CAPLAG     PMPLAG     DELLAG
    ---------- ---------- ----------
        2.304362   2.004874   1.869005
    SQL> SELECT CAPLAG,PMPLAG, DELLAG FROM GGATE_ADMIN.GGS_HEARTBEAT_
    HISTORY;
        CAPLAG     PMPLAG     DELLAG
    ---------- ---------- ----------
       17.88579  13.066255   3.620444
        2.189226   1.970397   1.748129
        2.304362   2.004874   1.869005
    ```

How it works...

Heartbeat mechanism is a procedure to measure the lag between the source and target systems in a reliable way. The basic idea is to have a table on the source system that gets updated at a regular interval. This table is then included in the replication process. All replication processes add some metadata tokens to the Heartbeat record. By the time the Heartbeat record is written to the target database, the timestamp and lag information of each process is added with the help of tokens. By querying the Heartbeat record in the target database we can see where the lag is and how much is the lag.

In this recipe, we cover various steps using which the Heartbeat mechanism is set up in the GoldenGate configuration.

For this, we first grant some privileges to the GGATE_ADMIN user to enable it to query the V$INSTANCE & V$DATABASE views. The Heartbeat table is created in the GGATE_ADMIN schema. This user must have the CREATE/UPDATE table privilege in both the databases. The Heartbeat setup in the source environment consists of creation of some new objects: Heartbeat Table (GGS_HEARTBEAT), procedure to generate a Heartbeat record (GG_UPDATE_HB_TAB), and database job to regularly run the procedure (GGS_HB). Since GGS_HEARTBEAT is a new table, we will also need to enable Supplemental Logging for this table in the source database. Without this, GoldenGate will not capture any changes generated for this table.

The next step is to create the necessary objects in the target environment. In the target environment, we have two tables for maintaining Heartbeat information. The first one is the GGS_HEARTBEAT table. This table is used for a regular up-to-date Heartbeat record. The second table is called the GGS_HEARTBEAT_HIST table. This table holds the historic Heartbeat record information. There is a trigger on both of these tables on INSERT or UPDATE. These triggers calculate and populate some of the crucial columns in these tables.

The GGS_HEARTBEAT table is added to the Extract and Datapump parameter files. As shown in step 15, the extract configuration for this table includes adding the DELTASTATS and timestamp information to the Heartbeat record. Similarly, in step 16, we saw how the Datapump configuration adds the timestamp information to the Heartbeat record which is extracted from the trail file.

The replicat configuration includes the mapping information defined for both the GGS_HEARTBEAT and GGS_HEARTBEAT_HISTORY tables. This is done to map the extracted token information from the Heartbeat record to the appropriate columns and also to generate additional tokens for the Replicat process itself and add them to the relevant columns in the table.

The information in the Heartbeat tables can be queried using standard SQL statements.

There's more...

The Heartbeat table contains one row per Replicat process in the target environment. Since it contains quite useful information, it is worth discussing the significance of each of its columns as shown in the following table:

Column	Data field
ID	This column gives the sequence ID of the Heartbeat record
SRC_DB	This column gives the name of the source database
EXTRACT_NAME	This column gives the name of the Extract process that extracts this Heartbeat record
SOURCE_COMMIT	This column gives the timestamp when the record was committed in the source database
TARGET_COMMIT	This column gives the timestamp when the record was committed in the target database
CAPTIME	This column gives the timestamp when the record was read by the Extract process
CAPLAG	This column gives the difference between the timestamp when the record was committed in the source database to the time it was read by the Extract process
PMPTIME	This column gives the timestamp when the Heartbeat record was processed by the Datapump
PMPGROUP	This column gives the name of the Datapump that read this record
PMPLAG	This column gives the difference between the timestamp when the record was processed by the Extract process to the time it was processed by the Datapump process
DELTIME	This column gives the timestamp when the Heartbeat record was processed by the Replicat
DELGROUP	This column gives the name of the Replicat process which wrote this Heartbeat record
DELLAG	This column gives the difference between the timestamp when the record was processed by the Datapump process to the time it was processed by the Replicat process
TOTALLAG	This column gives the difference between the timestamp when the record was committed in the source database to the time it was committed in the target database
THREAD	This column gives the thread number of the source redo log
UPDATE_TIMESTAMP	This column gives the timestamp when the Heartbeat record was updated by the Heartbeat procedure
EDDLDELTASTATS	This column gives the number of DDL operations since the last stats command on the Extract process

Column	Data field
EDMLDELTASTATS	This column gives the number of DML operations since the last `stats` command on the Extract process
RDDLDELTASTATS	This column gives the number of DDL operations since the last `stats` command on the Replicat process
RDMLDELTASTATS	This column gives the number of DML operations since the last `stats` command on the Replicat process

The following queries can be run in the target database to query the Heartbeat information:

▶ Check the lifecycle of the last replicated Heartbeat record as follows:

```
SQL> SET LINES 180
SQL> COLUMN SOURCE_COMMIT FOR A30
SQL> COLUMN TARGET_COMMIT FOR A30
SQL> COLUMN CAPTIME FOR A30
SQL> COLUMN PMPTIME FOR A30
SQL> COLUMN DELTIME FOR A30
SQL> SELECT SOURCE_COMMIT,CAPTIME, PMPTIME, DELTIME, TARGET_COMMIT
FROM GGATE_ADMIN.GGS_HEARTBEAT;

SOURCE_COMMIT        CAPTIME          PMPTIME              DELTIME        TARGET_
COMMIT

------------------------------------ ------------------------------- ------------------

13-MAR-13 06.50.05.045893 PM    13-MAR-13 06.50.07.074299 PM

13-MAR-13 06.50.08.296275 PM    13-MAR-13 06.50.09.902099 PM

13-MAR-13 06.50.09.948094 PM
```

▶ Query the current lag information for each process as follows:

```
SQL> SELECT CAPLAG,PMPLAG,DELLAG,TOTALLAG FROM GGATE_ADMIN.GGS_
HEARTBEAT;

    CAPLAG      PMPLAG      DELLAG     TOTALLAG
---------- ---------- ---------- ----------
  2.679754    1.721918    1.069694    5.514485
```

Similarly, these queries can be run in the Heartbeat history table to query the historic information and measure the lag trends.

See also

▶ See the recipe *Steps to measure throughput of a GoldenGate configuration* earlier in this chapter

7

Advanced Administration Tasks – I

In this chapter we will cover the following recipes:

- ▸ Upgrading Oracle GoldenGate binaries
- ▸ Table structure changes in GoldenGate environments with similar table definitions
- ▸ Table structure changes in GoldenGate environments with different table definitions
- ▸ Resolving GoldenGate errors using the logdump utility
- ▸ Undoing the applied changes using the reverse utility
- ▸ Creating an Integrated Capture with a downstream database for compressed tables

Introduction

So far in the previous chapters we have seen how to implement GoldenGate in various configurations to replicate data. The job of the person responsible for managing GoldenGate environments does not end here. Once the system goes live like any other IT infrastructure component, GoldenGate requires maintenance. This includes applying newly released patches, and upgrading to newer GoldenGate versions. In this chapter, we will cover how to upgrade GoldenGate environments to newer versions. We will also go through how to apply application patches including DDL changes in GoldenGate environments.

GoldenGate uses a proprietary format for writing to trail files. Usually the administrator does not need to worry as to how the data is written to these trail files, however, when there is an issue in replication, the administrator would need to verify the value of the record in the trail file, and check the state of the data in the target database to identify the cause of the error. GoldenGate provides a utility called logdump for this purpose. In this chapter we will go through how one can use this utility to read the trail file data.

We will also cover how to reverse the changes that were applied to the target database. This is done using the reverse utility. Last, we will see how we can set up an **Integrated Capture Extract** to read data from compressed tables using a downstream database.

Upgrading Oracle GoldenGate binaries

In this recipe you will learn how to upgrade GoldenGate binaries. You will also learn about GoldenGate patches and how to apply them.

Getting ready

For this recipe, we will upgrade the GoldenGate binaries from version 11.2.1.0.1 to 11.2.1.0.3 on the source system, that is `prim1-ol6-112` in our case. Both of these binaries are available from the Oracle Edelivery website under the part number V32400-01 and V34339-01 respectively. 11.2.1.0.1 binaries are installed under `/u01/app/ggate/112101`.

How to do it...

The steps to upgrade the Oracle GoldenGate binaries are:

1. Make a new directory for 11.2.1.0.3 binaries:

   ```
   mkdir /u01/app/ggate/112103
   ```

2. Copy the binaries ZIP file to the server in the new directory.

3. Unzip the binaries file:

   ```
   [ggate@prim1-ol6-112 112103]$ cd /u01/app/ggate/112103
   [ggate@prim1-ol6-112 112103]$ unzip V34339-01.zip
   Archive:  V34339-01.zip
   inflating: fbo_ggs_Linux_x64_ora11g_64bit.tar
   inflating: Oracle_GoldenGate_11.2.1.0.3_README.doc
   inflating: Oracle GoldenGate_11.2.1.0.3_README.txt
   inflating: OGG_WinUnix_Rel_Notes_11.2.1.0.3.pdf
   ```

4. Install the new binaries in `/u01/app/ggate/112103`:

   ```
   [ggate@prim1-ol6-112 112103]$ tar -pxvf fbo_ggs_Linux_x64_
   ora11g_64bit.tar
   ```

5. Stop the processes in the existing installation:

   ```
   [ggate@prim1-ol6-112 112103]$ cd /u01/app/ggate/112101
   [ggate@prim1-ol6-112 112101]$ ./ggsci
   ```

```
Oracle GoldenGate Command Interpreter for Oracle

Version 11.2.1.0.1 OGGCORE_11.2.1.0.1_PLATFORMS_120423.0230_FBO

Linux, x64, 64bit (optimized), Oracle 11g on Apr 23 2012 08:32:14


Copyright (C) 1995, 2012, Oracle and/or its affiliates. All rights
reserved.


GGSCI (prim1-ol6-112.localdomain) 1> stop *


Sending STOP request to EXTRACT EGGTEST1 ...

Request processed.

Sending STOP request to EXTRACT PGGTEST1 ...

Request processed.
```

6. Stop the manager process:

```
GGSCI (prim1-ol6-112.localdomain) 2> STOP MGR

Manager process is required by other GGS processes.

Are you sure you want to stop it (y/n)? y

Sending STOP request to MANAGER ...

Request processed.

Manager stopped.
```

7. Copy the subdirectories to the new binaries:

```
[ggate@prim1-ol6-112 112101]$ cp -R dirprm /u01/app/ggate/112103/

[ggate@prim1-ol6-112 112101]$ cp -R dirrpt /u01/app/ggate/112103/

[ggate@prim1-ol6-112 112101]$ cp -R dirchk /u01/app/ggate/112103/

[ggate@prim1-ol6-112 112101]$ cp -R BR /u01/app/ggate/112103/

[ggate@prim1-ol6-112 112101]$ cp -R dirpcs /u01/app/ggate/112103/

 [ggate@prim1-ol6-112 112101]$ cp -R dirdef /u01/app/ggate/112103/

[ggate@prim1-ol6-112 112101]$ cp -R dirout /u01/app/ggate/112103/

[ggate@prim1-ol6-112 112101]$ cp -R dirdat /u01/app/ggate/112103/

[ggate@prim1-ol6-112 112101]$ cp -R dirtmp /u01/app/ggate/112103/
```

8. Modify any parameter files under dirprm if you have hardcoded old binaries path in them.

9. Edit the `ggate` user profile and update the value of the GoldenGate binaries home:

   ```
   vi .profile

   export GG_HOME=/u01/app/ggate/112103
   ```

10. Start the manager process from the new binaries:

    ```
    [ggate@prim1-ol6-112 ~]$ cd /u01/app/ggate/112103/
    [ggate@prim1-ol6-112 112103]$ ./ggsci

    Oracle GoldenGate Command Interpreter for Oracle
    Version 11.2.1.0.3 14400833 OGGCORE_11.2.1.0.3_
    PLATFORMS_120823.1258_FBO
    Linux, x64, 64bit (optimized), Oracle 11g on Aug 23 2012 20:20:21

    Copyright (C) 1995, 2012, Oracle and/or its affiliates. All rights
    reserved.

    GGSCI (prim1-ol6-112.localdomain) 1> START MGR

    Manager started.
    ```

11. Start the processes:

    ```
    GGSCI (prim1-ol6-112.localdomain) 18> START EXTRACT *

    Sending START request to MANAGER ...
    EXTRACT EGGTEST1 starting
    Sending START request to MANAGER ...
    EXTRACT PGGTEST1 starting
    ```

How it works...

The method to upgrade the GoldenGate binaries is quite straightforward. As seen in the preceding section, you need to download and install the binaries on the server in a new directory. After this, you would stop the all GoldenGate processes that are running from the existing binaries. Then you would copy all the important GoldenGate directories with parameter files, trail files, report files, checkpoint files, and recovery files to the new binaries. If your trail files are kept on a separate filesystem which is linked to the `dirdat` directory using a softlink, then you would just need to create a new softlink under the new GoldenGate binaries home. Once all the files are copied, you would need to modify the parameter files if you have the path of the existing binaries hardcoded in them. The same would also need to be done in the OS profile of the `ggate` user. After this, you just start the manager process and rest of the processes from the new home.

GoldenGate patches are all delivered as full binaries sets. This makes the procedure to patch the binaries exactly the same as performing major release upgrades.

Table structure changes in GoldenGate environments with similar table definitions

Almost all of the applications systems in IT undergo some change over a period of time. This change might include a fix of an identified bug, an enhancement or some configuration change required due to change in any other part of the system. The data that you would replicate using GoldenGate will most likely be part of some application schema. These schemas, just like the application software, sometimes require some changes which are driven by the application vendor. If you are replicating DDL along with DML in your environment then these schema changes will most likely be replicated by GoldenGate itself. However, if you are only replicating only DML and there are any DDL changes in the schema particularly around the tables that you are replicating, then these will affect the replication and might even break it.

In this recipe, you will learn how to update the GoldenGate configuration to accommodate the schema changes that are done to the source system. This recipe assumes that the definitions of the tables that are replicated are similar in both the source and target databases.

Getting ready

For this recipe we will refer to the setup done in the *Setting up a simple GoldenGate replication configuration between two single node databases* recipe in *Chapter 2, Setting up GoldenGate Replication*. For this recipe we are making the following assumptions:

1. GoldenGate is set up to replicate only DML changes between the source and target environments.

2. The application will be stopped for making schema changes in the source environment.

3. The table structures in the source and target database are similar.

4. The replication is configured for all objects owned by a SCOTT user using a SCOTT.* clause.

5. The GoldenGate Admin user has been granted SELECT ANY TABLE in the source database and INSERT ANY TABLE, DELETE ANY TABLE, UPDATE ANY TABLE, SELECT ANY TABLE in the target database.

The schema changes performed in this recipe are as follows:

1. Add a new column called DOB (DATE) to the EMP table.

2. Modify the DNAME column in the DEPT table to VARCHAR(20).

3. Add a new table called `ITEMS` to the `SCOTT` schema:

   ```
   ITEMS

   ITEMNO     NUMBER(5)     PRIMARY KEY
   NAME       VARCHAR(20)
   ```

4. Add a new table called `SALES` to the `SCOTT` schema:

   ```
   SALES

   INVOICENO   NUMBER(9)        PRIMARY KEY
   ITEMNO      NUMBER(5)        FOREIGN KEY     ITEMS(ITEMNO)
   EMPNO       NUMBER(4)        FOREIGN KEY     EMP(EMPNO)
   ```

5. Load the values for the `DOB` column in the `EMP` table.

6. Load a few records in the `ITEMS` table.

How to do it...

Here are the steps that you can follow to implement the preceding schema changes in the source environment:

1. Ensure that the application accessing the source database is stopped. There should not be any process modifying the data in the database.

2. Once you have stopped the application, wait for 2 to 3 minutes so that all pending redo is processed by the GoldenGate extract.

3. Check the latest timestamp read by the Extract and Datapump processes and ensure it is the current timestamp:

   ```
   GGSCI (prim1-ol6-112.localdomain) 9> INFO EXTRACT EGGTEST1


   GGSCI (prim1-ol6-112.localdomain) 10> INFO EXTRACT *


   EXTRACT     EGGTEST1   Last Started 2013-03-25 22:24    Status
   RUNNING
   Checkpoint Lag          00:00:00 (updated 00:00:07 ago)
   Log Read Checkpoint   Oracle Redo Logs
           2013-03-25 22:35:06   Seqno 350, RBA 11778560
           SCN 0.11806849 (11806849)


   EXTRACT     PGGTEST1   Last Started 2013-03-25 22:24    Status
   RUNNING
   Checkpoint Lag          00:00:00 (updated 00:00:04 ago)
   ```

```
Log Read Checkpoint  File /u01/app/ggate/dirdat/st000010

      2013-03-25 22:35:05.000000  RBA 7631
```

4. Stop the Extract and Datapump processes in the source environment:

```
GGSCI (prim1-ol6-112.localdomain) 1> STOP EXTRACT *

Sending STOP request to EXTRACT EGGTEST1 ...
Request processed.

Sending STOP request to EXTRACT PGGTEST1 ...
Request processed.
```

5. Check the status of the Replicat process in the target environment and ensure that it has processed the timestamp noted in step 3:

```
GGSCI (stdby1-ol6-112.localdomain) 54> INFO REPLICAT *

REPLICAT    RGGTEST1  Last Started 2013-03-25 22:25    Status
RUNNING
Checkpoint Lag        00:00:00 (updated 00:00:04 ago)
Log Read Checkpoint  File ./dirdat/rt000061
             2013-03-25 22:37:04.950188  RBA 10039
```

6. Stop the Replicat process in the target environment:

```
GGSCI (stdby1-ol6-112.localdomain) 48> STOP REPLICAT *

Sending STOP request to REPLICAT RGGTEST1 ...
Request processed.
```

7. Apply the schema changes to the source database:

```
SQL> ALTER TABLE SCOTT.EMP ADD DOB DATE;
Table altered.

SQL> ALTER TABLE SCOTT.DEPT MODIFY DNAME VARCHAR(20);
Table altered.

SQL> CREATE TABLE SCOTT.ITEMS (
ITEMNO NUMBER(5) PRIMARY KEY,
NAME VARCHAR(20));
Table created.
```

```
SQL> CREATE TABLE SCOTT.SALES (
INVOICENO NUMBER(9) PRIMARY KEY,
ITEMNO NUMBER(5) REFERENCES SCOTT.ITEMS(ITEMNO),
EMPNO NUMBER(4) REFERENCES SCOTT.EMP(EMPNO));
Table created.

SQL> UPDATE SCOTT.EMP SET DOB=TO_DATE('01-01-1980','DD-MM-YYYY');
14 rows updated.

SQL> INSERT INTO SCOTT.ITEMS VALUES (1,'IRON');
1 row created.

SQL> INSERT INTO SCOTT.ITEMS VALUES (2,'COPPER');
1 row created.

SQL> INSERT INTO SCOTT.ITEMS VALUES (3,'GOLD');
1 row created.

SQL> INSERT INTO SCOTT.ITEMS VALUES (4,'SILVER');
1 row created.

SQL> COMMIT;
Commit complete.
```

8. Apply the schema changes to the target database:

```
SQL> ALTER TABLE SCOTT.EMP ADD DOB DATE;
Table altered.

SQL> ALTER TABLE SCOTT.DEPT MODIFY DNAME VARCHAR(20);
Table altered.

SQL> CREATE TABLE SCOTT.ITEMS (
ITEMNO NUMBER(5) PRIMARY KEY,
NAME VARCHAR(20));
Table created.
```

```
SQL> CREATE TABLE SCOTT.SALES (
INVOICENO NUMBER(9) PRIMARY KEY,
ITEMNO NUMBER(5) REFERENCES SCOTT.ITEMS(ITEMNO),
EMPNO NUMBER(4) REFERENCES SCOTT.EMP(EMPNO));
Table created.

SQL> UPDATE SCOTT.EMP SET DOB=TO_DATE('01-01-1980','DD-MM-YYYY');
14 rows updated.

SQL> INSERT INTO SCOTT.ITEMS VALUES (1,'IRON');
1 row created.

SQL> INSERT INTO SCOTT.ITEMS VALUES (2,'COPPER');
1 row created.

SQL> INSERT INTO SCOTT.ITEMS VALUES (3,'GOLD');
1 row created.

SQL> INSERT INTO SCOTT.ITEMS VALUES (4,'SILVER');
1 row created.

SQL> COMMIT;
Commit complete.
```

9. Add supplemental logging for the newly added tables:

```
GGSCI (prim1-o16-112.localdomain) 4> DBLOGIN USERID GGATE_ADMIN@
DBORATEST
Password:
Successfully logged into database.

GGSCI (prim1-o16-112.localdomain) 5> ADD TRANDATA SCOTT.ITEMS

Logging of supplemental redo data enabled for table SCOTT.ITEMS.

GGSCI (prim1-o16-112.localdomain) 6> ADD TRANDATA SCOTT.SALES

Logging of supplemental redo data enabled for table SCOTT.SALES.
```

10. Alter the Extract and Datapump processes to skip the changes generated by the Application Schema Patch:

```
GGSCI (prim1-ol6-112.localdomain) 7> ALTER EXTRACT EGGTEST1 BEGIN NOW

EXTRACT altered.


GGSCI (prim1-ol6-112.localdomain) 8> ALTER EXTRACT PGGTEST1 BEGIN NOW

EXTRACT altered.
```

11. Start the Extract and Datapump in the source environment:

```
GGSCI (prim1-ol6-112.localdomain) 9> START EXTRACT *


Sending START request to MANAGER ...
EXTRACT EGGTEST1 starting


Sending START request to MANAGER ...
EXTRACT PGGTEST1 starting
```

12. Start the Replicat process in the target environment:

```
GGSCI (stdby1-ol6-112.localdomain) 56> START REPLICAT RGGTEST1


Sending START request to MANAGER ...
REPLICAT RGGTEST1 starting
```

How it works...

The preceding steps cover a high level procedure that you can follow to modify the structure of the replicated tables in your GoldenGate configuration. Before you start to alter any processes or parameter file, you need to ensure that the applications are stopped and no user sessions in the database are modifying the data in the tables that you are replicating. Once the application is stopped, we check that all the redo data has been processed by GoldenGate processes and then stop. At this point we run the scripts that need to be run to make DDL changes to the database. This step needs to be run on both the source and target database as we will not be replicating these changes using GoldenGate. Once this is done, we alter the GoldenGate processes to start from the current time and start them.

There's more...

Some of the assumptions made in the earlier procedure might not hold true for all environments. Let's see what needs to be done in such cases where the environment does not satisfy these conditions:

Specific tables defined in GoldenGate parameter files

Unlike the earlier example, where the tables are defined in the parameter files using a schema qualifier for example SCOTT.*, if you have individual tables defined in the GoldenGate parameter files, you would need to modify the GoldenGate parameter files to add these newly created tables to include them in replication.

Individual table permissions granted to the GoldenGate Admin user

If you have granted table-specific permissions to the GoldenGate Admin user in the source and target environments, you would need to grant them on the newly added tables to allow the GoldenGate user to read their data in the source environment and also to apply the changes to these tables in the target environment.

Supplemental logging for modified tables without any keys

If you are adding or deleting any columns from the tables in the source database which do not have any primary/unique keys, you would then need to drop the existing supplemental log group and read them. This is because when there are no primary/unique keys in a table, GoldenGate adds all columns to the supplemental log group. This supplemental log group will have to be modified when the structure of the underlying table is modified.

Supplemental log groups with all columns for modified tables

In some cases, you would need to enable supplemental logging on all columns of the source tables that you are replicating. This is mostly applicable for consolidation replication topologies where all changes are captured and converted into INSERTs in the target environment, which usually is a Data warehouse. In such cases, you need to drop and read the supplemental logging on the tables in which you are adding or removing any columns.

See also

▸ See the next *Table structure changes in GoldenGate environments with different table definitions* recipe

Table structure changes in GoldenGate environments with different table definitions

In this recipe you will learn how to perform table structure changes in a replication environment where the table structures in the source and target environments are not similar.

Getting ready

For this recipe we will refer to the setup done in *Setting up a GoldenGate replication between tables with different structures using defgen* in *Chapter 2, Setting up GoldenGate Replication*. For this recipe we are making the following assumptions:

1. GoldenGate is set up to replicate only DML changes between the source and target environments.

2. The application will be stopped for making schema changes in the source environment.

3. The table structures in the source and target databases are not similar.

4. The GoldenGate Admin user has been granted `SELECT ANY TABLE` in the source database and `INSERT ANY TABLE`, `DELETE ANY TABLE`, `UPDATE ANY TABLE`, `SELECT ANY TABLE` in the target database.

5. The definition file was generated for the source schema and is configured in the replicat parameter file.

The schema changes performed in this recipe are as follows:

1. Add a new column called `DOB (DATE)` to the `EMP` table.

2. Modify the `DNAME` column in the `DEPT` table to `VARCHAR(20)`.

3. Add a new table called `ITEMS` to the `SCOTT` schema:

   `ITEMS`

`ITEMNO`	`NUMBER(5)`	`PRIMARY KEY`
`NAME`	`VARCHAR(20)`	

4. Add a new table called `SALES` to the `SCOTT` schema:

   `SALES`

`INVOICENO`	`NUMBER(9)`	`PRIMARY KEY`	
`ITEMNO`	`NUMBER(5)`	`FOREIGN KEY`	`ITEMS(ITEMNO)`
`EMPNO`	`NUMBER(4)`	`FOREIGN KEY`	`EMP(EMPNO)`

5. Load the values for the DOB column in the EMP table.

6. Load a few records in the ITEMS table.

How to do it...

Here are the steps that you can follow to implement the previous schema changes in the source environment:

1. Ensure that the application accessing the source database is stopped. There should not be any process modifying the data in the database.

2. Once you have stopped the application, wait for 2 to 3 minutes so that all pending redo is processed by the GoldenGate extract.

3. Check the latest timestamp read by the Extract and Datapump process, and ensure it is the current timestamp:

```
GGSCI (prim1-ol6-112.localdomain) 9> INFO EXTRACT EGGTEST1


GGSCI (prim1-ol6-112.localdomain) 10> INFO EXTRACT *


EXTRACT      EGGTEST1   Last Started 2013-03-28 10:12   Status RUNNING
Checkpoint Lag        00:00:00 (updated 00:00:07 ago)
Log Read Checkpoint   Oracle Redo Logs
         2013-03-28 10:16:06   Seqno 352, RBA 12574320
         SCN 0.11973456 (11973456)


EXTRACT      PGGTEST1   Last Started 2013-03-28 10:12     Status
RUNNING
Checkpoint Lag        00:00:00 (updated 00:00:04 ago)
Log Read Checkpoint   File /u01/app/ggate/dirdat/st000010
         2013-03-28 10:15:43.000000   RBA 8450
```

4. Stop the Extract and Datapump processes in the source environment:

```
GGSCI (prim1-ol6-112.localdomain) 1> STOP EXTRACT *


Sending STOP request to EXTRACT EGGTEST1 ...
Request processed.


Sending STOP request to EXTRACT PGGTEST1 ...
Request processed.
```

5. Check the status of the Replicat process in the target environment and ensure that it has processed the timestamp noted in step 3:

```
GGSCI (stdby1-ol6-112.localdomain) 54> INFO REPLICAT *


REPLICAT    RGGTEST1   Last Started 2013-03-28 10:15    Status
RUNNING
Checkpoint Lag         00:00:00 (updated 00:00:04 ago)
Log Read Checkpoint   File ./dirdat/rt000062
            2013-03-28 10:15:04.950188   RBA 10039
```

6. Stop the Replicat process in the target environment:

```
GGSCI (stdby1-ol6-112.localdomain) 48> STOP REPLICAT *


Sending STOP request to REPLICAT RGGTEST1 ...
Request processed.
```

7. Apply the schema changes to the source database:

```
SQL> ALTER TABLE SCOTT.EMP ADD DOB DATE;
Table altered.


SQL> ALTER TABLE SCOTT.DEPT MODIFY DNAME VARCHAR(20);
Table altered.


SQL> CREATE TABLE SCOTT.ITEMS (
ITEMNO NUMBER(5) PRIMARY KEY,
NAME VARCHAR(20));
Table created.


SQL> CREATE TABLE SCOTT.SALES (
INVOICENO NUMBER(9) PRIMARY KEY,
ITEMNO NUMBER(5) REFERENCES SCOTT.ITEMS(ITEMNO),
EMPNO NUMBER(4) REFERENCES SCOTT.EMP(EMPNO));
Table created.


SQL> UPDATE SCOTT.EMP SET DOB=TO_DATE('01-01-1980','DD-MM-YYYY');
14 rows updated.
```

```
SQL> INSERT INTO SCOTT.ITEMS VALUES (1,'IRON');
1 row created.


SQL> INSERT INTO SCOTT.ITEMS VALUES (2,'COPPER');
1 row created.


SQL> INSERT INTO SCOTT.ITEMS VALUES (3,'GOLD');
1 row created.


SQL> INSERT INTO SCOTT.ITEMS VALUES (4,'SILVER');
1 row created.


SQL> COMMIT;
Commit complete.
```

8. Apply the schema changes to the target database:

```
SQL> ALTER TABLE SCOTT.EMP ADD DOB DATE;
Table altered.


SQL> ALTER TABLE SCOTT.DEPT MODIFY DNAME VARCHAR(20);
Table altered.


SQL> CREATE TABLE SCOTT.ITEMS (
ITEMNO NUMBER(5) PRIMARY KEY,
NAME VARCHAR(20));
Table created.


SQL> CREATE TABLE SCOTT.SALES (
INVOICENO NUMBER(9) PRIMARY KEY,
ITEMNO NUMBER(5) REFERENCES SCOTT.ITEMS(ITEMNO),
EMPNO NUMBER(4) REFERENCES SCOTT.EMP(EMPNO));
Table created.


SQL> UPDATE SCOTT.EMP SET DOB=TO_DATE('01-01-1980','DD-MM-YYYY');
14 rows updated.
```

```
SQL> INSERT INTO SCOTT.ITEMS VALUES (1,'IRON');
1 row created.


SQL> INSERT INTO SCOTT.ITEMS VALUES (2,'COPPER');
1 row created.


SQL> INSERT INTO SCOTT.ITEMS VALUES (3,'GOLD');
1 row created.


SQL> INSERT INTO SCOTT.ITEMS VALUES (4,'SILVER');
1 row created.


SQL> COMMIT;
Commit complete.
```

9. Add supplemental logging for the newly added tables:

```
GGSCI (prim1-ol6-112.localdomain) 4> DBLOGIN USERID GGATE_ADMIN@
DBORATEST
Password:
Successfully logged into database.


GGSCI (prim1-ol6-112.localdomain) 5> ADD TRANDATA SCOTT.ITEMS


Logging of supplemental redo data enabled for table SCOTT.ITEMS.


GGSCI (prim1-ol6-112.localdomain) 6> ADD TRANDATA SCOTT.SALES


Logging of supplemental redo data enabled for table SCOTT.SALES.
```

10. Update the parameter file for generating definitions as follows:

```
vi $GG_HOME/dirprm/defs.prm


DEFSFILE ./dirdef/defs.def
USERID ggate_admin@dboratest, PASSWORD XXXX
TABLE SCOTT.EMP;
TABLE SCOTT.DEPT;
TABLE SCOTT.BONUS;
```

```
TABLE SCOTT.DUMMY;
TABLE SCOTT.SALGRADE;
TABLE SCOTT.ITEMS;
TABLE SCOTT.SALES;
```

11. Generate the definitions in the source environment:

    `./defgen paramfile ./dirprm/defs.prm`

12. Push the definitions file to the target server using `scp`:

    `scp ./dirdef/defs.def stdby1-ol6-112:/u01/app/ggate/dirdef/`

13. Edit the Extract and Datapump process parameter to include the newly created tables if you have specified individual table names in them.

14. Alter the Extract and Datapump processes to skip the changes generated by the Application Schema Patch:

    ```
    GGSCI (prim1-ol6-112.localdomain) 7> ALTER EXTRACT EGGTEST1 BEGIN
    NOW

    EXTRACT altered.


    GGSCI (prim1-ol6-112.localdomain) 8> ALTER EXTRACT PGGTEST1 BEGIN
    NOW

    EXTRACT altered.
    ```

15. Start the Extract and Datapump in the source environment:

    ```
    GGSCI (prim1-ol6-112.localdomain) 9> START EXTRACT *


    Sending START request to MANAGER ...
    EXTRACT EGGTEST1 starting


    Sending START request to MANAGER ...
    EXTRACT PGGTEST1 starting
    ```

16. Edit the Replicat process parameter file to include the tables:

    ```
    ./ggsci
    EDIT PARAMS RGGTEST1
    REPLICAT RGGTEST1
    USERID GGATE_ADMIN@TGORTEST, PASSWORD GGATE_ADMIN
    DISCARDFILE /u01/app/ggate/dirrpt/RGGTEST1.dsc,append,MEGABYTES
    500
    SOURCEDEFS ./dirdef/defs.def
    ```

```
MAP SCOTT.BONUS, TARGET SCOTT.BONUS;
MAP SCOTT.SALGRADE, TARGET SCOTT.SALGRADE;
MAP SCOTT.DEPT, TARGET SCOTT.DEPT;
MAP SCOTT.DUMMY, TARGET SCOTT.DUMMY;
MAP SCOTT.EMP, TARGET SCOTT.EMP;
MAP SCOTT.EMP,TARGET SCOTT.EMP_DIFFCOL_ORDER;
MAP SCOTT.EMP, TARGET SCOTT.EMP_EXTRACOL, COLMAP(USEDEFAULTS,
LAST_UPDATE_TIME = @DATENOW ());
MAP SCOTT.SALES, TARGET SCOTT.SALES;
MAP SCOTT.ITEMS, TARGET SCOTT.ITEMS;
```

17. Start the Replicat process in the target environment:

```
GGSCI (stdby1-ol6-112.localdomain) 56> START REPLICAT RGGTEST1

Sending START request to MANAGER ...
REPLICAT RGGTEST1 starting
```

How it works...

You can follow the previously mentioned procedure to apply any DDL changes to the tables in the source database. This procedure is valid for environments where existing table structures between the source and the target databases are not similar.

The key things to note in this method are:

1. The changes should only be made when all the changes extracted by GoldenGate are applied to the target database, and the replication processes are stopped.
2. Once the DDL changes have been performed in the source database, the definitions file needs to be regenerated.
3. The changes that you are making to the table structures needs to be performed on both sides.

There's more...

Some of the assumptions made in the earlier procedure might not hold true for all environments. Let's see what needs to be done in cases where the environment does not satisfy these conditions:

Individual table permissions granted to the GoldenGate Admin user

If you have granted table-specific permissions to the GoldenGate Admin user in the source and target environments, you would need to grant them on the newly added tables to allow the GoldenGate user to read their data in the source environment and also to apply the changes to these tables in the target environment.

Supplemental logging for modified tables without any keys

If you are adding or deleting any columns from the tables in the source database which do not have any primary/unique keys, you would then need to drop the existing supplemental log group and read them. This is because when there are no primary/unique keys in a table, GoldenGate adds all columns to the supplemental log group. This supplemental log group will need to be modified when the structure of the underlying table is modified.

Supplemental log groups with all columns for modified tables

In some cases, you would need to enable supplemental logging on all columns of the source tables that you are replicating. This is mostly applicable for consolidation replication topologies where all changes are captured and converted into INSERTs in the target environment, which usually is a Data warehouse. In such cases, you need to drop and read the supplemental logging on the tables in which you are adding or removing any columns.

Resolving GoldenGate errors using the logdump utility

So far we have learned in previous recipes how to use various GoldenGate commands to manage GoldenGate processes and scan the logs. If there is an issue in the replication and the processes have abended, you can always restart them. But if the processes abended due to some data error, then a restart will not resolve the issue and you would then need to drill down further to find the exact cause of the data error. GoldenGate uses a proprietary format to write data to the trail files. Because of this you cannot just open the trail file in an editor and see its contents.

In this recipe we will learn how to use a tool called logdump using which you can view the contents of a trail file. If the replication abends due to a particular record, you can evaluate the values of the failing record and then understand why it is failing. This will help you to decide the further course of action to fix the replication.

Getting ready

In this recipe we will go through a simple replication setup between the tables of a SCOTT schema which is failing due to a missing row in the target table. GoldenGate extract has mined a DELETE record from the source environment, but when the replicat is trying to apply this to the target environment, it is failing. Because of this missing row in the target environment the replication is unable to continue further.

How to do it...

The steps to resolve this issue and resume the replication are as follows:

1. The last statements that ran in the source environment were:

    ```
    SQL> DELETE SCOTT.EMP WHERE EMPNO=7369;


    1 row deleted.


    SQL> INSERT INTO SCOTT.EMP VALUES (8800,'ROGER','ANALYST',7934,'23-
    DEC-1972',2300,0,10);


    1 row created.


    SQL> COMMIT;
    ```

2. The replicat is abended in the target environment. Let's verify its status:

    ```
    GGSCI (stdby1-ol6-112.localdomain) 2> status *
    REPLICAT RGGTEST1: ABENDED
    ```

3. The error from the replicat report file is:

    ```
    2013-05-01 00:41:11  WARNING OGG-01431  Aborted grouped
    transaction on 'SCOTT.EMP', Mapping error.


    2013-05-01 00:41:11  WARNING OGG-01003  Repositioning to rba 7874
    in seqno 65.


    2013-05-01 00:41:11  WARNING OGG-01151  Error mapping from SCOTT.
    EMP to SCOTT.EMP.


    2013-05-01 00:41:11  WARNING OGG-01003  Repositioning to rba 7874
    in seqno 65.


    Process Abending : 2013-04-30 22:57:07
    ```

4. Further details of the error can be checked from the discard file as follows:

```
Oracle GoldenGate Delivery for Oracle process started, group
RGGTEST1 discard file opened: 2013-04-30 22:59:57


Key column ENAME (1) is missing from delete on table SCOTT.EMP
Key column JOB (2) is missing from delete on table SCOTT.EMP
Key column MGR (3) is missing from delete on table SCOTT.EMP
Key column HIREDATE (4) is missing from delete on table SCOTT.EMP
Key column SAL (5) is missing from delete on table SCOTT.EMP
Key column COMM (6) is missing from delete on table SCOTT.EMP
Key column DEPTNO (7) is missing from delete on table SCOTT.EMP
Missing 7 key columns in delete for table SCOTT.EMP.
Current time: 2013-04-30 23:24:10
Discarded record from action ABEND on error 0


Aborting transaction on ./dirdat/rt beginning at seqno 63 rba
315017
                          error at seqno 63 rba 315017
Problem replicating SCOTT.EMP to SCOTT.EMP
Mapping problem with delete record (target format)...
*
EMPNO = 7369
*
Process Abending : 2013-04-30 23:24:10
```

5. Let's check whether this record exists in the target database or not:

```
SQL> SELECT * FROM SCOTT.EMP WHERE EMPNO=7369;


no rows selected
```

6. The current position of the Replicat process is:

```
GGSCI (stdby1-ol6-112.localdomain) 2> INFO RGGTEST1


REPLICAT    RGGTEST1   Last Started 2013-05-01 00:39    Status
ABENDED
Checkpoint Lag        00:00:00 (updated 00:00:23 ago)
Log Read Checkpoint  File ./dirdat/rt000065
                     2013-05-01 00:40:17.764177  RBA 7874
```

7. Start the logdump utility:

   ```
   [ggate@stdby1-ol6-112 ggate]$ cd /u01/app/ggate
   [ggate@stdby1-ol6-112 ggate]$ ./logdump
   ```

8. Open the trail file sequence 65:

   ```
   Logdump 10 >open ./dirdat/rt000065
   Current LogTrail is /u01/app/ggate/dirdat/rt000063
   ```

9. Set up the logdump utility to show the additional useful information:

   ```
   Logdump 11 >ghdr on
   Logdump 12 >detail on
   Logdump 13 >detail data
   ```

10. Position the logdump to the position of the failing record in the trail file:

    ```
    Logdump 16 >pos 7874
    Reading forward from RBA 7874
    ```

11. Now list the failing record:

    ```
    Logdump 17 >n
    ```

    ```
    Hdr-Ind     :     E  (x45)    Partition  :      . (x04)
    UndoFlag    :     .  (x00)    BeforeAfter:      B (x42)
    RecLength   :    14  (x000e)  IO Time    : 2013/05/01
    00:41:06.681.212
    IOType      :     3  (x03)    OrigNode   :    255 (xff)
    TransInd    :     .  (x00)    FormatType :      R (x52)
    SyskeyLen   :     0  (x00)    Incomplete :      . (x00)
    AuditRBA    :        356      AuditPos   : 23233552
    Continued   :     N  (x00)    RecCount   :      1 (x01)


    2013/05/01 00:41:06.681.212 Delete           Len    14 RBA
    7874
    Name: SCOTT.EMP
    Before Image:                                        Partition
    4    G  b
     0000 000a 0000 0000 0000 0000 1cc9            |
    . . . . . . . . . . . . .
    Column       0 (x0000), Len    10 (x000a)
    ```

12. We want to skip this record and find the position of the next one:

```
Logdump 164 >n
```

```
:     E   (x45)       Partition  :      .   (x04)

UndoFlag    :       .  (x00)      BeforeAfter:      A   (x41)

RecLength   :     123  (x007b)    IO Time    : 2013/05/01
00:41:06.681.212

IOType      :       5  (x05)      OrigNode   :     255  (xff)

TransInd    :       .  (x02)      FormatType :       R   (x52)

SyskeyLen   :       0  (x00)      Incomplete :       .  (x00)

AuditRBA    :         356         AuditPos   : 23234576

Continued   :       N  (x00)      RecCount   :       1  (x01)


2013/05/01 00:41:06.681.212 Insert              Len    123 RBA
8002

Name: SCOTT.EMP

After   Image:                                       Partition
4   G   e
 0000 000a 0000 0000 0000 0000 2260 0001 0009 0000 |
. . . . . . . . . . . ." `. . . . . .

 0005 524f 4745 5200 0200 0b00 0000 0741 4e41 4c59 |
. .ROGER. . . . . . . .ANALY

 5354 0003 000a 0000 0000 0000 0000 1efe 0004 0015 |
ST. . . . . . . . . . . . . . . . .

 0000 3139 3732 2d31 322d 3233 3a30 303a 3030 3a30 | ..1972-12-
23:00:00:0

 3000 0500 0a00 0000 0000 0000 0382 7000 0600 0a00 |
0. . . . . . . . . . . . . .p. . . . .

 0000 0000 0000 0000 0000 0700 0a00 0000 0000 0000 |
. . . . . . . . . . . . . . . . . .

 0000 0a                                            |  . . .

Column      0 (x0000), Len    10 (x000a)

Column      1 (x0001), Len     9 (x0009)

Column      2 (x0002), Len    11 (x000b)

Column      3 (x0003), Len    10 (x000a)

Column      4 (x0004), Len    21 (x0015)

Column      5 (x0005), Len    10 (x000a)

Column      6 (x0006), Len    10 (x000a)

Column      7 (x0007), Len    10 (x000a)
```

13. Position the replicat to the RBA of this record that is 8002:

```
GGSCI (stdby1-ol6-112.localdomain) 1> alter replicat rggtest1,
extrba 8002
REPLICAT altered.
```

14. Start the replicat:

```
GGSCI (stdby1-ol6-112.localdomain) 2> start replicat rggtest1


Sending START request to MANAGER ...
REPLICAT RGGTEST1 starting
```

15. Verify the newly inserted record in the target environment:

```
SQL> SELECT * FROM EMP WHERE EMPNO=8800;


EMPNO ENAME   JOB     MGR HIREDATE    SAL  COMM    DEPTNO
---------- ------  ----  ---------  ------ ----  -----------
8800 ROGER  ANALYST  7934 23-DEC-72  2300  0        10
```

How it works...

This is a very simple example of a typical data mismatch issue in a GoldenGate environment. A record was deleted from the EMP table in the source database and this record was extracted by the GoldenGate processes. When the Replicat process tried to apply it to the target environment, it failed as the record does not exist in the target environment.

While troubleshooting such issues, the first thing that one should check is why is the data different in the target database. There could be something else modifying the data in the target database. Once you have identified the source of the second modification and taken care of that, you need to fix this data anamoly and continue the replication. For this we use a GoldenGate tool called logdump. Using logdump you can scan through the trail files to see their contents and you can move through various records in the trail file.

In the earlier example, we first check the status of the Replicat process and verify that it is abended. Since the process is abended, we check the reason from the report/discard file. From steps 3 and 4, it is quite clear that the process abended as it could not apply the delete record. Next we note the current sequence number and RBA of the Replicat process. We will then use logdump to dump the contents of this trail file and this RBA. In steps 7 and 8, we start the logdump and open this trail file. By default, logdump does not display the header record when you view a data record. We instruct logdump in step 9 using ghdr on and detail the data command to output the metadata information as well. After this we move the current pointer in the trail file to where the Replicat process was failing and then we dump the next record using the n command. This is the failing record and we want to skip this, so we run the n command again to move to the next record. You can see in step 12 that this is the Insert record that was executed in the source database after this delete. This is the point from which we want the Replicat process to continue. So we alter the Replicat process to start from this RBA and resume it. Once the process is resumed it continues working fine. In step 15, we verify that the Insert record was applied to the target database by checking the Insert record from the database.

There's more...

Logdump is a very handy tool when it comes to troubleshooting various data issues in a GoldenGate replication. There are a few other important commands in the logdump which we will discuss here:

Count

With the `count` command you can count the number of records in a GoldenGate trail file:

```
Logdump 166 >count
LogTrail /u01/app/ggate/dirdat/rt000065 has 33 records
Total Data Bytes              5363
   Avg Bytes/Record            162
Delete                          1
Insert                          1
FieldComp                      28
RestartOK                       2
Others                          1
Before Images                   1
After Images                   31


Average of 6 Transactions
       Bytes/Trans .....      1157
       Records/Trans ...         5
       Files/Trans .....         1
```

Scan for timestamp

Scan for timestamp is useful when you want to find a record that was modified at a particular timestamp in a trail file:

```
Logdump 167 >sfts 2013-05-01 00:33:00
Scan for timestamp >= 2013/04/30 23:33:00.000.000 GMT


2013/05/01 00:35:14.710.374 FieldComp              Len   121 RBA 1920
```

```
Name: SCOTT.EMP
After  Image:                                                    Partition 4   G
b
  0000 000a 0000 0000 0000 0000 1cc9 0001 0009 0000 |  ....................
  0005 534d 4954 4800 0200 0900 0000 0543 4c45 524b |  ..SMITH........CLERK
  0003 000a 0000 0000 0000 0000 1ede 0004 0015 0000 |  ....................
  3139 3830 2d31 322d 3137 3a30 303a 3030 3a30 3000 |  1980-12-17:00:00:00.
  0500 0a00 0000 0000 0000 0138 8000 0600 0aff ff00 |  ...........8........
  0000 0000 0000 0000 0700 0a00 0000 0000 0000 0000 |  ....................
  14                                                 |  .
```

Filter on SCN

If you know the SCN from the source database, you can scan the trail file for the SCN using the logdump `filter on csn` command as follows:

```
Logdump 210 >filter on csn 11910911
Logdump 211 >n

2013/05/01 00:11:46.633.724 FileHeader          Len   1786 RBA 0
Name: *FileHeader*
  3000 047d 3000 0008 4747 0d0a 544c 0a0d 3100 0002 | 0..}0...GG..TL..1...
  0003 3200 0004 2000 0000 3300 0008 02f2 01cf 94d4 | ..2... ...3.........
  4bfc 3400 0035 0033 7572 693a 7072 696d 312d 6f6c | K.4..5.3uri:prim1-ol
  362d 3131 323a 6c6f 6361 6c64 6f6d 6169 6e3a 3a75 | 6-112:localdomain::u
  3031 3a61 7070 3a67 6761 7465 3a31 3132 3130 3135 | 01:app:ggate:1121015
  0002 bb35 0000 3500 3375 7269 3a70 7269 6d31 2d6f | ...5..5.3uri:prim1-o
  6c36 2d31 3132 3a6c 6f63 616c 646f 6d61 696e 3a3a | 16-112:localdomain::
```

See also

> ▸ See the next recipe *Undoing the applied changes using the reverse utility*

Undoing the applied changes using the reverse utility

Part of the job of setting a GoldenGate replication consists of defining what to replicate. Once these rules are in place, GoldenGate processes scan the redo data for any records for the replicated tables. Most of the time, these changes are intended and generated by some application. However, sometimes some data updates are performed in the source environment by mistake and you would ideally not want them to be replicated to the target environment. In such scenarios, the administrator might want to roll back the changes performed. You can perform such tasks using the latest database technologies, for example, flashback. However, it is very difficult to roll back only a set of transactions from the database especially when you have applied complex filtering in the GoldenGate configuration. In such cases, you need another approach which will reverse the changes that were applied using GoldenGate. GoldenGate provides a reverse utility using which you can undo the changes in the target database. In this recipe we will go through how to configure and use this utility. We will do this by following a simple scenario in which a few statements are applied to the target database and then reversed.

Getting ready

For this recipe we will refer to the setup done in *Setting up a simple GoldenGate replication configuration between two single node databases* in *Chapter 2, Setting up GoldenGate Replication*. We will perform a few simple `INSERT/UPDATE/DELETE` operations on some tables owned by the SCOTT user. Once these changes are applied to the target database, we will verify them and then reverse those using the reverse utility.

How to do it...

In order to demonstrate reversing the changes applied by GoldenGate, let's first perform some changes in the source environment:

1. List the records in the `EMP` and `DEPT` table in the target database:

   ```
   SQL> SELECT * FROM EMP;
   ```

EMPNO	ENAME	JOB	MGR	HIREDATE	SAL	COMM	DEPTNO
7934	MILLER	CLERK	7782	23-JAN-82	1300		10
7902	FORD	ANALYST	7566	03-DEC-81	3000		20
7900	JAMES	CLERK	7698	03-DEC-81	950		30
7876	ADAMS	CLERK	7788	12-JAN-83	1100		20
7844	TURNER	SALESMAN	7698	08-SEP-81	1500	0	30
7839	KING	PRESIDENT		17-NOV-81	5000		10
7788	SCOTT	ANALYST	7566	09-DEC-82	3000		20
7782	CLARK	MANAGER	7839	09-JUN-81	2450		10
7698	BLAKE	MANAGER	7839	01-MAY-81	2850		30
7654	MARTIN	SALESMAN	7698	28-SEP-81	1250	1400	30
7566	JONES	MANAGER	7839	02-APR-81	2975		20
7521	WARD	SALESMAN	7698	22-FEB-81	1250	500	30

```
7499 ALLEN     SALESMAN   7698 20-FEB-81 1600   300        30
7369 SMITH     CLERK      7902 17-DEC-80  800              20

14 rows selected.

SQL> SELECT * FROM DEPT;

    DEPTNO  DNAME        LOC
---------- ------------- -------------
    10    ACCOUNTING   NEW YORK
    20     RESEARCH    DALLAS
    30       SALES     CHICAGO
    40     OPERATIONS  BOSTON
```
Run the following statements in the source database
```
SQL> SELECT TO_CHAR(SYSDATE,'DD-MON-YYYY HH24:MI:SS') FROM DUAL;

TO_CHAR(SYSDATE,'DD-MON-YYYYH
----------------------------
01-MAY-2013 21:22:36

SQL> DELETE EMP;

14 rows deleted.

SQL> INSERT INTO SCOTT.EMP VALUES (8800,'ROGER','ANALYST',7934,'23-
DEC-1972',2300,0,10);

1 row created.

SQL> INSERT INTO DEPT VALUES (50,'MARKETING','SAN JOSE');

1 row created.

SQL> COMMIT;

Commit complete.

SQL> SELECT TO_CHAR(SYSDATE,'DD-MON-YYYY HH24:MI:SS') FROM DUAL;

TO_CHAR(SYSDATE,'DD-MON-YYYYH
```

```
------------------------------
01-MAY-2013 21:23:52
```

2. Verify the current data in the EMP and DEPT table in the target database:

```
SQL> SELECT * FROM EMP;

EMPNO  ENAME   JOB     MGR  HIREDATE   SAL   COMM   DEPTNO
------ ------- --- ---- --------- ---- ---- ------
8800   ROGER   ANALYST 7934 23-DEC-72  2300  0      10

SQL> SELECT * FROM DEPT;

DEPTNO     DNAME       LOC
------ ---------- ---------------
    50     MARKETING   SAN JOSE
    10     ACCOUNTING  NEW YORK
    20     RESEARCH    DALLAS
    30     SALES       CHICAGO
    40     OPERATIONS  BOSTON
```

Now, we will run through the following steps to reverse the preceding changes:

1. Stop the Extract and Datapump processes in the source environment:

```
GGSCI (prim1-ol6-112.localdomain) 1> STOP EXTRACT *

Sending STOP request to EXTRACT EGGTEST1 ...
Request processed.

Sending STOP request to EXTRACT PGGTEST1 ...
Request processed.
```

2. Stop the Replicat process in the target environment:

```
GGSCI (stdby1-ol6-112.localdomain) 4> STOP RGGTEST1

Sending STOP request to REPLICAT RGGTEST1 ...
Request processed.
```

3. Set up an Extract in the source environment just to read the records between the timestamps that we noted in step 1:

    ```
    GGSCI (prim1-ol6-112.localdomain) 1> EDIT PARAMS EGGREVERSE
    EXTRACT EGGREVERSE
    USERID GGATE_ADMIN@DBORATEST, PASSWORD GGATE_ADMIN
    NOCOMPRESSDELETES
    GETUPDATEBEFORES
    END 2013-05-01 21:23:52
    RMTHOST stdby-ol6-112 , MGRPORT 8809
    RMTTRAIL /u01/app/ggate/dirdat/reverse/rt
    TABLE SCOTT.*;
    ```

4. Add the Extract to the source GoldenGate config:

    ```
    GGSCI (prim1-ol6-112.localdomain) 1> ADD EXTRACT EGGREV, TRANLOG,
    BEGIN 2013-05-01 21:22:36
    EXTRACT added.
    ```

5. Add the remote trail for the Extract:

    ```
    GGSCI (prim1-ol6-112.localdomain) 2> ADD RMTTRAIL /u01/app/ggate/
    dirdat/reverse/rt, EXTRACT EGGREV

    RMTTRAIL added.
    ```

6. Start the Extract process, it will only extract the records for the timestamps noted in step 1:

    ```
    GGSCI (prim1-ol6-112.localdomain) 3> start eggrev

    Sending START request to MANAGER ...
    EXTRACT EGGREV starting
    ```

7. The Extract process in step 8, created a trail file on the target system.

8. We will use the reverse utility to generate a trail file with reverse records:

    ```
    [ggate@stdby1-ol6-112 ggate]$ ./reverse ./dirdat/reverse/rt000000
    ./dirdat/reverse/st000000

    Oracle GoldenGate Dynamic Rollback
    Version 11.2.1.0.1 OGGCORE_11.2.1.0.1_PLATFORMS_120423.0230
    Linux, x64, 64bit (optimized) on Apr 23 2012 04:59:01
    ```

```
*Warning* Source file contained Deletes which maybe compressed
Reversed ./dirdat/reverse/rt000000 to /u01/app/ggate/dirdat/
reverse/st000000
Total Data Bytes          1890
  Avg Bytes/Record         118
Delete                      14
Insert                       2
Before Images               14
After Images                 2
```

9. Now we will create a Replicat process to apply the records generated in the ./
   dirdat/reverse/st000000 trail file:

```
GGSCI (stdby1-ol6-112.localdomain) 1> EDIT PARAMS RGGREV

REPLICAT RGGREV

USERID GGATE_ADMIN@TGORTEST, PASSWORD GGATE_ADMIN

END 2013-05-01 21:23:52

DISCARDFILE /u01/app/ggate/dirrpt/RGGREV.dsc,append,MEGABYTES 500

ASSUMETARGETDEFS

MAP SCOTT.*, TARGET SCOTT.*;
```

10. Add the replicat to the target GoldenGate configuration:

```
GGSCI (stdby1-ol6-112.localdomain) 3> ADD REPLICAT RGGREV,
EXTTRAIL ./dirdat/reverse/st, CHECKPOINTTABLE GGATE_ADMIN.
CHECKPOINT

REPLICAT added.
```

11. Start the replicat to apply the changes generated by the reverse utility:

```
GGSCI (stdby1-ol6-112.localdomain) 4> START REPLICAT RGGREV

Sending START request to MANAGER ...
REPLICAT RGGREV starting
```

12. Verify that the changes have been reversed in the target database and the data is as it was before the changes made in step 1:

```
SQL> SELECT * FROM EMP;
```

EMPNO	ENAME	JOB	MGR	HIREDATE	SAL	COMM	DEPTNO
7934	MILLER	CLERK	7782	23-JAN-82	1300		10
7902	FORD	ANALYST	7566	03-DEC-81	3000		20
7900	JAMES	CLERK	7698	03-DEC-81	950		30
7876	ADAMS	CLERK	7788	12-JAN-83	1100		20
7844	TURNER	SALESMAN	7698	08-SEP-81	1500	0	30
7839	KING	PRESIDENT		17-NOV-81	5000		10
7788	SCOTT	ANALYST	7566	09-DEC-82	3000		20
7782	CLARK	MANAGER	7839	09-JUN-81	2450		10
7698	BLAKE	MANAGER	7839	01-MAY-81	2850		30
7654	MARTIN	SALESMAN	7698	28-SEP-81	1250	1400	30
7566	JONES	MANAGER	7839	02-APR-81	2975		20
7521	WARD	SALESMAN	7698	22-FEB-81	1250	500	30
7499	ALLEN	SALESMAN	7698	20-FEB-81	1600	300	30
7369	SMITH	CLERK	7902	17-DEC-80	800		20

```
14 rows selected.

SQL> SELECT * FROM DEPT;
```

DEPTNO	DNAME	LOC
10	ACCOUNTING	NEW YORK
20	RESEARCH	DALLAS
30	SALES	CHICAGO
40	OPERATIONS	BOSTON

How it works...

The reverse utility is quite useful to roll back accidental changes that might have happened in an environment. You would need to determine a time slot during which the unwanted changes happened. Once you have determined the timeslot you can use GoldenGate to extract the changes occurred, reverse them, and apply the deltas to bring the data back to the state where it was.

In this recipe we first verify the current state of the data in the source and the target database, and then make some data modifications. We also capture the timestamps before and after making these changes. We then stop the current GoldenGate processes and create a new extract called EGGREV specifically to extract the changes for that timeslot. This extract also transfers the data to the remote trail file. So once the extract has stopped, we get a new trail file in the target system. This trail file is then fed into the reverse utility in step 8. The reverse utility reads this trail file and generates opposite records. These records are written to a new trail file. In steps 9 and 10, we create a new Replicat process called RGGREV using which the changes in this trail file are applied to the target database. Once the Replicat process has stopped we verify the data in the target database.

There's more...

The reverse utility reverses the operations by:

- Converting INSERTs to DELETEs
- Converting DELETEs to INSERTs
- Running UPDATEs with old values
- Reversing the sequence in which the statements were run

In order to enable the reverse utility to complete the preceding operations successfully, it is very crucial that you run the Extract process for capturing changes for reversing operations with the NOCOMPRESSDELETES and GETUPDATEBEFORES options.

> Always run the Extract process for reverse operations using the NOCOMPRESSDELETES and GETUPDATEBEFORES options, else the data might not be reversed to its original state.

There are a few data types for which reversing is not supported in Oracle. This is because GoldenGate does not generate/capture the before images of these data types. The unsupported data types for the reverse utility are:

- CLOB
- BLOB
- NCLOB

- ▸ LONG
- ▸ LONG RAW
- ▸ XMLType
- ▸ UDT
- ▸ Nested Tables
- ▸ VARRAY

Creating an Integrated Capture with a downstream database for compressed tables

Logical replication between two databases is a complex task. The level of complexity is quite dependent on the data types of the underlying data that you are replicating. When you add additional features offered by an Oracle database, for example compression, the complexity increases further. Until quite recently, Oracle GoldenGate did not support replicating data from a source database where the data was stored in compressed tables. With the launch of Oracle GoldenGate 11gR2, Oracle has added a new capture mode called Integrated Capture using which you can extract data from compressed tables. The Integrated Capture uses a logminer dictionary which you can either place in the source database itself, or in a separate database called the downstream database. In this recipe we will see how we can create an Integrated Capture extract to read data from compressed tables with a logminer dictionary created in a downstream database. The downstream mining will be set up in real-time mode so the downstream database will be configured with standby redo logs.

Getting ready

For this recipe we will refer to the setup done in *Setting up a simple GoldenGate replication configuration between two single node databases* in *Chapter 2, Setting up GoldenGate Replication*. For this recipe the EMP and DEPT tables in the SCOTT schema are compressed. We also have an additional database called downstrm which will hold the logminer dictionary. The downstrm database is a shell database in which archiving is enabled. We will perform some additional setup for GoldenGate in this database. The recipe does not cover the steps to create the shell database but does explain the additional steps required to set up the downstream mining and logminer dictionary in the downstream database. For this recipe, the downstream database is created on the same host as the source database. In a real world scenario, you would create the downstream database on a different host.

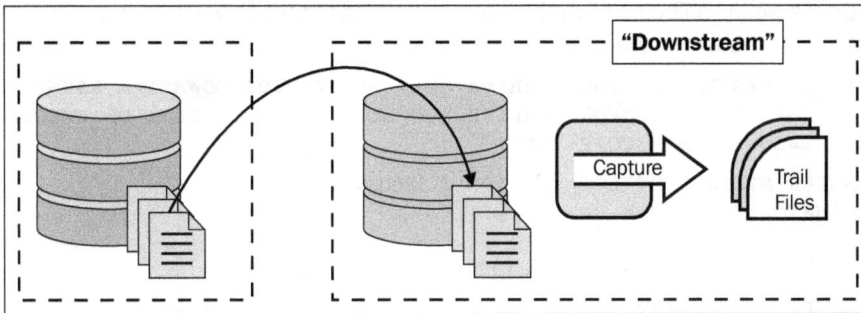

How to do it...

The steps to set up an Integrated Capture with a downstream database are as follows:

1. Compress the EMP and DEPT tables in the source database:

   ```
   ALTER TABLE EMP COMPRESS;
   ALTER TABLE DEPT COMPRESS;
   ```

2. Set up a tns entry for the downstrm database:

   ```
   DOWNSTRM =
   (DESCRIPTION =
   (ADDRESS = (PROTOCOL = TCP)(HOST = prim1-ol6-112)(PORT = 1521))
   (CONNECT_DATA =
   (SERVER = DEDICATED)
   (SERVICE_NAME = downstrm)))
   ```

3. Create standby redo log files in the downstrm database:

   ```
   alter database add standby logfile group 4 ('/u01/app/oracle/
   oradata/downstrm/std_redo04.log') size 50m;

   alter database add standby logfile group 5 ('/u01/app/oracle/
   oradata/downstrm/std_redo05.log') size 50m;

   alter database add standby logfile group 6 ('/u01/app/oracle/
   oradata/downstrm/std_redo06.log') size 50m;

   alter database add standby logfile group 7 ('/u01/app/oracle/
   oradata/downstrm/std_redo07.log') size 50m;
   ```

4. Configure log shipping from the source database to the downstream mining database. Login to the `dboratest` database and run the following commands:

```
ALTER SYSTEM SET log_archive_dest_2='SERVICE=DOWNSTRM ASYNC
NOREGISTER VALID_FOR=(ONLINE_LOGFILES,PRIMARY_ROLE) DB_UNIQUE_
NAME=downstrm' SCOPE=BOTH;

ALTER SYSTEM SET LOG_ARCHIVE_CONFIG='DG_
CONFIG=(dboratest,downstrm)';
```

5. Configure the log archive config in the downstrm database:

```
ALTER SYSTEM SET log_archive_config='DG_
CONFIG=(downstrm,dboratest)' SCOPE=MEMORY;
```

6. Configure an archive destination for standby log files in the `downstrm` database:

```
ALTER SYSTEM SET LOG_ARCHIVE_DEST_2='LOCATION=/u01/app/oracle/
oradata/downstrm/stdby_archive VALID_FOR=(STANDBY_LOGFILE,PRIMARY_
ROLE)';
```

7. Set up a GoldenGate user in the downstream database for mining:

```
CREATE USER GGATE_ADMIN identified by GGATE_ADMIN;

GRANT CREATE SESSION, ALTER SESSION to GGATE_ADMIN;

GRANT ALTER SYSTEM TO GGATE_ADMIN;

GRANT CONNECT, RESOURCE to GGATE_ADMIN;

GRANT SELECT ANY DICTIONARY to GGATE_ADMIN;

GRANT FLASHBACK ANY TABLE to GGATE_ADMIN;

GRANT SELECT ANY TABLE TO GGATE_ADMIN;

GRANT SELECT ON DBA_CLUSTERS TO GGATE_ADMIN;

GRANT EXECUTE ON DBMS_FLASHBACK TO GGATE_ADMIN;

GRANT SELECT ANY TRANSACTION To GGATE_ADMIN;

EXEC DBMS_GoldenGate_AUTH.GRANT_ADMIN_PRIVILEGE('GGATE_ADMIN');

GRANT SELECT ON SYS.V_$DATABASE TO GGATE_ADMIN;
```

8. Next we set up an Integrated Capture in the `DOWNSTRM` database:

```
GGSCI (prim1-ol6-112.localdomain) 1> DBLOGIN USERID GGATE_ADMIN@
DBORATEST, PASSWORD GGATE_ADMIN
Successfully logged into database.


GGSCI (prim1-ol6-112.localdomain) 2> miningDBLOGIN USERID GGATE_
ADMIN@DBORATEST, PASSWORD GGATE_ADMIN
Successfully logged into mining database.


GGSCI (prim1-ol6-112.localdomain) 3> REGISTER EXTRACT EGGINT
```

DATABASE

```
2013-05-02 15:59:02  INFO   OGG-02003  Extract EGGINT
successfully registered with database at SCN 12037817.
```

9. Create a parameter file for Integrated Capture `EGGINT`:

   ```
   EXTRACT EGGINT

   USERID GGATE_ADMIN@DBORATEST, PASSWORD GGATE_ADMIN

   TRANLOGOPTIONS MININGUSER GGATE_ADMIN@DOWNSTRM MININGPASSWORD
   GGATE_ADMIN

   TRANLOGOPTIONS INTEGRATEDPARAMS (downstream_real_time_mine Y)

   EXTTRAIL /u01/app/ggate/112101/dirdat/it

   TABLE SCOTT.*;

   RMTHOST stdby1-ol6-112 , MGRPORT 8809

   RMTTRAIL /u01/app/ggate/dirdat/rt
   ```

10. Add the Integrated Capture Extract process to the GoldenGate configuration:

    ```
    GGSCI (prim1-ol6-112.localdomain) 1> ADD EXTRACT EGGINT INTEGRATED
    TRANLOG BEGIN NOW

    EXTRACT added.
    ```

11. Add a local and remote trail:

    ```
    GGSCI (prim1-ol6-112.localdomain) 82> ADD EXTTRAIL ./dirdat/it,
    EXTRACT EGGINT, MEGABYTES 50

    EXTTRAIL added.


    GGSCI (prim1-ol6-112.localdomain) 83> ADD RMTTRAIL /u01/app/ggate/
    dirdat/rt, EXTRACT EGGINT

    RMTTRAIL added.
    ```

12. We already have a Replicat process (`RGGTEST1`) in the target environment; let's just reset it to start from the current time:

    ```
    GGSCI (stdby1-ol6-112.localdomain) 8> ALTER REPLICAT RGGTEST1,
    BEGIN NOW

    REPLICAT altered.
    ```

13. Now start the Extract process:

    ```
    GGSCI (prim1-ol6-112.localdomain) 84> START EXTRACT EGGINT

    Sending START request to MANAGER ...

    EXTRACT EGGINT starting
    ```

14. Start the Replicat process:

```
GGSCI (stdby1-ol6-112.localdomain) 9> START REPLICAT RGGTEST1

Sending START request to MANAGER ...
REPLICAT RGGTEST1 starting
```

15. Now perform some updates on the source database:

```
SQL> UPDATE EMP SET COMM=5000 WHERE EMPNO=7876;

1 row updated.

SQL> UPDATE DEPT SET DNAME='MARKETING' WHERE DEPTNO=30;

1 row updated.

SQL> DELETE EMP WHERE EMPNO=7782;

1 row deleted.

SQL> COMMIT;
Commit complete.
```

16. Now verify the changes in the target database:

```
SQL> SELECT COMM FROM EMP WHERE EMPNO=7876;

      COMM
----------
      5000

SQL> SELECT DNAME FROM DEPT WHERE DEPTNO=30;

DNAME
--------------
MARKETING

SQL> SELECT * FROM EMP WHERE EMPNO=7782;

no rows selected
```

How it works...

In this recipe we go through the procedure to set up a replication for compressed tables. For this we first compress two tables in the source database. There is an additional database in the source environment called DOWNSTRM. This database is used for setting up the logmining server. The source database DBORATEST sends the redo log data to the mining database. In this example, the mining database is set up to receive the redo log data in real time. For this we create standby redo logs in the mining database.

In this recipe we go through the procedure to set up an Integrated Capture Extract process with the logmining server set up in a downstream database. In step 4, we set up the log shipping from the source database. In steps 5 and 6, we configure the local archiving for the mining database.

GoldenGate requires a mining user in the mining database to be able to read the logminer dictionary. This user is set up in step 7. In the next steps, we set up an Integrated Capture Extract and start it. We then perform some data changes in the EMP and DEPT tables and verify that these are replicated across to the target database.

> When you set up an Integrated Capture with a downstream mining database, the compatible parameter in the downstream database must be at least 11.2.0.3.

8
Advanced Administration Tasks – Part II

In this chapter we will cover the following recipes:

- ▶ Creating a GoldenGate configuration with a consistent state behind target database
- ▶ Replicating data from an active standby database in Archivelog mode only
- ▶ Migrating from an Oracle Streams environment to Oracle GoldenGate
- ▶ GoldenGate Administration role separation from the DBA team
- ▶ Cross RDBMS replication using GoldenGate
- ▶ Creating a multimaster GoldenGate replication configuration

Introduction

If you are working in a very busy database environment in a large organization, you would probably come across some additional challenges in implementing GoldenGate, particularly due to the way team responsibilities are structured. If the GoldenGate management is done by a separate team other than the DBA team, then the security policies would need to be set up so that there is no risk of teams overlapping each other's areas. If the source database is quite busy, it could be that the DBA team would not allow any additional load on the source database server. In such a scenario, you would need to implement GoldenGate on a separate server without having any impact on the source database.

In this chapter, we will look at how we can separate the GoldenGate management responsibilities from the DBA team and also how we can implement GoldenGate on a different server without putting additional load on the source database server. We will also go through the procedure to set up replication between two different database platforms and also how to migrate from an Oracle Streams environment to Oracle GoldenGate.

Finally, we will look at the steps using which you can set up an active-active GoldenGate replication.

Creating a GoldenGate configuration with a consistent state behind the target database

In this recipe you will learn how to set up an Oracle GoldenGate configuration with a deferred apply state target database. You will also learn about some scenarios where such a configuration can be useful.

Getting ready

For this recipe we will refer to the setup done in the *Setup a simple GoldenGate replication configuration between two single node databases* recipe in *Chapter 2, Setting up GoldenGate Replication*. For the purpose of this recipe, we will modify the replication to replicate only the records for the EMP table in the SCOTT schema. We will also modify the structure of the EMP table in the target database to add the following two new columns:

- ▸ SOURCE_COMMIT_TIME   TIMESTAMP
- ▸ TARGET_COMMIT_TIME   TIMESTAMP

This can be done as follows:

```
SQL> ALTER TABLE EMP ADD(SOURCE_COMMIT_TIME TIMESTAMP);

Table altered.

SQL> ALTER TABLE EMP ADD(TARGET_COMMIT_TIME TIMESTAMP);

Table altered.
```

How to do it...

The steps to perform this setup are as follows:

1. Create an Extract process parameter file as follows:

```
EXTRACT EGGTEST1
USERID GGATE_ADMIN@DBORATEST, PASSWORD GGATE_ADMIN
EXTTRAIL /u01/app/ggate/dirdat/st
TABLE SCOTT.EMP, TOKENS (ORIG_TS = @GETENV("GGHEADER" ,
"COMMITTIMESTAMP" ));
```

2. The Datapump process parameter file any should look like this:

```
EXTRACT PGGTEST1
USERID GGATE_ADMIN@DBORATEST, PASSWORD GGATE_ADMIN
RMTHOST stdby1-ol6-112 , MGRPORT 8809
RMTTRAIL /u01/app/ggate/dirdat/rt
TABLE SCOTT.EMP;
```

3. Start the Extract and Datapump processes.

The steps to be performed in the target environment are as follows:

1. Edit the Replicat process configuration as follows:

```
./ggsci
EDIT PARAMS RGGTEST1
REPLICAT RGGTEST1
USERID GGATE_ADMIN@TGORTEST, PASSWORD GGATE_ADMIN
DISCARDFILE /u01/app/ggate/dirrpt/RGGTEST1.dsc,append,MEGABYTES
500
ASSUMETARGETDEFS
DEFERAPPLYINTERVAL 3MINS
MAP SCOTT.EMP, TARGET SCOTT.EMP, COLMAP(USEDEFAULTS, SOURCE_
COMMIT_TIME = @TOKEN ("ORIG_TS"), TARGET_COMMIT_TIME=@DATE ("YYYY-
MM-DD HH:MI:SS.FFFFFF","JTS",@GETENV ("JULIANTIMESTAMP")));
```

2. Start the Replicat process.

3. Insert a row in the source EMP table as follows:

```
SQL> SELECT SYSTIMESTAMP FROM DUAL;

SYSTIMESTAMP
-----------------------------------------------------------
06-JUN-13 08.11.02.161644 PM +01:00

SQL> INSERT INTO EMP VALUES('8888','TEST','CLERK',7369,TO_
DATE('30-SEP-1971','DD-MON-YYYY'),950,0,10);
```

```
1 row created.

SQL> COMMIT;

Commit complete.
```

4. Wait for 3 minutes and query the target EMP table:

```
SQL> SELECT * FROM EMP WHERE EMPNO=8888;

EMPNO ENAME   JOB    MGR   HIREDATE    SAL   COMM   DEPTNO SOURCE_COMMIT_
TIME          TARGET_COMMIT_TIME
---------- ---------- --------- ---------- --------- ----
8888 TEST    CLERK 7369 30-SEP-71 950 0      10         06-JUN-13
08.11.07.000000 PM    06-JUN-13 08.14.09.302649 PM
```

How it works...

We just saw a simple demonstration of a GoldenGate configuration in which the target database is maintained with a consistent deferred time. The example uses a modified EMP table in the target database with extra columns to store the commit timestamp of the source and target environments. In step 1, we modify the Extract parameter file to only extract the records for the EMP table and also add a token called ORIG_TS with commit timestamp information to the trail records. In step 2, we modify the Datapump process to only replicate the EMP table records. After this we start both the processes in the source environment.

In the target environment, we modify the Replicat process to only replicate the records for the EMP table. With this change, we have also added the mapping information of the two new columns (SOURCE_COMMIT_TIME and TARGET_COMMIT_TIME). The first column SOURCE_COMMIT_TIME is assigned the token information that was extracted in step 1 in token ORIG_TS. The second column TARGET_COMMIT_TIME gets the newly extracted current timestamp information. Also in the Replicat parameter file, there is a new parameter called DEFERAPPLYINTERVAL. This parameter controls how long the Replicat process should wait before the record is applied to the target database. This interval is added to the commit timestamp of the record in the source database. In order to demonstrate the functioning of this setup, we then insert a new row in the EMP table in the source database and verify when it's replicated to the target database.

There's more...

Let's look at the deferred apply in a bit more detail:

Why use deferred apply

The main feature of Oracle GoldenGate is its ability to replicate the data in real time. One might wonder as to what is the point of deliberately introducing a delay in replication. The key benefit of such a configuration is that if any data is modified by mistake in the source database, those changes will not be replicated to the target database for the time specified in this parameter. This gives the administrator a chance to save such data from the target environment which might otherwise require performing complex database recovery from the backups.

DEFERAPPLYINTERVAL UNITS

The defer interval can be specified using different units. These units are SECS, MINS, MINUTES, HOURS, and DAYS. You can specify the unit in singular as well. The syntax of specifying the units is:

```
DEFERAPPLYINTERVAL <n><UNIT>
```

Where <n> is the number of units and UNIT is the unit of time for the delay. For example:

```
DEFERAPPLYINTERVAL 1DAY
```

See also

▶   The *Undoing the applied changes using the reverse utility* recipe in *Chapter 7, Advanced Administration Tasks – I*

Replicating data from an active standby database in Archivelog mode only

In this recipe you will learn how to set up a GoldenGate configuration to replicate the data from the archived logs on an active standby database.

Getting ready

The setup used for this recipe consists of a primary database called DBORATES running on prim1-ol6-112. A physical standby database for DBORATES has been created with Oracle Active Dataguard on stdprim1-ol6-112. The standby database is configured to write its archived logs to /u01/app/oracle/fast_recovery_area/STDDB. The target database called TGORTEST is running on stdby1-ol6-112. GoldenGate binaries are already installed on stdprim1-ol6-112 and stdby1-ol6-112 and a Manager process has been set up on both of these servers. A GoldenGate Administrator has already been created in both the DBORATES and TGORTEST databases. A TNS entry DBORATEST has been set up on stdprim1-ol6-112 which resolves to the DBORATES database running on prim1-ol6-112.

How to do it...

The steps to perform this setup are as follows:

1. Log in to the `sprim1-ol6-112 server` as the `ggate` user.

2. Create a GoldenGate classic Extract process as follows:
   ```
   ./ggsci
   EDIT PARAMS EGGTEST1
   EXTRACT EGGTEST1
   USERID GGATE_ADMIN@STDDB, PASSWORD GGATE_ADMIN
   TRANLOGOPTIONS ARCHIVEDLOGONLY ALTARCHIVELOGDEST /u01/app/oracle/
   fast_recovery_area/STDDB
   EXTTRAIL /u01/app/ggate/dirdat/st
   TABLE scott.*;
   ```

3. Create a GoldenGate Datapump process in the source environment:
   ```
   ./ggsci
   EDIT PARAMS PGGTEST1
   EXTRACT PGGTEST1k
   USERID GGATE_ADMIN@STDDB, PASSWORD GGATE_ADMIN
   RMTHOST stdby1-ol6-112 , MGRPORT 8809
   RMTTRAIL /u01/app/ggate/dirdat/rt
   TABLE scott.*;
   ```

4. Add the Extract process to the source manager configuration:
   ```
   ADD EXTRACT EGGTEST1, TRANLOG, BEGIN NOW
   ```

5. Add the local trail to the Extract process:
   ```
   ADD EXTTRAIL /u01/app/ggate/dirdat/st, EXTRACT EGGTEST1
   ```

6. Add the Datapump process to the source manager configuration:
   ```
   ADD EXTRACT PGGTEST1, EXTTRAILSOURCE /u01/app/ggate/dirdat/st
   ```

7. Add the remote trail location to the Datapump process:
   ```
   ADD RMTTRAIL /u01/app/ggate/dirdat/rt, EXTRACT PGGTEST1
   ```

8. Log in to `stdby1-ol6-112` server as the `ggate` user.

9. Create a Checkpoint table in the target database:
   ```
   ./ggsci
   DBLOGIN, USERID GGATE_ADMIN@TGORTEST PASSWORD GGATE_ADMIN
   ADD CHECKPOINTTABLE
   ```

10. Create a GoldenGate Replicat process in the target environment:

```
./ggsci
EDIT PARAMS RGGTEST1
REPLICAT RGGTEST1
USERID GGATE_ADMIN@TGORTEST, PASSWORD GGATE_ADMIN
DISCARDFILE /u01/app/ggate/dirrpt/RGGTEST1.dsc,append,MEGABYTES
500
ASSUMETARGETDEFS
MAP SCOTT.*, TARGET SCOTT.*;
```

11. Add the Replicat process to the target manager configuration:

```
ADD REPLICAT RGGTEST1, EXTTRAIL /u01/app/ggate/dirdat/rt,
CHECKPOINTTABLE GGATE_ADMIN.CHECKPOINT, BEGIN NOW
```

12. Start the Extract and Datapump processes:

```
START EXTRACT EGGTEST1
START EXTRACT PGGTEST1
```

13. Start the Replicat process:

```
START REPLICAT RGGTEST1
```

14. Check the row in the source database that we will update later.

```
SQL> show parameter db_unique_name

NAME                        TYPE          VALUE
----------------------------------- -----------
db_unique_name              string        dboratest

SQL> SELECT SAL FROM SCOTT.EMP WHERE ENAME='KING';

       SAL
----------
      5000
```

15. Update the salary for an employee in the source database:

```
SQL> UPDATE SCOTT.EMP SET SAL=7500 WHERE ENAME='KING';

1 row updated.

SQL> COMMIT;

Commit complete.
```

16. Perform a log switch in the source database to generate an archive logfile:

    ```
    SQL> ALTER SYSTEM SWITCH LOGFILE;

    System altered.
    ```

17. Now verify the update in the standby database by logging on to `sprim1-ol6-112`:

    ```
    SQL> SHOW PARAMETER DB_UNIQUE_NAME

    NAME                                 TYPE          VALUE
    ------------------------------------ -----------db_unique_name
    string           stddb

    SQL> SELECT SAL FROM SCOTT.EMP WHERE ENAME='KING';

           SAL
    ----------
          7500
    ```

18. Now verify the update in the target database by logging on to `stdby1-ol6-112`:

    ```
    SQL> SHOW PARAMETER DB_UNIQUE_NAME

    NAME                                 TYPE          VALUE
    ------------------------------------ -----------  -----------
    db_unique_name                       string        tgortest

    SQL> SELECT SAL FROM SCOTT.EMP WHERE ENAME='KING';

           SAL
    ----------
          7500
    ```

How it works...

We know that GoldenGate Extract processes do not consume a lot of resources in terms of memory/CPU and do not degrade the performance of the source database significantly. But if the production database in your environment is a very busy transactional database, it would not be desirable to add any further additional processes to the production server. In such a case, you can configure the GoldenGate Extract process to connect to a standby database and extract the changes by reading the archive logs. The Extract process also requires connecting to the source database to query the data dictionary to query object structure information. This is why before Oracle 11g, GoldenGate required a connection to the source database even when you configured the Extract process to read archive logs from a standby database. From 11g onwards, the GoldenGate license includes the license for Oracle Active Dataguard and this allows the administrator to keep the standby database open in read-only mode while the logs are being applied. With Active Dataguard, you can configure the Extract process to connect to the standby database, and for an 11g database you can configure GoldenGate to work purely from a standby site without any connection to the primary database.

In the preceding setup, we have a standby database called `stddb` running on `sprim1-ol6-112` for our source database `DBORATES`. GoldenGate binaries are installed on `sprim1-ol6-112` and a Manager process has been configured. In this setup, we create an Extract process to read the redo records from the archive log which are generated at `/u01/app/oracle/fast_recovery_area/STDDB`. This is done by specifying the following parameters in the Extract parameter file:

```
TRANLOGOPTIONS ARCHIVEDLOGONLY ALTARCHIVELOGDEST /u01/app/oracle/fast_
recovery_area/STDDB
```

After this, we create a Datapump process to transfer the trail files to the target server, `stdby1-ol6-112`. We also create a Replicat process on the target server called `RGGTEST1` which will write the trail file records to the target database, `TGORTEST`.

When the Extract process is started and it reads the first archive log record with an update for the `SCOTT.EMP` table, we see the following lines in the Extract report file:

```
2013-06-12 20:13:19  INFO    OGG-01516  Positioned to Sequence 2193,
RBA 201728, SCN 0.0, Jun 12, 2013 8:12:28 PM.
2013-06-12 20:13:19  INFO    OGG-01517  Position of first record
processed Sequence 2193, RBA 201744, SCN 0.12490857, Jun 12, 2013
8:12:28 PM.
Wildcard TABLE resolved (entry scott.*):
  TABLE "SCOTT"."EMP";
```

Once all the processes are running, we update a row in the `EMP` table and verify the change as it progresses to the standby database and from there on to the target database.

Migrating from an Oracle Streams environment to Oracle GoldenGate

Sometime back, Oracle announced in its statement of direction that it is no longer going to enhance Oracle Streams further. Although the existing Oracle Streams is still supported, many companies have started migrating the Oracle Streams based replication environments to Oracle GoldenGate. In this recipe, we will go through a step-by-step procedure for performing such migration.

Getting ready

The setup in this recipe consists of a Streams environment configured between two Oracle databases called DBORATES and TGORTEST running on prim1-ol6-112 and stdby-ol6-112 virtual machines. The streams replication has been set up as table-level replication for the SCOTT.EMP table between both databases. The setup presented does not cover the steps required for setting up a Streams environment.

How to do it...

The steps to migrate a streams replication setup to GoldenGate are as follows:

1. Follow the steps from the *Installing Oracle GoldenGate in a x86_64 Linux-based environment* recipe in *Chapter 1, Installation and Initial Setup*, to install GoldenGate binaries on prim1-ol6-112 and stdby1-ol6-112.

2. Follow the steps from the *Preparing the source database for GoldenGate setup* recipe in *Chapter 1, Installation and Initial Setup*, to create a GoldenGate Administrator user in the dborates database and grant necessary privileges to it.

3. Follow the steps from the *Preparing the target database for GoldenGate replication* recipe in *Chapter 1, Installation and Initial Setup*, to create a GoldenGate Administrator user in the TGORTEST database and grant necessary privileges to it.

4. Create a Manager process parameter file as follows:

```
EDIT PARAMS MGR
PORT 7809
DYNAMICPORTLIST 7810-7820, 7830
AUTOSTART ER *
AUTORESTART ER *, RETRIES 4, WAITMINUTES 4
PURGEOLDEXTRACTS /u01/app/ggate/dirdat/st*, USECHECKPOINTS,
MINKEEPHOURS 2
```

5. Create an Extract process parameter file as follows:

```
EDIT PARAMS EGGTEST1
EXTRACT EGGTEST1
USERID GGATE_ADMIN@DBORATEST, PASSWORD ******
EXTTRAIL /u01/app/ggate/dirdat/st
TABLE SCOTT.EMP;
```

6. Add the Extract process to the GoldenGate instance:

```
ADD EXTRACT EGGTEST1, TRANLOG, BEGIN NOW
```

7. Add the local trail to the Extract process configuration:

```
ADD EXTTRAIL /u01/app/ggate/dirdat/st, EXTRACT EGGTEST1
```

8. Create a Datapump process parameter file as follows:

```
EXTRACT PGGTEST1
USERID GGATE_ADMIN@DBORATEST, PASSWORD *****
RMTHOST stdby1-ol6-112.localdomain, MGRPORT 7809
RMTTRAIL /u01/app/ggate/dirdat/rt
TABLE SCOTT.EMP;
```

9. Add the Datapump extract to the GoldenGate instance:

```
ADD EXTRACT PGGTEST1, EXTTRAILSOURCE /u01/app/ggate/dirdat/st
```

10. Add the remote trail to the Datapump configuration:

```
ADD RMTTRAIL /u01/app/ggate/dirdat/rt, EXTRACT PGGTEST1
```

11. Create a Manager process on `stdby1-ol6-112` as follows:

```
EDIT PARAMS MGR
PORT 7809
DYNAMICPORTLIST 7810-7820, 7830
AUTOSTART ER *
AUTORESTART ER *, RETRIES 4, WAITMINUTES 4
PURGEOLDEXTRACTS /u01/app/ggate/dirdat/rt*, USECHECKPOINTS,
MINKEEPHOURS 2
```

12. Create a Replicat process as follows:

```
EDIT PARAMS RGGTEST1
REPLICAT RGGTEST1
USERID GGATE_ADMIN@TGORATST, PASSWORD ******
DISCARDFILE /u01/app/ggate/dirrpt/RGGTEST1.dsc, APPEND, MEGABYTES
500
ASSUMETARGETDEFS
MAP SCOTT.*, TARGET SCOTT.*;
```

13. Add a Checkpoint table to the target database as follows:

```
DBLOGIN USERID GGATE_ADMIN@DBORATEST
ADD CHECKPOINTTABLE CHECKPOINT
```

14. Add the Replicat process to the Manager configuration on the `stdby1-ol6-112` server:

```
ADD REPLICAT RGGTEST1, EXTTRAIL /u01/app/ggate/dirdat/rt,
CHECKPOINTTABLE CHECKPOINT
```

15. Start a `sqlplus` session in the `DBORATES` database and run the following command. Do not issue a commit.

```
SQL> UPDATE EMP SET SAL=SAL+150 WHERE EMPNO=7934;

1 row updated.
```

16. Start the Extract and Datapump process on `prim1-ol6-112`.

```
GGSCI (prim1-ol6-112.localdomain) 24> start EXTRACT *

Sending START request to MANAGER ...
EXTRACT EGGTEST1 starting

Sending START request to MANAGER ...
EXTRACT PGGTEST1 starting
```

17. Check the GoldenGate event log to find the timestamp of the Extract process startup.

```
[ggate@prim1-ol6-112 ggate]$ grep "EXTRACT EGGTEST1 starting"
ggserr.log | tail -1
2013-06-25 23:04:25  INFO    OGG-00975  Oracle GoldenGate Manager
for Oracle, mgr.prm:  EXTRACT EGGTEST1 starting.
```

18. Check for any current open transactions in the database that started before the timestamp noted in the preceding step:

```
SELECT s.username, s.program,s.machine,t.xidusn, t.xidslot,
t.xidsqn, t.start_time
FROM v$transaction t, v$session s
WHERE t.addr = s.taddr
and to_date(t.start_time,'MM/DD/YY HH24:MI:SS') < to_date('2013-
06-25 23:04:25','YYYY-MM-DD HH24:MI:SS')
ORDER BY start_time
/

USERNAME    SCOTT
PROGRAM     sqlplus@prim1-ol6-112.localdomain(TNS V1-V3)
MACHINE     prim1-ol6-112.localdomain
XIDUSN      9
XIDSLOT     19
XIDSQN      5510
START_TIME  06/25/13 23:02:49
(The above output has been reformatted to make it readable)
```

19. Wait for these transactions to finish as they will be processed by the Streams Capture process.

20. Run commit in the `sqlplus` window that was started in step 15.

21. Re-run the query from step 18 to ensure no rows are returned.

22. Run the following command in the `TGORTEST` database to stop the Streams Apply process.

```
SQL> exec dbms_apply_adm.stop_apply('APPLY$_DBORATES_4');

PL/SQL procedure successfully completed.
```

23. Check the SCN number of the last transaction that was applied by the Streams Apply process in the target database:

```
SQL> select APPLIED_MESSAGE_NUMBER from DBA_APPLY_PROGRESS;


APPLIED_MESSAGE_NUMBER
----------------------
               5312999
```

24. Verify that the record updated in step 15 was updated in the target database:

```
From dborates
SQL> SELECT SAL FROM EMP WHERE EMPNO=7934;


       SAL
----------
      1450


From tgortest
SQL> SELECT SAL FROM EMP WHERE EMPNO=7934;


       SAL
----------
      1450
```

25. Now start the Replicat process in the target environment from this SCN number noted in step 23 as follows:

```
GGSCI (stdby1-ol6-112.localdomain) 2> start replicat RGGTEST1
AFTERCSN 5312999


Sending START request to MANAGER ...
REPLICAT RGGTEST1 starting
```

26. Ensure that the transactions running in the source system are getting replicated to the target system using GoldenGate. We do this by running a DML statement in the source database and checking the data in the target database.

```
SQL> UPDATE EMP SET SAL=SAL+100 WHERE EMPNO=7934;


1 row updated.


SQL> COMMIT;


Commit complete.
```

27. Now verify the data in the target database.

```
SQL> SELECT SAL FROM EMP WHERE EMPNO=7934;

       SAL
----------
      1550
```

28. At this point, you have a working GoldenGate configuration so we are no longer reliant on the Streams setup. Let us stop the Streams Capture and Propagate process in the dborates database.

```
SQL> exec dbms_capture_adm.stop_capture('DBORATEST$CAP');

PL/SQL procedure successfully completed.
SQL> exec dbms_propagation_adm.stop_propagation('PROPAGATION$_9');

PL/SQL procedure successfully completed.
```

29. Drop the Capture process, Propagation process, and Capture Queue in the source database:

```
SQL> exec dbms_capture_adm.drop_capture('DBORATEST$CAP');

PL/SQL procedure successfully completed.

SQL> exec dbms_propagation_adm.drop_propagation('PROPAGATION$_9');

PL/SQL procedure successfully completed.
SQL> exec dbms_streams_adm.remove_queue('DBORATEST$CAPQ',cascade=>
true,drop_unused_queue_table=>true);

PL/SQL procedure successfully completed.
```

30. Drop the Apply process and Apply Queue in the target database:

```
SQL> exec dbms_apply_adm.drop_apply('APPLY$_DBORATES_4');

PL/SQL procedure successfully completed.
SQL> exec dbms_streams_adm.remove_queue('DBORATEST$APPQ',cascade=>
true,drop_unused_queue_table=>true);


PL/SQL procedure successfully completed.
```

31. Drop the Streams Administrator user in both the databases by running the following command:

```
SQL> drop user strmadmin ;

User dropped.
```

How it works...

In order to migrate an existing Oracle Streams environment to GoldenGate, you first need to install and set up Oracle GoldenGate on both the source and target servers. In this setup, we are performing these tasks in steps 1 to 14. These tasks include the GoldenGate binaries setup, Administrator user configuration, and the creation of necessary GoldenGate processes that are required for replication. Once the processes are set up we start the GoldenGate Extract and Datapump processes on the source server.

The key thing to note about the migration is that any existing open transactions that were started before starting the Extract process would be ignored by the Extract process. They would be replicated across to the target database by the Streams Apply process. In order to demonstrate this, we start a transaction in step 15 and run an update but do not commit it. In step 16, we start the Extract and Datapump processes. In step 17, we verify that the transaction that we started in step 15 is still open. The GoldenGate Replicat process in the target environment is still not started so at this point, GoldenGate is not replicating any data to the target environment. After this we complete the transaction that was started in step 15. Since the Streams processes are still running, this transaction is replicated across by the Streams Apply process.

We again check if there are any open transactions that were started prior to starting the Extract process by rerunning the query from step 18. Once we know there are no such transactions, it is a good time to stop the Streams Apply process. The Apply process is stopped in step 22. At this point, we need to find out the SCN of the last transaction that was applied by the Oracle Streams processes. We then use this SCN number to resume the replication using the Oracle GoldenGate Replicat process. By doing so, we ensure that no transactions are missed in the migration process.

Once the replication is set up using GoldenGate we test it by running an UPDATE statement in the source database and verifying that the change has been replicated to the target database. At this point, we have a working GoldenGate replication between the source and target databases so we can safely remove the Oracle Streams processes, queues, and Streams Administrator user from both databases.

> The steps 15 and 20 have been included in this setup to demonstrate that the existing transactions will be replicated by the Streams Apply process. Steps 26 and 27 have been included only to demonstrate that the replication is working once GoldenGate processes are started.

GoldenGate Administration role separation from the DBA team

When GoldenGate is used for Oracle databases, it is quite closely integrated with the database. Due to this, in most organizations, the responsibility of managing the GoldenGate environments rests with the DBA team. We know that the GoldenGate OS user requires being a member of the OS DBA group. With this access, an administrator who logs in as a GoldenGate OS user can also log in to any of the databases on that server. So, if the responsibility of managing GoldenGate environments lies with a different team, the DBA would not want/allow the GoldenGate team to log in to the databases with privileged user access. In this recipe, you will learn how to set up the GoldenGate environment in order to separate the GoldenGate management responsibilities to a dedicated team without giving them the DBA access to the databases.

Getting ready

For this recipe, we will set up GoldenGate binaries on a Linux server called `prim1-ol6-112`. Some of the steps for this setup need to be run as the `root` user, so for a production environment these would need to be run by a system administrator. The GoldenGate administation team will log in to the OS using the `oggate` user.

How to do it...

Follow these steps to set up the OS and GoldenGate environment:

1. Log in as `root` to `prim1-ol6-112`.

2. Create the following groups:
   ```
   groupadd oggate
   groupadd oggdba
   ```

3. Create the following users:
   ```
   useradd oggate -g oggate
   useradd oggdba -g oggdba -G oggate, dba
   ```

4. Set the password for the `oggate` and `oggdba` users:
   ```
   passwd oggate
   passwd oggdba
   ```

5. Create a directory for GoldenGate home:
   ```
   mkdir /u01/app/oggate
   chown oggate:oggate /u01/app/ggate
   ```

6. Copy the GoldenGate binaries to `/u01/app/oggate`.

Perform the following steps as the `oggate` user:

1. Add the following environment variables to `.bash_profile`:

   ```
   export GG_HOME=/u01/app/oggate
   export ORACLE_HOME=/u01/app/oracle/product/11.2.0/dbhome_1
   export LD_LIBRARY_PATH=$LD_LIBRARY_PATH:$ORACLE_HOME/lib
   ```

2. Install GoldenGate binaries:

   ```
   cd /u01/app/oggate/
   [oggate@prim1-ol6-112 oggate]$ unzip ogg112101_fbo_ggs_Linux_x64_
   ora11g_64bit.zip
   Archive:  ogg112101_fbo_ggs_Linux_x64_ora11g_64bit.zip
     inflating: fbo_ggs_Linux_x64_ora11g_64bit.tar
     inflating: OGG_WinUnix_Rel_Notes_11.2.1.0.1.pdf
     inflating: Oracle GoldenGate 11.2.1.0.1 README.txt
     inflating: Oracle GoldenGate 11.2.1.0.1 README.doc
   [oggate@prim1-ol6-112 oggate]$ tar -xvf fbo_ggs_Linux_x64_
   ora11g_64bit.tar
   ```

3. Create GoldenGate subdirectories:

   ```
   [oggate@prim1-ol6-112 oggate]$ ./ggsci

   Oracle GoldenGate Command Interpreter for Oracle
   Version 11.2.1.0.1 OGGCORE_11.2.1.0.1_PLATFORMS_120423.0230_FBO
   Linux, x64, 64bit (optimized), Oracle 11g on Apr 23 2012 08:32:14

   Copyright (C) 1995, 2012, Oracle and/or its affiliates. All rights
   reserved.

   GGSCI (prim1-ol6-112.localdomain) 1> create subdirs

   Creating subdirectories under current directory /u01/app/oggate

   Parameter files      /u01/app/oggate/dirprm: already exists
   Report files              /u01/app/oggate/dirrpt: created
   Checkpoint files          /u01/app/oggate/dirchk: created
   Process status files      /u01/app/oggate/dirpcs: created
   SQL script files          /u01/app/oggate/dirsql: created
   Database definitions files/u01/app/oggate/dirdef: created
   Extract data files        /u01/app/oggate/dirdat: created
   Temporary files           /u01/app/oggate/dirtmp: created
   Stdout files              /u01/app/oggate/dirout: created
   ```

4. Create a GoldenGate Manager process parameter file as follows:

```
./ggsci
EDIT PARAMS MGR
PORT 7809
DYNAMICPORTLIST 7810-7820, 7830
AUTOSTART ER *
AUTORESTART ER *, RETRIES 4, WAITMINUTES 4
```

5. Create a GoldenGate Extract process:

```
./ggsci
EDIT PARAMS EGGTEST1
EXTRACT EGGTEST1
USERID GGATE_ADMIN@DBORATEST, PASSWORD GGATE_ADMIN
EXTTRAIL /u01/app/oggate/dirdat/st
TABLE scott.*;
```

6. Add the Extract process to the Manager configuration:

```
ADD EXTRACT EGGTEST1, TRANLOG, BEGIN NOW
```

7. Add the local trail to the Extract process:

```
ADD EXTTRAIL /u01/app/oggate/dirdat/st, EXTRACT EGGTEST1
```

8. Create a CMDSEC file under GoldenGate home as follows:

```
cd /u01/app/oggate/
vi CMDSEC
# Command    Object    OS_Group    OS_User    Allow
START          *        OGGDBA        *         YES
STOP           *        OGGDBA        *         YES
START          *        OGGATE        *         NO
STOP           *        OGGATE        *         YES
STATUS         *        OGGATE        *         YES
VIEW           *        OGGATE        *         YES
```

9. Log in as an Oracle user and grant read permission on tnsnames.ora to the oggate user:

```
chmod a+r /u01/app/oracle/product/11.2.0/dbhome_1/network/admin/
tnsnames.ora
```

Run the following steps as the oggdba user:

1. Add the following environment variables to .bash_profile:

```
export GG_HOME=/u01/app/oggate
export ORACLE_HOME=/u01/app/oracle/product/11.2.0/dbhome_1
export LD_LIBRARY_PATH=$LD_LIBRARY_PATH:$ORACLE_HOME/lib
```

2. Create a script as follows:

```
cd ~
vi startmgr
#!/bin/bash
cd ~oggdba
. ./.bash_profile
cd $GG_HOME
ggsci <<EOF >> $GG_HOME/dirrpt/startmgr_oggdba.log
start mgr
exit
EOF
```

Run the following steps as the `root` user:

1. Modify the ownership of the CMDSEC file and allow the `oggate` user to read it:

```
chown oggdba:oggdba /u01/app/oggate/CMDSEC
chmod a+r /u01/app/oggate/CMDSEC
```

2. Modify the ownership and permissions on the `startmgr` script:

```
chown root:oggdba /home/oggdba/startmgr
chmod 750 /home/oggdba/startmgr
```

3. Modify the `sudoers` file and add the following line to it:

```
oggate ALL= (oggdba) NOPASSWD: /home/oggdba/startmgr
```

4. Lock the `oggdba` account:

```
passwd -l oggdba
```

5. Log in as the `oggate` user and try to start the Manager process using `ggsci`:

```
[oggate@prim1-ol6-112 ~]$ cd /u01/app/oggate
[oggate@prim1-ol6-112 oggate]$ ./ggsci

Oracle GoldenGate Command Interpreter for Oracle
Version 11.2.1.0.1 OGGCORE_11.2.1.0.1_PLATFORMS_120423.0230_FBO
Linux, x64, 64bit (optimized), Oracle 11g on Apr 23 2012 08:32:14

Copyright (C) 1995, 2012, Oracle and/or its affiliates. All rights
reserved.

GGSCI (prim1-ol6-112.localdomain) 1> start MGR
ERROR: Command not authorized for this user.

GGSCI (prim1-ol6-112.localdomain) 2>
```

6. Start the Manager process using `sudo` as the `oggdba` user:

```
[oggate@prim1-ol6-112 ~]$ sudo -u oggdba /home/oggdba/startmgr
```

7. Check the log under `/u01/app/oggate/dirrpt/` to verify that the Manager process has started successfully:

```
[oggate@prim1-ol6-112 oggate]$ cat /u01/app/oggate/dirrpt/
startmgr_oggdba.log

Oracle GoldenGate Command Interpreter for Oracle
Version 11.2.1.0.1 OGGCORE_11.2.1.0.1_PLATFORMS_120423.0230_FBO
Linux, x64, 64bit (optimized), Oracle 11g on Apr 23 2012 08:32:14

Copyright (C) 1995, 2012, Oracle and/or its affiliates. All rights
reserved.

GGSCI (prim1-ol6-112.localdomain) 1>
Manager started.
```

How it works...

As discussed in the introduction of this recipe, this setup can be followed to separate the GoldenGate management responsibilities to a team other than the DBA team, without giving them access to the OS DBA group. The security model described in this recipe is illustrated in the following diagram:

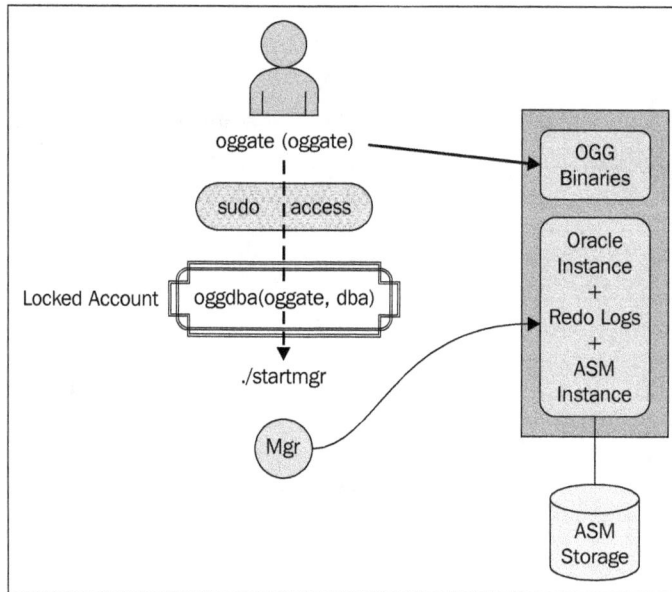

As we can see from the preceding diagram, GoldenGate binaries are owned and managed by the `oggate` OS user. This is the user using which the GoldenGate administration team will log in to the system and run all the commands for the day-to-day management of GoldenGate configurations. In the setup, we have also created another OS user called `oggdba` which is a member of the OS DBA group. This user account is used to start the GoldenGate Manager process. The startup of the Manager process is done using a script called `startmgr`. This script is owned by the `oggdba` user and the `oggate` user can run it using sudo access as `oggdba`. This setup allows the `oggate` user to start the GoldenGate processes as `oggdba` without having to log in as the `oggdba` user.

In order to restrict the `oggate` user to run the `START` command in `GGSCI`, we use the GoldenGate command security file called `CMDSEC`. In this file you can define what commands can be run by different users on different objects. In this setup we have defined that the `oggate` user cannot run a start command from `GGSCI` and due to this the only way the `oggate` user can start the GoldenGate processes is through the `startmgr` script.

Cross RDBMS replication using GoldenGate

One of the very popular uses of GoldenGate is to replicate data between databases running in different RDBMS. Different RDBMS systems have different data types and use different data structures to store the data. It is due to these complications that replicating between different systems becomes a complex task. GoldenGate extracts data from a database and stores it in its proprietary format. This data in proprietary format can then be replayed in any other supported database. You can use this feature to perform a one-off data migration from one RDBMS to another or you can use it to set up a permanent replication between a data set from one RDBMS to another.

In this recipe we will set up a continuous replication between an Oracle database and an SQL Server database. We will also cover the steps to install and configure GoldenGate in an SQL Server environment.

Getting ready

For this recipe, we will set up GoldenGate replication between an Oracle instance called `dboratest` which is running on an Oracle Enterprise Linux server called `prim1-ol6-112`, and SQL Server 2012 database which is running on a Windows server called `oggwin.localdomain`. The setup does not cover the steps to install SQL Server 2012 binaries, set up an SQL Server instance and to create the `oggtest` database. It is assumed that you have already installed and configured both the source and target databases and a `SCOTT` schema with the `EMP` table has been created. The `EMP` table has similar rows in both databases therefore the setup does not require any initial load.

We will be installing Oracle GoldenGate on the Windows server in this recipe. For this we have downloaded Oracle GoldenGate V 11.2.1.0.1 for SQL Server 2008 on Windows 2003 and 2008 (64 bit). We will also be referring to some steps from previous recipes about installing GoldenGate in the Linux environment.

How to do it...

The steps to set up the replication between the Oracle database and the SQL Server database are as follows:

Perform the following steps on the prim1-ol6-112 (source server):

1. Follow the steps from the *Installing Oracle GoldenGate in an x86_64 Linux-based environment* recipe in *Chapter 1, Installation and Initial Setup*, to install Oracle GoldenGate 112101 on `prim1-ol6-112`.

2. Follow the steps from the *Enabling supplemental logging in the source database* and *Preparing the source database for GoldenGate setup* recipes in *Chapter 1, Installation and Initial Setup*, to set up a GoldenGate Administrator user in the DBORATES database on the `prim1-ol6-112 server`.

3. Create a Manager process parameter file as follows:
    ```
    EDIT PARAMS MGR
    PORT 7809
    DYNAMICPORTLIST 7810-7820, 7830
    AUTOSTART ER *
    AUTORESTART ER *, RETRIES 4, WAITMINUTES 4
    PURGEOLDEXTRACTS /u01/app/ggate/dirdat/st*, USECHECKPOINTS,
    MINKEEPHOURS 2
    ```

4. Create an Extract process parameter file as follows:
    ```
    EDIT PARAMS EGGTEST1
    EXTRACT EGGTEST1
    USERID GGATE_ADMIN@DBORATEST, PASSWORD ******
    EXTTRAIL /u01/app/ggate/dirdat/st
    TABLE SCOTT.EMP;
    ```

5. Add the Extract process to the GoldenGate instance:
    ```
    ADD EXTRACT EGGTEST1, TRANLOG, BEGIN NOW
    ```

6. Add the local trail to the Extract process configuration:
    ```
    ADD EXTTRAIL /u01/app/ggate/dirdat/st, EXTRACT EGGTEST1
    ```

7. Create a Datapump process parameter file as follows:

```
EXTRACT PGGTEST1
USERID GGATE_ADMIN@DBORATEST, PASSWORD *****
RMTHOST oggwin.localdomain, MGRPORT 7809
RMTTRAIL C:\ggate\dirdat\rt
TABLE SCOTT.EMP;
```

8. Add the Datapump extract to the GoldenGate instance:

```
ADD EXTRACT PGGTEST1, EXTTRAILSOURCE /u01/app/ggate/dirdat/st
```

9. Add the remote trail to the Datapump configuration:

```
ADD RMTTRAIL c:\ggate\dirdat\rt, EXTRACT PGGTEST1
```

10. Create a parameter file for the `defgen` utility as follows:

```
cd /u01/app/ggate/dirprm
vi defs.prm
DEFSFILE ./dirdef/scott_defs.def
USERID ggate_admin@dboratest, PASSWORD GGATE_ADMIN
TABLE SCOTT.EMP;
```

11. Generate the definitions using the parameter file:

```
[ggate@prim1-ol6-112 ggate]$ ./defgen paramfile ./dirprm/defs.prm
***********************************************************
    Oracle GoldenGate Table Definition Generator for Oracle
                   Version 11.2.1.0.1
       OGGCORE_11.2.1.0.1_PLATFORMS_120423.0230
Linux, x64, 64bit (optimized), Oracle 11g on Apr 23 2012 05:08:19

Copyright (C) 1995, 2012, Oracle and/or its affiliates. All rights
reserved.



                  Starting at 2013-06-18 10:01:48
***********************************************************
Operating System Version:
Linux
Version #1 SMP Sat Jun 23 02:39:07 EDT 2012, Release
2.6.39-200.24.1.el6uek.x86_64
Node: prim1-ol6-112.localdomain
Machine: x86_64
                        soft limit    hard limit
Address Space Size   :    unlimited    unlimited
Heap Size            :    unlimited    unlimited
File Size            :    unlimited    unlimited
```

```
CPU Time                    :    unlimited    unlimited

Process id: 2855


************************************************************
**              Running with the following parameters
**
************************************************************
DEFSFILE ./dirdef/scott_defs.def
USERID ggate_admin@dboratest, PASSWORD **********
TABLE SCOTT.EMP;
Retrieving definition for SCOTT.EMP

Definitions generated for 1 table in ./dirdef/scott_defs.def
```

Perform the following steps on oggwin.localdomain (target server):

1. Copy the GoldenGate binaries to the Windows server.

2. Install GoldenGate binaries to c:\ggate by unzipping the downloaded binaries file.

3. Create GoldenGate subdirectories as follows:

```
C:\ggate>ggsci

Oracle GoldenGate Command Interpreter for SQL Server
Version 11.2.1.0.2 OGGCORE_11.2.1.0.2T3_PLATFORMS_120724.2205
Windows x64 (optimized), Microsoft SQL Server on Jul 25 2012
03:04:52

Copyright (C) 1995, 2012, Oracle and/or its affiliates. All rights
reserved.

GGSCI (oggwin) 1> create subdirs

Creating subdirectories under current directory C:\ggate

Parameter files               C:\ggate\dirprm: already exists
Report files                  C:\ggate\dirrpt: created
Checkpoint files              C:\ggate\dirchk: created
Process status files          C:\ggate\dirpcs: created
SQL script files              C:\ggate\dirsql: created
Database definitions files    C:\ggate\dirdef: created
Extract data files            C:\ggate\dirdat: created
Temporary files               C:\ggate\dirtmp: created
Stdout files                  C:\ggate\dirout: created
```

4. Add the GoldenGate Manager process as a Windows service:

```
C:\ggate>INSTALL ADDSERVICE
Service 'GGSMGR' created.
Install program terminated normally.
```

5. Create the GoldenGate Administrator user in the Oggtest database in the SQL Server Management Studio. For this, login to the SQL Server Management Studio as sa.

6. Expand the **Security** option and right-click on **Logins**.

7. Click on **New Login**:

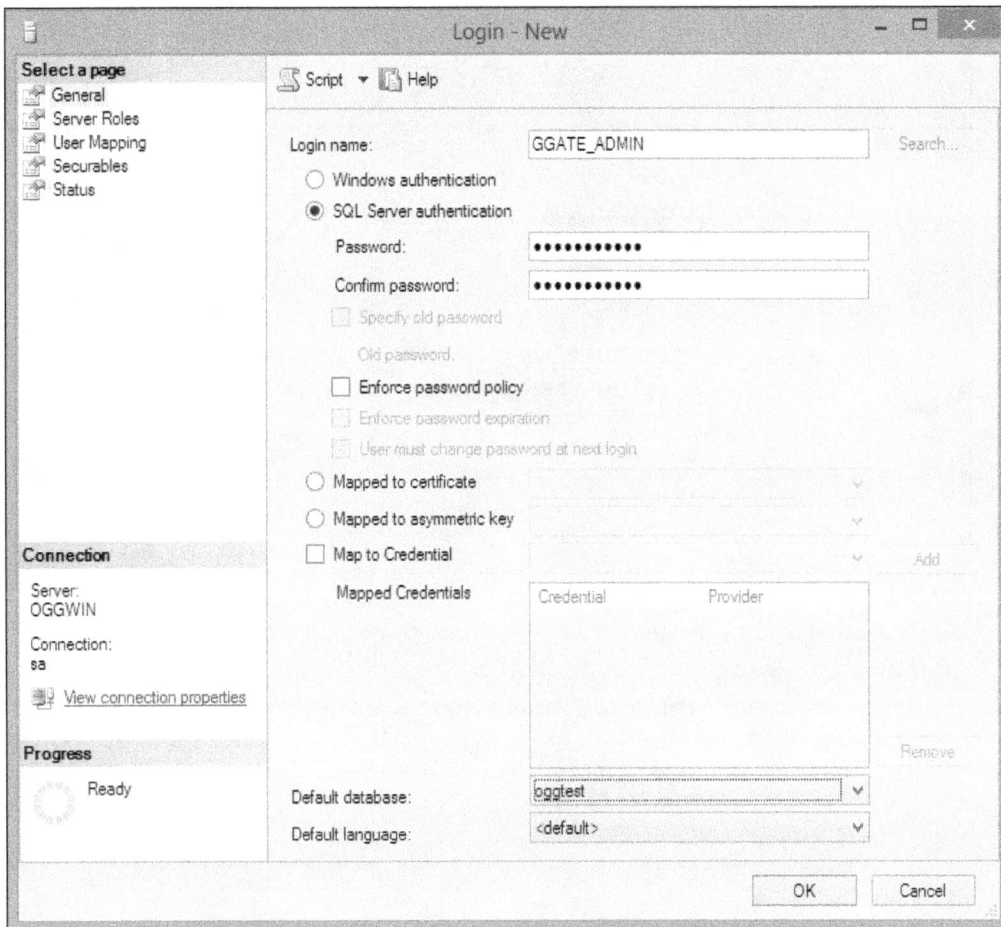

8. Enter the login name, password, select default database as oggtest.

9. Next, click on **User Mapping** and select the `oggtest` database and `db_owner` role as follows:

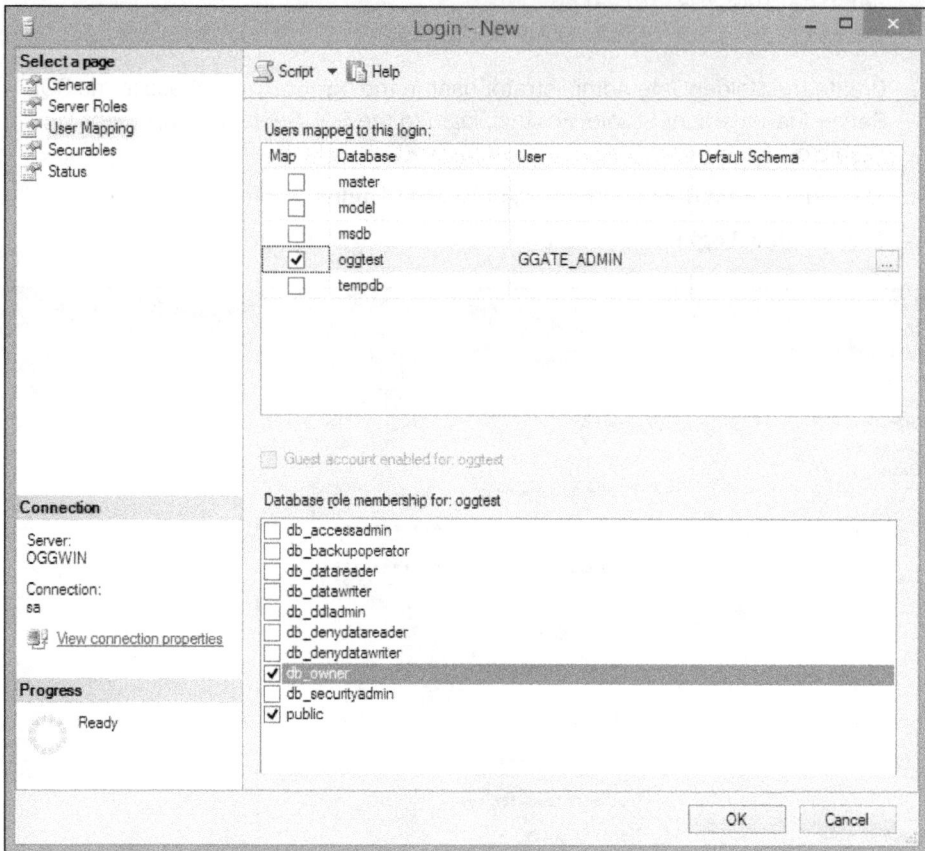

10. Click **OK** to create the user.

11. Next, create an ODBC data source to enable GoldenGate to access the SQL Server database. For this go to **Control Panel | Administrative Tools | Data Sources (ODBC):**

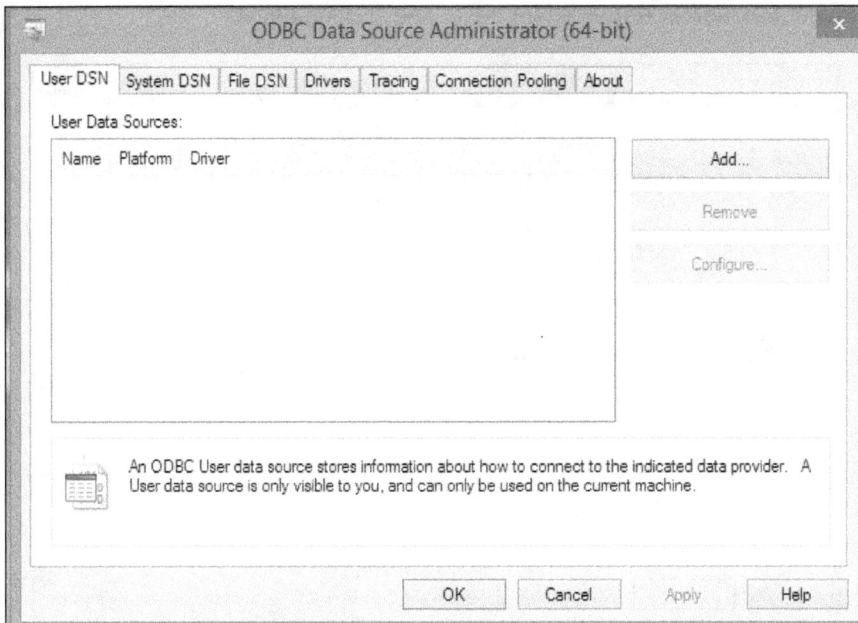

12. Click on **System DSN** and then on **Add**.

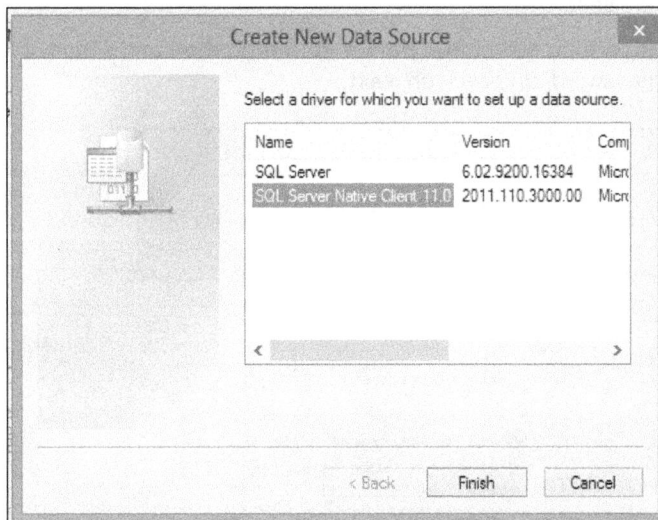

13. Select **SQL Server Native client** driver and click on **Finish**:

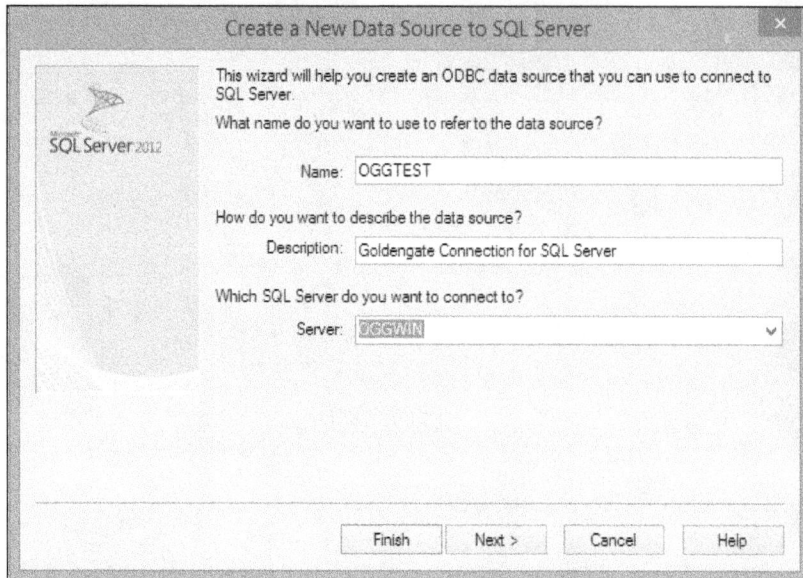

14. Enter a name for this connection, a description, and select local sql server instance and click on **Next**.

15. On the next window select **SQL Server Authentication** and specify the GGATE_ADMIN user and password, and click on **Next**:

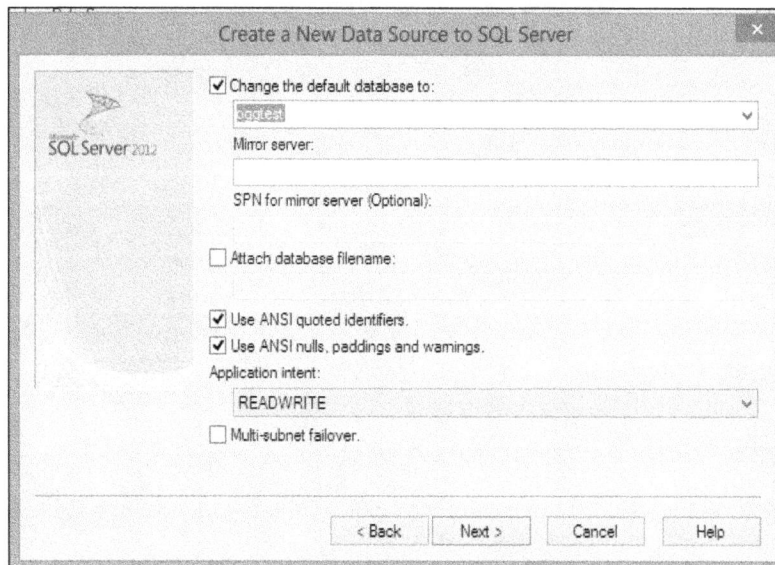

16. Change the default database to `oggtest` and click on **Next**.

17. Click on **Finish** in the next window:

```
                   ODBC Microsoft SQL Server Setup              [×]

              A new ODBC data source will be created with the following
                                  configuration:

     Microsoft SQL Server ODBC Driver Version 06.02.9200

     Data Source Name: oggtest
     Data Source Description: Goldengate Connection to OGGTEST
     Server: (local)
     Database: oggtest
     Language: (Default)
     Translate Character Data: Yes
     Log Long Running Queries: No
     Log Driver Statistics: No
     Use Regional Settings: No
     Prepared Statements Option: Drop temporary procedures on
     disconnect
     Use Failover Server: No
     Use ANSI Quoted Identifiers: Yes
     Use ANSI Null, Paddings and Warnings: Yes
     Data Encryption: No

           Test Data Source...              OK        Cancel
```

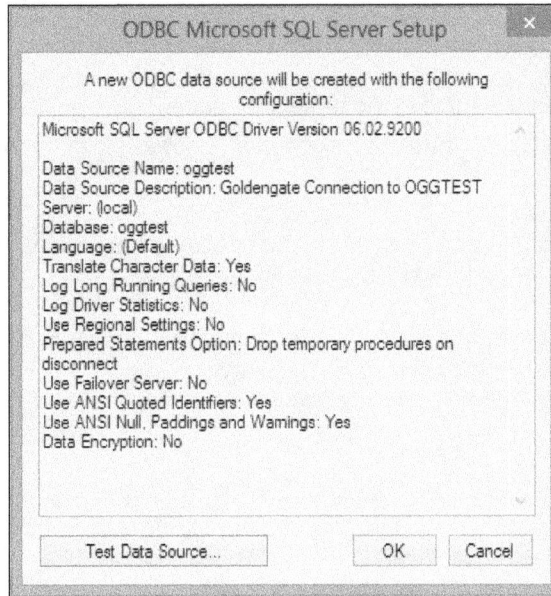

18. You should see the data source creation summary. Click on **Test Data Source** to test it and click on **OK** to create the data source.

19. Copy the source definitions file `/u01/app/ggate/dirdef/scott_defs.def` from `prim1-ol6-112` to `c:\ggate\dirdef\` on the `oggwin` server.

20. Create a Manager process as follows:

```
C:\ggate>ggsci

Oracle GoldenGate Command Interpreter for SQL Server
Version 11.2.1.0.2 OGGCORE_11.2.1.0.2T3_PLATFORMS_120724.2205
Windows x64 (optimized), Microsoft SQL Server on Jul 25 2012
03:04:52

Copyright (C) 1995, 2012, Oracle and/or its affiliates. All rights
reserved.

GGSCI (oggwin) 1> edit params mgr
PORT 7809
DYNAMICPORTLIST 7810-7820, 7830
AUTOSTART ER *
AUTORESTART ER *, RETRIES 4, WAITMINUTES 4
PURGEOLDEXTRACTS C:\GGATE\DIRDAT\tt*, USECHECKPOINTS, MINKEEPHOURS
2
```

21. Start the Manager process:

```
GGSCI (oggwin) 3> start mgr

Starting Manager as service ('GGSMGR')...
Service started.
```

22. Create a Checkpoint table in the target database:

```
GGSCI (oggwin) 8> DBLOGIN SOURCEDB OGGTEST, USERID ADMIN
Password:

2013-06-18 17:32:14  INFO    OGG-03036  Database character set
identified as windows-1252. Locale: en_US.

2013-06-18 17:32:14  INFO    OGG-03037  Session character set
identified as windows-1252.
Successfully logged into database.
GGSCI (oggwin) 10> ADD CHECKPOINTTABLE CHECKPOINT

Successfully created checkpoint table CHECKPOINT.
```

23. Create a Replicat process parameter file as follows:

```
GGSCI (oggwin) 2> edit params rggtest1
REPLICAT RGGTEST1
TARGETDB OGGTEST, USERID ADMIN, PASSWORD ADMIN
SOURCEDEFS ./dirdef/scott_defs.def
DISCARDFILE ./dirrpt/RGGTEST1.DSC, PURGE
MAP SCOTT.EMP, TARGET SCOTT.EMP;
```

24. Add the Replicat process to the Manager configuration:

```
GGSCI (oggwin) 4> ADD REPLICAT RGGTEST1, EXTTRAIL ./dirdat/rt,
CHECKPOINTTABLE CHECKPOINT
REPLICAT added.
```

25. Start the Extract, Datapump, and Replicat processes.

26. Let's perform some sample DML operations on the EMP table in the source database.

```
SQL> SELECT ENAME FROM EMP WHERE EMPNO=7782;

ENAME
-------------------------
CLARK

SQL> UPDATE EMP SET ENAME='JAMES' WHERE EMPNO=7782;

1 row updated.
```

```
SQL> SELECT COUNT(*) FROM EMP WHERE EMPNO=7566;

  COUNT(*)
----------
     1

SQL> DELETE EMP WHERE EMPNO=7566;

1 row deleted.

SQL> INSERT INTO EMP VALUES(8888,'ROBIN','CLERK',7788,TO_DATE('14-
01-1985','DD-MM-YYYY'),9850,NULL,20);

1 row created.

SQL> commit;

Commit complete.
```

27. Verify the DML changes in the target database.

	EMPNO	ENAME	JOB	MGR	HIREDATE	SAL	COMM	DEPTNO
1	7369	SMITH	CLERK	7902	1980-12-17	800.00	NULL	20
2	7499	ALLEN	SALESMAN	7698	1981-02-20	1600.00	300.00	30
3	7521	WARD	SALESMAN	7698	1981-02-22	1250.00	500.00	30
4	8888	ROBIN	CLERK	7788	1985-01-14	9850.00	NULL	20
5	7654	MARTIN	SALESMAN	7698	1981-09-28	1250.00	1400.00	30
6	7698	BLAKE	MANAGER	7839	1981-05-01	2850.00	NULL	30
7	7782	JAMES	MANAGER	7839	1981-06-09	2450.00	NULL	10
8	7788	SCOTT	ANALYST	7566	1982-12-09	3000.00	NULL	20
9	7839	KING	PRESIDENT	NULL	1981-11-17	5000.00	NULL	10
10	7844	TURNER	SALESMAN	7698	1981-09-08	1500.00	NULL	30
11	7876	ADAMS	CLERK	7788	1983-01-12	1100.00	NULL	20
12	7900	JAMES	CLERK	7698	1981-12-03	950.00	NULL	30
13	7902	FORD	ANALYST	7566	1981-12-03	3000.00	NULL	20
14	7934	MILLER	CLERK	7782	1982-01-23	1300.00	NULL	10

How it works...

In this recipe we went through the steps to set up a replication between an Oracle database environment and a SQL server database environment. In steps 1 and 2, the setup begins with GoldenGate installation in the Linux environment for which you should refer to some recipes from *Chapter 1, Installation and Initial Setup*. In the next steps we created a Manager process, and set up an Extract and a Datapump process for the GoldenGate setup in the Oracle environment. Both the Oracle and SQL Server systems use different data types and have their own ways of storing table structures. Copying data from one system to another requires these table definitions to be converted. This is done by generating a definitions file, which is done in steps 11 to 13.

Alter this under the steps for target server, we install GoldenGate binaries on the Windows machine. The installation is straightforward and only requires extracting the binaries from the ZIP file and creating subdirectories. GoldenGate requires an Administrator user to be set up in the database to be able to apply the extracted records and read the required metadata. This user is created in steps 5 to 10. In a SQL server environment, the client connectivity is performed by creating an ODBC connection at the operating-system level. This connection has the relevant details; for example, the default database to connect to, the user ID and password to be used for connection, and so on. In this setup we have created this ODBC connection in steps 11 to 18. Once the connection is in place and it is tested, we need to configure the target's GoldenGate setup. For this we copied the definitions file to the target server and create a Manager process. We also created a Checkpoint table in the target SQL Server database by connecting from GoldenGate using the GoldenGate Administrator user. In steps 23 to 24, we create a Replicat process and then start all the processes.

In order to test the replication, we perform some DML transactions in the source database and then verify the data in the target database.

Creating a multimaster GoldenGate replication configuration

Most of the configurations that we have discussed so far in this book had a one way replication stream. There are a few scenarios where such a setup will not be adequate. A very common usage where a single stream of replication will not be sufficient is a distributed environment where the database is divided into region-specific databases but the users can access the information of any region from any database. In order to keep the tables in sync in such an environment, you need multiple streams to synchronize the data both ways. Such a setup is called active-active or multimaster replication setup.

Another popular use of using active-active replication is maintaining a replicated system which could also be used to serve the complete production load in the event of a failover. Although, you can create a read-only standby database which is kept in sync with the primary database using Active Dataguard, but cannot perform any changes in the standby database without converting it into primary. If the business requirement is to keep a replicated copy of the database which would also serve production traffic with write operations and be kept in sync with the primary database, then you can set up an active-active GoldenGate replication between both the databases.

In this recipe, we will look into the steps that you can follow to set up an active-active replication. We will also go through some of the challenges that one might face when using active-active GoldenGate replication.

Getting ready

The setup for this recipe consists of two virtual machines called `prim1-ol6-112` and `stdby1-ol6-112` running OEL 6.3. Both virtual machines have an Oracle 11.2.0.3 binaries installed and an Oracle database running on them. The GoldenGate binaries are already installed under `/u01/app/ggate`. The setup assumes that you already have a `SCOTT` user and an `EMP` table in both databases.

How to do it...

The steps to set up an active-active GoldenGate replication are:

1. Follow the steps from the *Enabling supplemental logging in the source database* and *Preparing the source database for GoldenGate setup* recipes in *Chapter 1, Installation and Initial Setup*, to set up a GoldenGate Administrator user in the `DBORATES` database on the `prim1-ol6-112` server.

2. Follow the steps from the *Preparing the target database for GoldenGate setup* recipe in *Chapter 1, Installation and Initial Setup*, to grant additional privileges to the GoldenGate Admin user in the `dborates` database on `prim1-ol6-112`.

3. Follow the steps from the *Enabling supplemental logging in the source database* and *Preparing the source database for GoldenGate setup* recipes in *Chapter 1, Installation and Initial Setup*, to set up a GoldenGate Administrator user in the `TGORATST` database on the `stdby1-ol6-112` server.

4. Follow the steps from the *Preparing the target database for GoldenGate setup* recipe in *Chapter 1, Installation and Initial Setup*, to grant additional privileges to the GoldenGate Administrator user in the `TGORATST` database on `stdby1-ol6-112`.

5. By now, the GoldenGate Administrator user should have privileges required for extracting and replicating data in both databases. Supplemental Logging should be enabled on the `SCOTT.EMP` table in both databases.

Run the following steps on the `prim1-ol6-112` server:

1. Create a Manager process parameter file as follows:

    ```
    EDIT PARAMS MGR
    PORT 7809
    DYNAMICPORTLIST 7810-7820, 7830
    AUTOSTART ER *
    AUTORESTART ER *, RETRIES 4, WAITMINUTES 4
    ```

2. Create an Extract process parameter file as follows:

    ```
    EDIT PARAMS EXTPRIM1
    EXTRACT EXTPRIM1
    USERID GGATE_ADMIN@DBORATEST, PASSWORD ******
    EXTTRAIL /u01/app/ggate/dirdat/st
    GETAPPLOPS
    IGNOREREPLICATES
    TABLE SCOTT.EMP;
    ```

3. Add the Extract process to the GoldenGate instance:

    ```
    ADD EXTRACT EXTPRIM1, TRANLOG, BEGIN NOW
    ```

4. Add the local trail to the Extract process configuration:

    ```
    ADD EXTTRAIL /u01/app/ggate/dirdat/st, EXTRACT EXTPRIM1
    ```

5. Create a Datapump process parameter file as follows:

    ```
    EDIT PARAMS PMPPRIM1
    EXTRACT PMPPRIM1
    USERID GGATE_ADMIN@DBORATEST, PASSWORD *****
    RMTHOST stdby1-ol6-112.localdomain, MGRPORT 7809
    RMTTRAIL /u01/app/ggate/dirdat/rt
    TABLE SCOTT.EMP;
    ```

6. Add the Datapump extract to the GoldenGate instance:

    ```
    ADD EXTRACT PMPPRIM1, EXTTRAILSOURCE /u01/app/ggate/dirdat/st
    ```

7. Add the remote trail to the Datapump configuration:

    ```
    ADD RMTTRAIL /u01/app/ggate/dirdat/rt, EXTRACT PMPPRIM1
    ```

8. Log in to the `dborates` database through GGSCI and add
    a Checkpoint table:

    ```
    DBLOGIN USERID GGATE_ADMIN@DBORATEST
    ADD CHECKPOINTTABLE CHECKPOINT
    ```

9. Create a Replicat process parameter file:

```
EDIT PARAMS REPPRIM1
REPLICAT REPPRIM1
USERID GGATE_ADMIN@DBORATEST, PASSWORD ******
DISCARDFILE /u01/app/ggate/dirrpt/REPPRIM1.dsc, APPEND, MEGABYTES
500
ASSUMETARGETDEFS
MAP SCOTT.*, TARGET SCOTT.*;
```

10. Add the Replicat extract to the GoldenGate instance:

```
ADD REPLICAT REPPRIM1, EXTTRAIL /u01/app/ggate/dirdat/rt,
CHECKPOINTTABLE CHECKPOINT
```

Run the following steps on the `stdby1-ol6-112` server:

1. Create a Manager process parameter file as follows:

```
EDIT PARAMS MGR
PORT 7809
DYNAMICPORTLIST 7810-7820, 7830
AUTOSTART ER *
AUTORESTART ER *, RETRIES 4, WAITMINUTES 4
```

2. Create an Extract process parameter file as follows:

```
EDIT PARAMS EXTSTBY1
EXTRACT EXTSTBY1
USERID GGATE_ADMIN@TGORTEST, PASSWORD ******
EXTTRAIL /u01/app/ggate/dirdat/st
GETAPPLOPS
IGNOREREPLICATES
TABLE SCOTT.EMP;
```

3. Add the Extract process to the GoldenGate instance:

```
ADD EXTRACT EXTSTBY1, TRANLOG, BEGIN NOW
```

4. Add the local trail to the Extract process configuration:

```
ADD EXTTRAIL /u01/app/ggate/dirdat/st, EXTRACT EXTSTBY1
```

5. Create a Datapump process parameter file as follows:

```
EDIT PARAMS PMPSTBY1
EXTRACT PMPSTBY1
USERID GGATE_ADMIN@TGORATST, PASSWORD *****
RMTHOST prim1-ol6-112.localdomain, MGRPORT 7809
RMTTRAIL /u01/app/ggate/dirdat/rt
TABLE SCOTT.EMP;
```

6. Add the Datapump extract to the GoldenGate instance:

   ```
   ADD EXTRACT PMPSTBY1, EXTTRAILSOURCE /u01/app/ggate/dirdat/st
   ```

7. Add the remote trail to the Datapump configuration:

   ```
   ADD RMTTRAIL /u01/app/ggate/dirdat/rt, EXTRACT PMPSTBY1
   ```

8. Log in to the TGORTEST database through GGSCI and add a Checkpoint table:

   ```
   DBLOGIN USERID GGATE_ADMIN@tgortest
   ADD CHECKPOINTTABLE CHECKPOINT
   ```

9. Create a Replicat process parameter file:

   ```
   EDIT PARAMS REPSTBY1
   REPLICAT REPSTBY1
   USERID GGATE_ADMIN@TGORATST, PASSWORD ******
   DISCARDFILE /u01/app/ggate/dirrpt/REPSTBY1.dsc, APPEND, MEGABYTES
   500
   ASSUMETARGETDEFS
   MAP SCOTT.*, TARGET SCOTT.*;
   ```

10. Add the Replicat extract to the GoldenGate instance:

    ```
    ADD REPLICAT REPSTBY1, EXTTRAIL /u01/app/ggate/dirdat/rt,
    CHECKPOINTTABLE CHECKPOINT
    ```

11. Start all processes on both machines.

    ```
    START ER*
    ```

Now, let us run some DML transactions in both environments and verify that the changes have replicated across. The key objective here is that the data should be the same on both sites after the DMLs have been replicated.

1. Run the following statements on prim1-ol6-112:

   ```
   SQL> DELETE EMP WHERE EMPNO=7566;

   1 row deleted.

   SQL> INSERT INTO EMP VALUES(8888,'ROBIN','CLERK',7788, TO_
   DATE('14-01-1985','DD-MM-YYYY'),9850,NULL,20);

   1 row created.

   SQL> commit;
   ```

2. Run the following statements on `stdby1-ol6-112`:

```
SQL> DELETE EMP WHERE EMPNO=7521;

1 row deleted.

SQL> INSERT INTO EMP VALUES(9888,'ROBERT','CLERK',7788, TO_
DATE('14-01-1975','DD-MM-YYYY'),19850,2200,20);

1 row created.

SQL> commit;
```

3. Verify the `EMP` table data from `prim1-ol6-112`:

```
SQL> SELECT * FROM EMP;

EMPNO   ENAME     JOB         MGR HIREDATE    SAL   COMM DEPTNO
-----   --------- ----------- ----- --------- ------ -----
8888    ROBIN     CLERK       7788 14-JAN-85  9850          20
9888    ROBERT    CLERK       7788 14-JAN-75  19850 2200    20
7369    SMITH     CLERK       7902 17-DEC-80  800           20
7499    ALLEN     SALESMAN    7698 20-FEB-81  1600  300     30
7654    MARTIN    SALESMAN    7698 28-SEP-81  1250  1400    30
7698    BLAKE     MANAGER     7839 01-MAY-81  2850          30
7782    JAMES     MANAGER     7839 09-JUN-81  2450          10
7788    SCOTT     ANALYST     7566 09-DEC-82  3000          20
7839    KING      PRESIDENT        17-NOV-81  5000          10
7844    TURNER    SALESMAN    7698 08-SEP-81  1500          30
7876    ADAMS     CLERK       7788 12-JAN-83  1100          20
7900    JAMES     CLERK       7698 03-DEC-81  950           30
7902    FORD      ANALYST     7566 03-DEC-81  3000          20
7934    MILLER    CLERK       7782 23-JAN-82  1300          10

14 rows selected.
```

4. Verify the `EMP` table data from `stdby1-ol6-112`.

```
SQL> SELECT * FROM EMP;

EMPNO   ENAME     JOB         MGR HIREDATE    SAL   COMM DEPTNO
-----   --------- ----------- ----- --------- ------ -----
8888    ROBIN     CLERK       7788 14-JAN-85  9850          20
9888    ROBERT    CLERK       7788 14-JAN-75  19850 2200    20
7369    SMITH     CLERK       7902 17-DEC-80  800           20
7499    ALLEN     SALESMAN    7698 20-FEB-81  1600  300     30
7654    MARTIN    SALESMAN    7698 28-SEP-81  1250  1400    30
```

7698	BLAKE	MANAGER	7839	01-MAY-81	2850	30
7782	JAMES	MANAGER	7839	09-JUN-81	2450	10
7788	SCOTT	ANALYST	7566	09-DEC-82	3000	20
7839	KING	PRESIDENT		17-NOV-81	5000	10
7844	TURNER	SALESMAN	7698	08-SEP-81	1500	30
7876	ADAMS	CLERK	7788	12-JAN-83	1100	20
7900	JAMES	CLERK	7698	03-DEC-81	950	30
7902	FORD	ANALYST	7566	03-DEC-81	3000	20
7934	MILLER	CLERK	7782	23-JAN-82	1300	10

14 rows selected.

How it works...

The following diagram is a representation of the previous active-active replication setup:

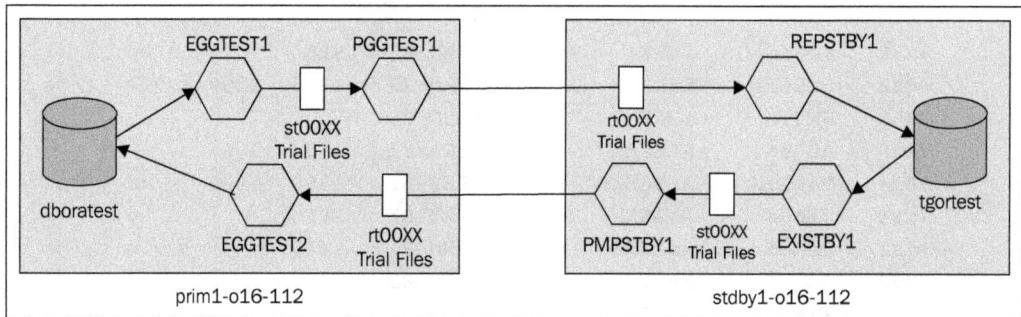

The two databases DBORATEST and TGORTEST are in a consistent state with an EMP table already created with default data in both of them. The GoldenGate setup in each site will consist of an Extract, Datapump, and a Replicat.

For this setup we need to prepare both the databases as if they were source and target for the GoldenGate replication. This requires granting the required privileges to read the changes for the EMP table and also to apply the DMLs for the EMP table to the GGATE_ADMIN user. We also need to enable Supplemental Logging in both databases, both at the database level and for the EMP table through GoldenGate.

After this, in steps 1 to 10 we set up a Manager process, Extract, Datapump, and Replicat processes on the prim1-ol6-112 server. Then we perform a similar setup on the stdby1-ol6-112 server. Once the setup is complete, we test it by performing some DMLs from both sites and verify the overall data in both databases in the end.

There are a few parameters which are quite important in an active-active replication:

▸ **IGNOREREPLICATES/GETAPPLOPS**: When you replicate the data between two databases both ways, there is a chance that the replication will fall into a loop as the changes that will be applied to a database will be extracted by the Extract process, thereby passing them back to the source database. This will cause the replication to fall into an endless loop. GoldenGate has the ability to identify which changes were generated by a Replicat process and which ones are coming from an application update. However, we need to configure GoldenGate to help it to decide what to do with these different types of changes that it will extract. Using IGNOREREPLICATES in conjunction with GETAPPLOPS allows GoldenGate to ignore any changes that are applied to the database by a Replicat process and only process the ones that are generated by an application.

▸ **GETREPLICATES/IGNOREAPPLOPS**: These parameters do the exact opposite of IGNOREREPLICATES/GETAPPLOPS. You can use these parameters to instruct GoldenGate to ignore any changes applied by anything other than the Replicat process and capture all the changes generated by the Replicat process. You might wonder why someone would need to do something like that. The most common use of these parameters is when you set up a cascading replication between three databases. In a cascading configuration, you replicate all the data from a system which gets updated by the application, to another system. The changes are then extracted from the second system and then applied to a third system. On the second system, all the changes are applied by the Replicat process so the Extract process configuration on that system would require these parameters so that it extracts only all the changes that are applied by the Replicat process. These would then be transferred to the third system where the Replicat process would apply them to the target environment.

There's more...

Implementing active-active replication between two systems comes with its own challenges. From a GoldenGate configuration perspective, it is quite straightforward. However, the biggest challenge in active-active configuration is how to handle the data collisions. Data collisions occur when the same data is updated by both sites at the same time. These need to be handled and resolved to prevent any data inconsistency between both sites. To understand a bit more about data collisions, let us take an example of two systems based in different countries offering an online shopping portal to local users. Imagine that there is only one piece of a particular item left in stock and both users place an order for that. If the replication system does not have any in-built intelligence to handle the data collision, both the users will be sent an order confirmation and the company will get two orders for a single item which will create further problems in the system. To avoid such situations, rules must be written to verify the data before confirming the order to the user.

Handling data collisions is complex and there is no right or wrong solution for them. At the first instance, you should try to avoid any data collisions. If even after deploying avoidance methodologies, there are some data collisions, then custom rules should be written for those scenarios depending on the application and the data. There are a few standard approaches that are used to writing such rules.

Data collision avoidance

If you want to guarantee that no data collisions ever occur in your system, then you need to ensure that there is only a single source of update for a piece of data. Ensuring a single source of update in a distributed system requires a logical partition of the data from an application perspective. Some examples of logical partitioning of the data are on the basis of some regions, even-odd number ranges, alphabetical ranges or even specific lists of the items. Such segregation at the application level ensures that two different applications will not update the same data and there are minimal chances of data collisions occurring.

Data collision resolution

There are two main principles of writing data collision resolution rules.

Timestamp-based

When using this technique the data collisions are resolved on the basis of timestamps of the changes that occur in the system. The key principle of this methodology is the change that occurred first wins. For this system to work, each change must be appended with the timestamp of when it happened.

Defined trusted source

Another methodology using which you can base your data collision resolution rules is a trusted source. In this system, you define a source as your trusted source system. In case of conflict, the change that occurred from the trusted source wins. All other changes that occurred from the other sources are discarded.

9
GoldenGate Veridata, Director, and Monitor

In this chapter we will cover the following recipes:

- Setting up the Oracle GoldenGate Monitor server
- Setting up Oracle GoldenGate Monitor Agents
- Installing Oracle GoldenGate Director
- Installing and using Oracle GoldenGate Director Client to manage the GoldenGate instances
- Steps to set up the GoldenGate monitoring using OEM 12c
- Steps to install Oracle GoldenGate Veridata
- Steps to compare data between the source and target environments using Oracle GoldenGate Veridata

Introduction

As a GoldenGate Administrator you would be monitoring, administering, and tuning the replication environments. These tasks can be performed with the basic GGSCI commands or through the ad-hoc scripts. Such mechanisms work well as long as the number of environments is small. Once the number of GoldenGate environments starts to grow and you want to see a consolidated picture of the overall replication, you would need some additional tools for this. Apart from Oracle GoldenGate, Oracle also offers a few other products under the data integration category, which can be used for maintenance and to perform other administration tasks by a GoldenGate Administrator. These tools are GoldenGate Monitor, GoldenGate Director, GoldenGate Veridata, and OEM 12c GoldenGate Plugin.

In this chapter, we will learn how to install, configure, and use these tools for performing various administration tasks.

Setting up the Oracle GoldenGate Monitor server

The Oracle GoldenGate Monitor server is used for monitoring Oracle instances remotely. The Monitor server works by communicating with various GoldenGate Monitor Agents, which are installed on the server where the GoldenGate instances are running. The Agents are instructed by the Monitor server to collect data about various metrics. Once the Agent has collected this data, it then pushes that data to the GoldenGate Monitor server. The Oracle GoldenGate Monitor server then stores this data in its repository, which it maintains in a backend database. It also allows you to set up various alerts when the threshold for a metric breaks.

In this recipe, you will learn how to set up the Oracle GoldenGate Monitor server. You will also learn how to configure the Monitor server access through SSL.

Getting ready

The setup in this recipe will be performed on a new **virtual machine** (**VM**) named mgmt1-ol6. The virtual machine was set up with OEL 6.3. The Oracle GoldenGate Monitor server requires a database for the repository purposes. In this example setup, we will be using an Oracle database for the repository. The Oracle 11.2.0.3 binaries have been installed on this VM under `/u01/app/oracle/product/11.2.0/dbhome_1`. A shell database named `oggmgmt` has been created under this Oracle Home. This database is registered with the default `LISTENER` running on the port 1521. This recipe does not cover the steps to install the Oracle binaries and to create the shell database. It is assumed that the reader is already familiar with the steps for these two tasks. You would also need to download Oracle GoldenGate Monitor binaries from the e-delivery website. The product number for these binaries is V27829-01. In order to install these binaries, you would need an X server set up on your PC.

How to do it...

The following are the steps to install the Oracle GoldenGate Monitor server:

1. Log in to sqlplus in the `oggmgmt` database as `sysdba`.

2. Create a tablespace for the GoldenGate Monitor repository objects.

   ```
   SQL> CREATE TABLESPACE OGGMON_DATA DATAFILE
     '/u01/app/oracle/oradata/oggmgmt/oggmon_data01.dbf' SIZE
      200M AUTOEXTEND ON;

   Tablespace created.
   ```

3. Create a new user for the GoldenGate Monitor repository schema.

```
SQL> CREATE USER OGGMON IDENTIFIED BY OGGMON DEFAULT
     TABLESPACE OGGMON_DATA QUOTA UNLIMITED ON OGGMON_DATA;

User created.
```

4. Grant the necessary privileges to the OGGMON user.

```
SQL> GRANT CREATE SESSION, RESOURCE, SELECT ANY TABLE TO
     OGGMON;

Grant succeeded.
```

5. Copy Oracle GoldenGate Monitor binaries to the mgmt1-ol6 server.

6. Unzip the binaries.

```
unzip Oracle_GoldenGate_Monitor_Linux_x64_11.1.1.1.0.zip
Archive: Oracle_GoldenGate_Monitor_Linux_x64_11.1.1.1.0.zip
  inflating: Oracle_GoldenGate_Monitor_unix_x64_11_1_1_1_0.sh
  inflating: README.txt
  inflating: ogg_monitor_rel_notes_11.1.1.1.pdf
```

7. Start GoldenGate Monitor installation.

```
./Oracle_GoldenGate_Monitor_unix_x64_11_1_1_1_0.sh
Unpacking JRE ...
Starting Installer ...
INFO {main} Starting Monitor Installation......
```

8. Click on **Next** on the initial screen.

9. Enter the directory where GoldenGate Monitor will be installed and click on **Next**.

10. Select **Oracle** on the next screen and click on **Next**.

11. Enter the details of the Oracle database that was created for the GoldenGate Monitor repository and click on **Next**.

```
Setup - Oracle GoldenGate Monitor 11.1.1.1.1      _ □ ✕

Oracle Database
  Enter repository connection information

  Enter the information needed to connect to the Oracle database repository.

  Oracle server host name:  mgmt1-ol6

  Oracle server port:       1521

  Oracle server SID:        oggmgmt

                                  < Back    Next >    Cancel
```

12. Enter the user ID and password for the GoldenGate Monitor repository schema and click on **Next**.

```
Setup - Oracle GoldenGate Monitor 11.1.1.1.1      _ □ ✕

Database User Credentials
  Enter a user name and password to access the repository

  Enter the credentials of an existing user with DML and DDL privileges. This is the
  user the installer will use to create the Oracle GoldenGate Monitor repository

  Database username:        oggmon

  Database user password:   ●●●●●●

                                  < Back    Next >    Cancel
```

13. Enter the details of the GoldenGate Monitor master **Username** and **Password** and click on **Next**.

14. Enter the port on which you want the Monitor server to listen for the HTTP requests and click on **Next**.

15. Enter the details for the JMX connection between GoldenGate Monitor Agents and the Monitor server and click on **Next**.

16. If you want to get an e-mail, SNMP, or CLI Alerts then enable them in the next windows, enter the relevant details, and click on **Next**.

17. On the summary window, click on **Next** to start the installation.

18. Click on **Finish** on the last screen.

How it works...

The Oracle GoldenGate Monitor architecture comprises of a GoldenGate Monitor server and GoldenGate Monitor Agents. The communication between the Agents and the servers is done using **JMX** (**Java Management Extensions**). The Monitor server stores its repository in a database. In this example, we are using an Oracle database named `oggmgmt` to store this repository. We also create a GoldenGate repository schema with its own tablespace in the steps 2, 3, and 4. The Monitor server installed has a graphics interface and hence requires the X windows. The installation is done in steps 5 to 18. During the installation, you can configure the way you want the GoldenGate Monitor server to send alerts. It supports e-mails, SNMP, and CLI Alerting mechanisms.

Once the Monitor server is installed, you can access it using the following link:

```
http://mgmt1-ol6:5500/monitor
```

You can log in to the GoldenGate Monitor interface using the master user ID and the password that was specified in step 13. Once you log in, you will get the following screenshot:

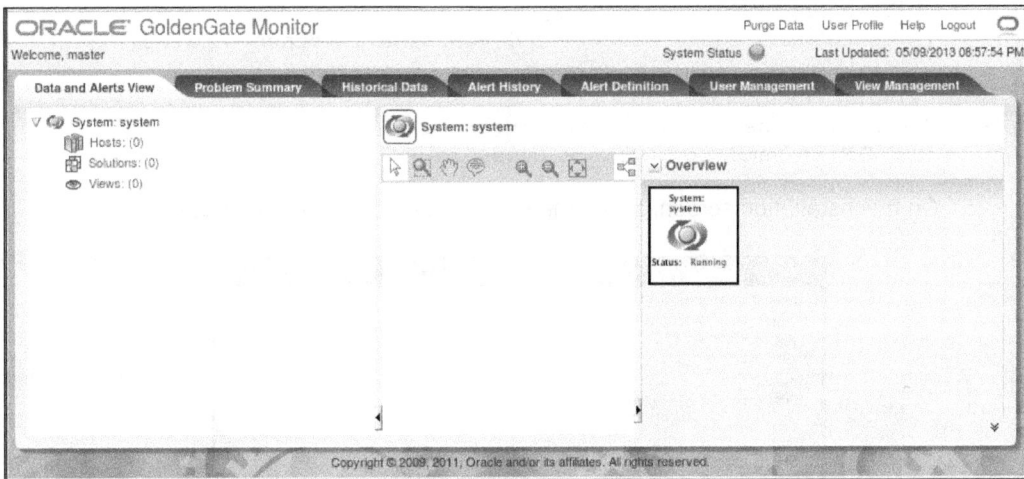

There's more...

You can also configure the Monitor server access in the secure mode using HTTPS as follows:

Installing the GoldenGate Monitor server using HTTPS

So far we have seen how to set up and access the GoldenGate Monitor server over HTTP. This is generally not accepted in any high-profile environment, as the security of the system will be a concern. For such cases, you have the option of configuring GoldenGate Monitor using HTTPs.

1. In order to configure the Monitor server to run over HTTPS, you first need to create a **Java Key Store** (**JKS**) with an identity certificate in it. For this example, we will just create a self-signed certificate using the default root certificate. For a real production environment, you would need to create a **Certificate Signing Request** (**CSR**) and get it signed from a recognized **Certificate Authority** (**CA**).

```
[ggate@mgmt1-ol6 monitor]$ keytool -genkey -keyalg RSA -
  alias monserver -keystore keystore.jks -storepass oggmon
    -keysize 2048
What is your first and last name?
  [Unknown]: Ankur Gupta
What is the name of your organizational unit?
  [Unknown]: IT
What is the name of your organization?
  [Unknown]: Fusion Infotech Limited
What is the name of your City or Locality?
  [Unknown]: Uxbridge
```

```
What is the name of your State or Province?
  [Unknown]: Middlesex
What is the two-letter country code for this unit?
  [Unknown]: GB
Is CN = Ankur Gupta, OU = IT, O = Fusion Infotech Limited,
  L = Uxbridge, ST = Middlesex, C = GB correct?
  [no]: Yes
Enter key password for <monserver>
(RETURN if same as keystore password):
```

2. On the installation screen, select the HTTPS protocol, and click on **Next**.

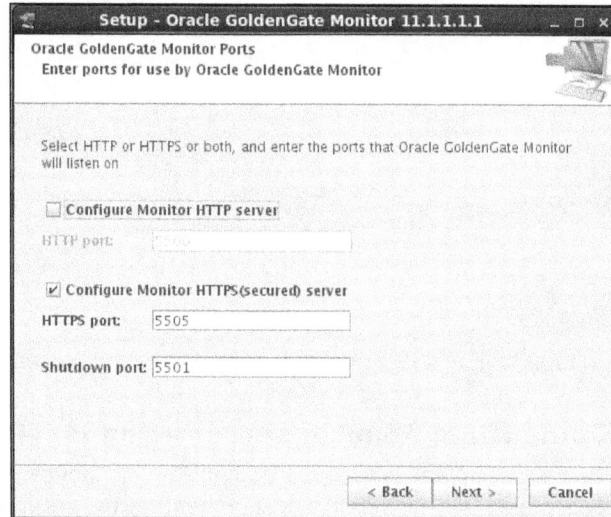

3. In the next window, select **Keystore file** that you created in step 1 and click on **Next**.

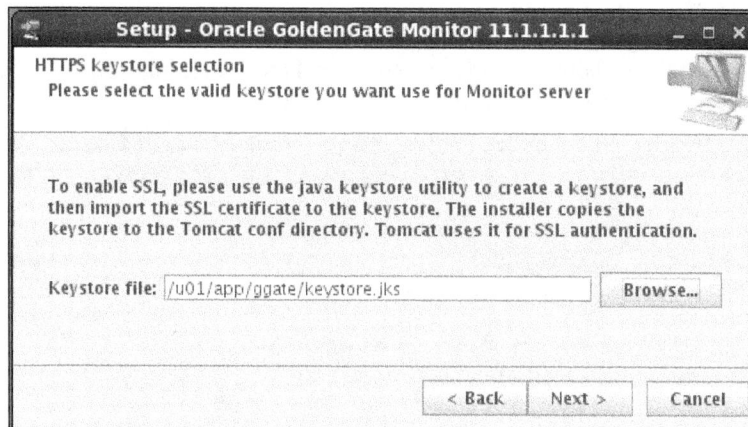

4. Do not start the Monitor server in the last window.

5. Modify the `server.xml` file to include the JKS password as follows:

```
<Connector SSLEnabled = "true" clientAuth = "false"
  keystoreFile = "${catalina.base}/conf/monitor.jks"
    keystorePass = "oggmon" maxThreads = "150" port =
      "5505" protocol = "HTTP/1.1" scheme = "https"
        secure = "true" sslProtocol = "TLS"/>
```

6. Start the Monitor server using `monitor.sh`.

```
[ggate@mgmt1-ol6 bin]$
  /u01/app/ggate/monitor/bin/monitor.sh start
Using CATALINA_BASE: /u01/app/ggate/monitor/tomcat
Using CATALINA_HOME: /u01/app/ggate/monitor/tomcat
Using CATALINA_TMPDIR: /u01/app/ggate/monitor/tomcat/temp
Using JRE_HOME: /u01/app/ggate/monitor/jre
Using CLASSPATH: /u01/app/ggate/monitor/cfg:/u01/app
  /ggate/monitor/tomcat/bin/bootstrap.jar
```

See also

▸ The next recipe *Setting up Oracle GoldenGate Monitor Agents*

Setting up Oracle GoldenGate Monitor Agents

In this recipe, you will learn how to set up Oracle GoldenGate Monitor Agents and configure them to communicate to the Monitor server.

Getting ready

For this recipe, we will refer to the GoldenGate setup done in the *Setting up a simple GoldenGate replication configuration between two single node databases* recipe in *Chapter 2, Setting up GoldenGate Replication*. We will set up GoldenGate monitoring for the source and target GoldenGate instance of this setup. For the GoldenGate Monitor server setup, we will refer to the set up performed in the previous recipe.

How to do it...

The steps to configure GoldenGate Monitor Agents are as follows:

1. Log in to the prim1-ol6-112 source server as a `ggate` user.

2. Edit the `config.properties` file as follows:

```
cd $GG_HOME/cfg
vi config.properties

jagent.host = prim1-ol6-112
jagent.jmx.port = 5555
interval.regular = 60
interval.quick = 30
monitor.host = mgmt1-ol6
monitor.jmx.port = 5502
monitor.jmx.username = jmxUser
agent.type.enabled = OGGMON
```

3. Install JDK Version 1.6 or higher.

```
[ggate@prim1-ol6-112 ggate]$ tar -xvf jdk-7u21-linux-x64
```

4. Set the environment variables to use the installed JDK.

```
[ggate@prim1-ol6-112 ggate]$ export JAVA_HOME =
   /u01/app/ggate/jdk1.7.0_21
[ggate@prim1-ol6-112 ggate]$ export PATH =
   $JAVA_HOME/jre/bin:$PATH
```

5. Create an Oracle wallet for the `jmxUser` password using `pw_agent_util.sh` as follows:

```
cd $GG_HOME
./pw_agent_util.sh - create

Please create a password for Java Agent:

Please confirm password for Java Agent:

Please enter Monitor Server JMX password:

Please confirm Monitor Server JMX password:

Wallet is created successfully.
```

6. After this, a `cwallet.sso` file will be created under `$GG_HOME/dirwlt`.

7. Modify the `ggate` user profile and add the following environment variables:

```
export JAVA_HOME = /u01/app/ggate/jdk1.7.0_21
export LD_LIBRARY_PATH = $JAVA_HOME/jre/lib/amd64/server:
  $LD_LIBRARY_PATH
export PATH = $JAVA_HOME/jre/bin:$PATH
```

8. Enable GoldenGate Monitor Agent.

```
cd $GG_HOME
vi GLOBALS
ENABLEMONITORING
```

9. Start GoldenGate Monitor Agent.

```
cd $GG_HOME
./ggsci
GGSCI (prim1-ol6-112.localdomain) 3> CREATE DATASTORE
Datastore created

GGSCI (prim1-ol6-112.localdomain) 4> STOP MGR
Manager process is required by other GGS processes.
Are you sure you want to stop it (y/n)? Y

Sending STOP request to MANAGER ...
Request processed.
Manager stopped.
GGSCI (prim1-ol6-112.localdomain) 5> START MGR
Manager started.

GGSCI (prim1-ol6-112.localdomain) 6> START JAGENT
GGCMD JAGENT started
```
2 target server as the `ggate` user.

10. Edit config.properties.

11. Log in to the `stdby1-ol6-112` file as follows:

```
cd $GG_HOME/cfg
vi config.properties

jagent.host = stdby1-ol6-112
jagent.jmx.port = 5555
interval.regular = 60
interval.quick = 30
monitor.host = mgmt1-ol6
monitor.jmx.port = 5502
agent.type.enabled = OGGMON
```

12. Install JDK Version 1.6 or higher.

```
[ggate@stdby1-ol6-112 ggate]$ tar -xvf jdk-7u21-linux-x64
```

13. Set the environment variables to use the installed JDK.

```
[ggate@stdby1-ol6-112 ggate]$ export JAVA_HOME =
   /u01/app/ggate/jdk1.7.0_21
[ggate@stdby1-ol6-112 ggate]$ export PATH =
   $JAVA_HOME/jre/bin:$PATH
```

14. Create an Oracle wallet for the `jmxUser` password using `pw_agent_util.sh` as follows:

```
cd $GG_HOME
./pw_agent_util.sh - create

Please create a password for Java Agent:

Please confirm password for Java Agent:

Please enter Monitor Server JMX password:

Please confirm Monitor Server JMX password:

Wallet is created successfully.
```

15. After this, a `cwallet.sso` file will be created under `$GG_HOME/dirwlt`.

16. Modify the `ggate` user profile and add the following environment variables:

```
export JAVA_HOME = /u01/app/ggate/jdk1.7.0_21
export LD_LIBRARY_PATH = $JAVA_HOME/jre/lib/amd64/server:
  $LD_LIBRARY_PATH
export PATH = $JAVA_HOME/jre/bin:$PATH
```

17. Enable GoldenGate Monitor Agent.

```
cd $GG_HOME
vi GLOBALS
ENABLEMONITORING
```

18. Start GoldenGate Monitor Agent.

```
cd $GG_HOME
./ggsci
GGSCI (stdby1-ol6-112.localdomain) 3> CREATE DATASTORE
Datastore created

GGSCI (stdby1-ol6-112.localdomain) 4> STOP MGR
Manager process is required by other GGS processes.
Are you sure you want to stop it (y/n)? Y

Sending STOP request to MANAGER ...
Request processed.
Manager stopped.
GGSCI (stdby1-ol6-112.localdomain) 5> START MGR
Manager started.

GGSCI (stdby1-ol6-112.localdomain) 6> START JAGENT
GGCMD JAGENT started
```

How it works...

The preceding procedure can be used to enable GoldenGate Monitor in a GoldenGate instance. For this, we first set the correct values for various parameters in the `config.properties` file for a GoldenGate instance. GoldenGate Monitor Agent binaries use the JDK executable. It is crucial that you have JDK installed of Version 1.6 or later on the machine, where the GoldenGate instance is running. Once the correct Java environment is set up, we generate an Oracle wallet with the password for `jmxUser`. After this, we enable the monitoring for the GoldenGate instance. These steps are repeated for both the source and target instances. When you enable the monitoring in both the instances, you will notice that they will appear in the GoldenGate Monitor server web interface as shown in the following screenshot:

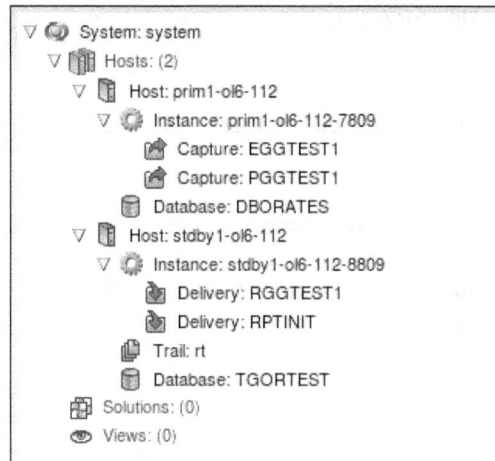

```
▽ 🌐 System: system
   ▽ 🗄 Hosts: (2)
      ▽ 🖥 Host: prim1-ol6-112
         ▽ ⚙ Instance: prim1-ol6-112-7809
              📷 Capture: EGGTEST1
              📷 Capture: PGGTEST1
              🗄 Database: DBORATES
      ▽ 🖥 Host: stdby1-ol6-112
         ▽ ⚙ Instance: stdby1-ol6-112-8809
              📦 Delivery: RGGTEST1
              📦 Delivery: RPTINIT
           📋 Trail: rt
           🗄 Database: TGORTEST
      🗄 Solutions: (0)
      👁 Views: (0)
```

You can also see the overall replication topology in an inverted tree form as follows:

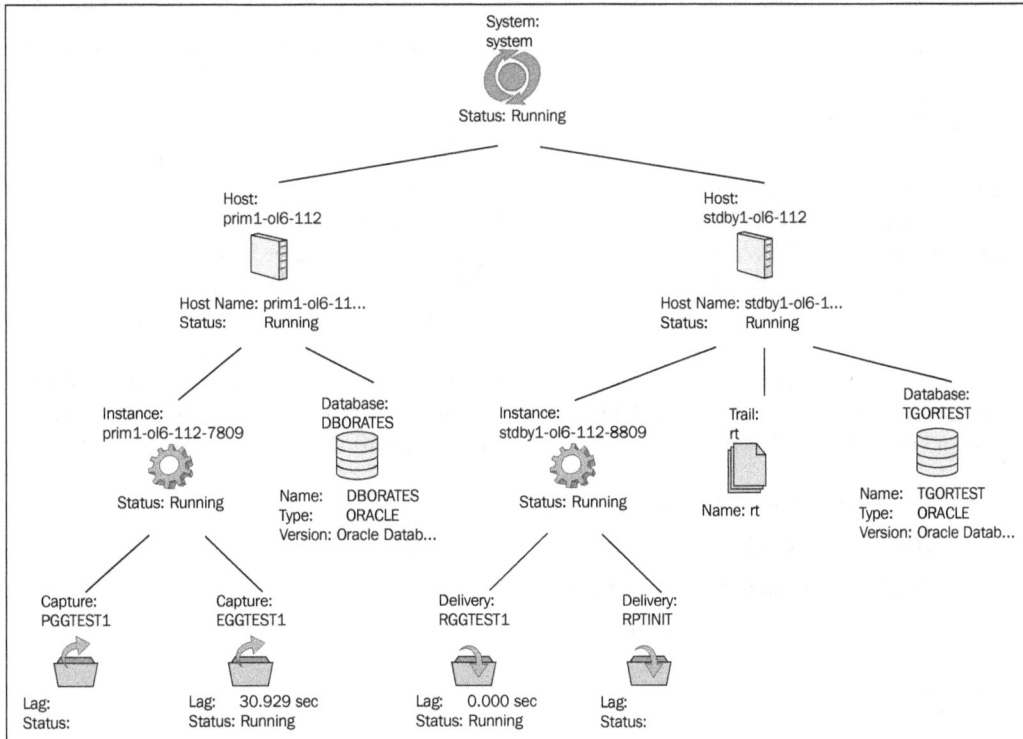

There's more...

The GLOBALS parameter file is a very important file in a GoldenGate instance. The parameter files in general are plain text files, which have specific parameters that the processes read on startup. Each process in GoldenGate has its own parameter file. The GLOBALS parameter file contains the parameters, which are applied to all the processes. This file is read by GGSCI and the parameters are passed on to the relevant processes. You can override the parameters in the GLOBALS file, by specifying the parameters in the process-specific parameter files.

Installing Oracle GoldenGate Director

In this recipe, you will learn how to set up an Oracle GoldenGate Director in your environment.

Getting ready

The setup in this recipe will be performed on a new VM named mgmt1-ol6. The VM was set up with OEL 6.3. The Oracle GoldenGate Director server requires a database for the repository purpose. In this example, we will be using an Oracle database for the repository. The Oracle 11.2.0.3 binaries have been installed on this VM under `/u01/app/oracle/product/11.2.0/dbhome_1`. A shell database named `oggmgmt` has been created under this Oracle Home. This database is registered with the default `LISTENER` running on the port 1521. This recipe does not cover the steps to install the Oracle binaries and to create the shell database. It is assumed that the reader is already familiar with the steps for these two tasks. You would also need to download the following binaries from the Oracle edelivery/otn website:

- Oracle Jrockit: Latest Version
- Oracle Weblogic 10.3.6
- Oracle GoldenGate Director server
- Oracle GoldenGate Director Client

How to do it...

The steps to install Oracle GoldenGate Director are as follows:

1. Install the Jrockit JDK binaries.

   ```
   [ggate@mgmt1-ol6 binaries]$ mkdir /u01/app/ggate/middleware
   [ggate@mgmt1-ol6 binaries]$ mkdir
     /u01/app/ggate/middleware/jrockit
   [ggate@mgmt1-ol6 director]$ ./jrockit-jdk1.6.0_45-R28.2.7-4.1.0-
   linux-ia32.bin
   Extracting
     0%..............................................100%
   ```

2. Click on **Next** on the initial screen.

3. Enter the installation directory for the Jrockit binaries, click on **Next**, and also click on **Next** on the next window. After this the Jrockit installation will be complete.

4. Install the Oracle Weblogic server.

```
[ggate@mgmt1-ol6 binaries]$ export JAVA_HOME =
  /u01/app/ggate/middleware/jrockit
[ggate@mgmt1-ol6 binaries]$ export PATH =
  $JAVA_HOME/bin:$PATH
[ggate@mgmt1-ol6 binaries]$ java -jar wls1036_generic.jar
```

5. Click on **Next** on the initial screen.

6. Enter the Middleware directory and click on **Next**.

7. Skip **Security Updates Registration** and click on **Next**.

8. Select **Typical** and click on **Next**.

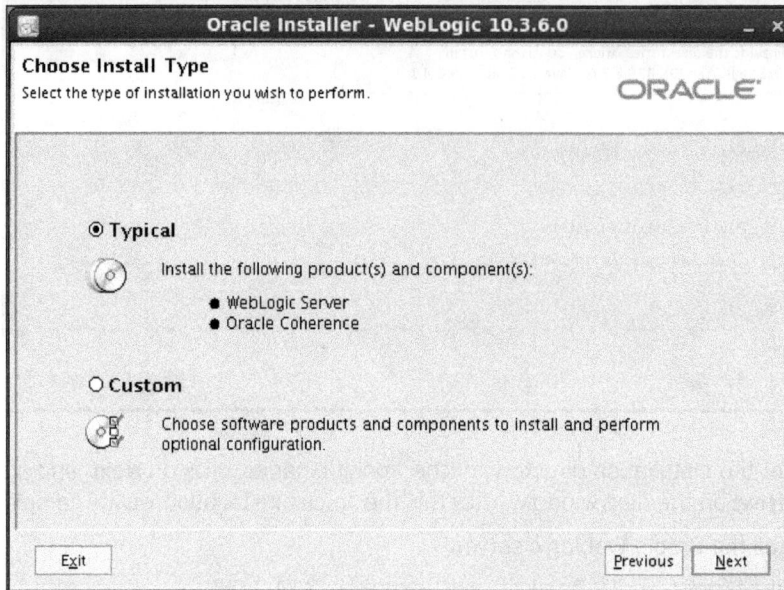

9. Ensure **Jrockit** is selected and click on **Next** on the summary screen to begin the installation.

10. Deselect **Run Quickstart** in the last window and click on **Done**.

11. Log in to sqlplus in the `oggmgmt` database as `sysdba`.

12. Create a tablespace for the GoldenGate Director server repository objects.

```
SQL> CREATE TABLESPACE OGGDIR_DATA DATAFILE
  '/u01/app/oracle/oradata/oggmgmt/oggdir_data01.dbf' SIZE
  200M AUTOEXTEND ON;

Tablespace created.
```

13. Create a new user for the GoldenGate Director repository schema.

```
SQL> CREATE USER OGGDIR IDENTIFIED BY OGGDIR123 DEFAULT
  TABLESPACE OGGDIR_DATA QUOTA UNLIMITED ON OGGDIR_DATA;

User created.
```

14. Grant the necessary privileges to the OGGDIR user.

```
SQL> GRANT CREATE SESSION, RESOURCE, SELECT ANY TABLE TO :OGGDIR;

Grant succeeded.
```

15. Copy the Oracle GoldenGate Director server binaries to the mgmt1-ol6 server.

16. Start the GoldenGate Director server installation.

```
[ggate@mgmt1-ol6 director]$ unzip V33190-01.zip
Archive: V33190-01.zip
  inflating: gg-director-
    serversetup_unix_v11_2_1_0_0_000.sh
  inflating: OGG_Dir_Rel_Notes_11.2.1.0.0.doc
  inflating: OGG_Dir_Rel_Notes_11.2.1.0.0.pdf
  inflating: README.txt
[ggate@mgmt1-ol6 director]$ mkdir /u01/app/ggate/director
[ggate@mgmt1-ol6 ~]$ ./gg-director-
    serversetup_unix_v11_2_1_0_0_000.sh
Starting Installer ...
```

17. Click on **Next** on the initial window.

18. Enter the location where you want to install the GoldenGate Director server and click on **Next**.

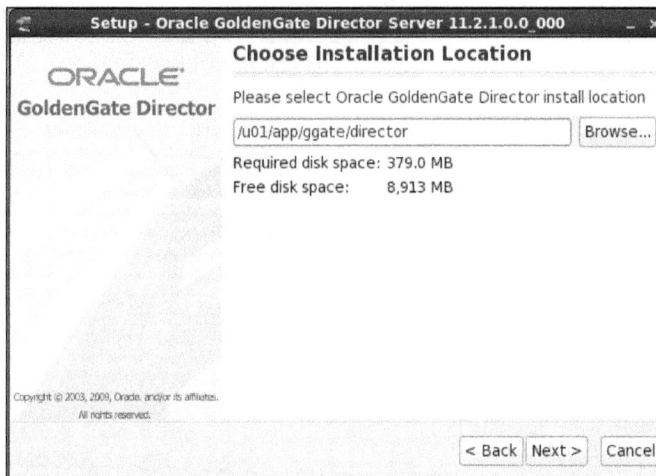

19. Select the parent directory where you installed the Weblogic server and click on **Next**.

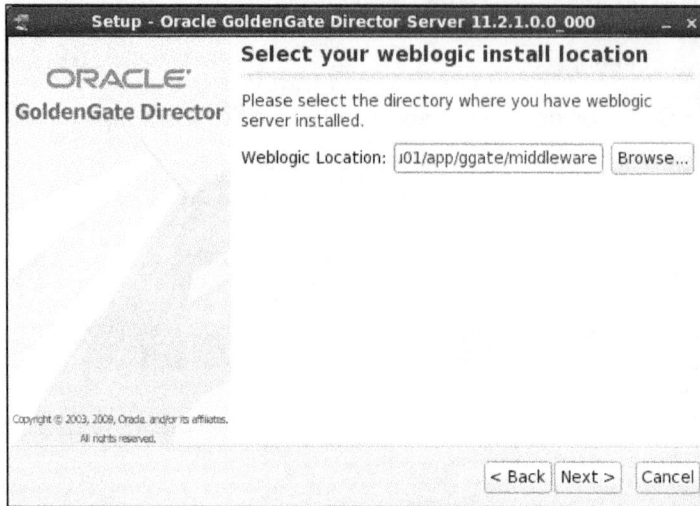

20. Enter the HTTP port for the Director server web interface and click on **Next**.

21. Select **Oracle Database** and click on **Next**.

22. Enter the details of the repository database and click on **Next**.

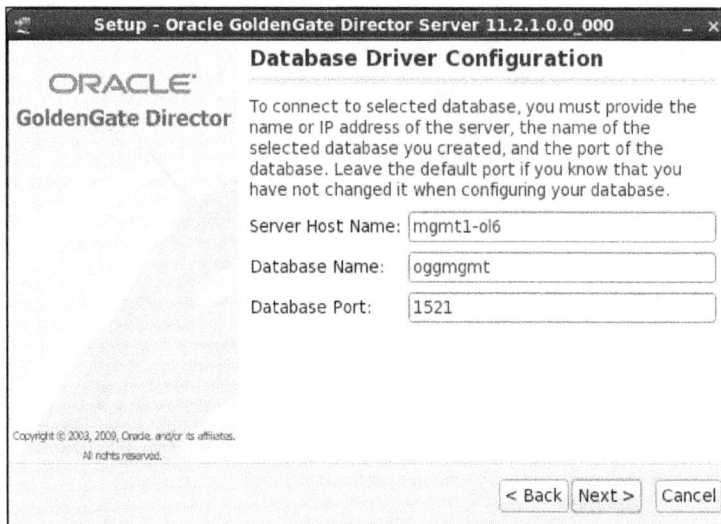

23. Enter the GoldenGate repository schema **User ID** and **Password** and click on **Next**.

24. Click on **Next** on the summary window to begin the installation.

25. Click on **Finish** to complete the installation.

26. Start the GoldenGate Director server.

```
[ggate@mgmt1-ol6 bin]$ ./directorControl.sh -b start
  nohup.out
Starting in background
Logging the output into the file nohup.out
Be careful about the size of the file, it grows regularly
```

27. You can check whether the GoldenGate Director server is running by accessing the GoldenGate Director Web Client as follows:

```
http://mgmt1-ol6:7001/acon
```

How it works...

The Oracle GoldenGate Director setup comprises of a Director server installation. The Director server is the main application through which all the admin requests are processed. GoldenGate Director uses a repository database to maintain its repository. In the preceding example, we are setting up a GoldenGate Director server on mgmt1-ol6. For this, we first install Jrockit JDK under `/u01/app/ggate/middleware/jrockit`. The JDK installed must be a 32-bit binary set, as GoldenGate Director does not support the use of a 64-bit JDK. After this, we install the Oracle Weblogic server 10.3.6 under `/u01/app/ggate/middleware/wlserver_10.3`.

The key thing to note in the Weblogic setup is that we only need to install the binaries and do not create any domain. In steps 12 to 15, we create a schema for the GoldenGate Director repository. After this, we start the Director server installation. The steps to run through the Director server installation wizard are shown previously. During the installation, the installer creates a default Weblogic domain under `/u01/app/ggate/director/domain`. Once the installation is complete, we need to start the Directory server from this domain folder.

See also

▶   The next recipe *Installing and using Oracle GoldenGate Director Client to manage the GoldenGate instances*

Installing and using Oracle GoldenGate Director Client to manage the GoldenGate instances

In this recipe, you will learn how to install the Oracle GoldenGate Director Client and then add the Oracle GoldenGate instances to the configuration. You will also learn how to manage the Oracle GoldenGate instances through the Oracle GoldenGate Director Client.

Getting ready

For this recipe, we will refer to the GoldenGate setup done in the *Setting up a simple GoldenGate replication configuration between two single node databases* recipe in *Chapter 2, Setting up GoldenGate Replication*. Both the source and target GoldenGate instances of this setup will be configured in the GoldenGate Director setup. For the GoldenGate Director server setup, we will refer to the set up performed in *Installing Oracle GoldenGate Director Server* in this chapter. The GoldenGate Director server must be up and running. You would also need to download the Oracle GoldenGate Director Client binaries from the Oracle edelivery/otn website.

How to do it...

The steps to install and configure a GoldenGate Director Client are as follows:

1.   Copy the GoldenGate Director Client binaries to the machine where you want to install Director Client. In this setup, we will install them on mgmt1-ol6 under `/u01/app/ggate/dirclient`.

2. Extract the binaries file and start the installation.

```
[ggate@mgmt1-ol6 director]$ unzip V33185-01.zip
Archive: V33185-01.zip
  inflating: gg-director-
    clientsetup_unix_v11_2_1_0_0_000.sh
  inflating: OGG_Dir_Rel_Notes_11.2.1.0.0.doc
  inflating: OGG_Dir_Rel_Notes_11.2.1.0.0.pdf
  inflating: README.txt
[ggate@mgmt1-ol6 director]$ ./gg-director-
  clientsetup_unix_v11_2_1_0_0_000.sh
Starting Installer ...
```

3. Click on **Next** on the initial screen.

4. Enter the full path of the directory where you want to install GoldenGate Director Client and click on **Next**.

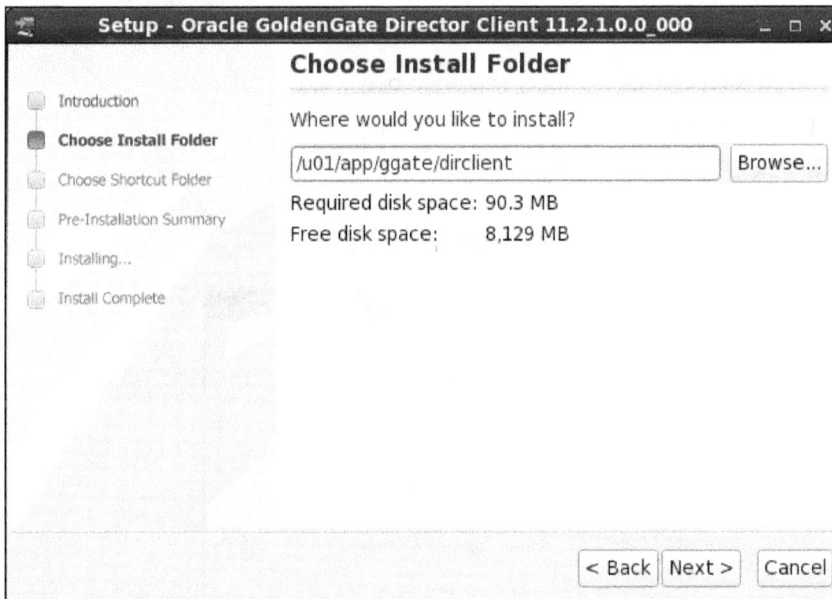

5. Enter the directory where you want to create the symbolic links and click on **Next**.

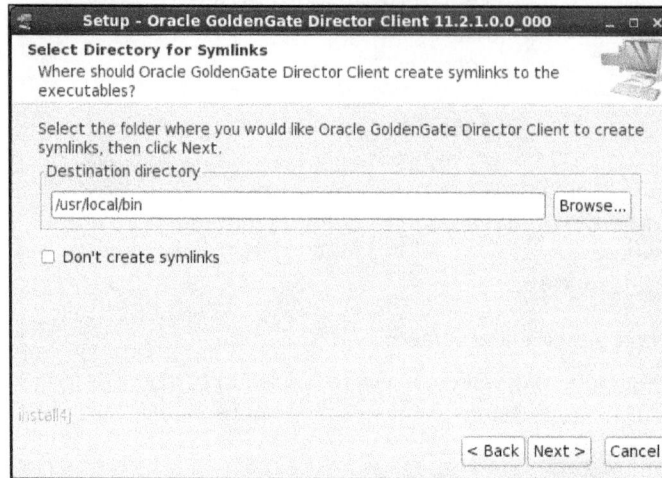

6. Click on **Next** on the summary screen to begin the installation.

7. Click on **Finish** to complete the installation.

8. Start the Director Client Admin tool.

```
[ggate@mgmt1-ol6 ~]$ cd /u01/app/ggate/dirclient/bin
[ggate@mgmt1-ol6 bin]$ ./run-admin.sh
```

9. Log in using the Admin **User Name** (admin), **Password**, and GoldenGate Director server details. The default password for the admin user is admin. The Director server should be specified as hostname.domain:Port.

10. Once you log in, you will see the preceding window. You can update the details of the Admin user and change its **Password**.

11. Click on **Data Sources** to add the GoldenGate instances.

12. Enter the details of the source GoldenGate instances as follows and click on **Save**:

```
FQDN - prim1-ol6-112.localdomain
Manager Port - 7809
Data Source Name - Source
Host Operating System - WU
Database - ORA
GoldenGate Version - 11.2.1.0
DSN
Username - GGATE_ADMIN
Password - GGATE_ADMIN
Owner - admin
```

13. Enter the details of the Target GoldenGate instance and click on **Save**.

```
FQDN - stdby1-ol6-112.localdomain
Manager Port - 8809
Data Source Name - Target
Host Operating System - WU
Database - ORA
GoldenGate Version - 11.2.1.0
DSN
Username - GGATE_ADMIN
Password - GGATE_ADMIN
Owner - admin
```

14. You can click on **Test Connection** to verify whether the GoldenGate instance is reachable from the GoldenGate Director server.

15. Click on **Monitor Agent** and then click on **Start All**.

16. Now that both the instances have been added to the GoldenGate Director server configuration, let's start the GoldenGate Director Client tool to check the status of the whole replication that will be as follows:

    ```
    [ggate@mgmt1-ol6 bin]$ ./run-director.sh
    ```

17. Navigate to **File** | **Login** and log in to the Director Server.

18. You should see both **Data Sources** in the Director Client window.

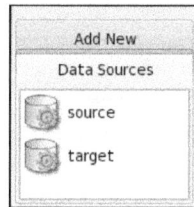

19. Click on the icon to add a diagram and specify a name, for example, Prod. You will see the diagram section in the Director Client window.

20. Drag-and-drop both **Data Sources** to the diagram window.

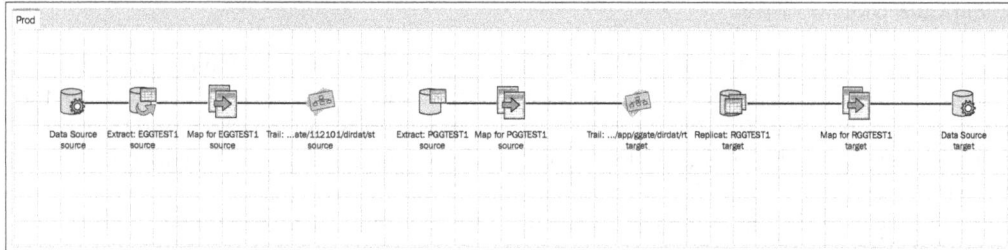

21. You can also log in to GoldenGate Director Web Client through the browser using the following URL:

```
http://mgmt1-ol6:7001/acon
```

How it works...

GoldenGate Director Client enables you to perform the day-to-day management of the GoldenGate instances and also monitor them. It allows the Administrator to issue various GGSCI commands to various GoldenGate instances centrally from a GoldenGate client. You can start, stop, check status, delete, and add various GoldenGate processes through GoldenGate Director Client.

In this recipe, we have installed the GoldenGate Director Client binaries in the `/u01/app/ggate/dirclient` directory on the mgmt1-ol6 server. These binaries are different from the Director server binaries. The Client binaries consist of two parts: Admin Client and Director Client. Once the installation is complete, we need to configure the GoldenGate instances in the Director configuration. This is done using Admin Client. In step 8, we invoke Admin Client and log in to the Director server. Then, we add both the source and target GoldenGate instances, and save them. The information regarding these two GoldenGate instances is saved in the Director repository database.

```
SQL> SELECT * FROM MANAGERREFB;

ID URISTRING                                        STAGE
5 manager://prim1-ol6-112.localdomain:7809          2
6 manager://stdby1-ol6-112.localdomain:8809         2
```

Once the instances are added, we log in to Director Client, and can then perform various management tasks. You can also log in to Director Client using the web interface.

Steps to set up the GoldenGate monitoring using OEM 12c

If you are using Oracle Grid Control in your organization for monitoring the database and application environments, you would most likely prefer to monitor the GoldenGate instances using Oracle Grid Control. Oracle has recently launched a new plugin for Oracle Grid Control to monitor the Oracle GoldenGate instances. In this recipe, you will learn how to monitor the Oracle GoldenGate instances using Oracle Grid Control 12c.

Getting ready

For the purpose of this recipe, we have an Oracle Grid Control 12c set up on a machine named `em12c.localdomain`. A database named `emrep` has been created on the `em12c.localdomain` server, which is used for the Grid Control repository. There are two additional schemas named `SCOTT` and `SCOTT_TARGET` in this database. A simple replication setup has been performed between the tables of these schemas following the steps in the *Setting up a simple GoldenGate replication configuration between two single node databases* recipe in *Chapter 2, Setting up GoldenGate Replication*.

The following setup assumes that you have already set up Oracle Grid Control 12c and installed the Oracle Grid Control agent on the server, where the GoldenGate instance is running. It also assumes that you have already downloaded and uploaded the GoldenGate monitoring plugin in the Grid Control software library. This recipe does not aim to cover the steps for the Grid Control administration, and hence the steps to install Oracle Grid Control 12c, uploading the GoldenGate management plugin to the Grid Control software library, and installing the Grid Control agent are out of the scope of this discussion.

How to do it...

The steps to set up the monitoring of a GoldenGate instance using OEM 12c are as follows:

1. Log in to the server where the GoldenGate instance is running. In this case, we will log in to `em12c.localdomain`.

2. You would need to perform an installation of JDK binaries Version 1.6 or higher on the server, where the GoldenGate instances are running. In this case, JDK binaries are installed under `/u01/app/oracle/Middleware/jdk16/jdk` on `em12c.localdomain`.

3. Add the following parameters to the login profile of the OS user and also run them in the current session:

```
export JAVA_HOME = /u01/app/oracle/Middleware/jdk16/jdk
export LD_LIBRARY_PATH =
  $JAVA_HOME/jre/lib/amd64/server: $LD_LIBRARY_PATH
export PATH = $JAVA_HOME/jre/bin: $PATH
```

4. Enable the monitoring in the GoldenGate instance.

```
cd /u01/app/ggate/112101
vi GLOBALS
ENABLEMONITORING
```

5. Create a wallet for the Agent password.

```
[oracle@em12c 112101]$ cd /u01/app/ggate/112101
[oracle@em12c 112101]$ ./pw_agent_util.sh -jagentonly
Please create a password for Java Agent:
Please confirm password for Java Agent:
Wallet is created successfully.
```

6. Update the GoldenGate monitoring properties to work with OEM.

```
[oracle@em12c 112101]$ cd /u01/app/ggate/112101/cfg
[oracle@em12c cfg]$ vi Config.properties
agent.type.enabled = OEM
jagent.host = em12c.localdomain
```

7. Enable and start GoldenGate Monitor Agent.

```
[oracle@em12c cfg]$ cd /u01/app/ggate/112101
[oracle@em12c 112101]$ ./ggsci

Oracle GoldenGate Command Interpreter for Oracle
Version 11.2.1.0.1
  OGGCORE_11.2.1.0.1_PLATFORMS_120423.0230_FBO
Linux, x64, 64bit (optimized), Oracle 11g on Apr 23 2012
  08:32:14

Copyright (C) 1995, 2012, Oracle and/or its affiliates.
  All rights reserved.
```

```
GGSCI (em12c.localdomain) 1> CREATE DATASTORE
Datastore created

GGSCI (em12c.localdomain) 2> STOP MANAGER
Manager process is required by other GGS processes.
Are you sure you want to stop it (y/n)? Y

Sending STOP request to MANAGER ...
Request processed.
Manager stopped.

GGSCI (em12c.localdomain) 3> START MANAGER

Manager started.

GGSCI (em12c.localdomain) 4> START JAGENT

GGCMD JAGENT started
```

8. Set up the credentials to deploy the GoldenGate monitoring plugin to the host Agent from the OEM 12c window.

9. Navigate to **Setup | Security | Preferred Credentials**.

10. Select **Host** and click on **Manage Preferred Credentials**.

11. On the **Preferred Credentials** page, under **Target Preferred Credentials**, click on `em12c.localdomain`, and click on **Set**.

12. Enter the OS **Username** and **Password** for the host and specify the name for the credentials. Click on **Save**.

13. Click on **Normal Host Credentials**.

14. Click on **Test** to test the credentials.

15. Select **Basic** in the drop-down box and click on **Test**. You should get a new pop-up window with the **Test Successful** message.

16. Navigate to **Setup | Extensibility | Plugins**.

17. On the **Plug-Ins** window, you should see **Oracle GoldenGate** under **Middleware**.

18. Select **Oracle GoldenGate**, click the arrow next to **Deploy on**, and select **Management Servers....**

ORACLE **Enterprise Manager** Cloud Control 12c

Enterprise ▾   Targets ▾   Favorites ▾   History ▾

Plug-ins

This page displays the list of plug-ins available, downloaded and deployed in the Enterprise Manager environment. Plug-in lifecycle action

Actions ▾   View ▾   Deploy On | ▾   Undeploy From | ▾   Check Updates   Deployment Activities

Name	Management Servers...	Version		Management Agent with Plug-in
	Management Agent... able	Latest Downloaded	On Management Server	
⊳ Databases				
▽ Middleware ⓘ				
Apache Tomcat	12.1.0.1.0	12.1.0.1.0		0
Microsoft .Net Framework	12.1.0.1.0	12.1.0.1.0		0
Microsoft Active Directory	12.1.0.1.0	12.1.0.1.0		0
Microsoft Biz Talk Server	12.1.0.1.0	12.1.0.1.0		0
Microsoft IIS	12.1.0.1.0	12.1.0.1.0		0
Oracle Fusion Middleware	12.1.0.3.0	12.1.0.3.0	12.1.0.3.0	1
Oracle GoldenGate	12.1.0.1.0	12.1.0.1.0		0
⊳ Servers, Storage and Network ⓘ				

Oracle GoldenGate

General   Recent Deployment Activities

Plug-in ID   oracle.fmw.gg
Vendor   oracle   Versions Downloaded   12.1.0.1.0
Version on Management Server   None   Description   Enterprise Manager for Oracle GoldenGate
Latest Available Version   12.1.0.1.0

Deploy Plug-in on Management Servers   ✕

General

Name   Oracle GoldenGate
Version   12.1.0.1.0   ▾
* Repository SYS Password   ●●●●●●●

Target Types

Name	Supported Target Versions
oracle_goldengate	12.1.0.1.0+
oracle_goldengate_extract	12.1.0.1.0+
oracle_goldengate_manager	12.1.0.1.0+
oracle_goldengate_replicat	12.1.0.1.0+

Continue   Cancel

19. Enter the system password for the OMS database (`emrep`) and click on **Continue**. In the next window, some prerequisite checks will be performed on the OMS server, and then the plugin will be installed.

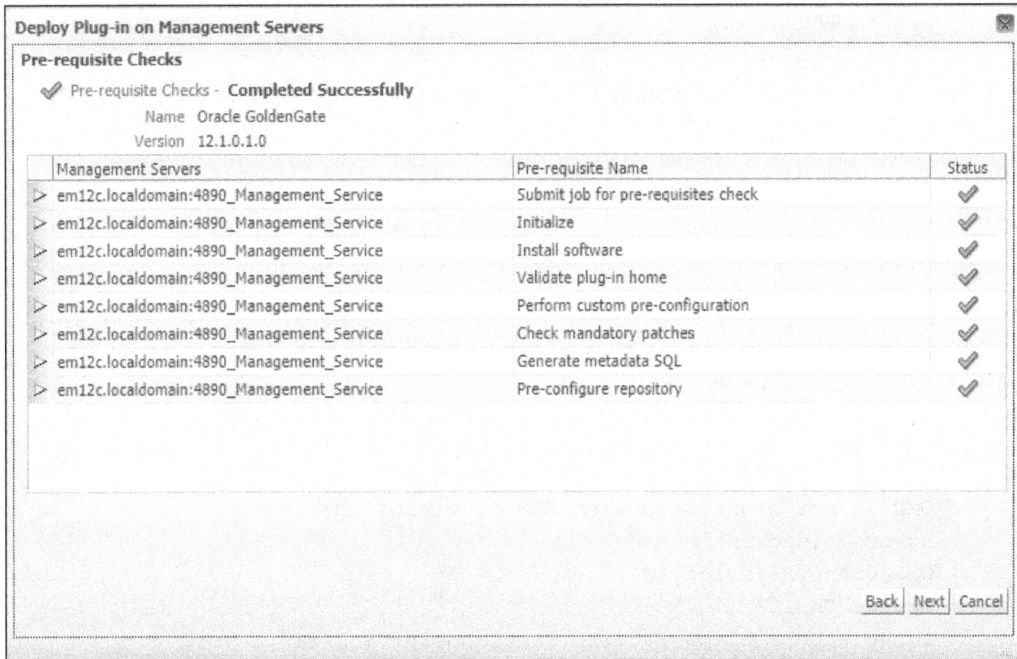

Deploy Plug-in on Management Servers

Pre-requisite Checks

✅ Pre-requisite Checks - **Completed Successfully**

Name Oracle GoldenGate

Version 12.1.0.1.0

Management Servers	Pre-requisite Name	Status
▷ em12c.localdomain:4890_Management_Service	Submit job for pre-requisites check	✅
▷ em12c.localdomain:4890_Management_Service	Initialize	✅
▷ em12c.localdomain:4890_Management_Service	Install software	✅
▷ em12c.localdomain:4890_Management_Service	Validate plug-in home	✅
▷ em12c.localdomain:4890_Management_Service	Perform custom pre-configuration	✅
▷ em12c.localdomain:4890_Management_Service	Check mandatory patches	✅
▷ em12c.localdomain:4890_Management_Service	Generate metadata SQL	✅
▷ em12c.localdomain:4890_Management_Service	Pre-configure repository	✅

Back | Next | Cancel

20. Click on **Next**.

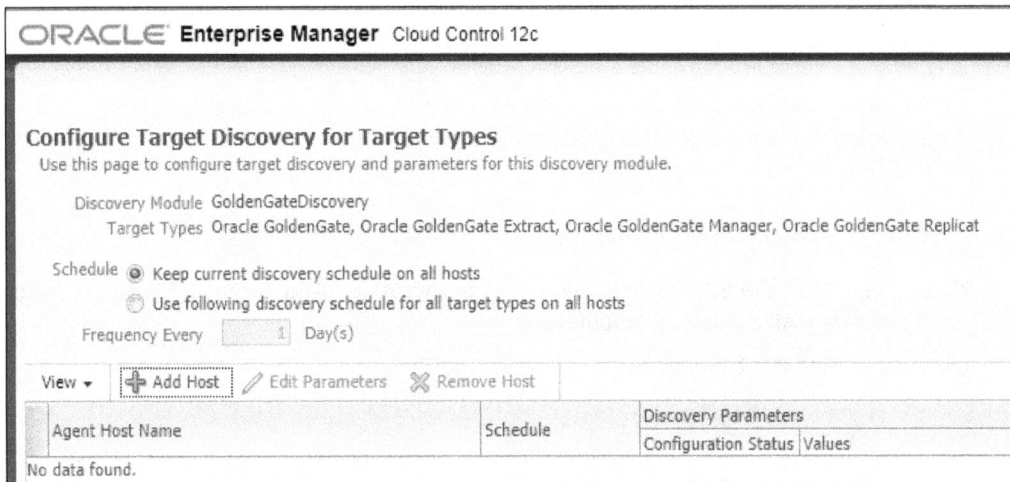

ORACLE Enterprise Manager Cloud Control 12c

Configure Target Discovery for Target Types

Use this page to configure target discovery and parameters for this discovery module.

Discovery Module GoldenGateDiscovery

Target Types Oracle GoldenGate, Oracle GoldenGate Extract, Oracle GoldenGate Manager, Oracle GoldenGate Replicat

Schedule ⦿ Keep current discovery schedule on all hosts

○ Use following discovery schedule for all target types on all hosts

Frequency Every [1] Day(s)

View ▾ | ➕ Add Host | ✎ Edit Parameters | ✖ Remove Host

Agent Host Name	Schedule	Discovery Parameters	
		Configuration Status	Values
No data found.			

21. Confirm that you have backed up the OEM repository and click on **Deploy**. The management server will be restarted once the deployment is complete. In order to check the progress of the plugin deployment, you can check it by running it. Once the management server has restarted, you should see the following output:

```
[oracle@em12c bin]$ ./emctl status oms -details
Oracle Enterprise Manager Cloud Control 12c Release 2
Copyright (c) 1996, 2012 Oracle Corporation.
  All rights reserved.
Enter Enterprise Manager Root (SYSMAN) Password:
Console Server Host       : em12c.localdomain
HTTP Console Port         : 7789
HTTPS Console Port        : 7801
HTTP Upload Port          : 4890
HTTPS Upload Port         : 4901
EM Instance Home          :
   /u01/app/oracle/Middleware/gc_inst/em/EMGC_OMS1
OMS Log Directory Location: /u01/app
   /oracle/Middleware/gc_inst/em/EMGC_OMS1/sysman/log
OMS is not configured with SLB or virtual hostname
Agent Upload is locked.
OMS Console is locked.
Active CA ID: 1
Console URL: https://em12c.localdomain:7801/em
Upload URL: https://em12c.localdomain:4901/empbs/upload

WLS Domain Information
Domain Name      : GCDomain
Admin Server Host: em12c.localdomain

Managed Server Information
Managed Server Instance Name: EMGC_OMS1
Managed Server Instance Host: em12c.localdomain
WebTier is Up
Oracle Management Server is Up
```

22. Log in to the OEM 12c console and navigate to **Setup | Add Target | Configure Auto Discovery | All discovery modules**.

23. Click on **Add Host**, select em12c.localdomain.

24. Click on **Run Discovery Now** and click on **Yes**.

Agent Host Name	Enabled Discovery Modules	Schedule	Discovered Targets	Managed Targets	Most Recent Ended On	Status
em12c.localdomain	GoldenGateDiscovery; Oracle Cluster a...	Every 1 Day(s)	18	22		

Configure Auto Discovery > Target Discovery (Agent Based)

Use this page to search and browse target discovery settings on hosts managed by Enterprise Manager, configure discovery settings on one or more hosts, or view the latest results.

> Search

View ▾ | Configure | Run Discovery Now | Refresh

25. Once it is finished, you will see some new targets discovered in the **Target Discovery** window.

Target Discovery (Agent Based)

Configure Auto Discovery > Target Discovery (Agent Based)

Use this page to search and browse target discovery settings on hosts managed by Enterprise Manager, configure discovery settings on one or more hosts, or view the latest results.

> Search

View ▾ | Configure | Run Discovery Now | Refresh

Agent Host Name	Enabled Discovery Modules	Schedule	Discovered Targets	Managed Targets	Most Recent Ended On
em12c.localdomain	GoldenGateDiscovery; Oracle Cluster a...	Every 1 Day(s)	10	22	

26. Click on the number below **Discovered Targets** and you will see a list of newly discovered targets as shown in the following screenshot:

> **Search**

View ▾ | Promote | Rename | Delete | Ignore | Refresh

Target Name	Target Type	Discovered On	Host
LISTENER_em12c.localdomain	Listener	17-May-2013 17:01:34 o'clock GMT-04...	em12c.localdomain
OraDb11g_home1_1_em12c	Oracle Home	25-Oct-2012 10:44:28 o'clock GMT-04:...	em12c.localdomain
common12c1_20_em12c	Oracle Home	25-Oct-2012 10:44:29 o'clock GMT-04:...	em12c.localdomain
emrep	Database Instance	25-Oct-2012 10:44:30 o'clock GMT-04:...	em12c.localdomain
extract:127.0.0.1:5559:EGGTEST1	Oracle GoldenGate Extract	17-May-2013 17:01:31 o'clock GMT-04...	em12c.localdomain
jdk1_2_em12c	Oracle Home	25-Oct-2012 10:44:29 o'clock GMT-04:...	em12c.localdomain
manager:127.0.0.1:5559:MGR	Oracle GoldenGate Manager	17-May-2013 17:01:31 o'clock GMT-04...	em12c.localdomain
ogg:127.0.0.1:5559	Oracle GoldenGate	17-May-2013 17:01:30 o'clock GMT-04...	em12c.localdomain
replicat:127.0.0.1:5559:RGGTEST1	Oracle GoldenGate Replicat	17-May-2013 17:01:31 o'clock GMT-04...	em12c.localdomain
sbin12c1_9_em12c	Oracle Home	25-Oct-2012 10:44:29 o'clock GMT-04:...	em12c.localdomain

27. Press the *Ctrl* key, select the manager target, and click on **Promote**. In the next window, Grid Control will list the subtargets of this Manager process.

Custom Promotion for GoldenGate Targets

GoldenGate Targets

Additional targets for the same Oracle GoldenGate instance host and port have been included for promotion. Deselect any Extract, Replicat, or Manager you do not want to promote.

View ▾

Target Type	Target Name	Host Name	Port Number	Select
Oracle GoldenGate	ogg:127.0.0.1:5559	127.0.0.1	5559	☑
Oracle GoldenGate Replicat	replicat:127.0.0.1:5559:RGGTEST1	127.0.0.1	5559	☑
Oracle GoldenGate Manager	manager:127.0.0.1:5559:MGR	127.0.0.1	5559	☑
Oracle GoldenGate Extract	extract:127.0.0.1:5559:EGGTEST1	127.0.0.1	5559	☑

28. Click on **Promote**.

29. Navigate to **Targets | GoldenGate**.

Oracle GoldenGate Homepage

Page Refreshed 17-May-2013 17:26:35 EDT ↻

Status: All   Lag: All   ⚙ Customize

Auto Refresh: 1 minute ▾

Target Name	Target Type	Status	Lag (Sec)	Lag Trend	Total Operations	Delta Operations	Delta Operations Per Second	Incidents ⊖ ⊗ ⚠ P				Seconds Since Last OGG Checkpoint	Last OGG Checkpoint
▽ 127.0.0.1:5559	Oracle GoldenGate	⬆	2					0	0	0	0	62	May 17, 2013 17:25:39 PM EDT
MGR	Manager	⬆						0	0	0	0		
EGGTEST1	Extract	⬆	2		97	0	0	0	0	0	0	62	May 17, 2013 17:25:39 PM EDT
RGGTEST1	Replicat	⬆	0		0	0	0	0	0	0	0	0	May 17, 2013 14:26:55 PM EDT

30. The GoldenGate instance and processes are now added to Oracle Grid Control.

How it works...

Oracle Grid Control 12c can be used to monitor the Oracle GoldenGate instances. The default installation does not contain the monitoring plugin that is required for monitoring the GoldenGate instances. The plugin needs to be downloaded from the Oracle website and added to the Grid Control software repository. Once the plugin is added to the software repository, it needs to be deployed to the management servers. This plugin is then deployed to the hosts, where the GoldenGate instances are running. The GoldenGate Monitor Agent on the hosts also needs to be configured and started so that it communicates with the Oracle Grid Control 12c Agent.

In the preceding 1 to 7 steps, we first configure the GoldenGate Agent on the host. This involves setting some environment variables to use the correct Java binaries, and then enabling GoldenGate Agent for monitoring. In step 5, we create a wallet to store a password for `Jagent`.

In steps, 8 to 19, we deploy the GoldenGate monitoring plugin to the OMS servers. For this, we first set the credentials for the host on which the plugin is to be deployed. Once the credentials are set, the plugin is pushed to the Oracle management server running on that host. This process restarts the management server instance. After this when you re-log in to the management server, you will see a new target type in the list of the targets named **Oracle GoldenGate**.

In steps 20 to 28, we discover and add the GoldenGate processes as the targets to the Oracle Grid Control. For this, the host is added to the target discovery list, and then the GoldenGate targets are promoted so that they are saved to the target list.

There's more...

Once the GoldenGate targets are added to the list, the thresholds for the metrics need to be configured to enable raising the appropriate alerts. An example of such configuration is setting an appropriate threshold for lag for the Replicat process. In this example, we will set the warning threshold for RGGTEST1 to 5 seconds and critical threshold to 10 seconds.

The steps to set the lag thresholds for the RGGTEST1 process are as follows:

1. Navigate to **Targets** | **GoldenGate Targets** | **RGGTEST1**.
2. Click on **Lag(Sec)** and click on **Modify Thresholds**.

⬆ **replicat:127.0.0.1:5559:RGGTEST1** ⓘ

⬡ Oracle GoldenGate Replicat ▾

⬆ **Replicat : RGGTEST1**

View ▾

Metric Name	Metric Value	Last Updated
Checkpoint Position	Current read position: Sequence #: 2 RBA: 1128 Timestamp: 2013-05-17 14:21:49.331042 Extract Trail: /u01/app/ggate/112101/dirdat/st	Fri May 17 18:40:16 EDT 2013
Delta Deletes	0	Fri May 17 18:40:16 EDT 2013
Delta Discards	0	Fri May 17 18:40:16 EDT 2013
Delta Executed DDLs	0	Fri May 17 18:40:16 EDT 2013
Delta Inserts	0	Fri May 17 18:40:16 EDT 2013
Delta Operation Per Second	0	Fri May 17 18:40:16 EDT 2013
Delta Operations	0	Fri May 17 18:40:16 EDT 2013
Delta Truncates	0	Fri May 17 18:40:16 EDT 2013
Delta Updates	0	Fri May 17 18:40:16 EDT 2013
End of File	true	Fri May 17 18:40:16 EDT 2013
Lag (Sec)	0	Fri May 17 18:40:16 EDT 2013
Last OGG Checkpoint Timestamp	Fri May 17 14:25:55 EDT 2013	Fri May 17 18:40:16 EDT 2013
Last Operation Timestamp		Fri May 17 18:40:16 EDT 2013
Last Processed Timestamp		Fri May 17 18:40:16 EDT 2013
Message		Fri May 17 18:40:16 EDT 2013
Name	RGGTEST1	Fri May 17 18:40:16 EDT 2013
Seconds Since Last OGG Checkpoint	0	Fri May 17 18:40:16 EDT 2013
Start Time	Fri May 17 14:21:41 EDT 2013	Fri May 17 18:40:16 EDT 2013
Status	Running	Fri May 17 18:40:16 EDT 2013
Total Deletes	0	Fri May 17 18:40:16 EDT 2013
Total Discards	0	Fri May 17 18:40:16 EDT 2013
Total Executed DDLs	0	Fri May 17 18:40:16 EDT 2013

3. Enter the value for the thresholds and number of occurrences for alerts and click on **Save Thresholds**.

Modify Thresholds

Data available from 17-May-2013 17:18:17 EDT to 17-May-2013 18:40:16 EDT

Warning Threshold	5	High Value	0	Time in warning (%)	0
Critical Threshold	10	Low Value	0	Time in critical (%)	0
Occurrences Before Alert	1	Average Value	0	Number of warning events	0
	[Test Thresholds]			Number of critical events	0

Thresholds suggestion chart

Past day   Day   2 hours   15 minutes   ▷ Slider

For a production environment where you have numerous GoldenGate instances, you can create a template with an appropriate threshold for various metrics and apply the template to the GoldenGate targets.

Steps to install Oracle GoldenGate Veridata

In this recipe, you will learn how to install and configure the Oracle GoldenGate Veridata server, using which you can validate data between the source and target systems.

Getting ready

The setup in this recipe will be performed on a new VM named mgmt1-ol6. The VM was set up with OEL 6.3. The Oracle GoldenGate Monitor server requires a database for the repository purposes. In this example setup, we will be using an Oracle database for the repository. The Oracle 11.2.0.3 binaries have been installed on this VM under `/u01/app/oracle/product/11.2.0/dbhome_1`. A shell database named `oggmgmt` has been created under this Oracle Home. This database is registered with the default `LISTENER` running on the port 1521. This recipe does not cover the steps to install the Oracle binaries and to create the shell database. It is assumed that the reader is already familiar with the steps for these two tasks. You would also need to download the Oracle GoldenGate Veridata server binaries from the e-delivery website. The product number for these binaries is V35572-01. In order to install these binaries, you would need an X server set up on your PC.

How to do it...

The steps to install the Oracle GoldenGate Veridata server are as follows:

1. Log in to sqlplus in the `oggmgmt` database as `sysdba`.

2. Create a tablespace for the GoldenGate Veridata repository objects.

   ```
   SQL> CREATE TABLESPACE OGGVER_DATA DATAFILE
     '/u01/app/oracle/oradata/oggmgmt/oggver_data01.dbf' SIZE
       200M AUTOEXTEND ON;

   Tablespace created.
   ```

3. Create a new user for the GoldenGate Monitor repository schema.

   ```
   SQL> CREATE USER OGGVER IDENTIFIED BY OGGVER DEFAULT
     TABLESPACE OGGVER_DATA QUOTA UNLIMITED ON OGGVER_DATA;

   User created.
   ```

4. Create Veridata Role.

   ```
   SQL> CREATE ROLE VERIDATA_ROLE;

   Role created.
   ```

5. Grant the necessary privileges to the OGGVER user.

   ```
   SQL> GRANT CREATE SESSION, RESOURCE, SELECT ANY TABLE TO
     VERIDATA_ROLE;

   Grant succeeded.
   ```

6. Grant Veridata Role to the OGGVER user.

   ```
   SQL> GRANT VERIDATA_ROLE TO OGGVER;

   Grant succeeded.
   ```

7. Copy the Oracle GoldenGate Veridata binaries to the mgmt1-ol6 server.

8. Unzip the binaries.

   ```
   [ggate@mgmt1-ol6 binaries]$ unzip V35572-01.zip
   Archive:  V35572-01.zip
     inflating: GoldenGate_Veridata_redhatAS40_x64.sh
     inflating: ogg_veridata_relnotes_11.2.1.0.0.pdf
     inflating: ogg_veridata_relnotes_11.2.1.0.0.doc
     inflating: ogg-veridata-readme-11.2.1.0.0.doc
     inflating: ogg-veridata-readme-11.2.1.0.0.txt
   ```

9. Start the GoldenGate Veridata installation.

   ```
   [ggate@mgmt1-ol6 binaries]$
     ./GoldenGate_Veridata_redhatAS40_x64.sh
   Unpacking JRE ...
   Starting Installer ...
   ```

10. Click on **Next** on the initial screen.

11. Enter the full path of the directory where you want to install the Veridata server for example, `/u01/app/ggate/veridata` and click on **Next**.

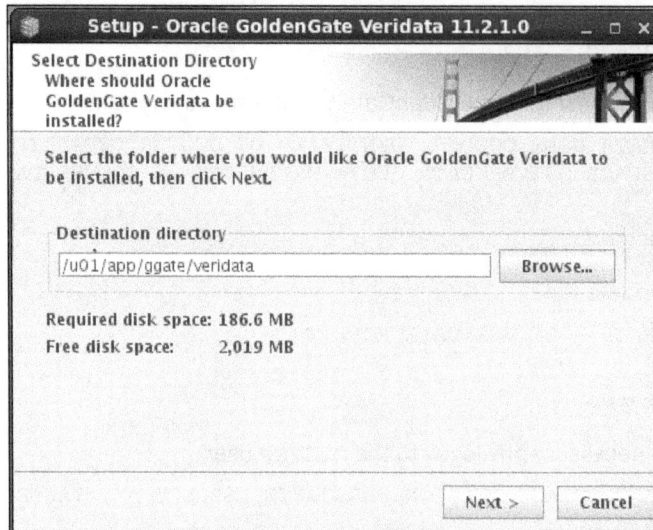

```
Setup - Oracle GoldenGate Veridata 11.2.1.0    _ □ ×

Select Destination Directory
Where should Oracle
GoldenGate Veridata be
installed?

Select the folder where you would like Oracle GoldenGate Veridata to
be installed, then click Next.

  Destination directory
  /u01/app/ggate/veridata                        Browse...

  Required disk space: 186.6 MB
  Free disk space:    2,019 MB

                                          Next >     Cancel
```

12. Click on **Next** on the next window.

```
Setup - Oracle GoldenGate Veridata 11.2.1.0    _ □ ×

Select Veridata Data Location
Please specify a location for
the Data

This screen retrieves the data folder location from the user. This will
typically be co-located with the rest of the application under the
Veridata installation folder, but can be located in a different location.

  /u01/app/ggate/veridata/shared/data             Browse...

                                          Next >     Cancel
```

13. Enter the **HTTP** and **Shutdown Port** in the next window and click on **Next**.

14. Enter the Admin user details in the next screen and click on **Next**.

15. Select **Oracle** and click on **Next**. Confirm Oracle Home on the next window.

16. Select the TNS service name from the drop-down list and click on **Next**.

17. Choose **Use an Existing Userid** and click on **Next**.

18. Enter the schema details for the Veridata repository and click on **Next**.

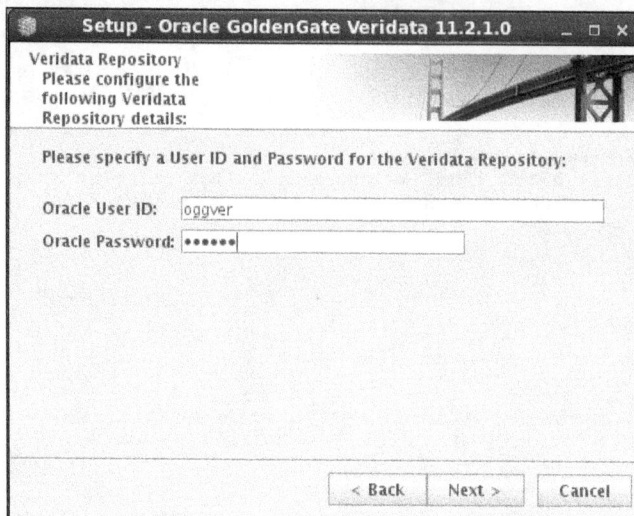

19. Click on **Next** on the next window to start the installation.

20. Click on **Finish** to complete the installation.

How it works...

The Oracle GoldenGate Veridata architecture comprises of a GoldenGate Veridata server and GoldenGate Veridata Agents. The Veridata server stores its repository in a database. In this example, we are using an Oracle database named oggmgmt to store this repository. We also create a GoldenGate repository schema with its own tablespace in steps 2 to 6. The Veridata server installer has a graphics interface and hence requires X windows. The installation is done in steps 8 to 20. You need to specify a Veridata Admin server username and password during the installation. You can also configure the HTTP on which you want the Veridata web interface to be accessible.

See also

▸ The next recipe *Steps to compare data between the source and target environment using Oracle GoldenGate Veridata*

Steps to compare data between the source and target environment using Oracle GoldenGate Veridata

In this recipe, you will learn how to use Oracle GoldenGate Veridata to compare data between the source and target environments.

Getting ready

For this recipe, we will refer to the GoldenGate setup done in the *Setting up a simple GoldenGate replication configuration between two single node databases* recipe in *Chapter 2, Setting up GoldenGate Replication*. We will set up GoldenGate Veridata Java Agents on these two GoldenGate instances and perform a data comparison through Veridata. For the GoldenGate Veridata server setup, we will refer to the previous recipe.

How to do it...

The steps to set up a Veridata comparison between the source and target databases are as follows:

1. Copy the Veridata Java client binaries to the source server (`prim1-ol6-112.localdomain`). The Java client binaries can be downloaded from the `oracle otn/edelivery` website.

2. Extract the contents of the Agent binaries into a temporary folder.

   ```
   [ggate@prim1-ol6-112 binaries]$ unzip V35569-01.zip
   Archive:  V35569-01.zip
   ```

3. Move the Agent folder into an appropriate location.

   ```
   [ggate@prim1-ol6-112 binaries]$ mkdir
     /u01/app/ggate/veridata
   [ggate@prim1-ol6-112 binaries]$ mv agent
     /u01/app/ggate/veridata/
   ```

4. Create an `agent.properties` file from `agent.properties.sample` and modify it.

   ```
   [ggate@prim1-ol6-112 agent]$ cp agent.properties.sample
     agent.properties
   [ggate@prim1-ol6-112 agent]$ vi agent.properties
   ```

5. The following four parameters need to be specified in this file.

```
server.port = 5999
database.url = jdbc:oracle:thin:
  @prim1-ol6-112:1521:dboratest
server.driversLocation = drivers
server.jdbcDriver = ojdbc6.jar
```

6. Start the Veridata Java Agent.

```
./agent.sh start
```

7. Perform steps 1 to 6 on the target server. The parameters to be specified in the `agent,properties` file are as follows:

```
server.port = 5999
database.url = jdbc:oracle:thin:
  @stdby1-ol6-112:1521:tgortest
server.driversLocation = drivers
server.jdbcDriver = ojdbc6.jar
```

8. Start the Veridata Java Agent on the target server as well.

9. Start the Veridata web interface on the GoldenGate Veridata server.

```
[ggate@mgmt1-ol6 bin]$ cd /u01/app/ggate/veridata/web/bin
[ggate@mgmt1-ol6 bin]$ ./startup.sh
CATALINA_HOME: /u01/app/ggate/veridata/web
JRE_HOME: /u01/app/ggate/veridata/jre
JAVA_OPTS: -Xms1024m -Xmx1024m -Djava.awt.headless =
  true -Dveridata.home = /u01/app/ggate/
    veridata -Dveridata.log.dir =
      /u01/app/ggate/veridata/shared/logs -
        Dveridata.log.file=veridataweb.log
Using CATALINA_BASE: /u01/app/ggate/veridata/web
Using CATALINA_HOME: /u01/app/ggate/veridata/web
Using CATALINA_TMPDIR: /u01/app/ggate/veridata/web/temp
Using JRE_HOME: /u01/app/ggate/veridata/jre
```

10. Log in to the Veridata web interface using the Admin account that was specified during the installation:

```
http://mgmt1-ol6.localdomain:8830/veridata
```

11. Once you log in to the web interface, click on **Connection Configuration**.

12. Now, click on **New**.

13. Enter the name of the source environment and description, and click on **Next**.

14. Enter the details of the source server and the port number on which the Agent was configured to run, and click on **Next**.

15. In the next window, you would need to specify the database user ID / password for the source database, and click on **Finish**.

16. Similarly add the target database in the Veridata configuration.

17. After this you should be able to see two data sources in the the configuration window as shown in the following screenshot:

18. Next, we will create a Group in Group Configuration. For this click on **Group Configuration**, and then click on **New**.

19. Enter the Group **Name** and **Description** and click on **Next**.

20. Select **Source** and **Target Connection** and click on **Finish**.

21. Select **Go to Compare Pair configuration** and click on **OK**.

22. Click on **Pattern Mapping**, specify the source and target schema names, and click on **Generate Mapping** at the bottom of this page. Veridata will generate mapping for all the four tables in the **SCOTT** schema. You can view these in the **Preview** tab.

23. Click on **Save** to save the mappings.

24. Click on **Job Configuration** and click on **New**.

25. Specify a name for the job and its description and click on **Next**.

26. Select the Group that we previously created and click on **Finish**.

27. You should now see a job in the **Job Configuration** window. Select the job and click on **Run** to run it.

28. On the next window you can see the data discrepancies.

How it works...

In this recipe, we looked into the steps required to set up a data comparison job using Oracle GoldenGate Veridata. For this, we first installed the GoldenGate Veridata Agent on the source and target server in steps 1 to 8. The next step is to start the GoldenGate Veridata web interface using which all the configurations will be done. At this stage, we have various components of the Veridata architecture ready; however, we still need to add the source and target databases to the Veridata configuration. This is done in steps 11 to 17. Once the data sources are added, we need to create a Group with the data sources, and also define a compare pair list. The compare pair list identifies which tables in the source database will be compared to the corresponding tables in the target database. After this, we create a job for the actual comparison and run it. The job will run the data comparison and show the results. If there are data discrepancies, then you need to fix them manually as that is outside the scope of of Veridata.

Index

configuring, to read from Oracle ASM instance 46, 47

Extracts processes 168

EXTTRAIL command 58

F

file
data, loading to database utility method 86-91

FILTER
used, for filtering records 114-117

FILTER clause 45, 117, 124

FILTER command 114-116

filter on csn command 232

FORMATASCII parameter 92

G

General Purpose File System option 139

GETAPPLOPS parameter 285

GETREPLICATES parameter 285

GETUPDATEBEFORES option 239

GETUPDATEBEFORES parameter 120

GGATE_ADMIN schema 38

GGSCI 56

GGSCI commands 173, 174

ggserr.log file 172

global mappings 107

GLOBALS parameter 301

global SQL procedure
running 114

global SQL statement
running 114

GoldenGate
schema changes, with different table definitions 218-224
schema changes, with similar table definitions 211-217
used, for performing initial load 72-76
used, for RDBMS replication 267-278

GoldenGate_action.scr script 140

GoldenGate Administration role
separating, from DBA team 262-267

GoldenGate Admin user
authentication 217, 225

GoldenGate configuration
creating, ACFS used 135-141

creating, DBFS used 148-162
creating, OCFS2 used 142-148
creating, Oracle Clusterware used 135-162
creating, to run Shell script 122-124
creating, with consistent state behind target database 248-251
failure, re-instantiating 187-192
healthcheck, performing 172-176
healthcheck, performing by script 176-179
network settings, optimizing 170-172
throughput, measuring 179-187

GoldenGate DDL replication
setting up 67-72

GoldenGate direct load
data, loading with 92-97

GoldenGate environment
configuring 34
used, for DDL replication 64-67

GoldenGate errors
resolving, logdump utility used 225-232

GoldenGate high availability option
choosing 132-135

GoldenGate instances
Oracle GoldenGate Director Client, installing 308-314
Oracle GoldenGate Director Client, using 308-314

GoldenGate monitoring
setting up, Oracle Grid Control 12c used 315-326

GoldenGate parameter files
specific tables, defining 217

GoldenGate replication
Heartbeat mechanism, implementing 193-206
setting up, between Oracle RAC databases 48-50
setting up, defgen used 60-62
setting up, with mapping between different columns 104-107
setting up, with multiple process groups 38-45

GoldenGate replication configuration
setting up, between two single node databases 34-38

GoldenGate resources
relocating, to other nodes 154, 155

TCPBUFSIZE parameter 172
TCPFLUSHBYTES option 170
TCPFLUSHBYTES parameter 171
THREAD column 205
throughput
  measuring, of GoldenGate configuration
      179, 180-184, 187
timestamp-based 286
tokens
  used, for adding custom field for replicated
      record 108-111
TOKENS clause 109
TOTALLAG column 205
totalsonly parameter 181
TRACE option 124
trail file
  about 168
  area size, calculating 51
  encrypting 58, 59
  used, for loading data to Replicat process
      method 81-86
TRANLOGOPTIONS INTEGRATEDPARAMS
      parameter 27
transaction history
  storing, in history table 117- 121

TRANSLOGOPTIONS DBLOGREADER
      parameter 50
TRANSLOGOPTIONS parameter 46-48
trusted source
  defining 286

U

Update statement 165
UPDATE_TIMESTAMP column 205

V

virtual machine (VM) 288

W

WHERE clause 116
  used, for filtering records 114-117
  using 116
Windows environment
  Oracle GoldenGate, installing 10

X

x86_64 Linux-based environment
  Oracle GoldenGate, installing 8, 9

[PACKT] enterprise

PUBLISHING

professional expertise distilled

Thank you for buying
Oracle GoldenGate 11*g* Complete Cookbook

About Packt Publishing

Packt, pronounced 'packed', published its first book "*Mastering phpMyAdmin for Effective MySQL Management*" in April 2004 and subsequently continued to specialize in publishing highly focused books on specific technologies and solutions.

Our books and publications share the experiences of your fellow IT professionals in adapting and customizing today's systems, applications, and frameworks. Our solution-based books give you the knowledge and power to customize the software and technologies you're using to get the job done. Packt books are more specific and less general than the IT books you have seen in the past. Our unique business model allows us to bring you more focused information, giving you more of what you need to know, and less of what you don't.

Packt is a modern, yet unique publishing company, which focuses on producing quality, cutting-edge books for communities of developers, administrators, and newbies alike. For more information, please visit our website: www.PacktPub.com.

About Packt Enterprise

In 2010, Packt launched two new brands, Packt Enterprise and Packt Open Source, in order to continue its focus on specialization. This book is part of the Packt Enterprise brand, home to books published on enterprise software – software created by major vendors, including (but not limited to) IBM, Microsoft and Oracle, often for use in other corporations. Its titles will offer information relevant to a range of users of this software, including administrators, developers, architects, and end users.

Writing for Packt

We welcome all inquiries from people who are interested in authoring. Book proposals should be sent to author@packtpub.com. If your book idea is still at an early stage and you would like to discuss it first before writing a formal book proposal, contact us; one of our commissioning editors will get in touch with you.

We're not just looking for published authors; if you have strong technical skills but no writing experience, our experienced editors can help you develop a writing career, or simply get some additional reward for your expertise.

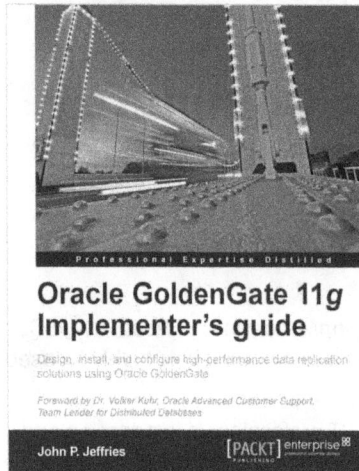

Oracle GoldenGate 11*g*
Implementer's guide

ISBN: 978-1-84968-200-8   Paperback: 280 pages

Design, install, and configure high-performance data
replication solutions using Oracle GoldenGate

1. The very first book on GoldenGate, focused on
    design and performance tuning in enterprise-wide
    environments

2. Exhaustive coverage and analysis of all aspects
    of the GoldenGate software implementation,
    including design, installation, and advanced
    configuration

3. Migrate your data replication solution from Oracle
    Streams to GoldenGate

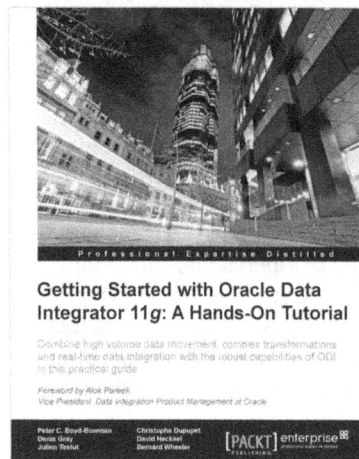

Getting Started with Oracle
Data Integrator 11*g*:
A Hands-On Tutorial

ISBN: 978-1-84968-068-4   Paperback: 384 pages

Combine high volume data movement, complex
transformations and real-time data integration with the
robust capabilities of ODI in this practical guide

1. Discover the comprehensive and sophisticated
    orchestration of data integration tasks made
    possible with ODI, including monitoring and
    error-management

2. Get to grips with the product architecture
    and building data integration processes with
    technologies including Oracle, Microsoft SQL
    Server, and XML files

3. A comprehensive tutorial packed with tips,
    images, and best practices

Please check **www.PacktPub.com** for information on our titles

Oracle BPM Suite 11*g* Developer's cookbook

ISBN: 978-1-84968-422-4   Paperback: 512 pages

Over 80 advanced recipes to develop rich, interactive business processes using the Oracle Business Process Management Suite

1. Full of illustrations, diagrams, and tips with clear step-by-step instructions and real-time examples to develop Industry Sample BPM Process and BPM interaction with SOA Components

2. Dive into lessons on Fault, Performance, and Rum Time Management

3. Explore User Interaction, Deployment, and Monitoring

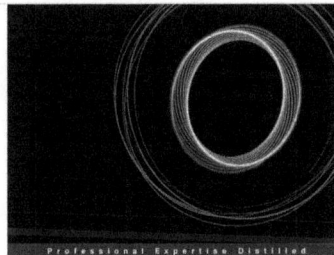

Oracle BPM Suite 11g Developer's Cookbook

Over 80 advanced recipes to develop rich, interactive business processes using the Oracle Business Process Management Suite

Vivek Acharya   [PACKT] enterprise

Oracle Database XE 11*g*R2 Jump Start Guide

ISBN: 978-1-84968-674-7   Paperback: 146 pages

Build and manage your Oracle Database 11*g* XE environment with this fast paced, practical guide

1. Install and configure Oracle Database XE on Windows and Linux

2. Develop database applications using Oracle Application Express

3. Back up, restore, and tune your database

4. Includes clear step-by-step instructions and examples

Oracle Database XE 11gR2 Jump Start Guide

Build and manage your Oracle Database 11g XE environment with this fast paced, practical guide

Asif Momen   [PACKT] enterprise

Please check **www.PacktPub.com** for information on our titles

www.ingramcontent.com/pod-product-compliance
Lightning Source LLC
Chambersburg PA
CBHW080904220326
41598CB00034B/5467